Medieval History and Archaeology

General Editors

JOHN BLAIR   HELENA HAMEROW

Beyond the Medieval Village

MEDIEVAL HISTORY AND ARCHAEOLOGY

General Editors

John Blair   Helena Hamerow

The volumes in this series bring together archaeological, historical, and visual methods to offer new approaches to aspects of medieval society, economy, and material culture. The series seeks to present and interpret archaeological evidence in ways readily accessible to historians, while providing a historical perspective and context for the material culture of the period.

BEYOND THE MEDIEVAL VILLAGE

The Diversification of Landscape Character in Southern Britain

STEPHEN RIPPON

OXFORD

UNIVERSITY PRESS

OXFORD

UNIVERSITY PRESS

Great Clarendon Street, Oxford OX2 6DP

Oxford University Press is a department of the University of Oxford.
It furthers the University's objective of excellence in research, scholarship,
and education by publishing worldwide in

Oxford New York

Auckland Cape Town Dar es Salaam Hong Kong Karachi
Kuala Lumpur Madrid Melbourne Mexico City Nairobi
New Delhi Shanghai Taipei Toronto

With offices in

Argentina Austria Brazil Chile Czech Republic France Greece
Guatemala Hungary Italy Japan Poland Portugal Singapore
South Korea Switzerland Thailand Turkey Ukraine Vietnam

Oxford is a registered trade mark of Oxford University Press
in the UK and in certain other countries

Published in the United States
by Oxford University Press Inc., New York

© Stephen Rippon 2008

The moral rights of the author have been asserted
Database right Oxford University Press (maker)

First published 2008

British Library Cataloguing in Publication Data

Data available

Library of Congress Cataloging in Publication Data

Rippon, Stephen, 1968–
Beyond the medieval village: diversification of landscape character in southern
Britain / Stephen Rippon.
p. cm.—(Medieval history and archaeology)
Includes bibliographical references and index.
ISBN 978–0–19–920382–6
1. England, Southern—Historical geography. 2. Land use—England, Southern—History—To
1500. 3. Landscape—England, Southern—History—To 1500. 4. Land settlement—England,
Southern—History—To 1500. 5. England, Southern—Social conditions—1066–1485.
6. Villages—England, Southern—History—To 1500. 7. Landscape changes—England,
Southern—History—To 1500. I. Title.
DA600.R48 2008
307.7209422′0902—dc22
2008041661

Typeset by Laserwords Private Limited, Chennai, India
Printed in Great Britain
on acid-free paper by
CPI Antony Rowe, Chippenham, Wiltshire

ISBN 978–0–19–920382–6

1 3 5 7 9 10 8 6 4 2

Preface and Acknowledgements

In the past twenty years I have lived in Essex, Berkshire, and Devon, and carried out research in areas as far apart as Cornwall, southern Wales, the Midlands, and East Anglia. My present house looks out over Devon countryside that is dotted with cottages, farmsteads, and small hamlets. This is a landscape that is very different in character from the compact villages of Buckinghamshire and Northamptonshire that I saw while involved with the Whittlewood Project, and is in turn very different from the sprawling green-side hamlets I remember from a childhood in Essex. It is the aim of this book to try to discover why these landscapes are so different in their character.

In recent years there have been a series of seminal studies into the origins and development of regional variation in the character of England's landscape including *Village, Hamlet and Field* (Lewis *et al.* 1997), *Region and Place* (Roberts and Wrathmell 2002), *Shaping Medieval Landscapes* (Williamson 2003), and *Medieval Villages in an English Landscape* (Jones and Page 2006). From the perspective of this son of Essex and now resident of Devon there has, however, been a rather 'Midland-centric' view of the medieval landscape, with most attention focusing on why England's 'central zone' developed villages and open fields in contrast to what was happening to the east and west of this region. There appears to be a growing consensus that villages and open fields did not spread into areas such as the South-East, East Anglia, and the South-West because communities living there chose not to emulate those living in the Midlands: it is argued by some that these peripheral areas had lower populations or experienced less pressure on land and so there was no need to restructure their landscapes. Some scholars have suggested that the nature of the pre-medieval ('antecedent') landscape was different in these areas, or the soils and topography lacked the characteristics that encouraged people to live together in villages, and manage their land in communally run meadows and open fields in the Midlands. This book will try to take a very different stance and rather than seeing areas such as the South-East, East Anglia, and the South-West as lying beyond the real focus of attention, it will explicitly concentrate on these areas at the margins of, and beyond, the 'central province' and explore whether these landscapes are different because they failed to experience developments seen in the Midlands, or because they were equally dynamic landscapes that had their own trajectory of change.

This book could not have been written without many long discussions with fellow landscape archaeologists and historians. During my own work on the North Somerset Levels I received great inspiration from Mick Aston and Chris

Gerrard in their Shapwick Project, while Chris Dyer, Mark Gardiner, Richard Jones, and Mark Page provided equally stimulating discussions throughout my involvement in the Whittlewood Project and since. I also thank Grenville Astill, Mike Fulford, and Tom Williamson for inspiring the undergraduate Rippon, Rick Turner for enabling me to develop my research in southern Wales, and Bob Higham for introducing me to the landscape of Devon. I would also like to thank the many friends, colleagues, and students with whom I have discussed the ideas in this book, and John Blair, Helena Hamerow, Peter Herring, Alan Lambourne, Tom Williamson, and the anonymous Oxford University Press reader for commenting on all or part of an earlier draft.

I am extremely grateful to the British Academy for supporting this project with a small research grant that enabled me to employ Adam Wainwright as a research assistant and draughtsman. This grant also supported a series of invaluable visits to the Historic Environment Records and Records Offices in Cornwall, Devon, Somerset, Essex, Suffolk, Norfolk, and Pembrokeshire, and I wish to thank all the staff there for their help, but particularly Peter Herring, James Gossip, Steve Hartgroves, Bryn Tapper, Nigel Brown, Ken Crowe, Maria Medlycott, Edward Martin, and David Gurney.

I am also grateful to Mike Rouillard of the Exeter University Archaeology Department Drawing Office for his help with the illustrations. Isabel Richardson of the National Trust Holnicote Estate kindly supplied the data used to prepare Figure 2.7. I would like to thank Philip Pearce (Figure 3.7) and Alan James (Figures 6.3, 6.9, and 6.11) for flying me over some of the study areas. Finally, I wish to thank the following for permission to reproduce illustrations: Paul Drury and the Council for British Archaeology (Figure 5.8), the Essex Records Office (Figure 5.15 and Ordnance Survey map behind Figure 5.16), the Gwent Records Office (Ordnance Survey maps used in Figures 6.4 and 6.6), Steve Hartgroves (Figure 4.10), Peter Herring (the landownership mapping in Figure 4.11), Maria Medlycott/Essex County Council (Figure 5.16), Bryn Morris (Figures 5.5 and 5.14), Harold Mytum and Cambrian Archaeology (Figure 6.13), the National Monuments Record (English Heritage) (Figures 1.4, 1.5, 3.4, and 3.12), the Pembrokeshire Records Office (estate map and Ordnance Surveys map used in Figures 6.18 and 6.21), Henrietta Quinnell (Figures 4.2 and 4.3), the Somerset Records Office (Ordnance Survey maps used in Figures 2.3, 2.7, 2.8, and 3.5), the Somerset Studies Library (Figure 2.5), and Bryn Tapper/Cornwall County Council (inset map in Figure 4.7).

Contents

List of Illustrations

List of Tables

1

Introduction: Beyond Villages and Common Fields

The great Cambridge historian, Maitland, regarded the Ordnance map of England as one of the finest records we have, if only we could learn how to decipher it, and indeed it is. But the landscape itself is an equally revealing document, equally full of significant detail, and equally difficult to interpret aright.

(Hoskins 1952, 289)

THE RICH AND VARIED LANDSCAPE OF SOUTHERN BRITAIN

Anyone who travels around Britain cannot fail to notice how the appearance of the countryside varies from region to region. In part this is due to the underlying geology with its influence on topography, drainage, soils, land-use, and traditional building materials, but to a far greater extent local and regional variation in landscape character is the product of many generations of farming communities working the land. In the East Midlands, for example, the settlement pattern is characterized by large villages, clustered around the parish church, and surrounded by large, carefully planned rectangular fields that result from the Parliamentary Enclosure of former common fields. The landscape of Devon, in contrast, has a very different appearance, with a predominantly dispersed settlement pattern of hamlets and isolated farmsteads, linked by winding sunken lanes, all set within a complex field boundary pattern with few straight lines. Regional variations in landscape character such as these contribute significantly to a modern community's sense of place and identity, but they are also deeply rooted in the history of British society, and it is the origins of this local identity that are the subject of this book.

If we go back in time such local and regional variations in landscape character would have been even more striking. The Midland villages were surrounded by extensive common fields while the more dispersed settlement patterns of areas such as the South-East and the South-West would have been associated with a complex mixture of smaller-scale open fields set within areas of closes (enclosed fields) held in severalty (that is owned or occupied by a single person). In the sixteenth century John Leland and his contemporaries described these respective areas as 'champion' and 'bosky' countryside, the wooded character of the latter being due to the presence of trees in hedgerows rather than extensive woodland and forest (Fig. 1.1). When Leland was writing, these different settlement patterns and field systems were already many centuries old, so where did they come from? Villages and common fields dominated the landscape of what is referred to here as the 'central zone' of England, stretching from Dorset in the south to Yorkshire in the north-east, so why are they not found to the south-east or the south-west? While focusing on the specific matter of regional variation in landscape character in southern Britain, this study addresses the far wider issue of how human society interacts with the natural environment within a complex and dynamic socio-economic context.

CHANGING INTERPRETATIONS OF THE ORIGINS OF LOCAL AND REGIONAL VARIATION IN LANDSCAPE CHARACTER

As Taylor (1983, 125) argues, villages are an aberration, not just in their limited spatial distribution, but also in their relatively late appearance in the British countryside: while there were some nucleated rural settlements in late prehistoric and Roman Britain, dispersed patterns were far more common. The question of when, and why, only part of the country developed a more communal approach towards managing the landscape has been much debated, with an emerging consensus that it originated in the East Midlands some time around the ninth to twelfth centuries, and that this approach was then adopted in adjacent areas through a process of emulation (e.g. Lewis *et al.* 1997, 3; Taylor 2002). Before examining this prevailing orthodoxy, it is useful to review how we have arrived at our present state of understanding.

Across western Europe as a whole, writers were aware of regional variation in landscape character from at least the thirteenth century (e.g. Bartholomeus Anglicus' *De Proprietatibus Rerum*: Cahn 1991). Perhaps the best-known early English writer to describe the landscape was John Leland in the mid sixteenth century, and although he never drew a map showing his areas of 'champion' countryside—characterized by villages and common fields—Slater (1907, 47) plotted those places he described in this way, thereby revealing that they were mostly found in a broad swathe through central England stretching from Wessex to the North-East (Fig. 1.1). The origins of this champion countryside were discussed by Seebohm (1890) and Vinogradoff (1892) as early as the late nineteenth century, although the first systematic attempt at mapping the former extent of common field was in Gonner's (1912) *Common Land and Enclosure*

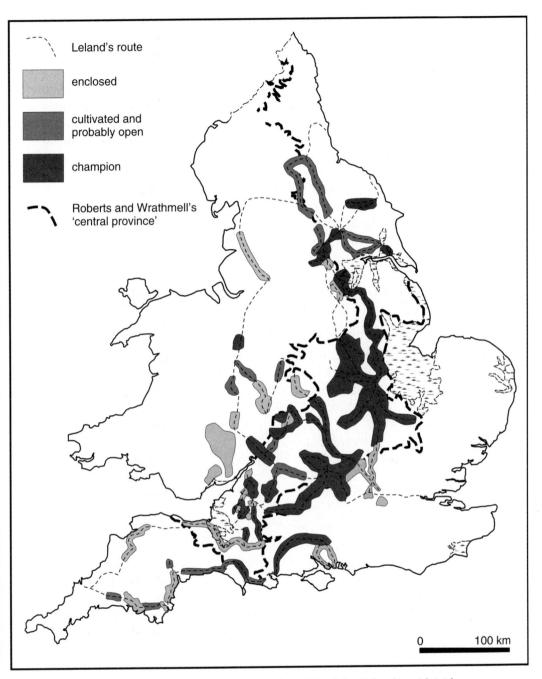

Fig. 1.1. An interpretation of references made within John Leland's mid 16th-century itineraries to enclosed and 'champion' countryside (after Slater 1907, 47). The divisions between the two broadly correspond with other attempts to map the extent of former common fields based on later sources (Fig. 1.2A–B) and confirm that Wessex should really be in Roberts and Wrathmell's (2000) 'central province' (Fig. 1.2D). Drawing by Adam Wainwright.

(Fig. 1.2A). In his book *English Field Systems* Gray (1915) discussed how the best-known system of common field farming, the 'Midland System'—whereby the strips of land held by the tenants within a manor were intermingled with the demesne (that is, land managed directly by the lord of the manor) and scattered fairly evenly across two or three extensive common fields, with one field lying fallow each year and being subject to communal grazing—was in fact restricted in its distribution to the Midlands (Fig. 1.2B). These regularly arranged two- and three-field systems were regulated through local custom, and often survived until the eighteenth and nineteenth centuries when they were enclosed through Act of Parliament (and see Ault 1972; Kain and Oliver 2004). Gray argued that the adjacent regions of East Anglia, Kent, and the Thames basin had their own, less regularly structured system of open field cultivation, often with larger numbers of smaller subdivided fields within which only a limited number of tenants had holdings, and which were therefore more amenable to relatively early enclosure by agreement. Gray believed that the west and north of Britain, in contrast, had a 'celtic' system with small hamlets (typically of less than six farms), associated with relatively small cultivated 'infields', surrounded by occasionally cultivated 'outfields' and extensive areas of rough grazing. While the cultivated landholdings of each farmstead in these hamlets may have taken the form of intermingled unenclosed strips, these open fields were on a far smaller scale than the vast common fields of the Midlands.

A wide range of terms have been used to describe field systems where an area of land is subdivided without the use of physical barriers such as ditches, hedges, or banks. In the same volume (Rowley 1981) the terms used included 'subdivided fields', 'commonfield', 'townfield', 'open field', and 'Midland system'. The reason for this varied use of terminology is that the authors were often talking about slightly different things. In the champion countryside there were vast common fields embracing most of the agricultural land in a parish (i.e. several square kilometres) and which were subject to communal regulations such as the grazing of livestock after the harvest, whereas beyond the central zone the fields containing land divided into unenclosed strips—open fields—usually covered just a few hectares. In the 'Midland' system the land of every tenant in a village might be spread across these two or three common fields, whereas elsewhere each of the many hamlets within a parish had its own subdivided field, with perhaps just three or four tenants holding land in each. Even within common field systems that cover an entire parish there are variants in how land was managed: in the 'Midland' system the strips of any individual tenant were scattered across the entire field system in a very 'regular' pattern, while in areas such as western Norfolk there were more irregular arrangements whereby the strips of a tenant were bunched in one or more parts of the field system (Dodgshon 1980, 47; and see Chapter 5).

While displaying certain common characteristics, these various field systems were clearly very different in their character and we must be careful with our

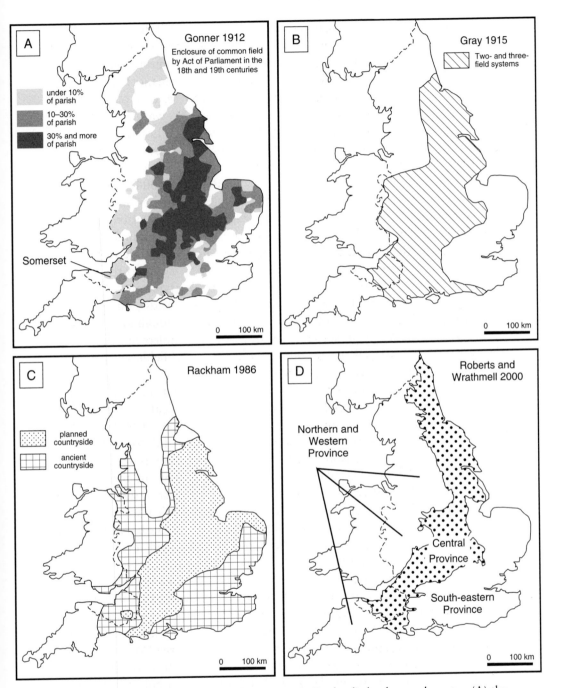

Fig. 1.2. Mappings of major regional variations in England's landscape character. (A) the enclosure of common field by Acts of Parliament in the 18th and 19th centuries (Gonner 1912); (B) documentary evidence for regularly arranged two- and three-field systems (Gray 1915); (C) Rackham's (1986a, fig. 1.3) 'ancient' and 'planned' countryside; (D) Roberts and Wrathmell's (2002, fig. 1.1) provinces.

use of terminology. While Roberts and Wrathmell (2002) use 'townfield' for the Midland-style two- and three-field system, that terminology is not really appropriate for a study focusing on southern Britain, and so 'common field' is preferred. In many cases, however, we lack the documentary research to be sure whether a field subdivided into strips was subject to the patterns of land tenure and communal regulation that characterize these common fields, and so in this study the term 'open field' is used as a general phrase for a field system of any scale that was divided into furlongs and strips that were shared between members of a community (following Campbell 1981).

After Gray's study, which considered the whole of England, there was a marked bias in later scholarship towards studies of the origins of villages and common fields, seen for example in the work of Bishop (1935), Orwin and Orwin (1938), and Homans (1941), at the expense of the other regional systems. These early twentieth-century scholars recognized that villages and common fields were of post-Roman origin, but believed that they were created through the clearing of woodland and waste by Anglo-Saxon immigrants during the fifth and sixth centuries. Believing that biennial rotation was a 'common-sense' approach to agriculture for any settled farming community, reducing the amount of fallow from a third to a half of the cultivated land, they assumed that Anglo-Saxons initially created a two-field system, with the three-field system emerging at a later date in order to intensify production.

The 1960s, however, saw a paradigm change in the way that historians perceived the origins of villages and common fields. Thirsk (1964; 1966) argued that the Midland system emerged as late as the twelfth and thirteenth centuries after a long process of evolution. She argued that in champion districts, population increase and partible inheritance led to the progressive disintegration of landholdings into strips and a growing shortage of grazing. As pastures were ploughed up, farmers needed to make more intensive use of the grazing available after the harvest and in fallow periods, although because arable lands lay in intermingled unhedged strips, this grazing could only be used effectively if neighbouring cultivators did the same. This pressure to use the scarce grazing resources effectively forced both peasants and the lord of the manor into increased levels of cooperation, culminating in the adoption of a simple two- or three-field system with its coordinated rotation of cultivation and fallow. Gray's other regional types of open field system, in areas such as East Anglia, were seen as examples of arrested development: what the Midlands might have looked like had that region not seen the development of the climactic form of common field farming: the two- and three-field system. There has also been a traditional view that areas of 'champion' countryside were amongst the first to be settled by medieval communities, in contrast to other areas that were colonized later, by individuals, with resulting landscapes that lacked the same degree of communal regulation, Roberts (1973, 229), for example, stating that 'open field land can therefore be viewed as a reflection of the extent and intensity of early settlement', while Everitt (1979, 85) suggests that 'in the fielden [champion] or "old arable" countrysides many settlements are certainly very ancient—although of course not all—and it seems likely that most of the earliest English and pre-English places are to be found in these valley areas'. Like Williamson (2003) before, it is one aim of this book to counter this often implicit assumption that the central zone of England was bordered by landscapes that were generally less favoured and colonized later.

Another important concept in the historiography of landscape research that developed in the 1960s and 1970s was that of *pays*: the idea that the countryside consists of discrete types of landscape such as marshland, fenland, downland, wolds, heathland, moorland, woodland, and clay vales that not only have a physical coherence but distinct communities too (Everitt 1977; 1979; 1986; Fox 1989a; 1989b; Thirsk 2000). The 'champion and 'woodland' landscapes described by Leland are also *pays* in the sense of distinctive *types* of landscape, while another sense of the term can be to identify discrete and unique districts, which the British landscape has in abundance and whose names are in common usage—Fenland, the Weald, the Chilterns, Breckland, etc.—and which often transcend the administrative convenience of the shires. It is also clear that many *pays* were recognized as distinct regions at least as far back as the medieval period, such as the wolds on the Leicestershire/Nottinghamshire borders (Fox 1989a), or Romney Marsh (Rippon 2000a). While *pays* are usually defined in terms of their geology and topography—what Everitt (1979, 88) referred to as 'natural regions'—they could also be defined in terms of their distinctive social and economic characteristics (e.g. Phythian Adams 1993). There remained, however, a tendency to generalize, such as Underdown's (1985; 1987) contention that cultural differences between sheep-corn and wood-pasture underpinned patterns of allegiance in the English Civil War, and Morrill (1987) is quite right to stress how the physical structure of the countryside with such land-use patterns can vary: while the sheep-corn country is often associated with nucleated villages, by the seventeenth century it could also be associated with dispersed settlement. Rather than seeing *pays* as types of countryside, we should instead think of local and regional variation in landscape character as producing a series of unique districts. The physical landscapes of southern Devon and northern Cornwall, for example, are very similar—lowlands with a series of estuaries extending far inland from the east coast, steep cliffs on the west coast, and surrounding a series of granite uplands—but culturally they are very different with distinctive languages and place names, and even a journal of *Cornish Studies* (the Journal of the Institute of Cornish Studies; and see Herring 2006a).

Until the 1970s discussion was dominated by historians and historical geographers, as reflected in Baker and Butlin's (1973a) *Studies of Field Systems in the British Isles*, although this started to change with the emergence of landscape archaeology and the development of large-scale, systematic field surveys in which the development of settlements and field systems was mapped across whole parishes. Large-scale rescue excavations were also beginning to reveal the character of 'Early Saxon' (fifth- to seventh-century) settlements, such as Mucking in Essex and West Stow in Suffolk (see Chapter 5), while there were also a growing number of excavations of deserted medieval villages, such as Goltho in Lincolnshire (see Chapter 7). The result was another paradigm shift, as it became clear that 'Early Saxon' settlements bore no resemblance to later medieval villages, and that deserted medieval villages did not have 'Early Saxon' settlements beneath them.

It is worth noting that the term 'Early Saxon' is quoted here simply because it reflects the terminology used by archaeologists at the time. Although 'early medieval' is the phrase now generally used for the fifth to eleventh centuries (*Medieval Archaeology*, 47 (2003), 199), 'Early Saxon' (400–650), 'Middle Saxon' (650–850), and 'Late Saxon' (850–1066) are still found in the literature, particularly in the east of the country. These are, however, clearly not appropriate period-specific terms for a study such as this, which embraces the whole of southern Britain from East Anglia through to Cornwall and South Wales, and so the term 'early medieval' is preferred. A crucial chronological horizon for this study is what historians such as Hanson and Wickham (2000) have referred to as the 'long eighth century' (the late seventh to early ninth centuries), when there were significant social, political, and economic changes across Europe, and which broadly corresponds to the 'Middle Saxon period'. In this study, the term 'earliest medieval period' is used for the early fifth to mid seventh century (and see Wickham 2005).

Returning to the historiography of research into the origins and development of regional variation in landscape character in southern Britain, some of the key early field surveys in the 1970s were carried out in the East Midlands, particularly Northamptonshire, where fieldwalking revealed that although the post-Roman period saw some contraction in the extent of settlement, with areas of heavier soil being abandoned, the basic character of the settlement pattern in areas of lighter soil remained the same, with a scatter of small sites associated with 'Early to Middle Saxon' pottery spread across what were to become medieval parishes (Foard 1978; Hall and Martin 1979; Hall 1981; Taylor 1983, 109–24). The dating of the pottery scatters suggested that this dispersed settlement pattern was abandoned sometime between the mid seventh and the mid ninth centuries, when 'Middle Saxon' pottery was in use, but before 'Late Saxon' pottery came into circulation. Excavation has since shown that the scatters were indeed related to settlements, in most cases simple farmsteads, although nothing is known about their associated field systems (e.g. Brixworth and Upton in Northamptonshire: Shaw 1993/4). The abandoned farmsteads are sometimes commemorated in the names of common field furlongs that eventually replaced them, such as the deserted site at Pennylands in Buckinghamshire that was associated with furlong names of Long Dunsteed and Short Dunsteed (*tun-stede* referring to a deserted settlement: R. Williams 1993, 97). Occasional finds of 'Middle Saxon' pottery from later medieval villages also suggested that in at least some cases nucleation occurred around a pre-existing settlement (e.g. Brixworth and Wollaston in Northamptonshire: Taylor 1977; Hall and Martin 1979; Lewis *et al.* 1997, 82). This evidence, together with Hall's (1981; 1982; 1983; 1985; 1988) suggestion that the furlongs within common fields were originally laid out in a planned fashion across whole townships, gave rise to a new hypothesis that there was a 'great replanning' of the landscape sometime in the late first millennium AD, with villages and common fields created at the same time.

The evidence from fieldwalking in the East Midlands appeared to suggest that this restructuring of the landscape took place sometime *before* the mid ninth century, as the scattered farmsteads lacked 'Late Saxon' pottery, and where such material had been found it was usually associated with later medieval villages (Hall 1983, 20; 1985, 64; Brown and Foard 1998; Williamson 2003, 67). A 'Middle Saxon' date for nucleation has, however, been challenged by those archaeologists and historians who argue that the restructuring of the landscape occurred somewhat later. Taylor (1983, 125), for example, suggested that few if any villages existed before the eleventh century, although this conclusion was largely based on the evidence from excavations carried out on deserted sites that are not necessarily typical. At much the same time historians were also reviewing the date when they believed that villages existed, with Fox (1981, 88) and Hooke (1981; 1998, 121–7) finding evidence for the existence of common fields that extended to the very edge of the estates described in tenth-century charters. The mid-tenth-century charter relating to Avon Farm, in Durnford, Wiltshire, for example, describes how three *cassati* of arable land consisted of 'single acres dispersed in a mixture here and there in common land' (Finberg 1964, No. 297; Sawyer 1968, No. 719). The context for this 'Late Saxon' reorganization of the landscape was widely seen as being the break-up of large estates that spread across a range of environmental zones, into smaller and more self-contained units that were to become medieval townships. Campbell (1981) argued that such a replanning of the landscape could only have occurred where there was strong lordship, with villagers being either unable or unwilling to bring about such a dramatic change, although this was contested by Dyer (1985) and Harvey (1989) who both saw peasant communities as being more important than lordship in shaping the countryside.

Following Foard and Hall's work in Northamptonshire, a number of other major archaeological projects were exploring the origins of villages and common fields. Since the 1950s, medieval archaeology's long-standing interest in deserted villages had led to a growing corpus of excavations, of which the most famous is Wharram Percy in Yorkshire (Beresford and Hurst 1990). The development of Milton Keynes new town, in Buckinghamshire (Croft and Mynard 1993), and the planned expansion of gravel quarrying at Raunds in Northamptonshire (Parry 2006), and Yarnton in Oxfordshire (Hey 2004), were all preceded by extensive programmes of survey and excavation. Lewis *et al.* (1997) studied the four East Midland counties of Bedfordshire, Buckinghamshire, Leicestershire, and Northamptonshire, while the development of the medieval landscape on the borders of Buckinghamshire and Northamptonshire was explored in greater detail by the Whittlewood Project (Jones and Page 2004; 2006; Page and Jones 2007). Hall (1995) continued his work on Northamptonshire field systems, while Foard (2001; Foard *et al.* 2005) surveyed Rockingham Forest in the north of the county, producing a remarkable reconstruction of the extent of common fields over an area of some 572 square kilometres. Major programmes of survey were also carried out at Rutland Water (Cooper 2000), and in Lincolnshire at Ropsley and Humby (Lane 1995) and the south western Fenland (Hayes and Lane 1992). Outside the East Midlands, there have also been a series of survey projects in Somerset at Shapwick (Aston and Gerrard 1999; Gerrard with Aston 2007) and Puxton (Rippon 2006), Berkshire (Gaffney and Tingle 1989; Tingle 1991), and in Cambridgeshire, East Anglia, and north-west Essex (see Chapter 5). Cumulatively, these research- and development-led projects have created a substantial body of data within areas that had seen villages and common fields in the medieval period.

There were also a number of attempts to map the major regional differences in landscape character. Oliver Rackham (1986a) pulled together various bodies of data to produce a schematic division of England into a central area of what he called 'planned countryside', with areas of 'ancient countryside' to the east and west (Fig. 1.2C): the planning to which Rackham referred was Parliamentary Enclosure although this phrase could equally apply to the late first-millennium restructuring of the countryside that produced villages and common fields in the first place. Roberts and Wrathmell (2000; 2002), however, produced the first systematic attempt at mapping these regional differences (Fig. 1.2D). Using nineteenth-century Ordnance Survey maps they characterized settlement patterns right across England, identifying a 'central province' with predominantly nucleated villages, and a 'south-eastern province' and a 'northern and western province' with more dispersed patterns. The broad correlation with Rackham's 'planned' and 'ancient' countryside is clear, as is the relationship between the 'central province' and those areas that saw extensive Parliamentary Enclosure. Roberts and Wrathmell have also examined the correlation between their nineteenth-century settlement provinces and a range of other data, notably the extent of early medieval woodland, 'Early Saxon' settlement and cemeteries, and Roman villas and other substantial buildings, suggesting that their 'central province' had an 'antecedent landscape' that was the most extensively cleared of woodland.

The past decade saw a series of major publications that sought to throw new light on why villages and common fields developed in the central part of England. Lewis *et al.* (1997) restated the view that scattered settlements on lighter soils associated with 'Early and Middle Saxon' pottery were abandoned 'sometime after 850' and were replaced by nucleated villages and common fields in the 'Late Saxon' period in what they refer to as the 'village moment' (Lewis *et al.* 1997, 198). The chronology of this process was challenged by Brown and Foard (1998, 75–90) who argued that, as the dispersed settlement pattern associated with 'Early to Middle Saxon' pottery was abandoned before the time when 'Late Saxon' pottery came into use (i.e. the mid ninth century), an initial nucleation of settlement must have occurred before that date. They argued that this initial nucleation often occurred around a pre-existing settlement, and that it pre-dated the creation of common fields around the tenth century when there was some restructuring of the already existing villages. The significance of pre-village nuclei was confirmed in the Whittlewood Project on the Buckinghamshire–Northamptonshire borders, although as a relatively well-wooded area it is not surprising that village formation here appears rather later than on the adjacent lowland areas (Jones and Page 2006).

In terms of the causes of regional variation in landscape character, a subject that is addressed in more detail below, a clear consensus had emerged by the 1990s that human society was solely responsible, with traditional 'environmentally deterministic' views—that human behaviour is shaped by the natural environment—being rejected outright. This sole emphasis on 'agency'—that 'the archaeological record is created through the actions of individuals' (Johnson 2007, 141; and see Tipping 2002) has, however, been challenged through the work of Williamson, most notably his *Shaping Mediev-al Landscapes* (2003; 2007). This study of the origins of common field farming suggests that it was particular soil conditions and an abundance of meadow in the English East Midlands that led to a more communal approach towards the practice of agriculture there. The significance of the 'natural environment in moulding social, economic and agrarian arrangements' also features in Williamson's (2002, 21) study of post-medieval agriculture and is a direct challenge to the increasingly dogmatic prevailing orthodoxy of social agency being the sole cause of landscape change.

On a wider level, Fleming's (2006; 2007) recent critiques of the post-processual approach to landscape, and specifically Johnson's (2007) *Ideas of Landscape*, also suggest that some of the traditional qualities of British landscape research still make a contribution to the discipline. Views on the relative roles of the environment and human society can be compared to a pendulum that has swung from the former to the latter, and it is interesting to note that Williamson is not alone in expressing concern that it has gone too far in the direction of social agency. There are very clear differences in settlement histories in some regions in which we are left in no doubt that many still feel that the topography and soils were a significant factor: Brown and Foard (1998, 73), for example, suggest that in Northamptonshire there was an 'intensive but dispersed pattern of [fifth- to eighth-century] settlement on the permeable geologies' but an 'almost complete loss of settlement from the marginal land, that is, from the claylands on the watersheds between the main river valleys'. A number of younger scholars have also recently argued that the significance of the natural environment may have been overlooked with the recent emphasis on social agency, including Draper (2006, 112), who suggests that the physical landscape is 'fundamental to understanding settlement and society', contrasting the very different patterns of settlement and agriculture in the chalk downland and clay vales of Wiltshire. Of his study of Somerset, Corcos (2002, 190) says, 'it must now be clear that a common thread is the importance of ecology and natural environment as important considerations in shaping the nature of medieval settlement, and by extension, the nature of human communities … This is not a "deterministic" conclusion, but one which accepts and indeed celebrates the extraordinary adaptive abilities of pre-industrial societies, and the symbiotic relationship between them and their ecological resource base.' While it is difficult to disagree with Johnson's (2007, 145) assertion that 'the landscape archaeologist … is examining the effects of real people leading real lives, and, further, doing so in active ways', and Lewis *et al.* (1997, 186) are right to remind us that 'human ingenuity is not *always* constrained by physical conditions' (italics added by the author), there is perhaps a tendency on the part of some not to consider whether the inherent properties of soil and topography *sometimes* influence landscape character. Overall, the early twenty-first century is an interesting time to be debating regional variation in landscape character, and this study sets out with an open mind as to what its causal factors were.

REGIONAL VARIATION IN LANDSCAPE CHARACTER: THE CURRENT DEBATES

As this overview has sought to demonstrate, the origins of the marked regional variation in landscape character that was such a feature of the English countryside over the second millennium AD remain a much disputed issue in landscape history. It is clear, however, that the central area of England had a distinctive *type* of landscape, structured around nucleated villages and common fields, and that this was described as 'champion' by sixteenth-century and later writers. Unfortunately, we do not have any contemporary maps showing its extent, and while various maps have been drawn up, using a variety of evidence, such as Rackham's (1986a) 'planned landscape' and Roberts and Wrathmell's (2000) 'central province', these are only in broad agreement with respect to their extent, and they have been subject to some criticism (e.g. Hinton 2005). The term 'central province' has, therefore, been avoided here in favour of the more neutral 'central zone' that refers to that part of the English landscape that had medieval settlement patterns characterized by a predominance of nucleated villages, and field systems that were overwhelmingly regularly arranged two- or three-field systems (i.e. champion-type countryside). With regard to the origins of these regional variations in landscape character, there are, perhaps, three crucial matters that are yet to be resolved: when were villages and common fields created; why was the landscape in the central zone restructured in this way; and why did this approach towards managing the countryside not spread across the whole of southern Britain?

The date of the creation of villages and fields

Two schools of thought have emerged as to when villages and common fields emerged in England's central zone. One view is that they post-date *c.*850, and were largely a tenth- or eleventh-century phenomenon which Lewis *et al.* (1997, 191–2) have called the 'village moment'. Dyer (2003, 21, 23), for example, suggests that the dispersed settlement patterns that preceded villages were abandoned 'soon after 850', that 'the first phase of occupation in many villages came no earlier than the eleventh century', but that 'some of the main elements of the common-field system were functioning in the tenth century' (and see Taylor 1992). The other view, presented by Brown and Foard (1998), and supported by Williamson (2003), is that settlement nucleation was a more drawn-out process starting before the mid ninth century (as the dispersed settlement patterns which were abandoned lack 'Late Saxon' pottery), followed by a phase of replanning and the creation of common fields around the tenth century. With these very different chronologies, it is not surprising that the process of change is also seen very differently, with Lewis *et al.* (1997, 201) arguing for an 'evolutionary upheaval', Hall (1981; 1982; 1985; 1988) for a 'great replanning', in contrast to Brown and Foard (1998) who allow for a more gradual process. We shall return to this issue in Chapter 7.

Causal factors: ethnicity

There has been much discussion as to why villages and common fields emerged in late first-millennium England. Seebohm (1890, 434–6) argued that many features of medieval society could be traced back at least as far as the Roman period, although the view soon prevailed that villages and common fields were introduced by Anglo-Saxon immigrants (e.g. Vinogradoff 1892, 162; Gray 1915, 415; Homans 1941, 83–107; 1969). We now know that this was not the case: the dispersed settlement patterns associated with 'Early and Middle Saxon' pottery are quite unlike those of the later village-based landscapes, while excavations of these earlier sites show that they lacked the stability and organization of medieval villages. Although explanations for cultural change based on invasion and migration have long since fallen out of favour, Martin (2007) recently argued that Scandinavian settlement and/or overlordship may have played a significant role in the tenth-century restructuring of landscapes in northern East Anglia.

Causal factors: the fragmentation of 'federative' estates

A number of historians suggest that the physical restructuring of the landscape may have taken place in the context of the fragmentation of earlier estates (e.g. Fox 1981, 99–100; Costen 1992a; Dyer 2003, 27; Williamson 2003, 37–46). In the fifth to seventh centuries most areas of southern Britain were probably divided up between a series of large autonomous or semi-autonomous tribal areas or folk-groups, possibly related to late Roman administrative districts or *pagi* (Bassett 1989, 17–21; Hooke 1998, 46–54). As more stratified societies evolved from around the seventh century, these territories, or *regiones*, developed into what Dyer (2003, 27) calls 'great estates' that became the property of the king, who in turn granted them to the Church or his major followers for the duration of an individual life. These 'great estates' were centred on a royal vill and straddled several different environmental zones so providing a range of resources. These estates were often assessed as 50 or even 100 hides, and where they can be reconstructed they covered tens or hundreds of square kilometres. They were based in fertile agricultural areas (the *inland*), often in river valleys, and extended out into adjacent environments that may have supported specialist settlements, for example in areas of low-lying wetland, and upland summer pasture or woodland (the *warland*). Their boundaries were often natural features such as rivers or streams, or they ran through areas of unenclosed 'waste' in interfluvial and upland areas (i.e. along watersheds). These territories have also been variously described as 'river estates' (Hoskins 1952, 303–4; and see Everitt 1986; Williamson 1993, 63–4), 'multiple estates' (Jones 1979; 1985), 'federal estates' (Lewis *et al.* 1997, 9, 20), 'federative estates' (Blair 1991, 24), and 'large terrains' (Fleming 1998, 51). These early estates may have been coterminous with the territories (*parochia*) of seventh- or eighth-century 'minster' churches that some have argued were founded on royal vills (Morris 1989; Hooke 1998, 70), although Blair (2005, 266–90) has recently questioned this on the basis that there were no stable royal centres during the seventh and eighth centuries.

From the late seventh century these great estates started to fragment as the king granted land in perpetuity to the Church (from the 670s) and noble families (from the 770s) as *bookland*. Some of those estates received by the Church survived intact, forming vast territories of 50 hides or more in the Domesday survey, although others appear to have been subdivided into smaller holdings typically of 5 or 6 hides. Secular estates were particularly prone to continued fragmentation through partible inheritance, and together this subdivision led to the formation of the multiplicity of manors that came to form the tenurial framework of post-Conquest England. The breaking up of these great estates was also associated with a decline in the status of the peasantry with relative free *ceorls*, who numerically dominated Middle Saxon society and typically held a 'yardland' of 30 acres (12 ha), being replaced by *geburs* and *cottars* that had owed regular labour services and a range of other dues to the lord of their manor (Faith 1997). This fragmentation of the secular territorial landscape was mirrored by the fission of early minster *parochiae* into smaller units that subsequently became medieval parishes.

It is entirely logical that the fragmentation of these estates and the creation of small, self-contained manors provided a *context* for the physical restructuring of the landscape, but this cannot in itself explain *why* villages and common fields were actually created, or why this happened in some areas but not others. There are plenty of examples of great estates being broken up in areas that did not go on to develop the 'Midland system', such as the Rodings in Essex (Bassett 1997), and so the crucial question is why, in the context of a common tenurial process—the fragmentation of the great estates—did some areas see landscape reorganization through the creation of villages and common fields, while others did not?

Causal factors: the balance of arable, pasture, and woodland

A widespread view is that villages and common fields were created in landscapes with large amounts of arable and a limited area of pasture (and indeed woodland). Hooke (1985, 105), for example, suggests that 'if the dominant land use of such areas [of dispersed settlement] was pastoralism, and there was an abundance of woodland and waste, there would be little incentive for massive reorganization of earlier settlement of field systems'. Lewis *et al.* (1997, 198) claim that 'the areas where the nucleated village was the dominant form of settlement in the middle ages, appear to have had consistently higher proportions of arable land in cultivation in 1086, which is likely to reflect a long standing bias towards cereal cultivation'. There is, however, a problem with this assumption that the champion districts had a long-standing bias towards arable cultivation: it is not borne out by the evidence in Domesday which shows little relationship between the central zone and areas that had a high density of ploughteams, with particular concentrations in places such as eastern Norfolk, the coastal plain of Sussex, the lowlands of central and eastern Devon, and large parts of Herefordshire (Darby 1977, fig. 41; Williamson 2003). That this assumption of a relationship between the development of villages and common fields, and areas with a high proportion of arable, is flawed is particularly significant as it also underlies two other ideas with regard to why some areas developed this approach towards structuring the landscape while others did not: first, that these were a response to pressures on agrarian resources such as rising population, and secondly that they reflect the character of the preceding, or 'antecedent' landscape.

Causal factors: rising population, a market economy, and the emergence of the English state

Thirsk (1964; 1966), along with other agrarian and economic historians of that generation (e.g. Postan 1972), was of the opinion that rising population was the driving force behind landscape change. Instead of seeing common fields as being the creation of Anglo-Saxon colonists, she argued that growing demographic pressure led to the progressive evolution and expansion of what had been small subdivided fields due to the fragmentation of landholdings through partible inheritance, alongside the steady conversion of pasture into arable that led to the need for agreed crop rotations, post-harvest grazing, and periods of fallow. Lewis *et al.* (1997, 179–86, 199–200) similarly argued that it was rising population which led to declining areas of pasture, as more land was put down to the plough, and the subdivision and intermixing of landholdings due to inheritance practices and exchange. They argued that villages and common fields were created when a certain set of socio-economic conditions prevailed—what they call the 'village moment'—and that the idea of structuring a landscape around nucleated villages and communally managed common fields then spread by emulation to other areas that saw similar pressure on their agrarian resources. Only where population levels were relatively low, and substantial areas of pasture remained, did dispersed settlement patterns survive. In addition to the rising population the conditions identified by Lewis *et al.* included the growing assertion of royal power over the newly formed kingdom of England from the late ninth century with its associated demands for taxation and military service. An added pressure was the growth of non-agriculturally productive urban centres, which provided the opportunity to gain profit through market-based exchange. The earlier great estates had not been 'geared towards squeezing the land and its people with any great intensity', with food rents representing just a small fraction of the total produce, but as royal demands and the potential for profit through market exchange increased, there was a growing incentive to exploit estates more efficiently (Dyer 2003, 29). The result was the progressive fragmentation of the old great estates, which had been assessed as up to 50 or 100 hides, into units of perhaps 20 to 40 hides which in turn were broken up into holdings of between 1 and 6 hides that were granted to individual thegns in return for military service (Dyer 2003, 31).

Causal factors: the process of emulation

Another common view is that structuring the countryside around villages and common fields was a concept that spread through emulation. Taylor (2002, 54), for example, suggests that the fashion for villages and common fields began in the East Midlands and spread outwards, 'overcoming and overlying the older dispersed pattern' until eventually the 'impetus was lost'.

This hypothesis implies that there was a 'moving frontier' as the new ideas spread, and we would therefore expect villages to be older in 'core areas' such as the East Midlands, and younger in areas towards the periphery of the central zone, as Roberts and Wrathmell (2002, fig. 5.11) have shown graphically (Fig. 1.3). Lewis *et al.* (1997, 200) have gone even further in suggesting that 'this adaptation, once introduced and established, probably spread by emulation: the nucleated settlements and regular open fields in so many communities across the east midlands show so many similarities as to suggest that, as the success of the nucleated open-field village became evident, the idea spread following a standard model'.

This hypothesis that a new form of structuring the agrarian landscape spread by emulation is entirely logical, although there is a danger of implying that areas which did not adopt the new ways were somehow remote, less well developed, and so conservatively retained an essentially older form of countryside. The suggestion that structuring the landscape around villages and common fields was a concept that spread across England's central zone in the late first millennium AD may indeed be correct, but it also does not explain why it did not extend into areas such as the South-East and the South-West. How do ideas about non-portable phenomena, such as agrarian practice and how to physically structure a landscape, spread through emulation? It is relatively easy to see how the exchange and trade in movable objects facilitates the diffusion of new fashions in some material culture, but villages and common fields cannot move in this way. It is well known that in the early medieval period, particularly the 'long eighth century', there was increasing contact between the social elites—both secular and ecclesiastical—in western Europe, and it is plausible that this was the means by which knowledge of new agricultural techniques and approaches to shaping settlements spread, by word of mouth and possibly even seeing evidence on the ground. This does, of course, imply that the key force behind landscape change in this case was lordship rather than community, but we do not really know the extent of mobility amongst the rural population and it is quite possible that the concept of villages and common fields could have spread through emulation at the level of peasant society, simply by a gradual process of copying one's neighbours.

Causal factors: antecedent landscapes

Roberts and Wrathmell (2002) have offered another potential explanation as to why only part of England saw the creation of villages and common fields. By mapping a series of different data sets, such as place names and Domesday woodland, and comparing them with the boundaries of their 'central province', they have observed a sometimes striking correlation between nucleated settlement in the nineteenth century and areas that were the most extensively cleared of woodland by the eleventh century, and they argue that

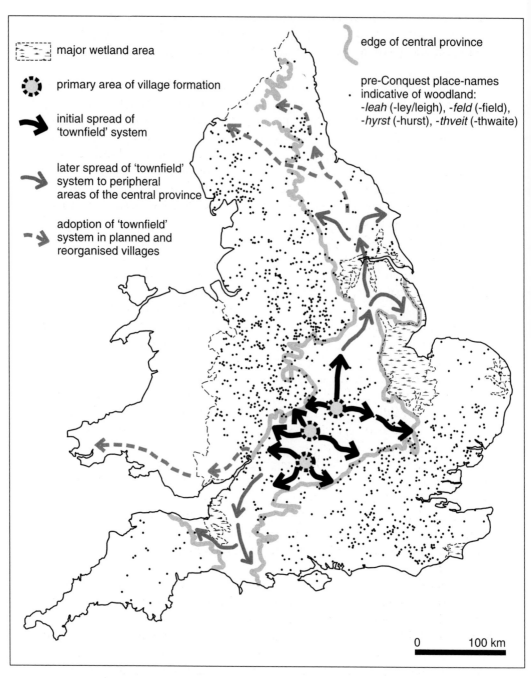

Fig. 1.3. Schematic representation of the spread of villages and common fields (after Roberts and Wrathmell 2002, fig. 5.11) in the context of place-name evidence for the extent of pre-Conquest woodland (Roberts and Wrathmell 2002, fig. 1.10).

the character of this 'antecedent landscape'—the area of England that was already the most extensively cultivated—contributed to the creation of villages and common fields in the Midlands (Robert and Wrathmell 2002, 18–24, 72–9).

Another important consideration with regard to the 'antecedent landscape' argument is that some form of open field agriculture clearly existed in southern England by at least the late seventh or early eighth century. King Ine's law code for Wessex (678–726), for example, records that 'If ceorls have a common meadow or other land divided into shares, and some have fenced their portion and some have not, and [if cattle] eat up their common crops or grass, those who are responsible for the gap are to go, and pay to the others, who have fenced their part, compensation for the damage that has been done there. They are to demand with regard to those cattle such reparation as is proper' (Whitelock 1955, 368–9, clause 42; Fox 1981, 86–7). It is not clear whether this communal approach to managing land was restricted to specific kin groups, as was the case in later medieval Wales, or extended to whole communities. This law code was written in the context of the emergence of stable kingdoms during the seventh century, at a time when rents, renders, and dues were being imposed and formalized, but there is nothing to suggest that this form of subdivided field was anything new: the law code appears to be stating current practice rather than trying to establishing a new one. There is also evidence for subdivided fields in the early Welsh law codes, which originated in the mid tenth century and clearly relate to areas beyond the 'great replanning' of the English Midlands (Seebohm 1890, 119–22; Jones 1981; Jenkins 1986, 198–202). These laws describe the communal ploughing of fields that appear to have been divided into strips, since church tithes were assessed by taking every tenth *erw*, the Old Welsh for acre. These *erws* were divided by grass balks, and were subject to the regulated rotation of ownership and cooperative ploughing. These Welsh open fields were, however, on a relatively small scale compared to the vast common fields of England, and were often associated with one family group, or *gwely*, in contrast to the English central zone where the landholdings of all members of a community were included within the two- or three-field system.

It is therefore clear that there was a crucial difference in scale between the early forms of communally managed landed resources found in Wales, and the 'Midland system' as it eventually emerged in the central zone of England. Subdivided fields, and cooperative practices such as communal ploughing and crop rotation, can occur at any scale, including the land held by small kin groups or that of a single community living in a hamlet with just a handful of tenements, which was one of many scattered across a parish or township. In the 'Midland system', in contrast, all of the arable land of an entire community was arranged in two or three huge common fields, one of which was put down to common grazing each year, while the other(s) saw a single crop being grown. These common fields were, therefore, on an altogether different scale from open fields in the Welsh landscape both in terms of their physical size, and in the degree of cooperation and communal regulation required. Roberts and Wrathmell (2002, 143) argue that hamlets with small subdivided fields were found right across early medieval Britain, and that what happened in their 'central province' was a magnification of this existing tendency because this area was 'anciently cleared land, already, by later prehistoric times, devoted to grain production'. Over time, they argue, 'the advantages of concentrated tenantry and a system of joint grain production was further stimulated by the inter-state frontier troubles of the eighth century, the Viking incursions of the ninth century and the demands of royal taxation' (ibid.).

Causal factors: lordship versus community and the process of change

While Thirsk saw the creation of common fields as a gradual, evolutionary process, others have argued for a more dramatic replanning of the landscape. In either case, we must return to the issue of social agency and the processes whereby landscapes are changed. The replacement of scattered farmsteads with a single, sometimes planned, nucleated village must have been a major dislocation for the rural population, unless of course there was a preceding period of widespread depopulation for which we have no evidence. While fieldwalking has revealed the dispersed settlement pattern that preceded nucleated villages in areas such as the East Midlands, unfortunately we know very little about their associated field systems that were replaced, although the lack of palaeoenvironmental evidence (that is, animal and plant remains preserved within recent geological deposits and the archaeological record) for widespread post-Roman woodland regeneration in lowland areas suggests that land remained open across large areas. There is also some evidence that medieval furlong boundaries perpetuate the lines of Romano-British and even prehistoric ditches (e.g. Taylor and Fowler 1978; Oosthuizen 1997a; 2003; 2005; Tolan-Smith 1997; Harrison 2002; Upex 2002; Percival and Williamson 2005; Jones and Page 2006; Gerrard with Aston 2007). Such examples of potential continuity can, however, be balanced by other cases where strips and furlongs clearly lie unconformably across earlier field systems (e.g. Mackreth 1996; Brown and Foard 1998, fig. 14; Hey 2004, figs. 1.5 and 11.5): what is not clear, however, is whether the earlier fields had fallen out of use for a brief period of time, or whether it was a working landscape that was restructured through the creation of common fields; there was still a pronounced discontinuity in the history of these landscapes. In essence, we do not understand the actual process whereby a landscape of dispersed settlement was transformed into one of villages and common fields.

Hall (1981, 27–34) has shown that the often complex blocks of strips within common fields sometimes resulted from the fragmentation of what had been far simpler, and seemingly planned, 'long furlong' boundaries (and see Foard *et al.* 2005, fig. 5). This suggests that the creation of common fields was a coordinated exercise, and not a gradual or piecemeal process. So who was responsible for this profound change in the landscape: the estate owners or the local communities? Campbell (1981) argues that lordship was a crucial factor in determining how landscapes evolved, suggesting that peasant communities were unlikely to have been capable of restructuring a landscape, and that the organized social structures that villages represent were the product of settlement nucleation rather than the cause. Archaeologists also generally assume that lordship was responsible for major changes in the landscape. Others, however, and in particular historians, have rejected the idea that lordly power was a prerequisite for landscape reorganization, citing documentary evidence for the remoteness of landowners from their often scattered estates, and the power and organization that a community could exert locally (e.g. Dyer 1985; Harvey 1989; Lewis *et al.* 1997, 172–9; Dyer 2003, 7). We therefore find ourselves in the paradoxical position that 'historians, working on documents, often see the lord of the manor as moving gingerly, pussyfooted even, among the intricacies of his tenants' rights and privileges. On the other hand archaeologists and geographers, working in the field, see this same lord sweeping all before him, uprooting entire villages and replanning lands and settlements in an almost arbitrary way' (Harvey 1989, 35). While the ability of a community to manage a landscape that already existed is in no doubt, this does not mean that they were also responsible for the initial creation of villages and common fields, as the documentary sources we have that illustrate the strength of local customary practices date from several centuries after this replanning is thought to have taken place. Lords may have exercised 'an intermittent and imperfect control over their subordinates' (Dyer 1985, 27) from the twelfth century onwards, but was this also the case during the eighth to tenth centuries?

Causal factors: soils and the practice of agriculture

Many early scholars explained the development of common fields in terms of agricultural practice, for example the need for a communal pooling of resources when using heavy mouldboard ploughs and the large teams of oxen that they require (co-aration) (e.g. Seebohm 1890; Orwin and Orwin 1938, 37–44). A rotated scatter of strips across two or three large common fields also shared out the good and bad land in a form of risk management (e.g. Vinogradoff 1892, 235–6; 1905; Gray 1915, 199–202; Thirsk 1964, 11–14; Baker and Butlin 1973b, 635–41), but why were these technologies and practices adopted in some areas but not others (Dodgshon 1980, 29–46; 1981, 132)?

In his thought-provoking analysis of East Anglia and the East Midlands, Williamson (2003) suggests that common fields were the response of human communities to different properties of the natural environment and the ways that they affect agricultural practice. He rejects any correlation between common fields and population density or the nature of lordship, and instead stresses the significance of soils, and specifically the need for communal grazing and manuring on areas of particularly light soil, and the problems of ploughing heavy clays that are prone to compaction and 'puddling' (forming a sticky mess which adheres to ploughs, harrows, and other implements, and which then dries hard and bricklike). The distribution of soils prone to 'puddling' is broadly similar to that of common fields and Williamson suggests, therefore, that where full advantage had to be taken of the limited times when such soils are suitable for ploughing or harrowing, ploughteams needed to be assembled with particular rapidity and this was much easier where farmsteads and ploughteams lay in close proximity, rather than scattered across the landscape. When the soils had dried out just enough to allow them to be worked without adverse effects, but further rain threatened, the time taken to gather together the beasts for the ploughteam would have been a matter of critical importance. Following from the detailed mapping of medieval agrarian resources of Campbell (2000, 75–6), who showed that meadow was consistently well represented in the clay vales of England's central zone, Williamson also suggests that settlement nucleation was encouraged by the greater efficiency that it affords hay making.

The correlation between farming practice and soil type has, however, been questioned along with Williamson's suggested ninth-century or earlier date for settlement nucleation (e.g. Dyer 2004). The hypothesis that landscape reorganization was essentially driven by agrarian practice—that is, the creation of common fields and common meadows—is also at odds with Brown and Foard's (1998) argument that settlement nucleation preceded the creation of common fields by perhaps several centuries. We are, therefore, seemingly no further forward in knowing when or why such marked regional variation in landscape character emerged in the late first millennium AD. The process may have been pre- or post-ninth century, and may have been due to the character of the natural environment, antecedent landscapes, or contemporary demographic, social, or economic conditions. About the only note of consensus is that most writers have focused on the Midlands, and favoured a single period and a single cause of the emergence of such a marked regional variation in landscape character.

Why did villages and common fields not spread beyond the central zone?

Possible explanations as to why villages and common fields were not found in areas such as the south-east, the south-west, and the north-west of England are mostly inherent in the arguments laid out above for why they were created in the central zone. Some suggest that these areas had a lower population than the Midlands, saw less economic development, and were less extensively cleared of woodland (e.g. Lewis *et al.* 1997; Roberts and Wrathmell 2002; Taylor 2002).

Archaeologists have traditionally believed that any major landscape change required lordly authority, so it is assumed that there must have been weaker manorial power where villages and common fields were not created. For his part, Williamson (2003) suggests that it was particular qualities of the soil, and the greater extent of meadow in the Midlands, that led to the restructuring of the countryside there. One philosophical viewpoint underlies all these arguments: that it was particular conditions in the central zone that led to the creation of villages and common fields there, while the remaining, peripheral, areas of England were somehow remote from the focus of agricultural innovation and so retained an essentially prehistoric landscape. This is the state of uncertainty and disagreement that we have arrived at, and from where this study hopes to move on to a new approach that accepts a greater diversity of causes and a far longer chronology for the development of regional variation in landscape character in southern Britain. This book hopes to challenge Midland-centric perspectives by focusing on the margins of the central zone where landscapes characterized by villages and common fields, and dispersed settlement and predominantly enclosed field systems, occur in close proximity (Figs. 1.4 and 1.5).

SOME PROCESSES OF LANDSCAPE CHANGE

So far a wide range of factors have been identified as possibly having led to the restructuring of the landscape in England's central zone during the late first millennium AD including ethnicity, population growth, the nature of lordship, the character of antecedent landscapes, and the way that communities adapted to local soil conditions and the communal effort needed to produce significant amounts of hay. It is now time to move away from the specific details of this particular region to consider in more general terms how regional differences in landscape character may have come about, and in particular what might have been happening in the south-east and west of the country since developments here may have contributed to the central zone having such a different appearance compared to the rest of southern Britain. Landscapes change in a variety of different ways. In some places, the dominant theme over a period of time is continuity, with only gradual evolution that does not fundamentally change the character of the landscape, such as the occasional amalgamation or subdivision of fields or the foundation and desertion of small numbers of settlements. At certain times the pace of change may accelerate and discontinuity becomes the dominant theme: areas of agricultural land can go out of use, areas of unenclosed land can be colonized (the classic idea of expansion and contraction within 'marginal' areas), and areas that are settled and farmed can be cleared and replanned (such as the Parliamentary Enclosure of common fields). In the context of early medieval southern Britain, it is therefore possible that the regional differences between the South-East,

Within the image:
Fig. 1.4

Fig. 1.5

Monk Wood

Stogursey

castle

0   1 km

Fig. 1.4. Vertical aerial photograph, taken in January 1947, of the nucleated settlement at Stogursey in western Somerset (bottom left) with an open field system to the north that was enclosed by agreement and preserves the outlines of the former strips as long narrow fields with reversed-S profiles (© National Monuments Record, English Heritage: CPE/UK 1944 23 Jan. 1947, frame 2171). In Domesday Stogursey was a large village with 38 villeins, 3 borders, and 3 freedmen (*DB Som.* 27,1), which later grew into a small borough with 15 burgesses in 1327 (Dickinson 1889, 276). The well-preserved motte and bailey castle, first recorded in 1204, lies to the south of the village. See Croft and Aston 1993, 88 for further interpretation of the village plan.

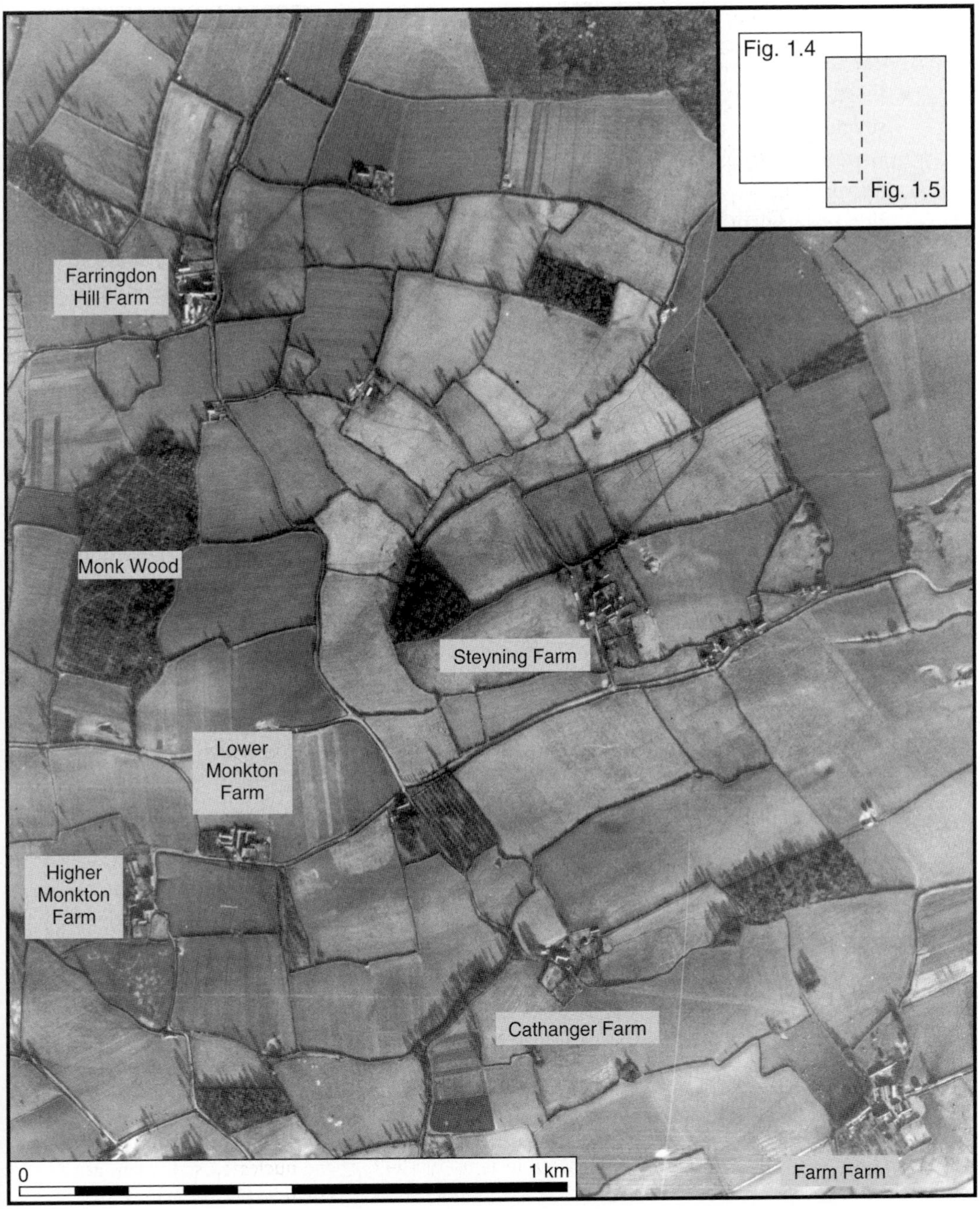
Fig. 1.4
Fig. 1.5
Farringdon Hill Farm
Monk Wood
Steyning Farm
Lower Monkton Farm
Higher Monkton Farm
Cathanger Farm
Farm Farm
0
1 km

Fig. 1.5. Vertical aerial photograph, taken in January 1947, of the area east of Stogursey (note that Monk Wood also appears on Fig. 1.4), with a contrasting landscape of dispersed settlement and fields that would appear to have always been closes held in severalty (© National Monuments Record, English Heritage: CPE/UK 1944 23 Jan. 1947, frame 2173).

the central zone, and the South-West could have developed in a number of different ways:

- First, there may have been late Romano-British and earliest medieval (fifth- to seventh-century) landscapes of relatively uniform character across southern Britain, although from around the eighth to tenth centuries (depending whose chronology is accepted), the central zone evolved in a different way from the rest, with landscapes in the South-East and South-West experiencing relative stability. In this scenario, the concept of villages and common fields spread out from the East Midlands but stopped at what subsequently became the edge of the central zone because the regions beyond had different environmental or socio-economic conditions: the landscape of the central zone would have continued to look much like that of the South-East or the South-West had it not experienced what others have referred to as the 'village moment' or 'great replanning'.

- A second possible scenario starts from the same assumption that there may initially have been landscapes of relatively uniform character across southern Britain, but then suggests that several regions subsequently evolved in their own separate ways, so that few or no landscapes of essentially prehistoric or Romano-British character have survived. That villages and common fields are not found outside the central zone is not because these areas were in any way less well developed, but because communities in each region had developed their own distinctive approaches to landscape management.

- A third possibility is that instead of there being a relatively uniform 'antecedent landscape' across southern Britain, each region may have had a different character long before villages and common fields emerged in the central zone, and in each of these regions local communities simply continued to manage the countryside in their own ways.

- Finally, it is possible that, whether or not there was a uniform 'antecedent landscape', there may initially have been a trend towards settlement nucleation across large areas giving rise to a convergence of landscape character, followed by a second phase of accelerated change in one or more of the regions leading to divergence in character.

The first of these scenarios is very much the prevalent view today, but in the case studies presented here these other possible trajectories of landscape change are explored.

A NEW APPROACH TO UNDERSTANDING THE ORIGINS OF LOCAL AND REGIONAL VARIATION IN LANDSCAPE CHARACTER

To date, various approaches towards studying the origins of the medieval landscape have been tried, including major thematic studies of individual landscape components, notably settlement (Roberts 1987; Lewis *et al.* 1997; Roberts and Wrathmell 2000) and field systems (e.g. Gray 1915; Baker and Butlin 1973a; Rowley 1981). Research projects have been carried out at a variety of scales, ranging from the mapping of various data sets across the whole country, such as soils, population density, and the extent of woodland and meadow (e.g. Roberts and Wrathmell 2000; 2002; Williamson 2007), through to detailed field-based surveys of specific regions (e.g. Whittlewood on the Buckinghamshire/Northamptonshire border: Jones and Page 2004) or even individual parishes (e.g. Shapwick in Somerset: Aston and Gerrard 1999; Gerrard with Aston 2007). As we have already seen, however, there was a tendency to focus on the origins of landscapes characterized by villages and common fields in the central zone, rather than the development of landscapes with more dispersed settlement patterns elsewhere, possibly due to the perception that the village, with its parish church, village green, and duck pond, was somehow central to our Englishness and typical of the 'good old days'. This bias in research is also a reflection of the visibility of the archaeological record and the opportunities to carry out large-scale survey and excavation in a region that has a continuous ceramic sequence from the Roman through to the medieval periods.

This volume will address these problems in three ways. First, it has as its focus the origins of regional variation in landscape character during the early medieval period in a series of study areas across southern Britain, and in particular focuses on the question of why areas adjacent to the central zone did not see the restructuring of their landscapes in this way: were areas such as the South-East and the South-West somewhat poorly developed regions that were not experiencing the same levels of arable cultivation, population growth, and agrarian innovation as seen in the Midlands?

The second aim of this study is to re-examine the chronology of landscape change in the later first millennium AD, and in particular to challenge what has become the prevailing view that it was the later ninth to eleventh centuries that saw the key developments. Instead, it argues that there was a significantly longer process of change that began with a widespread period of innovation during what historians have referred to as the 'long eighth century' (the later seventh to early ninth centuries: Hanson and Wickham 2000), which included the emergence of stable kingship, increasing definition of territorial jurisdictions—both secular and ecclesiastical (e.g. Reynolds 1999; Blair 2005)—the adoption of new agricultural techniques, and a move towards settlement nucleation. This is a period whose rural landscape was somewhat neglected by archaeologists in favour of the 'Early Saxon' period, for which we have a large number of cemeteries and a growing number of large-scale settlement excavations, and the 'Late Saxon' period to which many have attributed the origins of villages and common fields (Reynolds 1999). In contrast, it is suggested here that the late seventh to early ninth centuries saw developments across southern Britain that laid the foundations of today's historic landscape, although following Brown and Foard (1998), it is argued that it was only later, during the late ninth to eleventh centuries, that the central zone saw another period of change that culminated in the further restructuring of settlement and the emergence of the 'Midland' system of regularly arranged common fields, as the evolution of this landscape diverged from that of adjacent areas.

The third aim of this study is to explain regional variation in landscape character not simply by seeking spatial correlations between different sets of data, but by using the landscape as a laboratory and approaching the problem in a more scientific way. If we are having difficulties untangling a large number of possible causes of regional variation in landscape character, such as whether it was lordship or local communities that were responsible, then it would be helpful if we could rule out other possibilities such as variations in the natural environment and 'antecedent' cultural landscapes.

This agenda is addressed through the examination of a series of case studies that address one or more of these thematic and methodological issues, while not attempting a definitive review of the origins of regional variation in landscape character right across early medieval southern Britain. This area was chosen as the focus for this study because the replanning of landscapes in the north of England is an even more complex issue, with several additional potential causal factors including Scandinavian influence and the post-Conquest 'harrying of the north'. Even within southern Britain attention focuses on selected areas for which an interesting story has emerged from recent work: the pre-1974 county of Somerset,[1] at the very south-western limit of the central zone; the south-west peninsula that lies just beyond this limit of landscapes characterized by villages and common fields; southern Cambridgeshire and what is referred to here as 'greater East Anglia' (Norfolk, Suffolk, and Essex) as a case study in England's 'south-eastern province'; and finally south-east and south-west Wales, where landscapes created following the Anglo-Norman Conquest are compared with those back in England (Fig. 1.6). This explicitly comparative approach will hopefully combine the benefits brought about by the detailed understanding of a particular region, so avoiding the sweeping generalizations that have afflicted some previous work, but also refrains from the parochialism that all too easily characterizes landscape research.

Another distinctive feature of this volume is that it has the whole landscape as its focus in contrast to previous books on the early medieval period that have tended to concentrate on burial practice, ethnicity, the development of elite social institutions—notably kingship and the Church—and individual sites (e.g. Dark 2000; Baker 2006b). Sites are of course discussed, but attention

[1] In 1974 the northern part of Somerset was removed and added to the newly created county of Avon, which in turn has been split into a series of unitary authorities including North Somerset, and Bath and North-East Somerset: both of these are included in this study as they formed part of the historic county of Somerset.

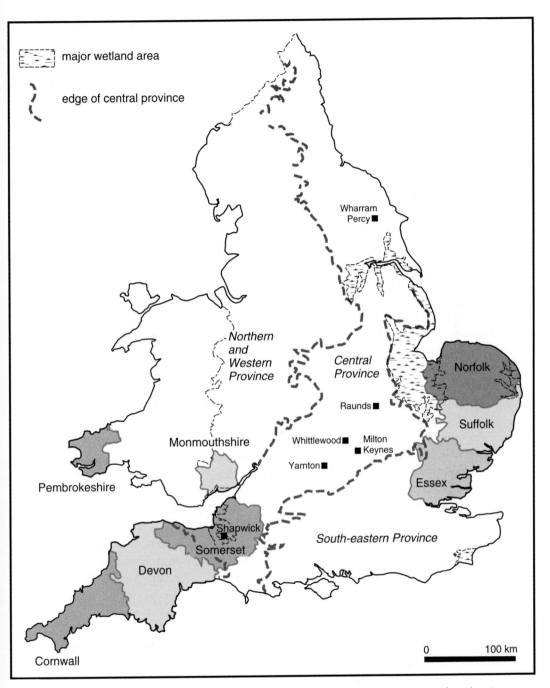

major wetland area

edge of central province

Wharram
Percy ■

Northern
and
Western
Province

Central
Province

Norfolk

Raunds ■

Suffolk

Monmouthshire

Whittlewood ■   Milton
                ■ Keynes

Yarnton ■

Pembrokeshire

Essex

Shapwick

Somerset

South-eastern Province

Devon

0   100 km

Cornwall

Fig. 1.6. The major case-study areas featured in this book, and other places referred to in the text, against a background of Roberts and Wrathmell's (2002, fig. 1.1) three provinces.

also focuses on the development of land-use, through using the available palaeoenvironmental evidence, and the neglected subject of field systems. As far as possible an attempt has been made to adopt the same approach in all areas—tracing the origins of the historic landscape back into the medieval period (and in some cases beyond), and looking at its relationship to the preceding, usually Romano-British and earliest medieval, landscape. There are, however, very different traditions of scholarship in the various case-study areas that affect what conclusions can be drawn about this period. Today, East Anglia and Essex, for example, have more extensive areas of arable cultivation, which have allowed for greater fieldwalking, than in the other areas, while larger-scale gravel quarrying and urban and infrastructure development has led to more excavations, mostly published in the local county journals, along with the monograph series East Anglian Archaeology. In all these areas the amount of unpublished, usually development-led, archaeological work is also considerable, and reports (so-called 'grey literature') on this were either supplied by the archaeological unit that carried out the work or consulted at Historic Environment Records (HERs). When visiting the HERs the author asked curatorial staff a series of standard questions in order to try and identify key recent projects, and these remain focal issues in this book: what became of the Romano-British landscape (how far into the medieval period did it survive); how far back can we trace the origins of today's historic landscape; and what palaeoenvironmental sequences are there which cover the first millennium AD?

Norfolk, Suffolk, and Essex also benefit from a continuous ceramic sequence throughout the Roman and medieval periods, whereas in Somerset, the South-West, and southern Wales the early medieval period is largely aceramic. In part, this problem is being overcome by the greater use of radiocarbon dating which in the South-West, for example, has dated a series of sites whose early medieval chronology would otherwise not have been expected (e.g. Gent and Quinnell 1999a). Several settlements in Essex have similarly only been identified as dating to around the eighth century through the use of radiocarbon dating (e.g. Timby *et al.* 2007, 152–6), although in all areas there is a need for greater use of scientific dating of the latest stratigraphic horizons on late Roman sites to see how far their occupation extended beyond the use of pottery and coins. Note that all radiocarbon dates cited here are calibrated to the two sigma standard deviation.

This, then, was the agenda behind this volume. In Chapter 2 we begin by looking at Somerset, where a characterization of the nineteenth-century landscape reveals that the county straddles the south-western boundary of the central zone, with villages and former common fields to the east, and a more dispersed settlement pattern and enclosed field systems to the west. A range of evidence shows that this broad division can be traced back at least as far as the High Middle Ages, and a number of possible causes of this regional variation are then reviewed. In Chapter 3, it will be described how the development of local differences in landscape character on land reclaimed from intertidal marshes can only be attributed to cultural factors, there having been a natural and antecedent landscape of uniform character. There is evidence that Glastonbury Abbey may have been a significant factor in some areas having villages and common fields, and this is then explored across Somerset, as is the role of other major landowners. It is suggested that the champion countryside in this, the south-west corner of England's central zone, originated in the fragmentation of 'great estates', and while the estate management policies of certain landowners, such as Glastonbury Abbey, may have been significant it appears to have been at a more local level that decisions were made as to how the landscape should be structured.

In Chapter 4 we move across the major watershed of the Blackdown and Quantock Hills (to the west of Bridgwater in Somerset, and Bridport in Dorset), which separates the south-west peninsula from the rest of Britain, to see why the idea of arranging a landscape around villages and common fields did extend this far. It is shown that there was a long-lived boundary of cultural significance along this watershed, but that around the eighth century there were major changes in the landscape. In the absence of a good ceramic sequence and large-scale archaeological fieldwork on sites of this period, palaeoenvironmental evidence is particularly important. Chapter 5 takes us across to East Anglia and Essex where another long-lived cultural boundary lies roughly along the line of the Lark and Gipping valleys (between Bury St Edmunds and Ipswich, in Suffolk). Important differences in the development of the landscape either side of this line are identified, with the area to the north also showing a major reorganization of the landscape around the eighth century. To the south there appears to have been greater continuity, with a pattern of gradual evolution rather than the significant changes seen further north. A review of recent work in Cambridgeshire, whose villages and common fields lay within England's central zone of champion countryside, also suggests that settlement nucleation began around the eighth century, although it was not until several centuries later that these settlements tended to acquire their modern village form.

In the final case study, Chapter 6 considers two areas in southern Wales where landscapes appear to have been transformed in the context of the Anglo-Norman lordships, while in both cases adjacent areas that remained in Welsh hands retained a very different character. This supports the notion that in the twelfth century, some in society had a clear concept of how a landscape should be structured with a nucleated village surrounded by common fields as its focus.

2

At the Margins of the Champion Countryside: The Emergence of Villages and Common Fields in Somerset

When the sixteenth-century traveller John Leland visited Somerset in 1542 he mostly travelled through 'pasture grounds and fields...largely enclosed with hedgerows of elm trees' (Toulmin-Smith 1906, 62; Slater 1907).[1] Had he ventured west of Glastonbury, however, he would have witnessed vast common fields surrounding a series of compact villages strung out along the Polden Hills which along with small areas of woodland on the poorer soils, and common meadows down in the valleys, comprised classic 'champion' countryside that would have been quite at home in an East Midland county such as Northamptonshire. Documentary sources and a careful analysis of the historic landscape show that in fact villages and common fields dominated the landscape of southern and eastern Somerset during the thirteenth century, before most were enclosed in the late medieval and post-medieval periods, yet just a few kilometres to the west, beyond the river Parrett, the landscape was very different in character. Here, the settlement pattern consisted of a scatter of small hamlets and isolated farmsteads, surrounded by a fieldscape dominated by ancient closes with just a few small areas of open field. So why was the landscape of central Somerset so similar to that of the East Midlands, and why was the countryside to the west so very different?

The pre-1974 county of Somerset straddles the boundary between Roberts and Wrathmell's (2000) 'central' and 'south-western' provinces, making it an ideal case study within which to explore the origins of this major regional difference in landscape character (Fig. 1.6). Initially, and in an approach familiar from previous studies (e.g. Roberts and Wrathmell 2002; Williamson 2003; forthcoming), this involves looking for correlations between variations in landscape character and a wide range of possible causal factors such as soils, the character of the countryside just before the creation of villages and common

---

[1] Leland specifically refers to an enclosed landscape between Midsomer Norton and Bishop Sutton in north-east Somerset, South Cadbury and Ilchester, around Montacute, and between Crewkerne and Hinton St George in south-east Somerset, and Culbone and Steart in west Somerset.

fields (the 'antecedent landscape'), population density, and economic development. We will then, however, move beyond this traditional approach and pursue a further line of enquiry that emphasizes how the landscape can be used as a laboratory within which the potential significance of the possible factors behind regional variation in character can be tested under controlled conditions. Following the emphasis that Roberts and Wrathmell (2000; 2002) have placed upon antecedent landscapes, and Williamson (2003; 2007) upon the suitability of soils for different forms of agriculture, we examine a third possible variable: the relationship between lordship and community. This is achieved by looking at areas where these other possible factors cannot have been significant as the medieval countryside was created through the reclamation of wetlands—where the soils and antecedent landscapes were all derived from a uniform saltmarsh environment—with the result that any local variation in the character of settlement patterns and field systems must have been due to other, cultural, factors. The results of this analysis show that social and tenurial variables were in fact crucial in shaping landscape character, and this is then explored further by examining variation in landscape character in the context of the fragmentation and rearrangement of large early medieval estates.

HILLS, VALES, FENS, AND MARSHES: THE PHYSICAL TOPOGRAPHY OF SOMERSET

The physical landscape of Somerset is one of great diversity, although it has a series of relatively clear natural boundaries (Fig. 2.1). To the west, south, and east there are a series of uplands that in the medieval period included large tracts of unenclosed and wooded land. To the west are the barren moors of Exmoor fringed by rolling hills and steep-sided valleys of the Brendon Hills, which are separated from the Quantock Hills by the Doniford Stream and Halse Water valleys. To the south lies the Vale of Taunton Deane beyond which lie the Blackdown Hills, an extensive area of relatively flat-topped uplands separated by a series of broad valleys. To the east of the Quantock and Blackdown Hills lies an extensive lowland plain that extends across much of southern and eastern Somerset, and which is drained by a series of rivers—the Tone, Isle, Parrett, Yeo, Cary, and Brue—that flow north and west into the Somerset Levels. The Levels dominate central Somerset, and before their reclamation this vast expanse of wetland comprised a mosaic of environments, notably saltmarshes and mudflats towards the coast, and freshwater peat bogs in the lower-lying inland 'backfens'. The eastern boundary of Somerset is marked by an extensively wooded ridge north of Penselwood that became the royal Forest of Selwood. To the north of the Somerset Levels lies a range of limestone hills, including Mendip, that extend from the coast in the west across almost two-thirds of the county towards Wells and Shepton Mallet in the east. The

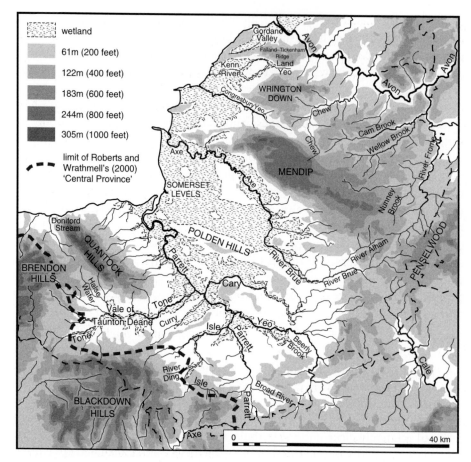

Fig. 2.1. The major topographical regions of Somerset.

landscape to the north of these hills is very different in character from the relatively flat lowland plains of the south of the county. North Somerset is an area of rolling hills and broad, gently sided valleys drained by the rivers Frome, Wellow, Cam, and Chew that all flow north into the Avon Valley, which marks the border with Gloucestershire. To the west lie two other wetland areas: the North Somerset Levels by the coast, into which flow the Congresbury Yeo and Land Yeo (Yeo being the local word for river), and the Gordano Valley that joins the estuary of the Avon north of the Failand–Tickenham Ridge.

REGIONAL VARIATIONS IN LANDSCAPE CHARACTER IN NINETEENTH-CENTURY SOMERSET

While at the national scale it is clear that Somerset straddles the boundary between England's 'central' and 'south-western' provinces, two questions immediately come to mind: how clear is this division in landscape character on the ground, and how far do the nineteenth-century sources used by Roberts and Wrathmell reflect landscape character in the medieval period? In contrast to much earlier work that has focused on just one landscape component, such as field systems (e.g. Gray 1915; Baker and Butlin 1973a; Rowley 1981), village morphology (e.g. for Somerset see Ellison 1983; Roberts 1987, fig. 96), or settlement patterns (e.g. Roberts 1987; Roberts and Wrathmell 2000), this study has undertaken a characterization of the landscape as a whole and in the context of the social/tenurial framework within which the countryside was managed. Roberts and Wrathmell, for example, used early nineteenth-century Ordnance Survey Old Series one inch to the mile maps of 1805–69, which only show settlements and roads, with the result that no account is taken of the character of the associated field systems, or their relationship to parish boundaries. The use of such small-scale maps (i.e. one inch to the mile, as opposed to six inches to the mile) can possibly be justified in an analysis carried out at a national scale, but in the county-based work presented here we are able to carry out a more multifaceted analysis.

A key characteristic of a village is that it was the single nucleated settlement from which the majority of the land of that community was exploited, in contrast to areas with dispersed settlement patterns where there were numerous hamlets and isolated farmsteads within that community's territory. The most important manifestation of the territories of rural communities in southern England is parishes, but when Roberts and Wrathmell were working there was no simple way of mapping their early nineteenth-century boundaries (before the local government reorganizations later in that century that altered some boundaries before they came to be depicted on the Ordnance Survey First Edition Six Inch maps). The result was that Roberts and Wrathmell categorized settlement nucleation and dispersion in a purely morphological way, counting the number of settlements within a 4 km^2 square. Since then, however, parish boundaries as depicted on the Tithe maps of *c.*1840 have become available in electronic form (Kain and Oliver 2001), and so in this study a very different approach could be adopted whereby the relationship between both settlement and field systems is characterized in the context of these territorial units within which communities managed their countryside. Tithe maps also provide us with the earliest complete depiction of settlement patterns and field systems but these are not, alas, available in such a user-friendly electronic form, and as it is impractical to transcribe all 498 Tithe maps in Somerset, the next best source for studying the character of settlement patterns and field systems is the Ordnance Survey First Edition Six Inch maps of *c.*1880 (e.g. Figs. 2.3, 2.7, 2.8, and 3.5).

In assessing the degree of settlement nucleation and dispersion it was important not to carry out the analysis in a too mechanistic way as some parishes in Somerset were very large and clearly embraced a number of separate communities known as tithings (equivalent to the 'townships' of northern England: Winchester 1990, 6–7). Unfortunately we do not have a definitive map of Somerset's tithings, although documentary sources allow them to be reconstructed with a fair degree of accuracy. In 1841, for example, the 6,930-acre parish and hundred of Martock (Fig. 2.2) consisted of the main village and the tithings of Bower Hinton & Hurst, Coat, Ash, Whitcombe, Milton, Long Load, and Stapleton, giving an average of 886 acres (360 ha) per tithing. The antiquity of this pattern is reflected in the *Nomina Villarum* of 1316 that records the manors of Martock (with the hamlets of 'Henton' (Bower Hinton), Hurst, and Coat), Ash (with the hamlet of Whitcombe), and Milton (with the hamlets of Long Load and Stapleton) (Dickinson 1889, 67). Overall, therefore, it would appear that across large areas of Somerset,

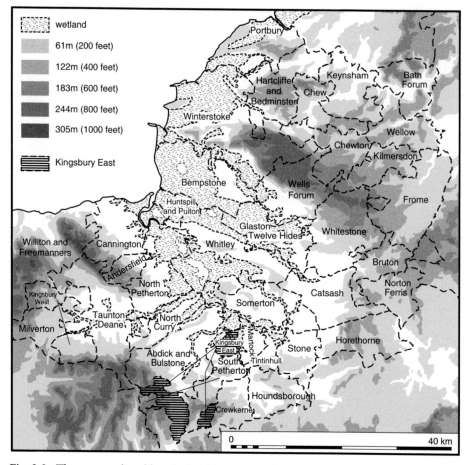

Fig. 2.2. The post-medieval hundreds of Somerset (after Thorn and Thorn 1980, 408–13).

excluding areas with extensive tracts of unreclaimed wetland and unenclosed upland, the average tithing was around 1,200 to 1,300 acres (485–525 ha), except in the central-southern lowlands where they were around 800–900 acres (325–65 ha).

We can now return to the question of how clear the boundary of England's central zone was as it crossed Somerset, by assessing the character of settlement patterns and field systems within these tithings and parishes. Based on an analysis of the First Edition Ordnance Survey Six Inch maps we can divide the landscape into four types of countryside:

- Settlement almost wholly restricted to a nucleated village, associated with the distinctive signatures of former common fields (Parliamentary Enclosure, or enclosure by agreement that preserved furlong boundaries and reversed-S-shaped fields) which covered most of the parish/tithing apart from areas of valley-bottom meadow and woodland on the steeper slopes (Fig. 2.3A). The majority of any isolated farmsteads clearly post-date the enclosure of the former common fields, although there were occasional isolated farmsteads/shrunken hamlets in the peripheral areas of some larger parishes within what appear to be closes always held in severalty (i.e. an enclosed plot of land in single ownership, as opposed to part of a common field). Within this category of settlement there are at least two clearly different forms: villages that have at their core a planned block of tenements that as such represent a distinct transformation of the landscape, and more amorphous plans, which include polyfocal villages that grew more slowly and in a piecemeal fashion.
- Hamlets associated with their own, smaller-scale, open or common fields (typically around a quarter to half a square mile; 65–130 ha), of which there were several within a parish/tithing (Fig. 2.3B). Occasionally also associated with isolated farmsteads and irregular closes in peripheral areas.
- Hamlets and isolated farmsteads associated with field systems that appear to have contained a mixture of small-scale open fields and closes held in severalty (Fig. 2.3C).
- Strongly dispersed settlement patterns (hamlets and isolated farmsteads) and closes that do not appear to have been former open fields (Fig. 2.3D).
- Parishes that are unclassified due to the loss of the medieval landscape, for example through urban expansion or the creation of landscape parks and gardens.

When mapped across the whole county a very clear pattern emerges (Fig. 2.4). In central and south-eastern Somerset, south of Mendip and as far west as the river Isle, type 'A' landscapes dominate, with almost wholly nucleated settlement patterns and each village surrounded by what were clearly extensive

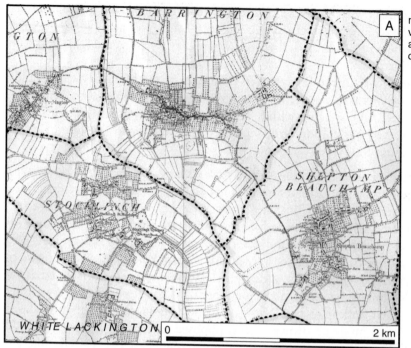

nucleated
villages
and former
open fields

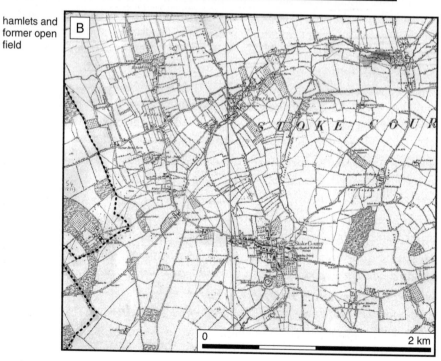

hamlets and
former open
field

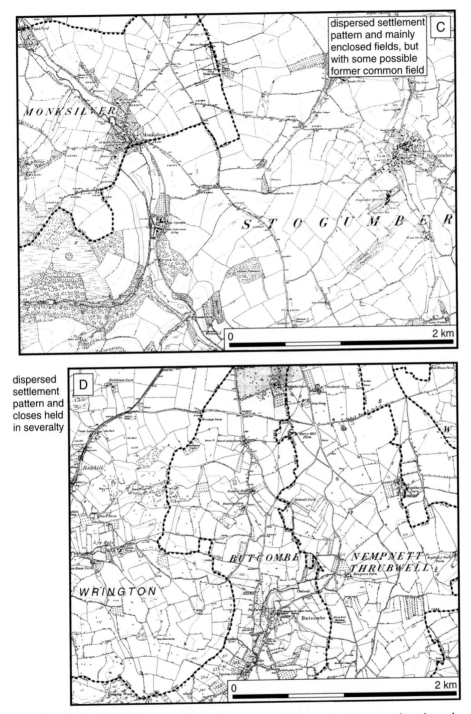

Fig. 2.3. Examples of major historic landscape character types in Somerset, based on the First Edition Ordnance Survey Six Inch maps of *c*.1880.

former common fields (the western boundary of this landscape character area runs immediately west of North Curry, Curry Mallet, Beercrocombe, Isle Abbots, and Ilton). A very small number of places within south-east Somerset had more hamlet-based landscapes (type B), although some of these may represent post-medieval creations that cannot otherwise be attributed to factors such as the growth of industry and the railways. Between the rivers Isle and Tone there are a mixture of landscapes with a small number of villages, a greater number of parishes and tithings with several hamlets and smaller-scale open field systems, and some places with predominantly dispersed settlement patterns: this is clearly the relatively narrow boundary zone of the central zone. West of a line drawn between the Parrett estuary, Bridgwater, Taunton, and the Blackdown Hills there are no landscapes characterized by villages or hamlets with common fields (types 'A' and 'B'): settlement was predominantly dispersed and associated with wholly enclosed field systems (type 'D'). While there are some areas of possible smaller-scale open fields (type 'C') in the Halse Valley north of Taunton they are of very limited extent. North of Mendip the picture is more complex. There are landscapes of villages and former common fields (type 'A'), although these are interspersed with areas of wholly dispersed settlement and fields that have clearly only ever been held in severalty (type 'D'). There are a scatter of hamlet-based landscapes (type 'B'), and a number of places where there may have been some common fields within a mostly enclosed landscape (type 'C'). At first sight this pattern appears fairly inexplicable although the villages tend to occur in lower-lying vales, and occasionally in clusters (planned blocks?) such as around Gordano in the far north-west, and on the northern flank of Mendip between Blagdon, and East and West Harptree. It is worth noting that the correlation between this multifaceted analysis of both settlement and field systems, and the boundary of Roberts and Wrathmell's 'central province', is variable: when mapped at the small (national) scale the correlation is reasonable, but when viewed in more detail only in the far south of Somerset is there a close match, while further north their boundary of village-based landscapes is around 10 to 20 kilometres too far west (Fig. 2.4).

In this particular county, the boundary of what had been champion countryside is therefore still relatively sharp, starting at the estuary of the river Parrett where the nucleated village and extensive former common fields of Pawlett[2] are in sharp contrast to the scattered settlements and irregularly shaped closes of Otterhampton and Cannington to the west. The Parrett flows south into the extensive wetland of Sedgemoor which once again marks a significant boundary in landscape character, with the dispersed settlement patterns and enclosed field systems in North Petherton to the west contrasting with Midland-style villages and former common fields on the island of Sowy

---

[2] Which are depicted in their unenclosed form on a parish map of 1658 (SRO T/PH/sfy2).

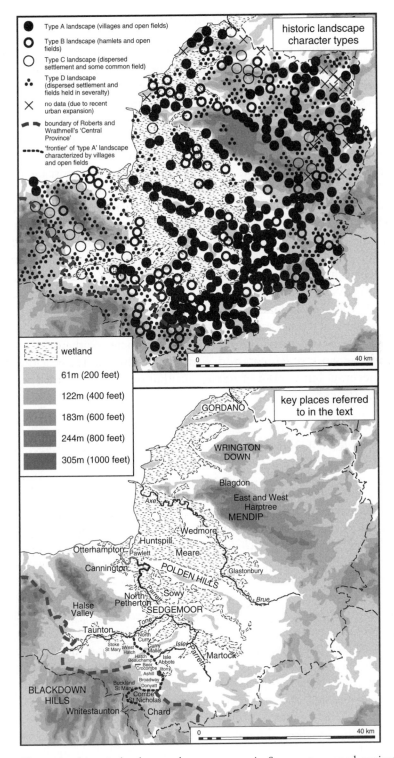

Fig. 2.4. The major historic landscape character types in Somerset mapped against topography.

and the Polden Hills to the east. Significantly, the boundary of this 'village zone' then diverges from natural features, running south across the lowland plain of southern Somerset (discussed further below) towards the Blackdown Hills where there is once again a remarkably sharp boundary in landscape character with Combe St Nicholas (Figs. 2.5 and 2.6) and Chard having compact villages and former common fields, in contrast to the highly dispersed settlement patterns and small, irregularly shaped closes of Buckland St Mary and Whitestaunton to the west. The boundary in historic landscape character in this latter area could be in part determined by topographical differences, and so the crucial area of interest is that between Sedgemoor and the Blackdown Hills where there is a similarly clear division in the character of settlement and field systems but on the flat lowland plain of central Somerset. To the east, North Curry, Curry Mallet, Beercrocombe, Isle Abbots, and Ilton represent former 'champion' countryside, while Stoke St Mary, West Hatch, Hatch Beauchamp, Ashill, Broadway, and Donyatt, just *c*.3 km to the west, had a dispersed settlement and ancient enclosures. A comparison with the results of this analysis, which takes into account not just settlement morphology within the context of parishes and tithings, but the character of the field systems as well, with the work of Roberts and Wrathmell (2000) shows that the latter is broadly accurate but in need of refinement that only more detailed work such as this can achieve.

RECONSTRUCTING REGIONAL VARIATION IN LANDSCAPE CHARACTER IN LATER MEDIEVAL (POST-CONQUEST) SOMERSET

The characterization above was based on the nineteenth-century landscape, and the reader might well ask how far this reflects the medieval pattern. In the case of both Parliamentary Enclosure and enclosure by agreement, the common fields were replaced by new landscapes that are instantly recognizable, as are some post-medieval changes in settlement patterns such as the development of villages associated with mining, the railways, and coastal recreation. The emergence of isolated farmsteads in areas of enclosed common fields and former common pasture can also be easily recognized. Other changes in the character of the countryside are, however, more difficult to detect purely from nineteenth-century maps, notably the shrinkage and desertion of some rural settlements, and the growth of others. There are also examples of small hamlets emerging in the late and post-medieval periods from what had been a more dispersed settlement pattern, such as where sub-infeudation and the decay of manorial authority allowed hamlets to emerge around areas of enclosed waste or where there was once just a single, often freehold, farmstead (e.g. in the southern part of Wedmore parish: Hudson 2002, 18–24). In other cases an isolated farmstead may be the surviving remnant of what had been a larger settlement, as is clearly demonstrated in parts of Devon and Cornwall through documentary research (Beresford 1964; Fox 1989b), and archaeological survey and excavation (e.g. the Roadford Reservoir in south-west Devon: Henderson and Weddell 1994). The same appears to be true in western Somerset and around Exmoor, for example on the Holnicote Estate (Richardson 2006; and see below) and at Lyshwell (Riley and Wilson-North 2001, fig. 5.11).

So does this fluidity in the character of some individual settlements invalidate the use of nineteenth-century sources when trying to characterize the medieval countryside as a whole? The answer is dependent on the scale at which research is undertaken, and the character of the landscapes in question. When research is carried out on a small scale (for example covering just a few parishes), and/or where settlement patterns include a mixture of both nucleated and dispersed elements, changes in landscape character within one or two parishes will be relatively significant and so the nineteenth-century sources may not be a reliable guide to the character of the medieval countryside. However, the larger the scale at which one works, the less significant these individual settlement biographies become as local detail is subsumed within the larger, regional picture. This is especially true where the nineteenth-century landscape is dominated by just one type of pattern: across large swathes of south-east Somerset, for example, there are parishes where even in the nineteenth century virtually all settlement was in a single village, surrounded by clear evidence for former common field, and a series of archaeological and standing building surveys are now confirming their medieval origins.

The Somerset village that has seen the most intensive investigation is Shapwick, where excavations, along with the collection of pottery from test pits and flower beds within the present village, have shown that it was laid out by or during the tenth century. The aceramic nature of early medieval Somerset[3] means that we cannot preclude there having been an earlier settlement focus beneath the later village, although the location of the eighth-century minster, which lies 800 m outside the village to the east, suggests that the site of the later village was not a significant location when this church was founded (Gerrard with Aston 2007). While a pre-tenth-century date is possible, the earlier weakness of Glastonbury's governance and turbulence caused by Viking raids makes

---

[3] The only early medieval pottery in Somerset before the 10th century is small amounts of 5th- to 6th-century material imported from the Mediterranean found on several well-known high-status sites such as the reoccupied hillforts at Cadbury Congresbury and South Cadbury, the possible monastic site at Glastonbury (the Mount and Tor), and the cemetery at Cannington (Thomas 1981). Two more recent discoveries, at Carhampton and Lyng (Webster and Croft 1994, 177; Bagwell and Webster 2006), are both from royal centres. The genuine absence of pottery from lower-status rural sites in the county between the 5th and the 9th centuries has recently been confirmed on a number of excavations where features containing domestic refuse but no ceramics have been radiocarbon dated to the early medieval period (e.g. Cheddar: Hollinrake and Hollinrake 1997; Evans and Hancock 2006, 109; Coronation Road in Highbridge: Hollinrake and Hollinrake 2004; Webster 2004, 209; St Michael's House in South Brent: Webster 2001, 231).

Fig. 2.5. The village and field systems at Combe St Nicholas, taken in March 1948 (© Somerset County Council: CPE/UK/2491. 11 Mar. 1948, frame 4077). The morphology of the blocks of long narrow fields surrounding the village is suggestive of former common field, and this is supported by the highly fragmented pattern of landownership and occupancy in the Tithe Survey (see Fig. 2.6).

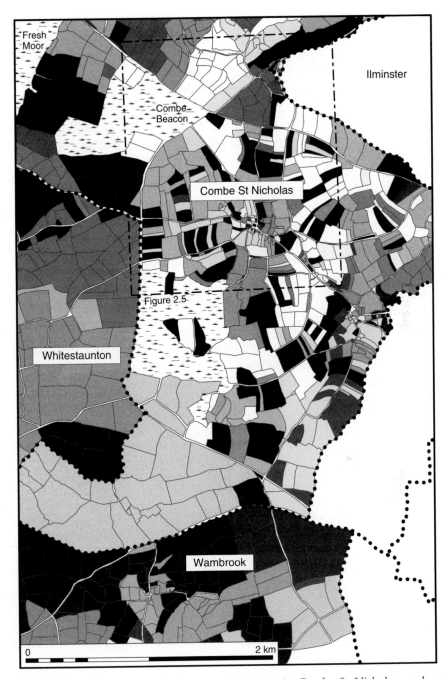

Fig. 2.6. Patterns of land occupancy (i.e. tenements) in Combe St Nicholas, and parts of Wambrook and Whitestaunton, based on their Tithe Surveys of *c*.1840. In Combe St Nicholas the highly fragmented pattern of landholding supports the hypothesis derived from historic landscape character that the village was surrounded by an extensive common field system. In contrast, in the north of the parish, and in Wambrook and Whitestaunton, isolated farmsteads held compact blocks of closes in severalty (drawing and research by Chris Smart, Jenny Viner, and Adam Wainwright).

this unlikely and it has been widely suggested that the most plausible context for the restructuring of this landscape was the 're-invigoration of monastic life under [Abbot] Dunstan in the 940s and subsequent monastic reforms' (Aston and Gerrard 1999, 29; and see Costen 1992c; Corcos 2002). To somewhat pre-empt later discussion, a tenth-century date for this planned village also fits in with the picture emerging across parts of southern Britain, of relatively unplanned settlement nucleation starting around the eighth century and then further restructuring of these villages several centuries later as proposed by Brown and Foard (1998) for Northamptonshire. Returning to Shapwick, and the question of how far nineteenth-century maps give an indication of the character of the medieval landscape, a standing building survey has shown that this village was the only settlement in the parish until the eighteenth century when several farms moved out to the more peripheral areas following the enclosure of the common fields: archaeology and buildings survey has confirmed the hypothesis derived from an analysis of nineteenth-century cartographic sources that Shapwick was a classic champion-type landscape during the medieval period (SVBRG 1996; Aston and Gerrard 1999; Gerrard with Aston 2007). That settlement nucleation across the rest of eastern and southern Somerset also occurred in or before the tenth century is also receiving increasing support from the growing number of evaluations, excavations, and watching briefs within still-occupied medieval villages that have revealed occupation from the tenth century.[4] There is also some palaeoenvironmental support for an increasing intensity of landscape use in central Somerset around the tenth century such as pollen sequences from Godney and Meare Heath that show a marked decline in dryland trees and an increase in herbs indicative of clearance and cultivation (Beckett and Hibbert 1979, 594; Housley *et al.* 2007). About the same time there was increased sedimentation in the palaeochannel of the former river Brue/Sheppey, just south of the Panborough–Bleadney Gap (Aalbersberg 1999, 93), and there also appears to have been an increase in alluviation in the Yeo Valley, in the south-western part of the Somerset Levels around Ilchester (Thew 1994).

The origins of the dispersed settlement pattern in the west of Somerset are unfortunately more difficult to establish as the predominantly pastoral modern land-use prevents large-scale fieldwalking surveys. The study of place names and standing buildings has, however, enabled a settlement pattern that in the nineteenth century was dispersed in character to be traced back at least as far as the thirteenth and fourteenth centuries (Aston 1983; Penoyre and Penoyre

[4] Aller (Webster 2003, 151); Bawdrip (Webster and Croft 1997, 149; Hollinrake and Hollinrake 2001; Bagwell and Webster 2006, 171); Bower Hinton in Martock (Webster 2004, 204–5); Dundon (Hollinrake and Hollinrake 1989); East Lyng (Bagwell and Webster 2005, 119); Glastonbury (Bagwell and Webster 2005, 119–20); Meare (Webster 2003, 157); Middlezoy (Webster 2001, 234; 2004, 210); Misterton (Webster 2003, 157–8); Shapwick (Aston and Gerrard 1999); Somerton (Webster 1999, 195); South Brent (Webster 2001; Gutiérrez 2007); Walton (Webster 2004, 215; Leach 2006); and Wedmore (Webster 1999, 196).

1999). This is most evident in the parishes of Luccombe and Selworthy, to the east of Porlock, large parts of which fall within the National Trust's Holnicote estate which was the subject of detailed documentary research and standing building survey by Isabel Richardson (2006). Twenty-two late medieval standing buildings have been recorded, the earliest dated through dendrochronology to 1315 (East Lynch Farm Cottage in Selworthy), and these structures are spread across the landscape confirming that what in the nineteenth century was a highly dispersed settlement pattern had the same character at least as far back as the fourteenth and fifteenth centuries (Fig. 2.7). This is in sharp contrast to a series of detailed surveys of standing buildings in a number of parishes in southern and eastern Somerset—for example in Chiselborough, West and Middle Chinnock, and Haselbury Plucknett (Fig. 2.8)—that have shown that surviving late medieval buildings are only found in villages and that all the outlying farms are post-medieval, post-dating the enclosure of the former common fields (SSAVBRG 1984; 1993; 1994).[5]

A range of other evidence similarly suggests that at a broad regional scale nineteenth-century differences in landscape character do reflect the medieval pattern. The existence of severely shrunken or wholly abandoned medieval settlements, for example, is a reminder of how the landscape is constantly changing, but it is significant that the nature of these settlements in different parts of Somerset is in keeping with the nineteenth-century landscape character of these areas: in central and south-east Somerset there are a number of deserted villages, while in the west there are deserted farmsteads and small hamlets (e.g. Aston 1982, 130; Croft and Aston 1993, 59, 61; Riley and Wilson-North 2001, figs. 4.8 and 5.11; Riley 2006, fig. 4.27). Another type of earthwork—ridge and furrow—can also be used to demonstrate the medieval origins of regional variation in landscape character. These earthworks were once common across large parts of central and south-east Somerset (Fig. 2.9A), although when interpreting such a distribution it must be remembered that in places where arable cultivation continued into the post-medieval period ridge and furrow will have been destroyed: its survival on the Royal Air Force photography of the late 1940s—the earliest we have with which to map its distribution—can at best be used to show its minimum extent. That said, it is remarkable how closely the extent of surviving ridge and furrow matches the western limit of countryside that in the nineteenth century was characterized by villages and former common field systems (cf. Figs. 2.4 and 2.9A).

A further strand of evidence that can be used to reconstruct the character of the medieval countryside is documentary material. As in any county, this has survived inconsistently across Somerset, although the well-preserved archives of Glastonbury Abbey provide us with a series of excellent sources for a

---

[5] For other standing building surveys in central and eastern Somerset see SSAVBRG 1982; 1986; 1988; SVBRG 1996; Dallimore 2001; SVBRG 2001; SVBRG 2004.

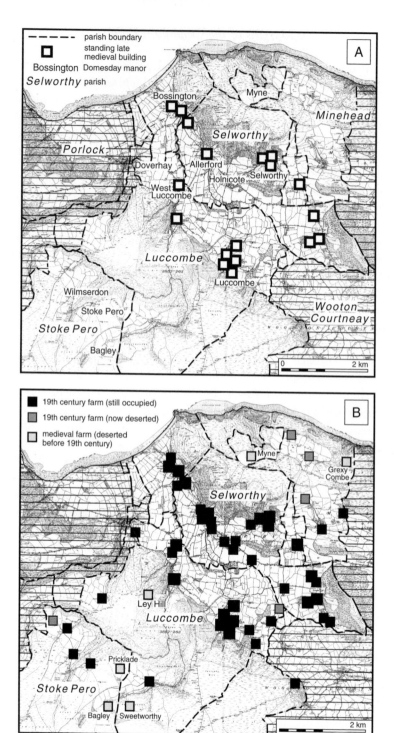

Fig. 2.7. (A) Standing domestic buildings dating to the late medieval period on the National Trust's Holnicote Estate near Porlock in western Somerset; (B) 19th-century farmsteads in the same area, along with sites of earlier, deserted settlement. Note how the standing buildings confirm the impression gained from 19th-century sources that this region has had a dispersed settlement pattern ever since at least the late medieval period. Based on research by Isabel Richardson (2006).

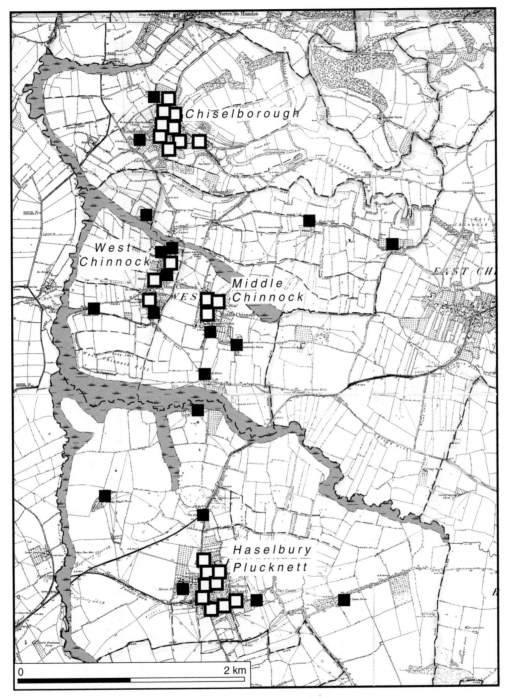

Fig. 2.8. The distribution of standing late medieval (white squares) and post-medieval buildings (black squares) in Chiselborough, West and Middle Chinnock, and Haselbury Plucknett in south-east Somerset, based on research by the Somerset and South Avon Vernacular Buildings Research Group (SSAVBRG 1984; 1993; 1994). Note how the late medieval buildings are restricted to the village centres, and that it is only post-medieval houses that are found out in the now enclosed former common fields.

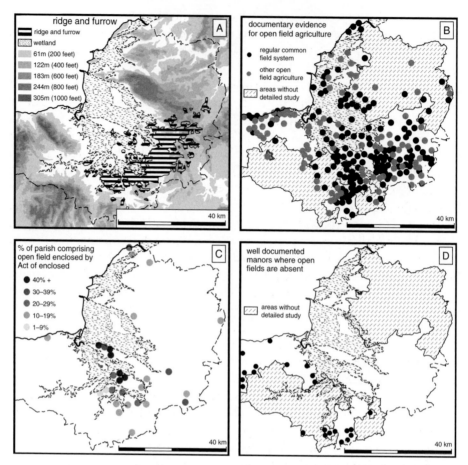

Fig. 2.9. Evidence for open and common fields in Somerset. (A) earthworks, both surviving and depicted on aerial photographs, of ridge and furrow (Aston 1988c, fig. 5.3); (B) documentary evidence (Rippon 2004a, fig. 27.8); (C) the percentage of parishes comprising open field enclosed by Act of Parliament (Turner 1978); (D) places for which there has been research into the medieval landscape but where open or common fields appear to have been absent (Rippon 2004, fig. 27.7).

broad swathe across the centre of the county. The evidence from these and other archives, mostly thirteenth and fourteenth century in date, suggest that regularly arranged common field systems were widespread in central and south-eastern parts of the county, and while there was some open field farming in parts of the west there were very few two- or three-field systems (Fig. 2.9B; Keil 1964; Dunning 1974; 1981; 1985; 1992; 1999; Whitfield 1981; Aston 1988c; Rippon 1993; 1997; Musgrove 1999; Corcos 2002). This pattern also corresponds to the distribution of common field that survived into the eighteenth and nineteenth centuries to be enclosed through Act of Parliament which once again concentrates in central and south-eastern Somerset (Fig. 2.9C; Turner 1978). While great care must be taken in using negative evidence, it is also striking that those places which have seen detailed documentary research but have failed to reveal evidence for common field agriculture are restricted to the foothills of the Blackdown, Brendon, and Quantock Hills in the far south and west of Somerset (Fig. 2.9D).

A final strand of evidence that can be used, with care, to reconstruct past field systems is that of patterns of landownership and tenancy that can be reconstructed using the Tithe maps and apportionments of *c*.1840. In areas where the field boundary pattern is clearly indicative of the enclosure of open or common field by agreement—resulting in blocks of long narrow fields (enclosed strips), laid out between long, sinuous, parallel boundaries (furlong blocks)—patterns of landownership and occupancy tend to be highly fragmented (e.g. around the village in Combe St Nicholas: Fig. 2.6). In contrast, in areas with more dispersed settlement associated with closes held in severalty, the land held by individual farmsteads tends to be held in compact blocks (e.g. Wambrook and Whitestaunton: Fig. 2.6). A crucial question is clearly how far back such different patterns in landownership can be traced, and in a detailed analysis of several parishes in north Somerset this was certainly as far as the late medieval period (Rippon 2006a, 94–7).

This overview of the archaeological, architectural, and documentary evidence in Somerset suggests that the broad regional difference in landscape character between eastern and western Somerset, as depicted on nineteenth-century cartographic sources, does indeed date back to the medieval period. This is certainly true for the thirteenth to fourteenth centuries when these sources start to become abundant, and there is growing evidence from central and south-eastern Somerset that the villages there existed by the later tenth century. At a local scale it is true that there was some settlement nucleation in areas that were formerly characterized by dispersed patterns, and in other places a scatter of isolated farmsteads has emerged around what were once wholly nucleated villages, but these individual changes do not affect the broad regional picture. Detailed historic landscape analysis, archaeological and standing building survey, and research into pre-nineteenth-century maps, documents, and place names confirms that in the medieval period central and south-eastern Somerset had 'champion' countryside, while there were more dispersed settlement patterns and a predominance of enclosed fields existed to the west.

THE PRE-VILLAGE LANDSCAPE

Unfortunately, the largely aceramic nature of the early medieval period in Somerset means that we know far less about the pre-village landscape here than we do in East Midland counties such as Northamptonshire, although at Shapwick we do have an insight into what appears to have been a dispersed settlement pattern. Fieldwalking has revealed an extensive scatter of

Romano-British settlement with a villa and at least nine farmsteads including those within medieval furlongs with the settlement-indicative names of Abchester (derived from OE *ceaster*: 'a fortification, an earthwork'), Chestell (derived from OE *ceastel*: 'a heap of stones'), and Blakelands (indicating areas of human habitation) (Field 1993, 212–13; Aston and Gerrard 1999, fig. 9). All the farmsteads were occupied in the fourth century and two (Church Field and Sladwick)—the only two that saw large-scale excavation—have produced archaeological evidence that they were occupied for some time thereafter, but as Somerset was aceramic during the fifth to ninth centuries all that can be said with certainty is that the rest were abandoned by the tenth century. A series of other settlement-indicative field and furlong names also point to an extensive dispersed settlement pattern that was swept away when the carefully planned village and common fields were created, four of which have yielded tenth-century pottery scatters (Buddell, Gracehay, Longenworthie, and Old Churche). Assuming these relate to settlement rather than manuring, they provide a *terminus post quem* for the desertion of these scattered farmsteads and their replacement by Shapwick's planned village and common fields.

There have been few other large-scale fieldwalking surveys in Somerset with which to test this model of a dispersed settlement pattern being replaced by nucleated villages, although around South Cadbury a number of settlement-indicative field names have revealed Romano-British sites that may have continued to be occupied into the early medieval period (e.g. Gilton and Stonechester in North Cadbury), and some that have produced a few sherds of 'Late Saxon' pottery (e.g. Henehill and Stonehill in Sutton Montis) (Davey 2005, 56). Excavations at Ash Boulogne, in Martock, have revealed traces of a settlement associated with tenth-century pottery, but which was then abandoned and replaced by common fields, although when the settlement started to be occupied is unclear due to the lack of fifth- to ninth-century pottery in Somerset (Graham 2005, 16–18).

EXPLAINING REGIONAL VARIATION IN LANDSCAPE CHARACTER

Having produced a broad characterization of nineteenth-century settlement patterns and field systems within the context of tithings and parishes across Somerset, and established that at a regional scale the major differences in landscape character can be traced back to at least the thirteenth and fourteenth centuries, we must now try and explain how these differences emerged by testing a variety of previously published hypotheses, notably that the emergence of villages and common fields was related to variations in soils, the character of antecedent landscapes, the extent of meadow, population density, and the degree of economic development.

A relationship with topography and soils?

At a very general level, that part of Somerset characterized by villages and common fields corresponds to the flat, low-lying plain in the central and south-eastern part of the county. This area also has soils that suffer from some impeded drainage, and which also occur across much of the central zone (Fig. 2.10; Mackney *et al.* 1983; Williamson 2003). Upon closer examination, however, this possible relationship weakens as villages and common fields in Somerset were not found on areas of the same soils in the Vale of Taunton Deane which also has plenty of flat or gently undulating land that would have been ideal for this type of farming. Overall, the possible correlation between the natural environment and the character of the medieval landscape, as identified by Williamson in East Anglia and the East Midlands, is only partially seen in medieval Somerset.

A relationship with the antecedent landscape?

Roberts and Wrathmell (2002) raise the possibility that villages and common fields were created in their 'central province' because of the character of its 'antecedent landscape'. In Somerset this may also have been significant, as there is a marked difference in the character of the Romano-British countryside between the highly Romanized east and the relatively un-Romanized west. To the east of the rivers Parrett and Isle there was a series of small towns, substantial roadside settlements, well-appointed villas, and stone-built Romano-Celtic temples, while even the lowest-status farmsteads are associated with large amounts of Romano-British material culture, reflecting society's engagement with a money-based market economy within which there was easy access to, and a desire to purchase, manufactured goods. This landscape extended to the fringes of the Blackdown and Quantock Hills, but to the west the landscape was very different, with just a handful of villas and no small towns: the *civitas* of the Dumnonii was far less Romanized than that of the Durotriges. This is explored further in Chapter 4.

The extent to which this regional difference in the character of the Romano-British landscape continued into the early medieval period is unclear, as the aceramic nature of settlement during the fifth to ninth centuries makes them very difficult to locate. Superficially, it appears that there was a major discontinuity in the landscape at the end of the Roman period, such is the large number of deserted settlements that lie in what were to become medieval fields; this very much fits the model, still adhered to by some, that in the early fifth century Britain was plunged into a 'dark age' (Faulkner 2004; though compare Henig 2004). It is certainly true that in the post-Roman world the most Romanized end of the settlement hierarchy—towns and villas—will have become increasingly unsustainable following the collapse of

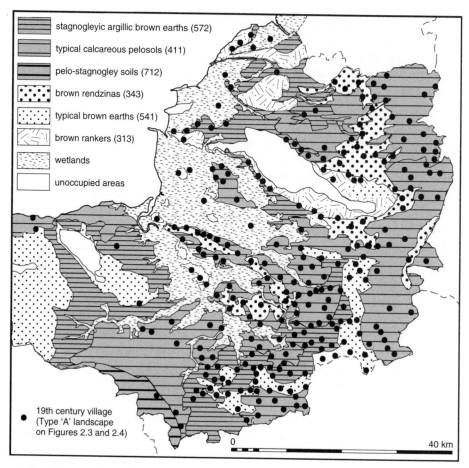

Fig. 2.10. The major soil types in Somerset (after Mackney *et al.* 1983), and distribution of settlements that in the 19th century were of the 'village and former common field' type. Note how there is only a limited correlation with the distribution of landscapes characterized by villages and common fields. Apart from the wetland areas with a permanently high water table, there are three types of soil in Somerset with impeded drainage. Stagnogleyic argillic brown earths are soils are loamy or clayey soils over a subsurface horizon with significant clay enrichment, leading to impeded drainage. Calcareous pelosols are slowly permeable clayey soils and a calcareous subsoil. Pelo-stagnogleys are slowly permeable, seasonally waterlogged clayey soils. There are also three types of well-drained soils. Brown rendzinas are shallow calcareous soils over limestone; brown rankers are shallow soils over non-calcareous rock; and typical brown earths are non-calcareous loamy soils without significant clay enrichment.

the market-based economy, but others have argued that this does not mean that there was a widespread desertion of the landscape. Leech (1982), for example, suggests there may have been a strong degree of continuity in the location of settlements, arguing that many medieval villages are the direct successors to Romano-British settlements, and that the deserted Romano-British sites simply represent a contraction from more marginal locations. Unfortunately, the lack of large-scale fieldwalking and excavation in Somerset means that this model is difficult to test. Recently, Roman occupation has been found under the medieval village at South Cadbury, while in the surrounding landscape the combination of cropmarks, extensive geophysical survey, and small-scale excavations suggests that elements of the late prehistoric and Romano-British fieldscape were incorporated into medieval field systems, implying some degree of continuity (Davey 2005). A further indication of continuity is that the palaeoenvironmental sequences we have for lowland Somerset do not indicate a woodland regeneration in the early medieval period (Beckett and Hibbert 1979, 594; Housley *et al.* 2007).

As a proxy for the intensity of landscape exploitation across England in the early medieval period, Roberts and Wrathmell have tried to map the distribution of woodland, as reflected in place names and Domesday, and this can be explored in Somerset (Fig. 2.11). *Lēah* place names are found across the county although there are noticeably fewer examples in the south-east where there was classic champion countryside by the thirteenth and fourteenth centuries. Whilst acknowledging the problems in assessing the extent of Domesday woodland, due to the variety of measures that are used in that survey (acres, leagues, furlongs, and rarely perches), the picture seems to be very broadly similar, although some parts of south-east Somerset (e.g. around Wincanton and South Petherton) appear to have had greater amounts of woodland compared to the lowlands of western Somerset (Welldon Finn and Wheatley 1967, 173–9). In Somerset, therefore, it appears that the distribution of early medieval woodland does not explain why some areas saw the creation of villages and common fields and others did not.

A relationship with meadow?

Williamson (2003; 2007) suggests that there is a correlation between 'champion' landscape and communities with access to relatively large areas of meadow. He observes that traditional hay making is very labour intensive as it requires the cutting, repeated turning, and stacking of the hay and then its carting from the meadows to a settlement. As the saying 'make hay while the sun shines' implies, there was also a relatively short 'window of opportunity' within which the scything, drying, turning, and carting could occur. Williamson therefore argues that where there were large areas of meadow it made sense to pool resources and harvest them communally and this encouraged people to live close together in villages. Conversely, he suggests, where meadow lay in smaller, more scattered parcels, or was generally less important in the agrarian economy, settlement could take a more dispersed form.

Somerset as a whole was certainly well endowed with meadow, due to its extensive wetlands (Fig. 2.12: Darby 1967, 380–2; Welldon Finn and

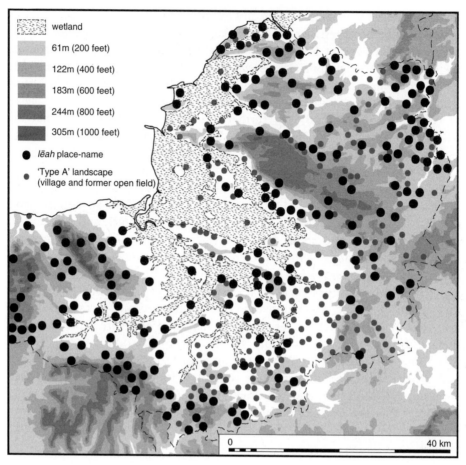

Fig. 2.11. Distribution of *lēah* place names in Somerset (Costen 1992a, fig. 4.5). Note how there is only a limited correlation with the distribution of landscapes characterized by villages and common fields.

Wheatley 1967, 181; Campbell 2000, 75–6), although there is no clear correlation between its distribution and the character of the settlement pattern. The village-dominated lowland plain of south-east Somerset was indeed well endowed with meadow, as was the north of the county where settlement patterns were more mixed. There were, however, also very large areas of meadow recorded in the lowlands between the Quantock Hills and the Parrett estuary, yet there is no evidence in the historic landscape or documentary sources that this area had nucleated villages or common fields. In contrast, in the Tone Valley to the south, Welldon Finn and Wheatley's (1967, fig. 42) mapping of Domesday meadow *appears* to show a sharper distinction between areas with abundant meadow to the east and very little meadow in the west, but this is in fact due to an error in the drawing of this map as the area actually

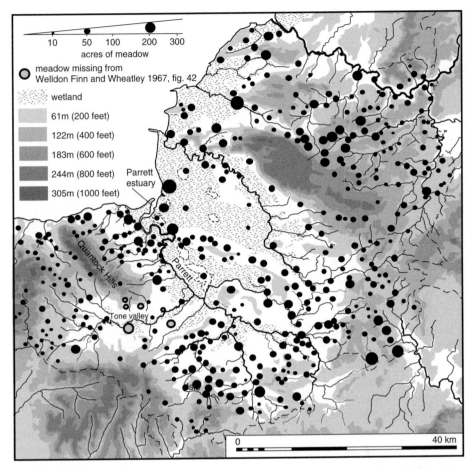

Fig. 2.12. Distribution of meadow recorded in the Domesday survey (after Welldon Finn and Wheatley 1967, fig. 42) with additional data from Thorn and Thorn (1980) for the Tone Valley.

had large areas of meadow: Durston, for example, had 15 acres (6 ha) (DB fo. 94^v; *DB Som.* 22,4),[6] while there were 78 acres (30 ha) in North Curry (DB fo. 86^v; *DB Som.* 1,19), and 141 acres (55 ha) in Taunton (DB fo. 87^v; *DB Som.* 2,1; 2,2; 2,6–8). Another problem with this Domesday data is the apparent absence of meadow on some manors lying close to the edge of the Levels, such as St Michael Church (DB fo. 98^v; *DB Som.* 46,13): it is inconceivable that such wetland-edge manors did not have any meadow, and so we must conclude that its recording was far from consistent. Overall, the correlation between Domesday meadow and villages and common fields is weak.

---

[6] The references 'DB fo. 95; *DB Som.* 22,4' refer to the folio number in Domesday (DB fo. 95) followed by the entry in the Phillimore edition (*DB Som.* 22,4).

A relationship with population density and economic development?

Two other possible, and related, factors behind the emergence of villages and common fields are population pressure and economic development (e.g. Lewis *et al.* 1997). At the time of the Domesday survey south-east Somerset was indeed a well-populated region with a density of around ten recorded tenants per square mile (260 ha) in most areas, although equally high population densities were found around Milverton and Taunton in the west (Fig. 2.13). The population density of 12.6 seen in Cannington Hundred, for example, with its dispersed settlement pattern and predominantly enclosed field systems, is second only to the 12.8 tenants per square mile in the champion district of Crewkerne and Houndsborough hundreds in south-east Somerset (Welldon Finn and Wheatley 1967, fig. 39; see Fig. 2.2 for the location of the hundreds referred to). At a regional scale, across the whole of south-west England, there is similarly no correlation between Domesday population density and the area of villages and common fields in the central zone (Darby 1967, figs. 84–5). There is also no correspondence between the density of ploughteams and Somerset's 'champion countryside' with the average of around three ploughteams per square mile in the south-east of the county being exactly the same as around Milverton and Taunton in the west; in Cannington Hundred the figure was 3.7 teams (Welldon Finn and Wheatley 1967, fig. 37). While in part this may reflect the less efficient use of ploughteams in areas of more dispersed settlement, it still demonstrates that the lowlands of western Somerset were not deficient in areas of arable cultivation.

Another index of economic development is the emergence of towns, mints, and markets, and in the eleventh century these too were spread right across lowland Somerset. There were eight boroughs recorded in Domesday, including Milverton and Taunton in the west.[7] Watchet may also have been a town as it was recorded as a *burh* in the Burghal Hidage and had a pre- and post-Conquest mint; the adjacent manor of Old Cleeve had the third penny of the *burgherist* [borough-right] from the hundreds of Cannington, Carhampton, North Petherton, and Williton for which no borough is recorded but within which Watchet lay (Welldon Finn and Wheatley 1967, 199). In addition there was a Domesday market at Ilminster, and short-lived pre-Conquest mints at the royal manors of Crewkerne and South Petherton, and the stronghold at South Cadbury (Aston 1986, 59–63). Overall, while central and south-east Somerset did have a relatively high population, and a series of mints and emerging towns, so did areas to the west that did not see the emergence of villages and common fields.

---

[7] Axbridge (32 burgesses), Bath (178), Bruton (17), Langport (39), Ilchester (107), Milborne Port (67), Milverton (the number of burgesses is not given), and Taunton (64). In addition, Frome had a pre-Conquest mint, Domesday market, and paid third penny to the king, and the '22 plots of land which 22 men held jointly before 1066' may also indicate the creation of a town at Yeovil (DB fo. 96ᵛ; DB Som. 26,6).

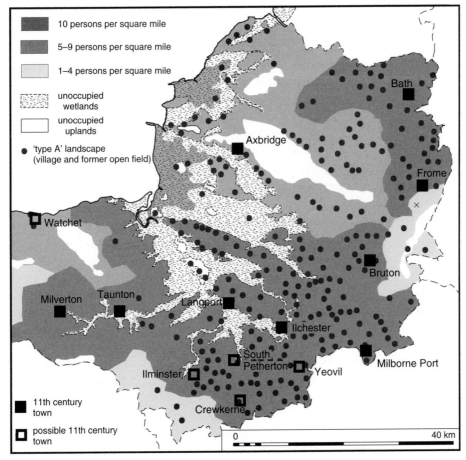

Fig. 2.13. Population density in 1086 from the Domesday survey (Welldon Finn and Wheatley 1967, fig. 39) and 11th-century towns (after Aston 1986). Note how there is no correlation with the distribution of landscapes characterized by villages and common fields.

DISCUSSION

This detailed analysis of the Somerset landscape in the nineteenth century, along with a range of evidence for the character of the settlement patterns and field systems in the later medieval period, suggests that the south-western boundary of the champion countryside of England's central zone did indeed run through the county. In broad terms this boundary also corresponds to the topography, soils, abundant meadow, high population, and economic development that it has been argued were conducive to the creation of villages and common fields elsewhere in the central zone. A closer examination of the evidence, however, reveals that the correspondence is far from exact, and that in particular similar conditions prevailed in the lowlands of western Somerset, notably in the Vale of Taunton Deane, which never saw this transformation.

While the character of the Romano-British countryside in western Somerset was also very different from that in the east, it is not clear how far this difference in the character of the 'antecedent landscape' continued into the early medieval period: while part of south-east Somerset, around Ilchester, appears to have been particularly well cleared of trees, overall there was little difference in the extent of woodland across the lowlands of Somerset. As none of these factors gives a clear explanation for the differences in landscape character seen in Somerset, we must now turn elsewhere, notably to the potential role of, and relationship between, lordship and community. In order to focus on these potential social factors we begin by examining a number of special landscapes—reclaimed coastal marshlands—where other potential factors, such as variations in physical topography, soils, and the 'antecedent' cultural landscape, cannot have been significant.

3

Abbots, Bishops, Thegns, or Communities:
Who was Responsible for Somerset's
Champion Countryside?

In the preceding chapter we saw that a variety of explanations for why central and south-eastern Somerset saw the creation of villages and common fields fail to be convincing. Part of the problem is that there are so many possible factors that it is difficult to untangle their potential significance. This chapter approaches the problem from a different angle by initially look- ing at a type of landscape, coastal wetlands, where several of the possible factors—the natural environment and the character of the antecedent cultural landscape—cannot have played a part as they were completely uniform, allow- ing us to focus on the issue of social agency: the potential roles of lordship and community.

WORKING ON A CLEANED SLATE: THE EMERGENCE OF LOCAL VARIATION IN LANDSCAPE CHARACTER ON THE SOMERSET LEVELS

Central Somerset is dominated by a series of wetlands collectively known as the Somerset Levels. Towards the coast these comprise alluvial soils derived from intertidal mudflats and saltmarshes, while further inland there is a range of freshwater peat bogs. The first occasion when the coastal marshlands were reclaimed was in the third and fourth centuries AD, although during the early medieval period the area reverted to a vast expanse of intertidal saltmarshes and mudflats (Rippon 1997; 2000a; 2000b; 2000c; 2006). The Levels must have been reclaimed for a second time by the eleventh century as Domesday shows that they were extensively settled and supported densities of population and ploughteams that were comparable to the adjacent dryland areas (Fig. 2.13). The date when the recolonization of these marshes began is not clear, although as the Roman ground surface is buried by c.0.7 m of later alluvium, there must have been a prolonged (lasting several centuries?) period when the area was an intertidal marsh. What is of particular interest here is that the settlement patterns and field systems that were created following reclamation show marked local variation in their character. Around Brent Knoll, for example, there were a series of large, nucleated villages, in contrast to the areas around Burnham and Huntspill to the south that had a more dispersed pattern: in a physically uniform environment, which had an equally uniform antecedent landscape character, why should the post-reclamation settlement patterns and field systems be so different?

First, we must establish the antiquity of these two very different nineteenth-century patterns. There has been no systematic archaeological survey in these areas, although from the 1950s through to the 1970s local amateur archaeologist Samuel Nash carried out extensive observations of building foundations, service trenches, and clay pits across the area. Fortunately he kept detailed records of his discoveries, and these reveal that the different settlement patterns around Brent, Burnham, and Huntspill can be traced back to at least the twelfth century, the earliest date when medieval pottery in Somerset was recognized at the time Nash was working (Rippon 1995; 1997, table 7.3). Since then tenth-century pottery has been recovered from South Brent village (Webster 2001, 231). The earthworks of shrunken and deserted settlements also confirm the antiquity of these different settlement patterns: nucleated in the north and dispersed in the south.

An analysis of the field boundary patterns also reveals significant differences. Around Brent large areas are covered with blocks of long narrow fields laid out between sinuous, parallel boundaries that are suggestive of the enclosure by agreement of common fields that once covered up to a square kilometre (Rippon 1997, fig. 50). This hypothesis, based on an analysis of the historic landscape, is confirmed by the abundant archives of Glastonbury Abbey which show that there was indeed a common field system in each of the manors that made up their Brent estate, although they had been almost entirely enclosed by 1567 (Stratton 1909; Gray 1915, 99; Rippon 1997, 253–5). Keil (1964, table A) suggests that each manor had a simple two-field system and although Harrison (1997, 123–72) could find no evidence for this, much of the land was certainly held in unenclosed strips, crops were rotated, there were jealously guarded rights in common, and a sophisticated system of regulation to maintain a balance between arable, meadow, and fallow. The field boundary patterns to the south of Brent, in Burnham and Huntspill, were, however, very different, and while we lack medieval sources that describe the patterns of agriculture that were practised, it is striking that the nineteenth-century field boundary pattern contains few of the distinctive traces of former common fields seen in Brent. The one exception is two blocks of long narrow fields that lie between a series of roughly parallel boundaries, each about a furlong apart. The names of two of these boundaries—Middle Westfield

Rhyne[1] and Middle Field Lane—suggests that they did indeed form a small open field, although covering just *c*.100 acres (*c*.0.5 km^2), in a parish of 5,010 acres (20.3 km^2), this was hardly a very significant part of the landscape.

It appears, therefore, that there was a marked difference in the way that the landscapes of Brent and Burnham/Huntspill were managed, with relatively nucleated settlements and extensive areas of common field in the former, and far more dispersed settlement and fields that were mostly held in severalty in the latter. As this marked difference in landscape character was clearly not due to variations in the natural environment or the antecedent cultural landscape—in both areas these were physically homogeneous reclaimed wetlands derived from alluvial saltmarshes—they can only be explained by cultural factors. A series of charters mean that we have some insights into the early tenurial development in this area. These charters are listed in Tables 3.1 and 3.2 which contain their dates, any area of hidage given, and their references in Sawyer (1968), Finberg (1964), Abrams (1996), and Domesday. Some charters survive in their original form, while others are only available in a later copy the authenticity of which is not in doubt. Others are 'available in later copy, thought to embody the substance of the original, but having some material, probably spurious, substituted or interpolated' (Finberg 1964, 23), and place names and hidages may have been altered.

The estate of Brent may have been held by the abbots of Glastonbury ever since King Baldred, and King Ine is said to have granted ten *cassati* there to Abbot Hæmgils in *c*.693. The boundary description—'On and around the hill which is called Brent, having to the west the Severn, on the north the Axe, on the east the *Ternuc*, and the *Siger* on the south'—shows that it was coterminous with the four parishes and manors of East Brent, South Brent, Berrow, and Lympsham that Glastonbury held from Domesday to the Dissolution (Abrams 1996, 69–72). As this area must have been an intertidal marsh for several centuries after the Roman period—during which the *c*.0.7 m of alluvium that seals the Romano-British landscape was deposited—it would appear that the recolonization of this landscape, and the creation of the villages and common fields, must have occurred when the estate was in the hands of Glastonbury.

In contrast, Glastonbury appears to have had little or no influence over the area to the south of Brent. Burnham was a royal estate, being granted by King Alfred to Edward the Elder in his will of 873 × 888 (S1507; Finberg 1964, 126).[2] In 1066 Burnham was held by Beorhtsige as four hides (DB fo. 95; *DB Som.* 24,27), while Cynsige and Ælfwig each held one virgate in the nearby

---

[1] 'Rhyne' is the local word for a major drainage ditch.

[2] It has been claimed that Abbot Guthlac's grant of part of one *cassatum in Brunham* to Eanulf in 824 relates to Burnham, though it is more likely that it was Brompton Ralph in west Somerset (Finberg 1964, No. 404; Abrams 1996, 71, 74).

hamlet of Huish (DB fo. 95; *DB Som.* 24,35–6). The early history of Huntspill is obscure,[3] although in 1066 Alwaker held one hide there, and Ælfwine three virgates (DB fo. 95; *DB Som.* 24,28; 24,43); Alstone, a hamlet in the north of Huntspill, was held by Ælfwold as one hide (DB fo. 95; *DB Som.* 24,33). With no evidence that Glastonbury ever held Burnham and Huntspill, in contrast to Brent which belonged to the Abbey from the late seventh century, is it therefore possible that this difference in lordship accounts for the divergent landscape character that developed after reclamation?

LANDSCAPE REORGANIZATION ON THE ESTATES OF GLASTONBURY ABBEY

Glastonbury Abbey is an ideal candidate through which to explore the relationship between landownership and landscape character as its lands were spread right across Somerset (Fig. 3.1). The core of its estates, mostly acquired during the late seventh to mid eighth centuries, covered a continuous swathe of territory embracing the Abbey itself and stretching from the Parrett estuary in the west, to Mells in the east. It also held outlying estates scattered across northern, southern, and western Somerset, as well as a few holdings in Devon, Dorset, Gloucestershire, and Wiltshire.

Central Somerset

The earliest recorded grant to Glastonbury was of a series of islands in the wetlands west of the Abbey, including Meare, in 670 or 680 (Finberg 1964, No. 353, 'a charter available in later copy, thought to embody the substance of the original, but having some material, probably spurious, substituted or interpolated'; Rippon 2004b, 99–102), while the substantial island at Brent, surrounded by a vast tract of what at the time was saltmarsh, was given to the Abbey in 693 (see above). The area immediately east of Glastonbury was acquired through a series of genuine or purported grants in 681 (Pennard), 705 (Pilton, which included Shepton Mallet and Croscombe), 705 or 706 (Doulting), 744 (Baltonsborough), and 746 (West Bradley) (see Table 3.1 for references). The area west of Glastonbury was acquired in the first half of the eighth century as the former estate of *Pouelt* (the Polden Hills) was progressively broken up and given to the Abbey by successive kings of Wessex

---

[3] King Offa of Mercia is said to have granted one hide at *Hunespulle* to his thegn Æthelmund, who then granted this hide to Abbot Beadwulf (793 × 800; Finberg 1964, No. 397; Abrams 1996, 142–3). William of Malmesbury also states that 10 hides at *Eswirht*, or *Inesuuyrth juxta Hunespulle*, was granted to Abbot Beadwulf in 794 by an unnamed laymen who had received it from King Offa (S1692; Abrams 1996, 142). *Hunespulle*, *Eswirht*, or *Inesuuyrth* cannot be located for certain though Finberg (1961, No. 47) places them at Insworth near Gloucester, and identifies Æthelmund as an ealdorman of the Hwicce (Finberg 1961, No. 49; Abrams 1996, 143).

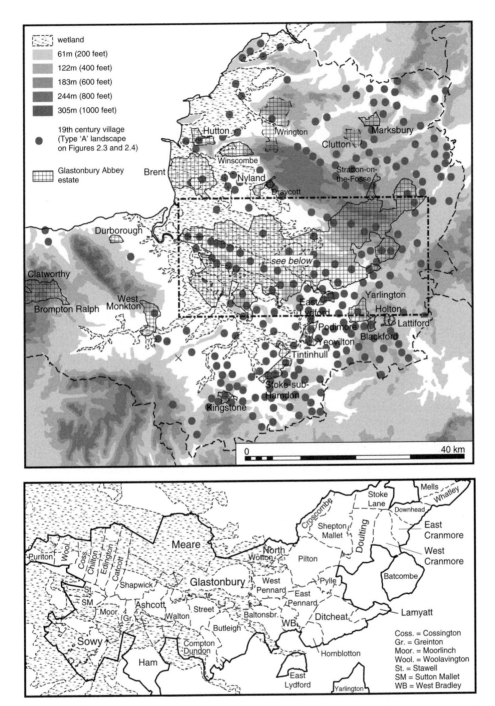

Fig. 3.1. Distribution of the estates in Somerset to which Glastonbury Abbey had a good claim (after Abrams 1996).

Table 3.1. Glastonbury Abbey's estates in central Somerset (see note 1 below)

Estate	Date acquired	Reliability (Finberg 1964, 23) and other references	Hidage in 1066
Beckery, Godney, Marchey, and Nyland	642 × 672	(lost) Finberg 1964, No. 354; Abrams 1996, 46–7	Nyland: 2 hides (DB fo. 90; *DB Som.* 8,1)
Meare	670 (1 *cassatum*) or 680 (2 *manentes*)	(**) S227; S1249; Finberg 1964, Nos. 353 and 357; Abrams 1996, 169–71	named under Glastonbury (DB fo. 90; *DB Som.* 8,1)
Glastonbury	678 (6 hides)	(lost) S1666; Finberg 1964, No. 356; Abrams 1996, 125	12 hides including Meare (DB fo. 90; *DB Som.* 8,1)
West Pennard (*Pengerd*)	681 (6 or 12 *manentes*)	(**) S236; Finberg 1964, No. 360; Abrams 1996, 195–9	not mentioned
Brent Edingworth	693 (10 *cassati*)	(**) S238; Finberg 1964, No. 364, 69–72	20 hides (DB fo. 90^v; *DB Som.* 8,33) / 2 hides (DB fo. 90^v; *DB Som.* 8,34)
Doulting	705 or 706 (20 *cassati*)	(* and lost) S247–8; Finberg 1964, Nos. 371, 407; Abrams 1996, 112–14	20 hides (DB fo. 90^v; *DB Som.* 8,23)
Charlton			3 hides 1 virgate (DB fo. 90^v; *DB Som.* 8,23)
Pilton	705 (20 *cassati*)	(**) S1671; Finberg 1964, No. 370; Abrams 1996, 200–4	20 hides (DB fo. 90; *DB Som.* 8,20)
Croscombe			3 hides (DB fo. 90; *DB Som.* 8,20)
North Wootton			5 hides (DB fo. 90; *DB Som.* 8,20)
Pilton			2 hides (DB fo. 90; *DB Som.* 8,20)
Pylle			5 hides (DB fo. 90; *DB Som.* 8,20)
Shepton Mallet			6.5 hides (DB fo. 90; *DB Som.* 8,20)
Pouelt Shapwick[2]			30 hides[1] and 20 ploughs that never paid tax (DB fo. 90; *DB Som.* 8,5)
Cossington	705 or 706 (20 *manentes*)	(*) S248; Finberg 1964, No. 371; Abrams 1996, 204–11; Corcos 2002	3 hides (DB fo. 90; *DB Som.* 8,7)

Stawell Walton[3]	729 (60 *manencia*)	(*) S253; Finberg 1964, No. 381; Abrams 1996, 204–11; Corcos 2002	2.5 hides (DB fo. 90; *DB Som.* 8,10) 30 hides[2] (DB fo. 90; *DB Som.* 8,11)
Greinton	754 (22 hides)	(lost) S1680; Finberg 1964, No. 387; Abrams 1996, 204–11; Corcos 2002	2.5 hides (DB fo. 90; *DB Som.* 8,15)
Ashcott			2 hides (DB fo. 90; *DB Som.* 8,14): a further 3 hides are listed under Walton (DB fo. 90; *DB Som.* 8,11)
Overleigh Puriton	754 (6 hides on the west side of *Pobolt*)	(lost) Finberg 1964, No. 387; Abrams 1996, 204–11; Corcos 2002	4 hides (DB fo. 90; *DB Som.* 8,16) had been lost: 6 hides by Queen Edith in 1066 (DB fo. 91; *DB Som.* 11,1)
Sowy	725 (12 *manentes*)	(*) S251; Finberg 1964, No. 379; Abrams 1996, 218–20	12 hides (DB fo. 90; *DB Som.* 8,6)
Baltonsborough and *Scobbanwirht*	744 (10 *manentes*)	(*) S1410; Finberg 1964, No. 384; Abrams 1996, 53–4	5 hides at Baltonsborough (DB fo. 90v; *DB Som.* 8,22)
Bradanleag (West Bradley?)	746 (4 hides)	(lost) S1679; Finberg 1964, No. 634; Abrams 1996, 66.	not listed: part of East Pennard?
North Wootton	760 or 946 (5 hides)	(*) S509; Finberg 1964, Nos. 389, 458; Abrams 1996, 181–5	5 hides listed under Pilton (see above: DB fo. 90v; *DB Som.* 8,20)
Compton	762 (5 hides)	(lost) S1685; S1705; Finberg 1964, No. 393; Abrams 1996, 94–5	5 hides added to Walton (see above: DB fo. 90; *DB Som.* 8,11)
Butleigh	801 (20 *mansiones*)	(**) S270a; Finberg 1964, No. 401; Abrams 1996, 76–7	20 hides (DB fo. 90; *DB Som.* 8,18; 8,41); and 3 virgates (DB fo. 90; *DB Som.* 8,12)
Ditcheat and Lottisham Hornblotton	842 (25 *cassati* in Ditcheat and 5 in Lottisham)	(*) S292; Finberg 1964, Nos. 405, 411, 109–12.	30 hides (DB fo. 90v; *DB Som.* 8,30) 5.5 hides (DB fo. 90v; *DB Som.* 8,30)

continued

Table 3.1. *continued*

Estate	Date acquired	Reliability (Finberg 1964, 23) and other references	Hidage in 1066
Alhampton	855 × 860	(lost) S1699; Finberg 1964, No. 411; Abrams 1996, 141, 163	6.5 hides (DB fo. 90ᵛ; *DB Som.* 8,30)
Lamyatt			5.5 hides (DB fo. 90ᵛ; *DB Som.* 8,30)
Downhead	854?	Abrams 1996, 115	3 hides (DB fo. 90ᵛ; *DB Som.* 8,35)
Whatley	940–6 (4 hides)	(lost) S1726; Finberg 1964, No. 452; Abrams 1996, 246	4 hides (DB fo. 90ᵛ; *DB Som.* 8, 26)
Mells	940–6 (20 *mansae*)	(*) S481; Finberg 1964, No. 445; Abrams 1996, 171–2	20 hides (DB fo. 90ᵛ; *DB Som.* 8,25)
East Pennard (*Pengeard Mynster*)	955 (20 *cassati*)	(+) S563; Finberg 1964, No. 469; Abrams 1996, 195–9	20 hides (DB fo. 90ᵛ; *DB Som.* 8,21)
Cranmore	955 × 959 (12 hides)	(both lost) S1746; Finberg 1964, Nos. 479, 504; Abrams 1996, 98–9	12 hides (DB fo. 90ᵛ; *DB Som.* 8,32)
Dundon	959–75 (5 hides)	(lost) Finberg 1964, No. 504; Abrams 1996, 117	5 hides (DB fo. 90; *DB Som.* 8,13)
Stratton-on-the-Fosse	959–75 (6 hides)	(lost) S1761; Finberg 1964, No. 501; Abrams 1996, 225	3 hides (DB fos. 88, 91; *DB Som.* 8,38; 5,43)
Wheathill	959–75 (3 hides)	(lost) S1770; Finberg 1964, No. 496; Abrams 1996, 246–7	3 hides (DB fo. 98; *DB Som.* 37,9)
Batcombe Westcombe	968 × 971 (20 *mansae*)	(*) S462; Finberg 1964, No. 441	20 hides (DB fo. 90ᵛ; *DB Som.* 8,24) 7 hides 3 virgates (DB fo. 90ᵛ; *DB Som.* 8,24)
High Ham (*Hamme*)	973 (17 hides)	(lost and *) S791; Finberg 1964, Nos. 490, 517; Abrams 1996, 134–5	17 hides (DB fo. 90; *DB Som.* 8,17)

| Draycott | by 1066 | *DB Som.* 8,39; 19,12 | 2 hides (DB fo. 91; *DB Som.* 8,39) |
| East Lydford | by 1066 | *DB Som.* 8,4 | 4 hides (DB fo. 90; *DB Som.* 8,4) |

Notes:

+ Original charter, authenticity not in doubt.

* Charter available only in a later copy or copies, authenticity not in doubt.

** Charter available in later copy or copies, thought to embody the substance of the original, but having some material, probably spurious, substituted or interpolated.

*** Charter thought to be fundamentally a fabrication, but which may embody some authentic material or record a genuine transaction.

lost: Charter no longer survives but is referred to in later sources (which for Glastonbury Abbey are likely to be unreliable).

[1] Of the other pre-Conquest estates in central Somerset that Glastonbury's archives make reference to, *Bocland* (Buckland Denham?), *Cedern* (Cheddar?), Clewer and Wedmore, Houndsborough, Huntspill (see above), Nunney, Orchardleigh, Ubley, and Westbury (-sub-Mendip?) were either held very fleetingly, cannot be identifed with any certainty, or appear to represent spurious claims (Abrams 1996, 62–3, 83–4, 90–2, 141, 142–3, 185, 188–9, 235, 242–4).

[2] Includes Catcott (5 hides), Chilton Polden (5 hides), Edington (5 hides), Sutton Mallet (5 hides), Woolavington (5 hides). Moorlinch is not otherwise mentioned, but was the mother church of Chilton Polden and Sutton Mallet, and so is probably the remaining 5 hides.

[3] Includes Ashcott (3 hides), Compton (Dundon) (5 hides), Pedwell (3 hides). Street is not otherwise mentioned, but was the mother church of Walton so is probably included under this entry or that for *Lega* (Overleigh): DB fo. 90; *DB Som.* 8,16).

(see below). The island-based estate at Sowy was granted to Glastonbury in 725, while Compton, to the south of the Poldens, may have been acquired in 762 (charter now lost), though if so it must have been subsequently lost as it was restored to them in 912. Twenty hides at Butleigh may have been given to Glastonbury in 801, while it acquired 25 hides at Ditcheat in 842, to which Hornblotton and Lamyatt may have been added in the late 850s (charter now lost). Around the edges of this core of early grants were further estates possibly added during the tenth century including Mells and Whatley in the east, and Dundon and High Ham to the south. Crucially, the acquisition of these estates was both before and after the tenth century, the date by which survey and excavations within one of these manors, Shapwick, show that a dispersed settlement pattern had been swept away and replaced by a single, planned, village (see above).

The Polden Hills

The most extensively studied evidence for the creation of villages and common fields on the estates of Glastonbury Abbey is on the Polden Hills, immediately west of Glastonbury, where an analysis of cartographic sources and the relatively abundant monastic archives reveal a 'champion' landscape where virtually all the agricultural land in each manor and parish was managed within regularly arranged common fields that surrounded a tightly nucleated and sometimes planned village (Figs. 3.2– 3.4; Keil 1964, table A; Costen 1992a, 115; Rippon 1997, 160–2; Aston and Gerrard 1999; Corcos 2002; Gerrard with Aston 2007). The clearest example of this is a block of parishes which included (from east to west) 20 hides at Shapwick, 5 hides at Catcott, 5 hides at Edington, 5 hides at Chilton [Polden], and 5 hides at Woolavington (DB fo. 90; *DB Som.* 8,5). Three hides at Cossington, lying between Woolavington and Chilton, have a separate entry (DB fo. 90; *DB Som.* 8,7). The striplike form of these parishes, the series of 'personal name + -*ingtun* or *cot*' place names (Catcott, Cossington, Edington, and Woolavington), and a degree of regularity in the resources described by Domesday, is suggestive of a planned division of the landscape by 1066. Pottery from excavations in Shapwick has shown that the villages existed by the tenth century (Somerset being aceramic before this date), while radiocarbon dating of aceramic features revealed through excavations in Edington suggests that the village was laid out in the late ninth or tenth centuries (see below: Aston and Gerrard 1999; Brigers 2006; Somerset Historic Environment Record PRNs 12750 and 14452). While it cannot be proved, this restructuring of the settlement pattern is the most logical context for the creation of the open fields that surrounded these villages.

If Domesday provides a *terminus ante quem* for the replanning of the landscape on the Polden Hills, can we provide a *terminus post quem*? A series of charters from the first half of the eighth century record several blocks of land at *Pouelt* or *Poholt* which were granted or sold by the kings of Wessex to Glastonbury and which probably represent the gradual breaking up of a single royal estate that amounted to around a hundred hides and stretched from Puriton in the west to Street in the east (see Table 2.1; Abrams 1996, 204–11). The former unity of the various places included in the four grants of land at *Pouelt/Poholt* is reflected in later ecclesiastical relationships, as Shapwick was the mother church of the chapel at Ashcott, while Moorlinch, itself probably part of Shapwick in Domesday, had chapelries at Catcott, Chilton Polden, Edington, Stawell, and Sutton Mallet (Aston 1986, 75). Woolavington, Cossington, Chilton Polden, Edington, Catcott, and Shapwick—which all lay on the northern side of the Polden Hills—also all had detached parochial parcels in the wetlands of Sedgemoor (i.e. to the south of Stawell, Sutton Mallet, and Moorlinch on the southern flanks of the Polden Hills), suggesting that these moors once provided common grazing for all the communities on the Polden Hills (Fig. 3.2).

So did the creation of villages and common fields in this area occur before or after the *Pouelt/Poholt* estate was fragmented and then reconfigured under the ownership of Glastonbury? The block of carefully laid out strip parishes that formed the 50 hides described under Shapwick in Domesday appears to have been created through a restructuring of the estates that Glastonbury had received in two separate grants in 705/6 and 729: the 20 ploughs which never paid tax at Shapwick probably relate to the grant of 20 *manentes* by King Ine in 705/6, while the remaining 30 hides (the block of manors between Catcott and Woolavington) were probably part of the 60 hides granted by King Æthelheard in 729, the remaining 30 hides being Walton (to the east of Shapwick).[4] An analysis of the historic landscape suggests that the field systems post-date the amalgamation of these two estates as the boundary between Catcott and Shapwick slices through a series of furlongs that run across both parishes. The boundary between Cossington and Woolavington similarly zigzags through, and so post-dates, a series of furlongs that run right across both parishes (Fig. 3.3). As it seems highly improbable that these common fields were laid out before the *Pouelt/Poholt* estate started to be broken up in 705/6, it would appear that the landscape between Shapwick and Woolavington was reorganized after the area came to be in the common ownership of Glastonbury (in 729), and before Cossington was detached (sometime before 1066). The major programme of survey and excavation in Shapwick has established that the planned village there was laid out by the tenth century, this being the earliest period for which there is medieval pottery in Somerset (Gerrard with Aston

---

[4] The bounds of the 729 charter refer to 'Chalkbrook' to the east: of the parishes on the Polden Hills the only one to follow a natural stream is that between Walton and Street. To the south lay 'carswell', the river Cary and Chedzoy, to the west lay 'land belonging to Cossington', while 'half the marsh' lay to the north (Abrams 1994, fig. 11).

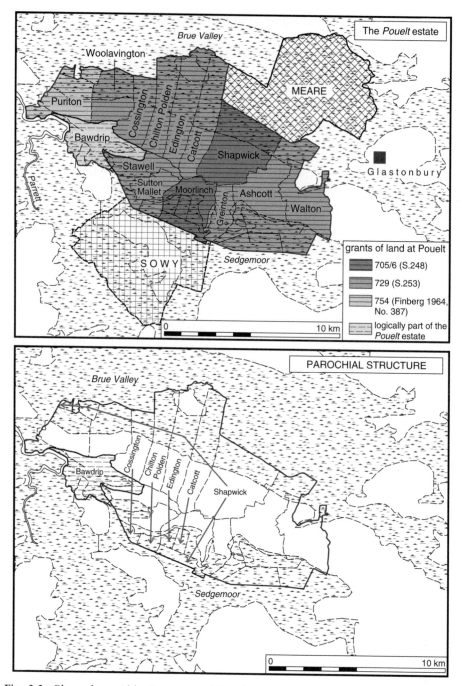

Fig. 3.2. Glastonbury Abbey's estates of *Pouelt*, Meare, and Sowy in central Somerset. The original extent of *Pouelt* appears to have included Shapwick and Moorlinch, granted to Glastonbury Abbey in 705/6, the blocks of land either side (which became the manors of Ashcott and Walton to the east, and Catcott, Edington, Chilton Polden, Cossington, Stawell, Sutton, and Woolavington to the west), which were granted to the Abbey in 729, and Puriton, which it acquired in 754. Logically, Bawdrip would have been part of the *Pouelt* estate but there is no evidence that it was granted to Glastonbury. That parishes on the northern slopes of the Polden Hills held detached areas of wetland to the south, in Sedgemoor, suggests that this was once an area of common grazing.

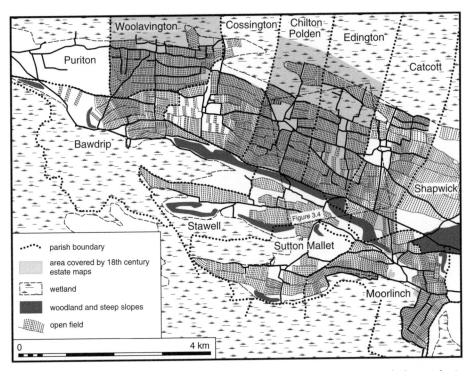

Fig. 3.3. A reconstruction of the landscape on the Polden Hills, west of Shapwick, in central Somerset. Alongside the enclosure maps for Catcott and Moorlinch, large areas of Catcott, Chilton Polden, Cossington, Edington, Moorlinch, and Woolavington have 18th-century estate maps showing surviving common fields (strips and furlong boundaries), while evidence contained within the historic landscape elsewhere allows the remaining furlong boundaries to be reconstructed. The strips depicted here are schematic in terms of their width, though the orientations and any curvature are correct. Apart from small areas of fen-edge meadow, most of the adjacent wetlands were unenclosed pasture (research and drawing by Adam Wainwright using the following sources (all estate maps unless otherwise indicated): Bawdrip, ?late 18th century: SRO DD/SAS/C/1696/3/2; 1795: SRO DD/CH/4547; Catcott, 1771: SRO DD\PR\56; 1799 (enclosure map) SRO Q/RDe 56; Chilton Polden, 1779: SRO DD\S\CD1; Cossington, 1771: SRO DD\PR\57; Edington, 1794: SRO DD\WG\\9; Moorlinch (enclosure map), 1800: SRP Q/RDe 169; Woolavington (with some land in Bawdrip), 1786: SRO DD\BR\Ely\14/4 and SRO DD\BR\Ely\20\3).

2007). An important, albeit smaller-scale, excavation in Edington has produced more conclusive evidence, revealing a set of boundary ditches aligned with the ladder-like layout of main streets and extant property divisions. Although these ditches were aceramic, two radiocarbon dates on animal bones provide a late ninth- or tenth-century *terminus post quem* for the laying out of the village (1079+/−88 BP, 760–1160 cal. AD; 1169+/−61 BP, 760–990 cal. AD: Brigers 2006).

It has been suggested that the most obvious context for this reorganization of the rural landscape was under the reforming Abbot Dunstan (940–57). When he became abbot, the Abbey was little more than an extension of the royal

Fig. 3.4. Aerial photograph of Edington (centre) and parts of Chilton Polden (top left) and Catcott (bottom right), taken in January 1947 (© National Monuments Record, English Heritage CPE/UK 1944 23 Jan. 1947 frame 1058). Note how the planned village of Edington is laid out on a north-east to south-west alignment, while the village of Chilton Polden appears to have developed along an east–west axis. As is the case in the adjacent settlements, including Shapwick to the east, a series of 18th-century enclosure and estate maps shows that these villages were associated with common field systems that covered virtually the entire dryland area of each parish (field and furlong names from the following maps: Chilton Polden, 1779: SRO DD\S\CD1; Edington, 1794: SRO DD\WG\9).

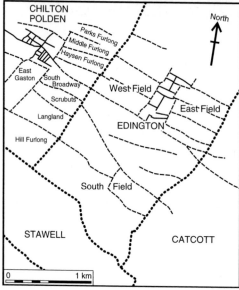

demesne, and a church much like any other minster, but he oversaw a spiritual revival, a major period of rebuilding, a consolidation of landholding, and the recovery of lost territory (Stacey 1972, 11; Carley 1988, 11–12; Costen 1992c, 26; Rahtz 1993, 36). There is, however, a problem with the hypothesis that Glastonbury was directly responsible for replanning the landscape on its Polden Hills estate: while each of these manors had a single village surrounded by a common field system, the layout of these settlements was far from uniform. Edington (Fig. 3.4), Shapwick, and possibly Cossington have a planned layout, with a series of tofts laid out around a ladder-like arrangement of two north to south oriented streets *c.*650 feet (*c.*200 m) apart. In contrast, Catcott, Chilton Polden (Fig. 3.4), and Woolavington have a more irregular east to west oriented plan. Had a single individual or institution been responsible for replanning these landscapes then we might expect there to have been a common design, suggesting that it may have been the subtenants who acquired each of the five hide manors that were responsible for restructuring their landscapes. Perhaps these were the tenants whose names are preserved in the place names of Catcott (Cada's *cot*), Cossington (Cosa's *tūn*), Edington (Eadwine's *tūn*), and Woolavington (Hunlaf's *tūn*) (Ekwall 1960, 532; Mills 1990, 68, 118), giving us a rare insight into the actual individuals who may have been responsible for restructuring these landscapes.

Glastonbury's other central Somerset estates

Landscapes characterized by nucleated villages and common fields are found across Glastonbury's other central Somerset estates. Meare may have been held by Glastonbury from at least 680, and possibly 670 (Table 3.1), and excavations have shown that this planned village was laid out by the late tenth or early eleventh century (Rippon 2004b, 110). The original village plan appears to have consisted of ten plots, each *c.*120 feet (36.6 m) wide, laid out to the north of the main road that crossed the island, and this single row plan is quite unlike the plans of Shapwick and Edington. Where villages and common fields are similarly found on estates that Glastonbury acquired in the early eighth century, it was also presumably during the period of the Abbey's control that the landscape was reorganized (i.e. Baltonsborough, Doulting, *Pengerd* (West Pennard), Pilton (with its sub-units of Croscombe, North Wootton, Pylle, and Shepton Mallet), and Walton (which has produced tenth-century pottery: Webster 2004, 215). The large island-based estate at Sowy is a further example, being granted to Glastonbury in 725 and recorded in Domesday as 12 hides (DB fo. 90; *DB Som.* 8,6). Sowy's historic landscape contains three nucleated villages—Westonzoyland, Middlezoy, and Othery—surrounded by common fields. Middlezoy has a planned layout very similar to Shapwick with a ladder-like arrangement of two parallel streets. Several excavations have revealed evidence for medieval occupation, including pre-Conquest pottery (Webster 2001, 234; 2004, 210). The villages at Westonzoyland and Othery are, in contrast, far more amorphous in their layout, and this lack of evidence for planning in two out of the three settlements may be a further indication that the Abbey itself was not responsible for reordering the landscape.

So far attention has focused on estates where we can be fairly certain that the creation of villages and common fields post-dated their acquisition by Glastonbury Abbey. Also of interest are the estates that Glastonbury acquired in the later tenth century as they may provide an indication of whether these estates had also seen their landscapes reorganized in this way, or whether it was the Abbey and its subtenants who were responsible after they had acquired these properties. The development of an estate south of Glastonbury is particularly informative (Fig. 3.5). Three hides at Wheathill, south of Baltonsborough, may have been given to Glastonbury by King Edgar (959–75), while 4 hides at East Lydford were acquired by the Abbey sometime before 1066. An analysis of the historic landscape shows that they were part of a block of at least five or six manors that had been created through the subdivision of an earlier estate that had included Alford, Lovington, West Lydford, and possibly Hornblotton (DB fos. 92ᵛ, 98, 99, 90ᵛ; *DB Som.* 19,65; 37,8; 47,21; 8,30). There is no difference in the character of the landscape on the Glastonbury manors compared to the others, and the way in which their boundaries zigzag through the common field systems between these villages clearly indicates that this landscape was laid out before the estate fragmented and two of its elements were given to Glastonbury.

Glastonbury's outlying estates in Somerset

In addition to its continuous block of territory in central Somerset, Glastonbury also held a series of detached manors elsewhere in Somerset, Devon, Dorset, Wiltshire, and Gloucestershire. These outlying properties are of interest because if Glastonbury was a great exponent of restructuring its estates and creating villages and common fields, it might be expected that the same approach would have been used in these places, some of which lay outside the central zone. It should be noted, however, that compared to Glastonbury's core estates, a far greater number of the charters have been lost and are only referred to in potentially unreliable later chronicles that may have invented them to explain the Abbey's ownership by the time of Domesday.

Glastonbury held a number of manors north of Mendip of which Hutton, Winscombe, Wrington, and Marksbury were the most important (Table 3.2).[5] Hutton contained two manors in 1066: 5 hides at Hutton itself, and 3 hides at Elborough, both of which were held by Glastonbury Abbey. Although no charters survive that name Hutton, it may have been part of King Ine's reputed grant of 'land at the foot of Mendip' in 705 × 712. A survey in 1309 describes

---

[5] Glastonbury's archives also claim that King Æthelwulf gave 10 hides at Clutton to another Æthelwulf, and that Æthelstan *comes*, son of Æthelnoth, gave it to Glastonbury with the consent of King Æthelwulf (839 × 855) (the charter is now lost; S1694; Finberg 1964, No. 406; Abrams 1996, 92–3). If the Abbey had indeed held Clutton it was lost by 1066 (DB fo. 88; *DB Som.* 5,14). The 19th-century landscape was one of dispersed settlement and small, irregularly shaped fields with no evidence that the medieval situation was any different. Of the other pre-Conquest estates in northern Somerset that Glastonbury's archives make reference to, those in Binegar, Camerton, *Ceollamwirthe* (Chelwood?), *Cympanhamme* (Shipham?), Portbury, Rowberrow, *Streton* (Statton-on-the-Fosse?), and Ubley were either held very fleetingly, or the claims were spurious (in the case of Camerton a forgery to provide proof of title to a post-Conquest acquisition: Abrams 1996, 58–9, 79–80, 85–6, 103–4, 204, 215, 225, 235).

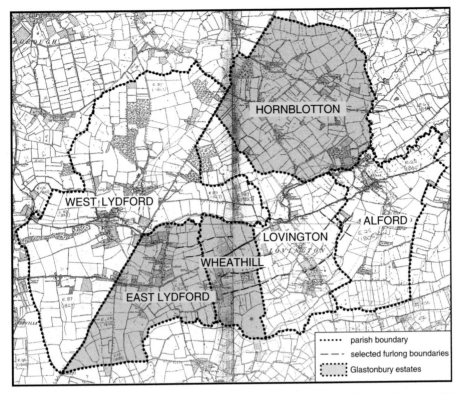

Fig. 3.5. Glastonbury Abbey's manors at East Lydford, Wheathill, and Hornblotton, which had clearly been carved out of a larger estate that included West Lydford, Lovington, and Alford. Note how the parish boundaries between the southern four parishes zigzag through an earlier set of furlong boundaries.

the manor in great detail and reveals a central zone landscape of two villages (Hutton and Elborough) surrounded by common fields and other common resources (Fig. 3.6; Coward 1978). The manor possessed demesne meadows of its own, as well as parcels in the common meadows along the fen-edge, while Hutton Hill was a common pasture 'for the lord and his men'. The lord's arable was partly in closes but largely spread throughout the common fields in a series of named furlongs, and which later sources suggest may have been cropped in three fields (East Field, West Field, and North Hills Field) whose extent can be reconstructed through an analysis of a map dated 1759.

Further east along the Mendip edge lay Winscombe, where King Edgar is said to have given Queen Ælfswith 15 hides in 959 × 975 that she subsequently gave to Glastonbury during the same reign. Winscombe is a large parish (3,900 acres; 1,600 ha) and not surprisingly contains several settlements of which Winscombe itself and Barton to the west were clearly associated with an open or common field (Fig. 3.7), while Sidcot and Woodborough were not, having dispersed settlement patterns and field systems that have the appearance

Table 3.2. Glastonbury Abbey's outlying estates in Somerset

Estate	Date acquired	Reliability (Finberg 1964, 23) and other references	Hidage in 1066
North Somerset			
Hutton and Elborough	705 × 712	(lost, lost, and *) S1670; Finberg 1964, Nos. 374, 391, and 465; Abrams 1996, 143	8 hides (DB fo. 88, 91^v; DB *Som.* 5,10–11; 8,38)
Clutton	839 × 855 (10 hides)	(lost) Finberg 1964, No. 406	(had been lost)
Wrington	925 × 940 (20 *cassati*)	(** and lost) S371; Finberg 1964, Nos. 423, 447; Abrams 1996, 76	20 hides (DB fo. 90^v; DB *Som.* 8,27)
Winscombe	959 × 975	(lost) S1762; Finberg 1964, No. 502; Abrams 1966, 248–2	15 hides (DB fo. 90; DB *Som.* 8,2)
Marksbury	936 (10 *manentes*)	(* and lost) S431; Finberg 1964, Nos. 434 and 506; Abrams 1996, 166–7	10 hides (DB fo. 90^v; DB *Som.* 8,29)
South-east Somerset			
Logderesdone (Montacute)	871 × 879 or earlier	(lost) Finberg 1964, No. 414	(had been lost)
Stoke (sub-Hamdon)	924 × 939		(DB fo. 91^v; DB *Som.* 8,39)
Stane (Kingstone?)	939 × 946 (8 hides)	(both lost) S1725; Finberg 1964, Nos. 442 and 449; Abrams 1996, 220–2	8 hides (DB fo. 91^v, 92; DB *Som.* 8,39; 19,10)
Kingestan	940 (8 hides)		
Yarlington (10 hides)	939 × 946 or later	(lost) S1731; Finberg 1964, No. 453; Abrams 1996, 256–7	(had been lost)
Tintinhull	959 × 975	(both lost) S1728; Finberg 1964, Nos. 451, 503; Abrams 1996, 229	5 hides (DB fo. 90^v, 91; DB *Som.* 8,31; 19,9)

Dinnington		Abrams 1996, 221	3 virgates (DB fo. 90^v; DB Som. 8,36)
Ilchester (St Andrews church)			3 hides (DB fo. 91; DB Som. 8,37)
Blackford	959 × 975 (3 or 6 hides)	(both lost) S1768; Finberg 1964, Nos. 477, 495; Abrams 1996, 59–60	4 hides (DB fo. 90; DB Som. 8,9)
Holton	959 × 975 or later (5 hides)	(lost) S1765; Finberg 1964, No. 497; Abrams 1996, 139	Not in Domesday but in Glastonbury's possession by 1189
Lodreford (Lattiford)		Abrams 1996, 162	2 hides (DB fo. 90; DB Som. 8,19)
Middeltone (Podimore)	966 and later	(*) S743; Finberg 1964, No. 493; Abrams 1996, 174–5	6 hides (DB fo. 90; DB Som. 8,3)
Stoke (sub-Hamdon)	979 × 1016		(DB fo. 91; DB Som. 8,39)
West Somerset			
West Monkton and Creechbarrow	682 (23 *mansiones* and 3 *cassati*)	(**) S237; Finberg 1964, No. 361; Abrams 1996, 80–2, 99–100	15 hides (DB Som. DB fo. 90; 8,28)
Brompton	729 × 740	(lost) S1677; Finberg 1964, No. 382; Abrams 1996, 74–5.	3.5 hides (DB fo. 95; DB Som. 25,7)
Clatworthy			1.5 hides (DB fo. 95; DB Som. 25,8)
Durborough	959 × 975	(lost) S1767; Finberg 1964, No. 499; Abrams 1996, 117	2 hides (DB fo. 90; DB Som. 8,8)

continued

Table 3.2. *continued*

Estate	Date acquired	Reliability (Finberg 1964, 23) and other references	Hidage in 1066
Devon			
Braunton	855 × 860	(*) S303; S1695; Finberg 1954, No. 13; Abrams 1996, 66–9	(lost 973)

Notes:
+ Original charter, authenticity not in doubt.
* Charter available only in a later copy or copies, authenticity not in doubt.
** Charter available in later copy or copies, thought to embody the substance of the original, but having some material, probably spurious, substituted or interpolated.
*** Charter thought to be fundamentally a fabrication, but which may embody some authentic material or record a genuine transaction.
lost: Charter no longer survives but is referred to in later sources (which for Glastonbury Abbey are likely to be unreliable).

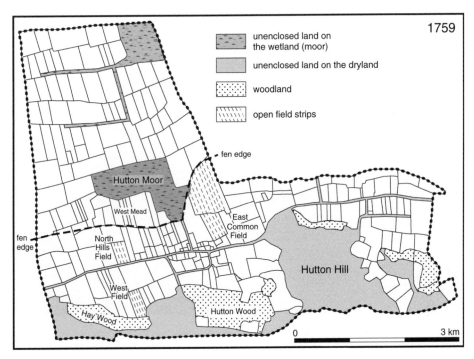

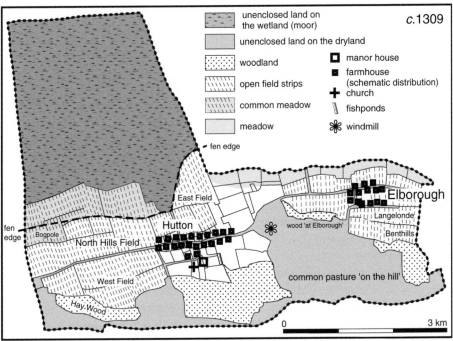

Fig. 3.6. The manor of Hutton in 1759 (based on a map of that date: BRO AC/M8/85/1), and reconstruction of the landscape in the early 14th century based on an Extent of 1309 (BRO AC/M8/10; Coward 1978).

Fig. 3.7. Aerial view of the hamlet and former open field system at Barton, in Winscombe parish, looking south-west down the Lox Yeo Valley, across the Somerset Levels, towards Bridgwater Bay.

of always being closes held in severalty. As with the Polden Hills, we are seeing a degree of diversity in landscape character within a single estate suggesting that the Abbey was either not directly involved in decisions to transform the landscape, or that it chose to develop areas in different ways.

North-east of Winscombe lay the 20-hide estate at Wrington that Æthelstan Half-King is said to have granted to Glastonbury in 925 × 940, and which presumably included Burrington, a chapelry of Wrington, which was confirmed as a possession of Glastonbury by William the Conqueror but which is not otherwise recorded in Domesday. Wrington was a large estate (7,570 acres; 3,000 ha) which contained areas of different landscape character. Around the substantial village at Wrington itself there are vestiges of a common field layout that in *c.*1300 was managed in a two-field system (Keil 1964, table A). Based on an analysis of the nineteenth-century field boundary pattern a further open or common field can be recognized north of Burrington, while other areas of the parish had very dispersed settlement patterns associated with closes held in severalty. The latter, however, mostly lie on the higher, steeper hillsides and would appear to represent piecemeal assarting of upland common and woodland, large areas of which remained unenclosed until 1813. When a retrogressive analysis of this landscape is carried out, removing these areas of relatively late assarting, it is possible to reconstruct an open field system of *c.*3 km^2 (*c.*750 acres) around Wrington and *c.*2 km^2 (*c.*500 acres) north of Burrington that are on the same scale as those in central and south-east Somerset (and as such are likely to have been managed as common fields).

Further to the east King Æthelstan gave his thegn Æthelhelm ten *man-entes* at Marksbury in 936, who in turn granted the estate to Glastonbury during the reign of the same king (i.e. before 940). In the nineteenth century the landscape consisted of a nucleated village surrounded by an enclosed fieldscape clearly derived from an extensive two-field common field system documented in *c.*1300 (Keil 1964, table A). As at Lydford, however, Glastonbury was granted a fragment of what had been a far larger estate, as Marksbury's northern boundary with Compton Dando zigzags through a series of former furlongs, which survived into the eighteenth century and must have existed before the estate was subdivided (Fig. 3.8). The configuration of the parish boundaries suggests that Farmborough was also part of this estate.

Glastonbury also held a number of manors in the south-east of Somerset (Table 3.2), although in several cases they were held very fleetingly, or the claims were spurious.[6] As we have already seen in Lydford and Marksbury, these mostly tenth-century grants were of manors created through the subdivision of larger estates within which the development of villages and common fields had already taken place, such as eight hides at Kingstone possibly granted to Glastonbury by King Edmund (939–46) or his wife Æthelflæd, and three virgates in the neighbouring Dinnington held by Glastonbury in 1066, the rest of which was in lay hands (DB fos. 90ᵛ, 99; *DB Som.* 8,36; 47,10). An analysis of the historic landscape reveals that Dinnington and Kingstone were once part of a single estate that appears to have been divided after the two villages and a common field system were laid out, the boundary between them zigzagging through the furlong boundaries. A similar situation appears to have occurred at Tintinhull, where King Edmund (939–46) is said to have granted 5 hides to one Wulfric—probably Abbot Dunstan's brother—who in turn gave it to Glastonbury, and whose boundary with Sock Denis once again clearly zigzags through strips and furlongs. Other examples of Glastonbury receiving manors that were created following the subdivision of an earlier estate are the 4 hides at Blackford (near Wincanton) said to have been granted to the Abbey by King Edgar (959–75), and Lattiford which in 1066 was a detached parcel of Glastonbury's manor at Butleigh.

Glastonbury also held a number of estates in western Somerset, beyond the edge of the central zone (Table 3.2). In 682 King Centwine is said to have granted Haemgils, abbot of Glastonbury, 23 *mansiones* by the wood called *Cantucwda* ('Quantock Wood'), whose bounds identify it as West Monkton,

---

[6] *Cantmel* (Queen and West Camel), Henstridge, Ilchester, and Yeovilton (Abrams 1996, 78–9, 137–9, 146–7, 257–8).

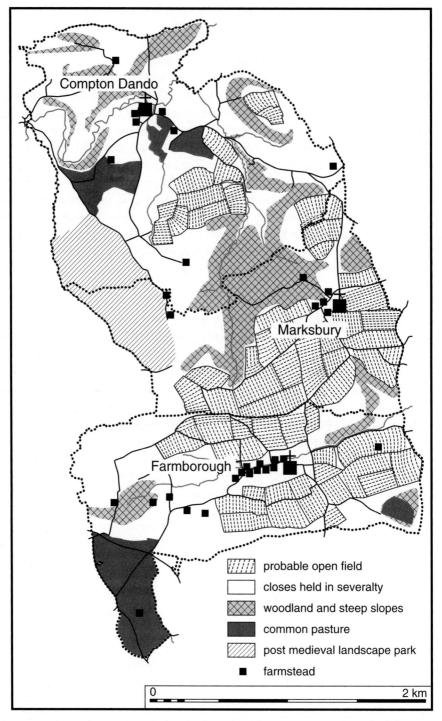

	probable open field
	closes held in severalty
	woodland and steep slopes
	common pasture
	post medieval landscape park
■	farmstead

0   2 km

Fig. 3.8. A reconstruction of the landscape of Compton Dando, Marksbury, and Farmborough in north-east Somerset. This landscape is typical of the region north of Mendip in having generally pre-18th-century enclosure of common fields that appear to have varied considerably in their extent. Research and drawing by Adam Wainwright using the following estate maps: Compton Dando, 1758 (SRO DD/PO 65); Marksbury, 1758 (SRO DD/PO 67); and Farmborough, 1758 (SRO DD/PO 66).

along with 3 *cassati* in 'the island by the hill that the British call *Cructan* and the Saxons *Crycbeorh*' (Creechbarrow). The latter was subsequently lost, being held by Gunhilda in 1066 as 10½ hides (DB fo. 86ᵛ; *DB Som.* 1,18), but (West) Monkton was still held by Glastonbury as 15 hides. Unlike its adjacent manors, which in the nineteenth century had dispersed settlement patterns and enclosed fields, West Monkton shows signs of being a shrunken village, surrounded by a substantial open or common field. Several of the outlying farmsteads and hamlets in the parish appear to be relatively late, for example Monkton Heathfield which clearly occupies a former common. Although we cannot say when the landscape was restructured, it was presumably after 682 as nowhere else in the country are village and common fields earlier than this date, suggesting that Glastonbury or its subtenants did indeed play a part in the creation of this landscape. Glastonbury's archives also make various claims to having held estates in the far west of Somerset of which those thought reliable are listed in Table 3.2.[7] None of the landscapes on these scattered estates appears to have been transformed through the creation of villages and common fields, although their small size and topographic context—on the Brendon Hills and the fringes of Exmoor—were not conducive to open field farming.

Devon: Braunton Great Field and the Glastonbury connection

Glastonbury also held several manors in Devon, of which Braunton is famous for its surviving open field (Fig. 3.9).[8] In 854 half a *hiwisc* at *Branuc* is included in the list of lands granted to the Abbey by King Æthelwulf (S303; Finberg 1964, No. 408), while in 855 × 860 the same king gave Glastonbury 10 hides at *Brannocmynstre* (Braunton) which in 973 the Abbey gave to King Edgar in exchange for High Ham in Somerset (S1695; S791; Finberg 1964, No. 517; Abrams 1996, 66–9). The surviving open field at Braunton is unique in the South-West (Finberg 1952, 265–8; Slee 1952; Griffith 1988, 96), and an analysis of the historic landscape reveals that it was once far more extensive. Lying well beyond the champion landscapes of England's central zone, it is tempting to see Glastonbury as having exported the concept of

---

[7] The other claims appear spurious. King Edgar is said to have granted 2 hides at Luccombe to the Abbey in 959 × 975, but it was held by Queen Edith in 1066 while another hide was also in lay hands (S1769; DB fos. 97, 98; *DB Som.* 32,1; 38,1; Abrams 1996, 162–3). King Edgar's alleged grant of land at *Cylfan* to the Abbey may be Old Cleve near Watchet, but there is no further reference to it in Glastonbury's archives (S1766; Abrams 1996, 89). The identification of King Æthelwulf's grant of 6 hides at *Cerawycombe* in 854 with Crowcombe is at best tenuous (S303; Abrams 1996, 86–7). In 891 King Alfred granted 2 hides at *Radingtone* to Glastonbury which may be Radington, several kilometres south of Clatworthy, where 2 hides in 1066 were in lay hands (DB fo. 94ᵛ; *DB Som.* 22,13; Abrams 1996, 215).

[8] The Abbey's other possible estates in the county—the land (half a hide?) at *Ocmund* (Monk Okehampton?; S1696; Abrams 1996, 177–8), and two hides at *Otheri* (Ottery St Mary?; S721; Abrams 1996, 189–91)—need not concern us due to doubts over their identification and limited extent.

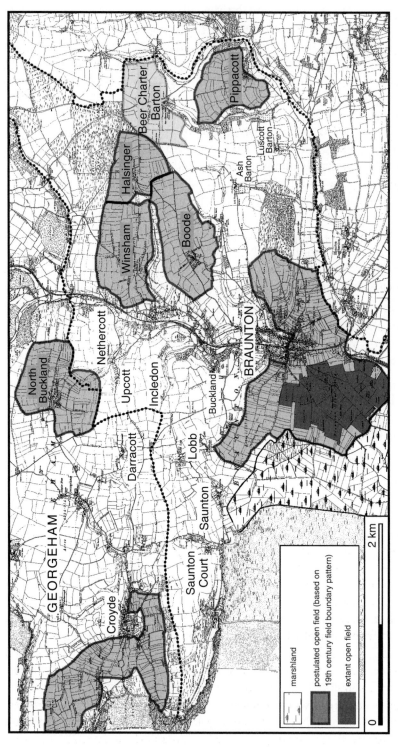

Fig. 3.9. An interpretation of the historic landscape of Braunton in north-west Devon. The surviving open field is probably around a third of its original extent, while smaller now-enclosed open fields can be identified around the hamlets and now isolated farmsteads (presumably shrunken hamlets) at Beer Charter Barton, Boode, Halsinger, Pippacott, and Winsham.

a Midland-style village and common field system into this outlying manor, but first we need to place this particular landscape in its wider context. Documentary evidence, earthworks, and analysis of the historic landscape reveal that strip-based open fields occurred widely across the South-West, with a particular concentration in the north-west of Devon (Fig. 3.10; Finberg 1952; Fox 1972; Riley and Wilson North 2001; Rippon 2004a, figs. 18, 19, 26). These open fields were arranged very differently from those in champion countryside and are discussed in Chapter 4. The large parish of Braunton is in fact typical of this region, as in addition to the large c.960 acre (1.5 mile^2; 3.88 km^2) open field associated with the main village, there appear to have been smaller open fields of c.320 acres (0.5 mile^2; 1.3 km^2) associated with the small hamlets of Winsham (which is recorded in Domesday: DB fo. 102^v; *DB Dev.* 3,43), and Hasinger, Pippacott, and Bode (first documented in 1167, 1311, and 1330 respectively: Gover *et al.* 1931, 32–4). The field boundary pattern around the Domesday manor of Beer Charter Barton does not contain individual striplike fields, although a number of dog-legged boundaries hint at the former presence of open field (DB fo. 102^v; *DB Dev.* 3,31). These small hamlets and open fields sat alongside areas with fields whose morphology suggest that they were always held in severalty, notably at North Buckland, Ash Barton, and Saunton, all of which are recorded in Domesday (DB fos. 110, 110^v, 115^v; *DB Dev.* 3,31; 19,13–14; 36,10), and Luscott and Incledon which are first recorded in 1167 and 1238 respectively (Gover *et al.* 1931, 32–4). Adjacent parishes have a similarly mixed landscape of small hamlets associated with former open field systems (e.g. North Buckland and Croyde) alongside areas whose morphology is suggestive of closes always held in severalty.

So, was the village and common field-based landscape at Braunton an innovation during Glastonbury's ownership of the manor in the mid ninth to mid tenth century that was subsequently emulated by neighbouring manors and/or communities, or did the Abbey happen to acquire an estate that either had already started to develop common field farming, or went on to do so, in line with developments within its local region? Three lines of argument may lend tentative support to the idea that Braunton's landscape was something somewhat different from the rest of north-west Devon. First, there is the sheer size of the open field: around three times larger than other examples in the vicinity. While there is a small cluster of former open fields around Braunton, these are far from typical of the north Devon and west Somerset landscape (Fig. 3.10). Secondly, that such a large proportion of it remained unenclosed into the nineteenth century—367 acres (150 ha) in 1843—might suggest that there was something embedded within local custom that was different from the adjacent areas where enclosure had clearly occurred much earlier. And thirdly, the morphology of the field systems was different, with Braunton having a relatively simple arrangement of long, regularly arranged furlongs up

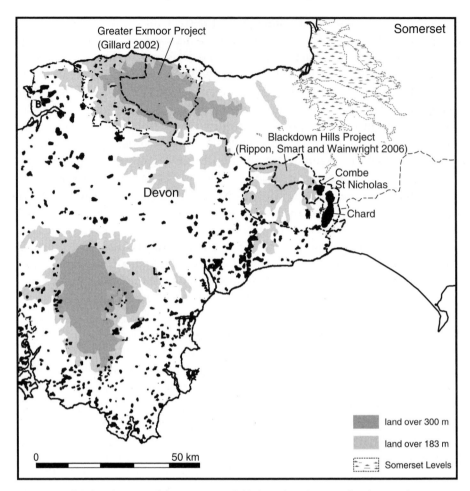

Fig. 3.10. The distribution of former open field, based on historic landscape character, in Devon (Shorter *et al.* 1969, fig. 26) and parts of western Somerset based on the results of the Greater Exmoor Project (Gillard 2002, fig. 5.39) and Blackdown Hills Project (Rippon *et al.* 2006b; Rippon 2007b). The extensive common fields in Chard and Combe St Nicholas in south-west Somerset represent the edge of England's 'central province'.

to three-quarters of a mile long, in contrast to the far smaller and irregularly laid out blocks of strips in the hamlet-based open fields nearby. All in all, the Braunton open field system does appear somewhat different from those elsewhere in north-west Devon, leading to the strong suspicion that it may have been created by Glastonbury based on the model being adopted across central Somerset.

In contrast, Glastonbury appears to have little or no impact on the landscape of its East Devon estates. The Abbey's claim to have held '24 hides'[9] at

---

[9] The '24 hides' may be a scribal error for 14 which is the number of hides in Domesday when the manor was in lay hands (DB fo. 111ᵛ; *DB Dev.* 23,9).

Uffculme from 854 (or 760 if Sulca's gift of land at *Culum* refers to Uffculme), to sometime before 1050 × 1053, appears to have been genuine, although by the mid eleventh century at least the manor appears to have been leased from the Abbey and then lost (S1697; Abrams 1996, 101–3, 235–41). While the historic landscape contains small areas of former open fields around the hamlets of Ashill and Craddock (both in existence in the thirteenth century: Gover *et al.* 1931, 538), there is certainly nothing comparable to the open fields of Braunton or central and south-eastern Somerset. Glastonbury's other substantial holding in Devon was the 6 hides that Ealdorman Æthelstan gave the Abbey at *Lim* (Uplyme) between 938 and 940 (S442; Abrams 1996, 155). Glastonbury still held the estate in 1066 (DB 103^v; *DB Dev.* 4,1) along with the adjacent manor of Colway in Lyme Regis (Dorset) that it must have received after 957 when King Eadwig granted 4 hides at *Lim* to one 'Huna' (S644; DB fo. 77^v; *DB Dor.* 8,6; Abrams 1996, 155). Once again, there is little evidence for open field in a landscape characterized by its highly dispersed settlement pattern.

Discussion: Glastonbury Abbey and the replanning of Somerset's landscape

While there are examples of estates acquired after *c.*930 where villages and common fields appear to have been created before Glastonbury acquired them, where the Abbey held estates from the late seventh or early eighth century until the eleventh century any restructuring of the landscape was presumably during their period of ownership (as nowhere else in the country has it been suggested that this transformation occurred before the eighth century). Although its lands were concentrated in central Somerset, the Abbey also held manors across the whole county and beyond, and it is noticeable that in all these areas where it was practical for common fields to be laid out this appears to have happened. Along with the planned villages on the Polden Hills, Meare, and Sowy, this might suggest that Glastonbury was a 'prime mover' in the introduction of villages and common fields into Somerset, but a number of the case studies above suggest that the picture was more complicated, as even within individual estates there was significant diversity in how the landscape was structured: the ladder-plan villages of Shapwick, Edington, and Middlezoy may be very similar, but they are very different from the adjacent but seemingly unplanned villages at Westonzoyland, Othery, Catcott, Edington, and Woolavington. The single-row plan at Meare is different again. There was clearly not a single 'Glastonbury' way of structuring the landscape, which raises a number of possibilities. It may be that the planned villages represent the handful of estates where the Abbey decided to directly intervene and redesign the landscape, the different forms of planned village representing separate phases of activity. Alternatively, the different settlement forms may reflect the fact that it was Glastonbury's subtenants who were responsible rather than the Abbey itself, and this idea can now be explored by looking at the estates of a number of other major landowners.

THE ROLE OF SUBTENANTS AND THE COMMUNITY: THE ESTATES OF THE BISHOPS OF WELLS

Another major landowner in Somerset was the bishop of Wells who held estates across the county (Fig. 3.11).[10] The character of the landscape on these estates invariably follows the local norm with villages and common fields in central and eastern Somerset (e.g. Wells itself, Westbury, Evercreech, Wanstrow, Wedmore, and Kingsbury Episcopi), and a dispersed settlement pattern associated with enclosed fields in Wiveliscombe and Wellington (which included West Buckland) in the west. The absence of villages and common fields on these western Somerset manors suggests that Wells also did not have a uniform approach towards estate management, which is supported by the form taken by their villages in eastern Somerset: Wanstrow and Winsham, for example, appear to be planned, whereas Evercreech and Westbury are more amorphous and probably grew more in a more piecemeal fashion.

One area of Wells's estates whose historic landscape character shows remark-able local variation is on the North Somerset Levels, the southern part of which lay within the manors of Banwell and Congresbury that were granted to the Welsh priest Asser by King Alfred in 885/6. Asser went on to become bishop of Sherborne and upon his death in 908–9 the see was divided in three, whereupon Banwell and Congresbury passed to the division based at Wells (Rippon 2006, 132–3). As with the areas around Brent, Burnham, and Huntspill described above, the North Somerset Levels were a reclaimed wetland, a process that started in the tenth and eleventh centuries, with the associated uniformity in soils and antecedent landscape character: any local variation in the character of the settlement patterns and field systems must be due to social factors. This landscape was studied as part of the North Somerset Levels Project, the results of which have been published in detail elsewhere (Rippon 2006). What is of particular interest here is that within the estates of this one landowner—the bishops of Wells—there was considerable variation in landscape character, including both nucleated and dispersed settlement patterns that fieldwalking, shovel test pitting, and the collection of pottery from the gardens of extant farmhouses have shown existed by the eleventh or twelfth century. At Puxton, for example, there was a nucleated village surrounded by two common fields, while immediately to the north, in a district known as Congresbury Marsh, there was a scatter of isolated farmsteads each associated with a compact block of fields held in severalty. Further to the west, in the chapelry of Wick

---

[10] This later became the See of Bath and Wells.

St Lawrence (part of the manor of Congresbury), there were two compact hamlets—Icelton [Easton] and Wick—that shared an open field, while a third hamlet—Bourton—appears to have had its own field system that included compact closes held in severalty and a large common meadow. In the bishops' neighbouring manor of Banwell, the reclaimed marshes were occupied by the compact hamlets of St Georges, Waywick, and West Wick in the north, along with a series of farmsteads that formed the very loosely arranged hamlets of East and West Rolstone in the south; all these settlements were once again associated with a mixture of small open fields and closes held in severalty. It is remarkable that in such close proximity, and on the same estate, these settlement patterns and field systems were so different, and it seems clear that the bishops of Wells did not have a determining hand in how the landscapes were created. Presumably, it was the bishops' (or the king's) subtenants and their local communities who decided whether they wanted to live in villages or isolated farmsteads, and to farm their land in communally managed open fields or closes held in severalty.

OTHER MAJOR LANDOWNERS

The bishops of Winchester

The bishops of Winchester held an extensive estate centred on Taunton, and stretching from Pitminster in the south to Kingston in the north (Fig. 3.11). In 737 King Æthelheard is said to have given the church at Winchester land at Withiel Florey and Cearn, in augmentation of Queen Frithogyth's gift of Taunton to the bishop (S383), and while Bishop Ælfsige gave Taunton to the king in his will (955 × 958), a few years later they were returned to the Church by King Edgar (?964 × 975: S1491; Finberg 1964, Nos. 85 and 119). Additions to the estate included Bishop's Trull being acquired in 1033 (S972; Finberg 1964, No. 530), and Pitminster as late as 1044 (S1006; Finberg 1964, No. 531).[11] In the context of this study what is significant is that both the core of the estate acquired in the early eighth century, and areas that were added in the eleventh century, have landscapes characterized by dispersed settlement and enclosed field systems: in common with the bishops of Wells's manors immediately to the west at Wiveliscombe and Wellington, there is no evidence for the nucleated villages and common fields that are so characteristic of the landscape just a few kilometres to the east. Winchester also held two other manors in Somerset: Rimpton, which it was given in 964 × 980 (S1512; Finberg 1964, No. 514), and Bleadon which it was allegedly given in 975 (S804; though this charter is 'fundamentally

---

[11] The charter purporting to record the granting of Orchard Portman, Ruishton, and Stoke St Mary in 854 is probably a forgery (S310; Finberg 1964, No. 409).

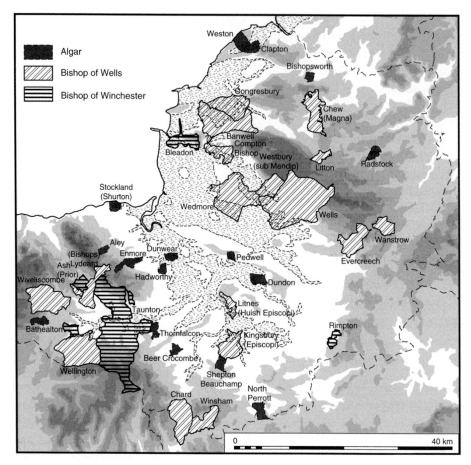

Fig. 3.11. Distribution of the Somerset estates held by the bishop of Wells, bishop of Winchester, and the thane Ælfgar in 1086.

a fabrication, but which may embody some authentic material or record a genuine transaction': Finberg 1964, No. 519). Both manors had nucleated villages and common fields whose character was very different from the landscape around Taunton, although this may well have resulted from a reorganization of the settlement pattern and field systems before Winchester received them.

The king

By 1066 the royal lands in Somerset had been significantly denuded through grants to the Church and the laity, although a series of manors survived which were scattered across the county (Rippon 2004a, fig. 27.13). A number of other estates were held by Queen Edith (wife of King Edward the Confessor and sister to King Harold), while the Godwinson family held a series of 'comital manors': royal estates set aside for officials, or as part of earldoms granted to members of the Godwinson family identifiable through the payment of third penny borough right and/or being listed in the Exeter Domesday as *mansiones de comitatu* (Baxter 2007, 141–5). There are no correlations, however, between these estates and landscape character, as they were spread across areas characterized by both villages and common fields, and dispersed settlement patterns associated with predominantly enclosed field systems (e.g. Fig. 3.12).

The laity

In 1066, those manors not held by the king and the major ecclesiastical institutions were divided amongst a large number of thegns. In some cases they are not named, but of those that are, just over half held a single manor in Somerset, while around a third held between two and four manors. There were a relatively small number of the aristocracy who held larger numbers of manors: around a tenth of the named landowners held between five and ten manors, with half this number holding between eleven and twenty. Eadmer Atser, for example, held six manors, and as we have seen on other lordships there was no common approach to structuring countryside, with landscapes characterized by villages (Camerton, East Chinnock, Odcombe, and Dinnington), hamlets (Mudford), and isolated farmsteads (Aldwick). There were five Saxon lords who held over twenty manors. Ælfgar, for example, held nineteen manors along with a furlong added to Timberscombe after 1066, and a virgate at Dunwear (Fig. 3.11; DB fos. 94, 95; *DB Som.* 22,14; 24,6). These manors were spread across the whole of Somerset and included small villages surrounded by common fields typical of central and south-eastern Somerset (Dundon, North Perrott, and Shepton Beauchamp), and small hamlets or farmsteads associated with closes held in severalty to the west of the Parrett at Alcombe (in Minehead), Aley (in Over Stowey), Bathealton, Hadworthy (in North Petherton), Enmore, Minehead, Porlock, Stockland (Stogursey), and 3 hides at Wootton (Courtenay). Two manors—Beercrocombe and Thornfalcon—lay on the interface of the medieval countryside characterized by villages and common fields to the east and more dispersed settlement patterns and predominantly enclosed fields to the west. In the north of Somerset he held Clapton (with its dispersed settlement and enclosed fields), Weston (a planned village with common fields), Bishopsworth (a hamlet possibly associated with a small open field but predominantly closes), and Radstock (whose landscape when first mapped in the post-medieval period was heavily industrialized, making it impossible to determine the character of the medieval countryside).

There are several important observations about the lordships of Eadmer Atser and Ælfgar. First, the manors were scattered right across Somerset which would have made it difficult for them or their predecessors to have

Fig. 3.12. Vertical aerial photograph, taken in January 1947, of the landscape south of the royal manor of Cannington (centre top), west of the Parrett estuary, showing a dispersed settlement associated with closes held in severalty including the Domesday manors of Chilton Trivett (centre), Clayhill (bottom right), and Gothelney (bottom left) (© National Monuments Record CPE/UK.1944, 23 Jan. 1947, frame 3106). The soils, extensive areas of meadow, and Domesday population are all comparable to those found in central Somerset that had medieval landscapes characterized by villages and common fields.

adopted a very 'hands-on' approach to management. Secondly, the characters of the landscapes were extremely diverse, with planned villages surrounded by common fields at one extreme and dispersed settlement patterns and enclosed fields at the other. Thirdly, these lordships were clearly created from the fragments of what had been far larger estates that were compact, not scattered: as we have seen in the case of Glastonbury Abbey's later acquisitions, the reorganization of the landscape occurred before the creation of these small manors, and so we must now consider whether it was in the context of these earlier estates that the landscape of eastern Somerset were reorganized.

RECONSTRUCTING EARLY MEDIEVAL ESTATES

Throughout this discussion of Domesday estates in Somerset, it has become clear that the manors existing in 1066 were usually produced through the fragmentation of larger territories. Examples discussed above have included Westonzoyland, Middlezoy, and Othery which were created out of Glastonbury's estate at Sowy; the Abbey's manor of Dinnington, which was clearly once part of a larger estate that also embraced Kingstone; and Wheathill and East Lydford, which were created through the subdivision of an estate that once embraced Alford, Lovington, and West Lydford. Analysis of the historic landscape in all these cases suggests that the creation of villages and common fields had started before the final fragmentation of these estates into the Domesday manors, as parish boundaries clearly zigzag through, and so post-date, furlong boundaries that run between the villages. In the case of the Polden Hills, discussed above, it appears that the *c.*100-hide area called *Pouelt* was progressively broken up in the early eighth century into several large 20- and 30-hide blocks, such as Shapwick, Walton, and the block of manors between Catcott and Woolavington. These estates were then further broken up into a series of typically 5-hide manors, each with its own village, although this appears to have been carried out after the laying out of common field systems that are cut by the manorial/parish boundaries. So was it these pre-manorial estates that provided the context for the replanning of landscapes elsewhere in eastern Somerset?

'Federative' estates

A variety of evidence suggests that across southern Britain the early medieval landscape was once divided up into large districts that may have originated as folk territories, sometimes referred to as *regiones*, and equating to around ten to twenty later parishes (Bailey 1989; Bassett 1989, 17; 1997; Brooks 1989, 71; Blair 1991, 12; Fleming 1994; 1998, 18–32; Hooke 1998, fig. 3). Similar-sized territories, which Jones (1979; 1985) has called 'multiple estates', are recorded in thirteenth-century Welsh lawbooks that describe a system of landscape exploitation whereby a hierarchical network of primary and subsidiary settlements lay within a territory that characteristically embraced a range of environments (e.g. straddling both uplands and lowlands). This 'multiple estate' model of landscape exploitation was widely applied to early medieval Britain, although Bassett (1989, 20) rejects the term as 'unhistorical' as there is no evidence that forms of agrarian organization based on ownership existed during the centuries in which the early English kingdoms developed (and see Gregson 1985; Jones 1985). What is clear is that, irrespective of whether the 'multiple estate' structure as described in the thirteenth-century lawbooks ever existed in that precise form during earlier periods, or indeed outside Wales, many of its underlying 'federative' principles towards exploiting a landscape are apparent in the earliest true estates that we can identify, based on late seventh-century and later charters that possessed a hierarchy of settlement, dependent on a single centre, spread across areas that embraced a diverse range of environments, leading to some specialist and even seasonal settlements that owed food, rent, and services to the centre (e.g. Blair 1991, 24–5; Faith 1997; Lewis *et al.* 1997, 23; Hooke 1998, 122–3; Dyer 2003, 25–30). Around the ninth century these great estates started to fragment, and while the king, Church, and great magnates often retained sizeable areas, usually on the best land, thegns were increasingly granted landed endowments of typically 1 to 6 hides (Dyer 2003, 30). These ultimately led to the multiplicity of manors that existed in 1066 as recorded in the Domesday survey. Following the Norman Conquest there was a major redistribution of land, with most estates of the English thegns being seized and granted to the king's followers, and some of the estates that Earl Harold had seized from the Church being restored (e.g. Banwell: see below).

Early territorial arrangements in Somerset

The Anglo-Saxon chronicle describes how the West Saxons conquered Somerset in AD 658 when Cenwalh 'fought at Pen[selwood][12] against the Welsh and drove them back as far as the Parrett' (Swanton 1996, 32). Surviving charters show that the kings of Wessex were granting estates in Somerset to the Church from the last two decades of the seventh century, including Centwine's purported gift in AD 682 of land at Creechbarrow Hill on the slopes of the Quantock Hills which shows that Saxon influence had already crossed the Parrett (S237). It is likely that the kingdom which the West Saxons were building could only be controlled if pre-existing territorial arrangements were initially retained for administrative purposes, and it is likely that new rulers took over the estates previously held by the native British elite, keeping the best

---

[12] Finberg (1974, 31) suggests that Pen may have been Pinhoe in Exeter, but this makes no sense as the Welsh would then have been driven east towards Somerset.

and largest estates, and distributing the rest to their followers and the Church (Costen 1992a, 85, 90). It is likely that by the ninth century many estates had been fragmented in order to grant land to the king's followers, and by the early tenth century there was increasing pressure for these tenants to perform military service, which led to further fragmentation, with a multiplicity of small estates that formed the basis of the post-Conquest manors being created for thegns. Originally these were around 6 hides, but they became even smaller as time went on and by 1066 there were 891 estates in Somerset, of which 485 were 3 hides or fewer, and 273 were under 1 hide (Costen 1992a, 115–17).

A number of attempts have been made to identify early royal estate centres in Somerset (e.g. Aston 1986; Costen 1992a), although Blair (2005, 266–90) has recently argued that such stable settlements did not exist in the seventh and eighth centuries. The emphasis here, therefore, is to try and reconstruct the territories themselves following the principles of retrogressive research, starting with the well-documented post-medieval period and working back towards the poorly recorded pre-Conquest period (the results of this analysis in north-west Somerset have been published in detail elsewhere: Rippon 2006). Evidence includes:

- Ecclesiastical relationships. In Somerset there are just seventeen churches in Domesday, five 'minster' place names (all from the tenth century, including Ilminster), and very little surviving pre-Conquest architecture. Early minster *parochiae* are, however, sometimes partially reflected in later ecclesiastical relationships, such as one place being a chapelry of, or owing other dues to, another church. In these documented examples of a mother church–chapel relationship, the parish boundary between the two is provably recent and invariably zigzags through, and so clearly post-dates, the historic landscape, and this same stratigraphic principle is evident in many other places, making it possible to identify other examples of where two parishes were once part of a single territory.
- The detaching of one parish from another similarly leads to a boundary that zigzags through the historic landscape, and detached parcels (e.g. Charlton Adam, which was carved out of Charlton Mackrell parish when William fitz Adam granted the land to Bruton Priory in 1258: Winchester 1990, 14–15).
- Detached parochial parcels are also indicative of when a former area of common was enclosed (e.g. Sedgemoor: Fig. 3.2; and see Winchester 1990, 14).
- Place names indicating the relative locations of primary and subsidiary settlements, such as Norton (North-ton) and Sutton (South-ton), and the subdivision of an earlier territory (e.g. East and West Lydford: Fig. 3.5).
- Place names indicative of secondary settlements (e.g. '-stock': Chard and Chardstock; Hoskins 1952, 289–333; Everitt 1977).

- Place names can also indicate a range of hierarchical relationships. A number of place names are suggestive of small estates granted by the king to his followers, such as Charlton ('the *tūn* [farmstead] of the *ceorls* [free peasant farmers who depended directly on the king]': Costen 1992a, 90). Other examples include Chilton ('farm of the young noblemen') and Hornblotton ('farm of the hornblower': Fig. 3.5) (Costen 1992a, 90–3). Several clusters of place names of the 'personal name + -ington' type also probably reflect the fragmentation of estates as seen on the Polden Hills (see above: Fig. 3.2) and around South Petherton (Fig. 3.13).

- Pre-Conquest charters giving estate boundaries (though these relate to the products of estate fragmentation.

For the purposes of this study the crucial area to study is between Sedgemoor and Blackdown Hills in southern Somerset where the boundary of landscapes characterized by villages and common fields does not appear to correspond to any feature of the natural environment (Fig. 3.13). The boundary between these areas of different landscape character falls within what appears to have been a large territory extending from the river Parrett in the east, the river Yeo and the wetlands of Sedgemoor in the north, the river Tone to the north-west, the Blackdown Hills to the south-west, and the river Axe to the south. Place names suggest four ancient centres: the simple topographical names of Crewkerne and Curry, and the 'river name + -ton' place names of Ilton and (South) Petherton. Of these Crewkerne, Curry (Rivel), and (South) Petherton were royal manors in Domesday. Ecclesiastical relationships suggest all of these places were minster churches, with others at Cudworth, Kingsbury Episcopi, and Seavington St Michael. Along with Chillington there are a noteworthy number of -ington place names around South Petherton. This is also an area that had a complex pattern of detached parochial parcels. West Sedgemoor was divided in half between North Curry and Curry Rivel, and that part to the south of this line contained detached parcels of six parishes (Isle Abbots, Fivehead, Curry Mallet, Hatch Beauchamp, Beercrocombe, and Broadway) suggesting that it was formerly an area of common. Several detached parcels in Broadway parish (belonging to Barrington, Ilton, Donyatt, and White Lackington) probably reflect former grazing rights on the commons of what was to become Neroche Forest. Domesday also records various dues paid to some of the lowland manors by places around the fringes of the Blackdown Hills.[13]

---

[13] Cricket (St Thomas) paid (South) Petherton six sheep with as many lambs and one bloom of iron from each free man (DB fo. 86; *DB Som.* 1,5). Ashill ought to pay Curry (Rivel) 30 pence (DB fo. 92; *DB Som.* 19,18), while the two manors of Bradon each paid Curry (Rivel) one sheep and a lamb (DB fo. 92; *DB Som.* 19,17; 19,23); Bickenhall paid Curry Rivel five sheep and as many lambs, while each freeman owed a bloom of iron (DB fo. 92; *DB Som.* 19,27). Seaborough paid Crewkerne twelve sheep with their lambs, a bloom of iron from every freeman (DB fo. 87ᵛ; *DB Som.* 3,1).

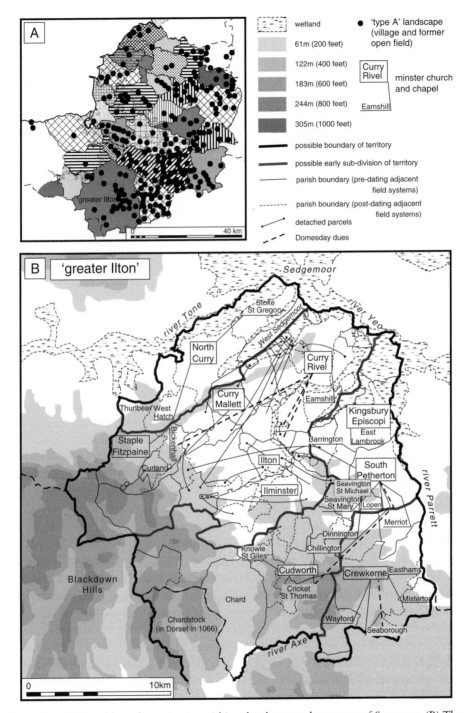

Fig. 3.13. (A) Possible early territories within what became the county of Somerset. (B) The evidence used to reconstruct the possible 'folk territory' potentially centred on Ilton. This appears to have been broken up into a series of smaller estates based at North Curry, Curry Rivel, South Petherton, and Crewkerne, which in turn fragmented into the manors recorded in Domesday.

An analysis of these various territorial and ecclesiastical relationships allows the identification of four early estates, each closely related to a minster church and early hundred: these may have been the estates into which the earlier folk territory was divided following the Saxon conquest. In the north there was North Curry, where the hundred and minster *parochia* were clearly coterminous. The hundred of Abdick and Bulstone appears to correspond to the royal manor and minster churches of Curry Rivel, Curry Mallet, Staple FitzPayne, and Ilminster. A third estate appears to have been based at the *villa regalis*, minster, and hundredal centre of South Petherton and probably embraced the split hundred of Kingsbury East that included Kingsbury Episcopi to the north of South Petherton and Chard and Combe St Nicholas to the south. Finally, in the south-east there was the royal manor, hundred, and minster of Crewkerne. In the context of this study, a crucial observation is that the western limit of landscapes characterized by villages and common fields shows no correspondence with these early territorial boundaries, suggesting that any restructuring of the landscape happened after these estates fragmented.

The restructuring of landscapes on early estates

In the case of the Polden Hills it has been shown that landscape reorganization appears to have occurred after the fragmentation of the *c.*100-hide *Pouelt* estate, and before the area's final division into a series of typically 5-hide manors. In this particular example, the stage at which the restructuring of settlement and field systems appears to have occurred was when the landscape was divided into blocks of around 20 to 30 hides, of which there are other possible examples across Somerset.

In the far south-east of Somerset, around Horsington, there are a series of strip parishes similar to those on the Polden Hills that were associated with a row of compact nucleated settlements each with its own common field system, laid out parallel with the river Cale. From north to south these parishes are North Cheriton, Horsington (which included the villages of South Cheriton and Horsington), Abbas Combe (which included the villages of Abbas Combe and Temple Combe), and Henstridge (which included the villages of Henstridge and Yenston). Each of these villages appears as a manor in Domesday (Yenston presumably being one of the two manors listed for Henstridge) (DB fos. 87, 91, 96^v, 97; DB *Som.* 1,25; 4,1; 14,1; 18,4; 25,56; 28,2; 36,14). Altogether, these villages may represent an estate of 57 hides that was fragmented into nine manors of 2, 3, 4, 5, 6, 8, 10 (with 8 that never paid tax), and 11 hides (which were two manors in 1066), which stretched from the floodplain of the Cale in the east to a watershed boundary in the west. The place name Horsington ('farmstead of the horse keepers or grooms': Mills 1990, 179) may reflect a manor created for one of the servants on this former federative estate. Little is known of the history of landownership within this early estate. The contents list of Glastonbury's *Liber Terrarum* contains three mid-tenth-century charters whereby the king granted land 'at Henstridge' to various thegns, the boundaries of which may correspond to the 5 hides at Abbas Combe. There is, however, no other record of the Abbey holding land in this area and as the text of one charter appears in the Shaftesbury cartulary, these charters may simply have been written or stored at Glastonbury and never involved any transfer of land to the Abbey (S570; S1712; S1736; Finberg 1964, Nos. 433, 460, and 467; Abrams 1996, 137–8). In 1066 these various manors were mostly in different hands: Ælfwold held two of the manors (both in Cheriton), while St Edward's church, Earl Harold, Earl Eadnoth, Earl Leofwine, and three thegns held the others.

Another area that demonstrates a degree of planning in its landscape is around Blagdon, which along with Ubley, Compton Martin, West and East Harptree forms a block of strip parishes that run from the watershed of Mendip to the south, down into the Chew and Yeo valleys in the north (what could be termed the 'greater Blagdon' estate). Each parish has a nucleated village, that in East Harptree having a ladder-like plan as seen in Shapwick, Edington, and Middlezoy. Ubley, Compton Martin, and East and West Harptree were clearly surrounded by common fields, although Blagdon, which in the nineteenth century at least had a more dispersed settlement pattern, had a field system that appears to have largely consisted of closes held in severalty. Several former furlongs are cut by the boundary between East and West Harptree, suggesting yet again that the laying out of the common fields pre-dated the final division of this landscape. We know little of the history of landownership in this area, although in 959 × 975 King Edgar is said to have granted an unspecified amount of land at Ubley to an unnamed thegn (S1771; Finberg 1964, No. 498). King Cynewulf's purported grant of an unspecified amount of land to an unnamed thegn at *Mertone* in 757 × 786 could relate to Compton Martin, but this charter is also lost (S1690; Finberg 1964, No. 635). In Domesday, Blagdon was assessed as 10 hides, while Ubley and Compton Martin were each 5 hides; East and West Harptree both contained two manors all of which were similarly assessed as 5 hides, and each valued at 40s. (Ubley and Compton Martin were valued at 100s. in 1066, and Blagdon £10.) In 1066 each of these manors was in different hands, while in 1086 they were divided between five lords: clearly, the subdivision of this estate occurred before 1066.

A further large, federative, estate that appears to have been broken up and then distributed to thegns was based at Portbury in north-west Somerset, which by 1066 had been broken down into Portbury (8 hides), Portishead (8 hides), Weston (manors of 7 and 3 hides), Walton (3½ hides), Clapton (5½ hides), and Easton (12 hides). These manors surround the Gordano Valley and their boundaries ran from the wetlands of the valley floor up to a long, sinuous watershed boundary on the adjacent hills to the east and the high cliffs of the coast to the west. In 1066 there were seven manors (there were two in Weston), held by six thegns (Ælfgar held Clapton and one of the Westons), amounting to 47 hides (DB fos. 88, 88ᵛ, 96, 97; DB Som. 5,22; 5,24–7; 5,33; 29,1). Only for Portbury do we have any pre-Conquest evidence, in the form of two charters (both now lost) whereby King Edward (899–925) and King Æthelred (979–1016) are said to have granted unspecified amounts of land to unnamed thegns (S1701; S1781; Finberg 1964, Nos. 426 and 522; Abrams 1996, 204). Of particular interest here is the difference in character of the historic landscape in these manors, ranging from planned villages and extensive common fields in Portishead and Weston (Rippon 1993, fig. 3.D.9), to far less nucleated settlement patterns and little evidence for former open fields around Clapton, Portbury, and Easton. Once again, it would appear that the recipients of the manors created out of 'greater Portbury' chose to structure their landscapes in rather different ways. In neither the 'greater Portbury' nor 'greater Horsington' estates is there any evidence for the regularity in the size of the 5-hide holdings seen on the Polden Hills and 'greater Blagdon', and while the morphology of the landscape around Horsington suggests some degree of planning, the irregular hidage of these manors may indicate that the break-up of these putative estates was a gradual process: perhaps the two charters referring to 'Portbury' do not relate to the Domesday manor of that name, but different parts of an estate of which Portbury was once its centre.

A final, smaller, example of an estate divided up in this way is perhaps Chinnock, to the west of Yeovil (Costen 1992a, 119, 126–7). In the will of Wynflaed of *c.*950 (S1539) this was probably still a single estate that by 1066 had been divided up into (East) Chinnock (7 hides), (Middle) Chinnock (3 hides), and West Chinnock (4 hides) (DB fo. 92ᵛ; DB Som. 19,44; 19,48–9). The boundary between East and Middle Chinnock clearly pre-dates the adjacent field systems, whereas the parish boundary between Middle and West Chinnock cuts across a series of furlong boundaries. The East Field of West Chinnock was also on the far side of Middle Chinnock, so that tenants in West Chinnock had to pass through Middle Chinnock to get there. As Costen (1992a, fig. 5.3) has observed, such planning suggests the role of an individual in a position of authority as no farming community would produce such an inconvenient layout for their field system.

DISCUSSION: THE SOCIAL CONTEXT FOR LANDSCAPE REORGANIZATION

During the medieval period, large parts of central and eastern Somerset were covered with champion countryside characterized by villages and common fields, in contrast to the west of the county which had a dispersed settlement pattern of small hamlets and isolated farmsteads surrounded by closes held in severalty. A wide range of evidence has shown that these broad local variations can be traced back into the medieval period with a growing list of villages having produced tenth-century pottery. Whilst unstratified material does not prove that these villages existed in their later form by this date—there may simply have been smaller 'pre-village' nuclei as have recently been identified in Whittlewood, on the Buckinghamshire/Northamptonshire border (Jones and Page 2006)—at Shapwick, at least, excavations have proved that the village plan dates back to this period. The aceramic nature of Somerset in the earlier medieval period means that we cannot be sure that there was not earlier occupation within these villages, though the small-scale work within Edington (radiocarbon dates from boundary ditches conforming to the village layout, and no earlier occupation) suggests a *terminus post quem* of the late ninth or tenth century. It has been shown that the south-western boundary of landscapes characterized by villages and common fields in Somerset was relatively sharp. Several of the possible explanations as to why villages and common fields did not occur in western Somerset can be dismissed. In places topography was clearly significant, for example in the south and west of the county where the edge of the champion countryside is marked by the Blackdown Hills and the Parrett estuary. In northern Somerset, in a region of relatively mixed landscape character, villages and common fields tend to occur on the flatter ground as opposed to the hillier districts. Topography was not, however, the sole determinant of cultural landscape character, as the flat lands around Taunton never saw the development of villages and common fields. That marked differences in settlement patterns and field systems were created on reclaimed coastal marshland, with its uniform physical characteristics, proves that local and regional variation in landscape character cannot be explained purely in terms of the natural environment. Some areas of south-east Somerset were also particularly extensively cleared of woodland, but most places that saw the creation of villages and common fields were no more or less wooded than areas that did not: once again there is not a clear correlation between this facet of the antecedent landscape and later landscape character. The variation in landscape character seen on reclaimed coastal wetlands with their uniform antecedent landscape once again shows that this was not the major factor behind local and regional variation in landscape character. It is, however, noteworthy that the boundary of the central zone appears to correspond very broadly to the south-western limit of landscape that was extensively Romanized by the fourth century AD, and this aspect of the antecedent landscape is addressed further in Chapter 4. Of the other possible factors that may have lain behind the variation in the character of Somerset's landscape, a correlation with the distribution of Domesday meadow and population can be dismissed, while another possible indicator of economic development—pre-Conquest towns—is similarly no stronger in areas that did have villages, compared to those that did not.

Attention has therefore focused upon the social context within which some landscapes were transformed. In the case of Shapwick the creation of a planned village and common fields appears to have occurred during the tenth century, when a dispersed settlement pattern of isolated farmsteads was swept away. Recent excavations within another of Glastonbury's villages—Meare—suggest that it also existed by the late tenth century. These replannings must have been carried out when the Abbey held those estates and there is some evidence that the Abbey may have actively encouraged the nucleation of settlement and laying out of common fields, as it was not only its central Somerset estates that experienced this change, but also its outlying properties in north Somerset (Hutton, Winscombe, Wrington, and Marksbury), western Somerset (West Monkton), and north Devon (Braunton). While there are also some similarities in the layout of villages such as Shapwick, Edington, and Middlezoy, these had a very different plan from Meare: there was not a single 'Glastonbury' way of restructuring a landscape. This suggests that in many cases the Abbey may not have been directly involved in the management of its estates, and that it was its subtenants and even the local communities that were more closely involved in determining how the countryside was physically structured on individual estates. This accords with Lewis *et al.*'s (1997, 174) conclusion that 'perhaps the type of lord most likely to have pursued order and efficiency might have been the numerous lesser aristocrats, thegns in the pre-Conquest period, knights and minor gentry in the succeeding centuries, whose small manors gave them the incentive to make the most profitable use of limited resources, and whose continued residence on the spot made them especially knowledgeable of the local terrain' (the latter comment an acknowledgement of the significance that variation in the natural environment could have in determining agricultural practice, and therefore landscape character).

Whereas on the estates of Glastonbury Abbey villages and common fields were the norm, the estates of a number of other major landowners in Somerset show a greater degree of variation in landscape character with the settlement patterns and field systems generally reflecting whatever the local norm was: there is nothing in the historic landscape to suggest that the king, bishops, or the major landholding thegns were particularly proactive in replanning their estates. It is also clear that in many if not all cases, the landscape was restructured sometime before the Domesday survey, as the manors described therein appear to have been the product of the fragmentation of larger estates which occurred sometime after the common fields were laid out (reflected in the way that their boundaries zigzag through the strips and furlongs). These pre-Domesday estates were in turn the product of the progressive disintegration of far larger folk territories, and where these can be reconstructed they also show very little correlation with those areas that went on to see the creation of villages and common fields. It therefore appears to have been in the context of the large estates of around 20 to 60 hides, derived from the breaking up of these folk territories, that many landscapes were replanned, which in turn were then subdivided further into blocks of typically 5-hide strip parishes/manors.

It would seem, therefore, that the reason why North Curry, Curry Mallet, Isle Abbots, and Ilton had classic 'champion' countryside, while Stoke St Mary, West Hatch, and Bickenhall, just 5 km to the west, had dispersed settlement and fields held in severalty is not because the topography or soils were different, the early medieval landscape was less wooded, or these areas had a greater amount of meadow, but because the communities living there, and their immediate overlords, decided not to adopt this communal approach towards managing their landscape. With the possible exception of Glastonbury Abbey, it does not appear that the major landowners in Somerset actively imposed the concept of villages and common fields, but that the idea of managing the countryside in this way spread through emulation at a lower level of society. At a local scale there were presumably local reasons why the idea did not continue right across the lowlands of southern Somerset as far as the Vale of Taunton, but at the larger, regional scale, it remains curious that having spread all the way down from the Midlands, and into southern Wales, it spread no further down the south-west peninsula, and it is to this issue that we must now turn.

4

Across the Watershed: The Development of Landscapes Characterized by Dispersed Settlement in the South-West

INTRODUCTION: THE DISTINCTIVE LANDSCAPES OF THE SOUTH-WEST PENINSULA

The Quantock and Blackdown Hills, rising up to the west of the river Parrett in the south and west of Somerset, form an important watershed within the landscape of southern Britain. Physically, they separate the south-west peninsula from the rest of central southern England, and today they mark the division between what are typically landscapes of villages and large arable fields to the east, and more dispersed settlement patterns associated with predominantly small pastoral fields to the west. This regional variation in landscape character was even more clearly evident in the eighteenth and nineteenth centuries, when our earliest cartographic sources show that central and eastern Somerset was characterized by nucleated villages and the last surviving fragments of what once had been extensive common fields, in contrast to the small hamlets, scattered farmsteads, and wholly enclosed field systems of western Somerset, Devon, and Cornwall. Documentary sources, archaeological survey and excavation, and studies of standing buildings suggest that this fundamental regional difference in the character of the countryside dates back to at least the later medieval period (see Chapter 2 and below), while a variety of evidence suggests that this border region was of great cultural significance long before the Norman Conquest. The Blackdowns–Quantock watershed marks the western limit of pre-mid-seventh-century Early Anglo-Saxon settlement, acculturation, and exchange networks at least as reflected in the distribution of burials and artefacts (Fig. 4.1; Arnold 1988; Eagles 1994; O'Brien 1999, 165–74; Rahtz *et al.* 2000, 359–64). In contrast, the fifth- to seventh-century cemeteries at Wembdon Hill, Cannington, and Stoneage Barton in the Quantocks belong firmly to the tradition of post-Roman cemeteries in south-west Britain seen, for example, at Kenn in south Devon (Webster and Croft 1990, 222; Rahtz *et al.* 2000; Weddell 2000; Webster and Brunning 2004). The Blackdown and

Quantock Hills also appear to have divided the Romano-British *civitas* and earlier tribal groupings of the Dumnonii in the west from the Durotriges in the east as reflected, for example, in the distributions of pottery, coins, heavily defended hillforts, and extent of Romanization (Fig. 4.1; Jones and Mattingly 1990; Rippon 2006b).

So why did the trend towards managing the landscape through nucleated villages and large common fields, which transformed eastern and central Somerset around the tenth century, not spread across the Blackdown and Quantock Hills into the South-West? Was this area a backwater that saw little agrarian innovation at this time? Recent archaeological and palaeoenvironmental work has certainly shown that the South-West, like the rest of southern Britain, was extensively settled and cultivated in the late prehistoric, Romano-British, and early medieval periods (Fox 2006; Rippon 2006b; Rippon *et al.* 2006a), so the natural environment clearly was suited to such arable-intensive forms of agriculture. Was it simply that there was a long tradition of societies in the South-West 'doing things differently', and that this 'antecedent landscape' they had created continued to influence the character of the later medieval countryside? Or were there active forces at work during the early medieval period which meant that the approach of structuring the landscape around villages and common fields was not adopted in this region?

After a brief introduction to the South-West's distinctive physical characteristics, and a consideration of how the history of archaeological and historical research in the region affects what we can say about the first millennium AD, the late prehistoric and Roman-British landscape is described in some detail as it is possible that this 'antecedent landscape' came to influence the character of the medieval countryside. It will be shown that there is, in fact, a clear discontinuity between the prehistoric and the historic landscapes in all areas except the far west of Cornwall, which archaeologically and historically can be dated to sometime between the seventh/eighth and tenth/eleventh centuries. Palaeoenvironmental research suggests that it was the start of this period that saw a significant change in land-use and this provides the most obvious context for the physical discontinuity in settlement patterns and field systems. Far from providing an example of what the central zones' landscape would have looked like if the 'village moment' had not occurred, the South-West was itself transformed in the early medieval period.

UPLANDS AND LOWLANDS: THE PHYSICAL TOPOGRAPHY ON THE SOUTH-WEST PENINSULA

The south-west peninsula extends for some 220 km beyond the Blackdown and Quantock Hills (Fig. 4.1). It is easy to assume that this was a somewhat remote region, battered by Atlantic storms, and it is commonly (and erroneously)

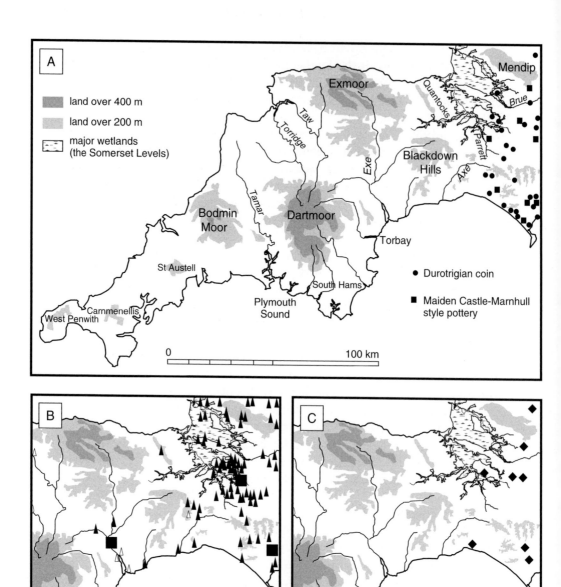

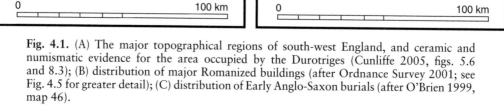

Fig. 4.1. (A) The major topographical regions of south-west England, and ceramic and numismatic evidence for the area occupied by the Durotriges (Cunliffe 2005, figs. 5.6 and 8.3); (B) distribution of major Romanized buildings (after Ordnance Survey 2001; see Fig. 4.5 for greater detail); (C) distribution of Early Anglo-Saxon burials (after O'Brien 1999, map 46).

included within the 'upland zone' of Britain (e.g. Fox 1952, map B; Rackham 1986a, fig. 1.3). The landscape of the South-West does indeed include a series of uplands: Exmoor in the north, the granite massif of Dartmoor in central Devon, and the smaller granite outcrops of Bodmin Moor, St Austell, Carnmenellis, and Penwith in Cornwall. The highest of these uplands—Exmoor, Dartmoor, and Bodmin Moor—certainly are physically and environmentally challenging areas, marginal in terms of settled agriculture, and although even the very highest uplands were cleared of woodland by the Early Bronze Age they were never permanently settled or enclosed (Fleming 1988, 94–100; Johnson and Rose 1994; Caseldine 1999b, 579; Riley and Wilson-North 2001). These unenclosed moors were covered in rough grassland, heather, and bracken, with woodland restricted to the steeper valley sides. The slightly lower slopes were enclosed during the Middle Bronze Age—evidenced by the famous relict field systems that on Dartmoor are known as reaves—although palaeoenvironmental evidence, the lack of lyncheting, and large amounts of clitter (loose stone boulders) in many of these fields suggest that the predominant land-use was grassland with very limited cereal cultivation (Fox 1954, 50; Smith *et al.* 1981, 240–5; Caseldine and Hatton 1994).

The Dartmoor reaves, and probably their equivalents on the South-West's other uplands, appear to have been abandoned in the Late Bronze Age (*c.*1400 to 1200 BC). There has been much debate over whether the lack of evidence for later settlement in these upland fringes is real, or due to the poor visibility of settlements at this time, although the palaeoenvironmental record does suggest that while there was a decline in the intensity of human activity, some grazing of livestock must have continued to prevent extensive woodland regeneration (Smith *et al.* 1981, 262–5; Balaam *et al.* 1982, 212; Caseldine and Hatton 1994, 41; Straker and Crabtree 1995, 43–51; Gearey and Charman 1996, 116–18; Gearey *et al.* 2000b, 504). The 'experiment' of intensive upland settlement had not proved worthwhile, but although these areas now lay beyond the settled agricultural landscape they continued to provide a rich reserve of summer grazing along with minerals such as tin.

All this would appear to confirm the 'upland' stereotype of south-west England but in fact this is far from the case. While visually dominating the region, the unoccupied uplands actually only cover *c.*10 per cent of its total landmass. The surrounding areas are typically gently rolling hills, the majority of which are classified as having soils with only 'moderate limitation' for modern agriculture (due to the climatic conditions, notably high rainfall), while areas such as the Exe Valley, Torbay, and the South Hams have fertile soils that provide excellent arable land (Caseldine 1999a). Palaeoenvironmental evidence shows that these lowlands were also largely cleared of woodland by the Early Bronze Age apart from small patches of alder carr in some of the wetter valley bottoms, and some oak and hazel woodland which was presumably restricted to the steeper hillsides (Gearey *et al.* 1997; Caseldine *et al.* 2000;

Fyfe *et al.* 2003a; 2003b; 2004). This was a densely settled landscape in later prehistory, and far from a marginal upland zone.

LANDSCAPES OF CONTINUITY: THE LATE PREHISTORIC, ROMANO-BRITISH, AND EARLY MEDIEVAL PERIODS

If we take a 'Midland-centric' view of the later first millennium AD, then the concept of villages and common fields spread from the East Midlands reaching Somerset and Dorset around the tenth century, but was then not adopted to the west of the Blackdown and Quantock Hills. This raises the possibility that the landscape of Devon and Cornwall simply continued its slow evolution and so, if the countryside of today has essentially prehistoric origins, it may bear some resemblance to what the central zone would have looked like before the creation of villages and common fields. Our story begins, therefore, with this prehistoric landscape.

The settlement pattern

Following a relatively uniform settlement pattern during the Middle Bronze Age, associated with a highly visible burial rite and extensive planned field systems on both the uplands and the lowlands (Fleming 1988; FitzPatrick *et al.* 1999; Herring forthcoming), the Iron Age saw the emergence of a very different landscape, most notably in its highly stratified settlement pattern. Hillforts and coastal promontory forts (locally known as 'cliff castles') are found throughout the South-West, although compared to their neighbours in Wessex they are relatively small, lightly defended, had comparatively small roundhouses, and a complete absence of grain storage pits. The hillforts of the Blackdown and Quantock Hills firmly belong to the South-West tradition, in being relatively small, univallate enclosures in sharp contrast to the massive multivallate 'developed hillforts' in Wessex, of which the westernmost examples include Brent Knoll, Cadbury Congresbury, Cannington, South Cadbury, and Ham Hill (Cunliffe 1982, fig. 59; Johnson and Rose 1982, 155; Todd 1987, 157–63; Cunliffe 1991, 260; Herring 1994; Gerrard 1997, 65–8; Riley and Wilson-North 2001, 56–64; Riley 2006, 52–60). The function of these South-West hillforts is likely to have varied in time and space, although where excavation has occurred evidence for domestic occupation has usually been found (Liddell 1930; 1931; 1932; 1935; Miles 1975; Gallant and Silvester 1985; 49; Todd 1992; Quinnell 1994, 80). Where dating evidence is forthcoming there appears to have been a long development starting in the Early Iron Age, although late second-millennium radiocarbon dates from a large hilltop enclosure at Liskeard in Cornwall may parallel the trend towards defended hilltop settlement seen further east in Late Bronze Age Wessex (Todd 1987, 153, 157; Jones 1998–9b; Gent and Quinnell 1999a; Pearce 1999, 72).

Lower down the Iron Age settlement hierarchy there are a range of enclosures that can be distinguished from hillforts by their smaller size, hillslope (not hilltop) location, and the modest scale of their enclosing banks and ditches. The most substantial of these sites—termed 'multiple enclosures'—have several circuits of widely spaced banks and ditches, defining an internal area of *c*.0.2 to 1.6 ha, which were mostly abandoned, along with the hillforts, by the first century AD.[1] The majority of identified Middle Iron Age to Romano-British settlements, however, were enclosed by a simple univallate, non-defensive ditch and/or bank enclosing an internal area of *c*.0.1 to 1.0 ha.[2] Excavated examples, such as Trethurgy in Cornwall (Figs. 4.2–3), show that collectively these form a distinctive pattern of enclosed settlements, probably containing several family groups, that as a type characterized the South-West's landscape through to the fifth and maybe the sixth centuries AD. In areas where conditions of preservation are good the density of enclosures can be as high as two or three per square kilometre, although excavated examples suggest that not all sites were occupied throughout this period. There was also another, poorly understood, tier in the settlement hierarchy, with a number of open settlements recently being recognized, such as that at Higher Besore, in Cornwall, which was contemporary with the occupation of a nearby round (Gossip 2005a; 2005b; 2006). The extent of such sites is unclear, although they are likely to have been more common than is currently appreciated, as those such as Long Range and Langland Lane in East Devon, and Littlehempston in the South Hams, were only discovered during road and pipeline construction and were not identifiable on air photographs (Fitzpatrick *et al.* 1999, 7, 130–59; Reed and Turton 2005). The relative scarcity of datable artefacts on excavated rural settlements of this period would have made them difficult to locate through fieldwalking (e.g. Balkwill 1976; Jarvis 1976; Simpson *et al.* 1989; Caseldine *et al.* 2000, 65; Horner 1993; Todd 1998; Uglow 2000, 238).

Agricultural expansion during the Middle to Late Iron Age

In recent years an increasing number of palaeoenvironmental sequences are transforming our understanding of the Iron Age, Roman, and medieval landscapes of Cornwall, Devon, and western Somerset, particularly because the newer examples come from small lowland mires that lay within areas that

---

[1] For further discussion see Fox 1952; Johnston and Rose 1982, 165–71; Quinnell 1986, 114–15; Cunliffe 1991, 252; Riley and Wilson-North 2001, 65–75; Riley 2006, 60–72.

[2] A large number of sites have been investigated, and key reports include Phillips 1966; Greene and Greene 1970; Pollard 1974; Jarvis 1976; Johnson and Rose 1982; Appleton-Fox 1992, 69–123; Griffith 1994; Carlyon 1998–9; Johnson *et al.* 1998–9; Gent 1997; Fitzpatrick *et al.* 1999; Uglow 2000; Riley and Wilson-North 2001, 65–75; Quinnell 2004; Passmore 2005; Wilkes 2004; 2006.

Fig. 4.2. Aerial view, from the east, of the excavations at Trethurgy Round, St Austell, in Cornwall, in September 1973 (© Henrietta Quinnell).

were settled and farmed during these periods, in contrast to 'traditional' pollen sequences taken from upland peat bogs that lay beyond the limits of past human settlement (Fig. 4.4).

For the Iron Age the general picture is one of a growing intensity with which the landscape was exploited agriculturally. At Broadclyst Moor, in the lowlands of central Devon, there was a marked phase of woodland clearance and an associated rise in pasture and meadow in the tenth to ninth centuries BC, followed by the appearance of wheat, oats, and rye around the fifth to sixth centuries several centuries later (Hawkins 2005b). At nearby Mosshayne, along with Bow and Newland Hill (North Tawton) in central Devon, the landscape was already extensively cleared of woodland by the mid first millennium BC, apart from small patches of alder carr on the wetter low-lying areas, and some oak and hazel woodland presumably restricted to the steeper hillsides (ibid.; Caseldine *et al.* 2000, 64; Passmore 2005, 38–40). The Blackdown Hills were, not surprisingly, more wooded, although there had already been some clearance at Bywood by the fourth century BC, and limited cultivation in a

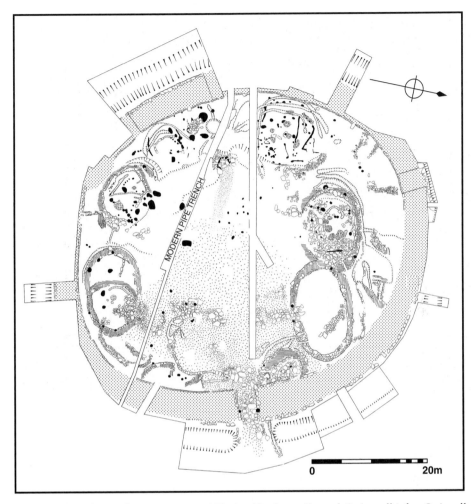

Fig. 4.3. Plan of Period 5 (*c.* AD 150–*c.*550+) at Trethurgy Round, St Austell (after Quinnell 2004, fig. 5; © Henrietta Quinnell).

largely open, pastoral, landscape at Greenway by the later first millennium BC (Hawkins 2005a). Elsewhere the Middle Iron Age (around the fifth to third centuries BC) may have seen some expansion of agriculture: at Hares Down near Rackenford in mid Devon, alder woodland was cleared from the valley bottom and replaced with grassland (Fyfe *et al.* 2004), while in the southern fringes of Exmoor there is evidence for woodland clearance around Codsend Moor and Molland Common (Francis and Slater 1992, 21; Fyfe *et al.* 2003b). On Bodmin Moor, there was a major clearance phase at Rough Tor (Gearey *et al.* 1997, 197–8). What late prehistoric woodland remained in the South-West was presumably managed with increasing intensity.

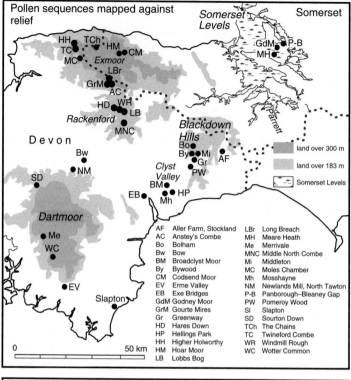

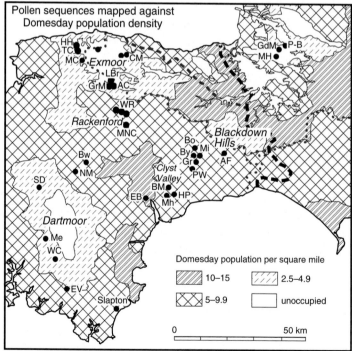

Fig. 4.4. Major palaeoenvironmental sequences from south-west England mapped against relief (top) and Domesday population density (bottom; after Darby 1967, fig. 84). In recent years the earlier bias towards work on the high uplands has started to be redressed through studies around Rackenford (Fyfe *et al.* 2004; Rippon *et al.* 2006a), the Blackdown Hills (Hawkins 2005a), and the Clyst Valley (Hawkins 2005b).

The impact of Conquest and the extent of Romanization

During the mid first century AD south-west Britain was drawn into the Roman world. The Second Legion established its base at *Isca Dumnoniorum* (modern Exeter) around AD 55, and a number of small forts were located across the region, but most notably in and around the lowlands of central and eastern Devon (Bidwell 1979; 1980; Fitzpatrick *et al.* 1999, 223–429; Maxfield 1999). This military occupation ceased around AD 80 and the legionary fortress at Exeter went on to become the *civitas* capital of the Dumnonii,[3] equipped with the normal range of civic amenities including a basilica-forum and public baths (Bidwell 1980; Henderson 1988; Holbrook and Bidwell 1991, 7). The South-West was a region rich in natural resources, most notably tin, and had a long history of trading contact with the Mediterranean world.[4] As such, it might be expected that this would have become a heavily Romanized area but this was far from the case, with features characteristic of the landscape of Roman Britain further east, such as small towns and Romano-Celtic temples, virtually absent from the South-West (Fig. 4.5). The *c.*12-ha roadside settlement at Woodbury, near Axminster, on the Roman road between Dorchester and Exeter, may have been a small town with a *mansio* but is the most westerly example known (Weddell *et al.* 1993). While a number of small villas are known in the far east of Devon, pottery styles suggest that they mostly fell within the economic sphere of the Durotriges (Miles 1977, 127–38, 147; and see Silvester 1981; Holbrook 1987; Todd 1987, 221; Brown and Holbrook 1989; Todd 2005). Within Dumnonia, several villas and highly Romanized farmsteads developed close to Exeter (Jarvis and Maxfield 1975; Griffith 1988a; Uglow 2000), although even here the native tradition of roundhouses continued into the third century (e.g. Pomeroy Wood near Honiton: Fitzpatrick *et al.* 1999, 243–63). Even the distribution of distinctively Roman burials, which are so common to the east of the Blackdown and Quantock Hills, is virtually absent from the South-West (apart from Exeter: Philpot 1991).

Beyond the hinterland of Exeter, the extent of Romanization is extremely limited, with the only other potential villa at Magor, near Camborne, in the far west of Cornwall (O'Neil 1933; Todd 1987, 222). This is a curious site that may in fact have been the residence of an official, perhaps from the

---

[3] The orthodox view is that the whole of modern Cornwall and Devon were controlled by the *ordo* of *Isca Dumnonium* though Quinnell (2004, 217) suggests that the area west of Bodmin Moor may have had a different arrangement; Mattingly (2007, 407) suggests it was *ager publicus* (public land).

[4] The evidence is summarized in Rippon 2006b, with more detailed discussion in Threipland 1956; Brown and Hugo 1983; Penhallurick 1986, 123–47; Todd 1987, 185–8; Cunliffe 1988; Beagrie 1989; Thomas 1990; Ratcliffe 1995; Griffith and Weddell 1996; Riley and Wilson-North 2001, 80–1; Gerrard 2000, 21–3; Herring 2000, 117–21; Bayley 2001; Holbrook 2001; Thorndycraft *et al.* 2002; 2004; S. Turner 2004.

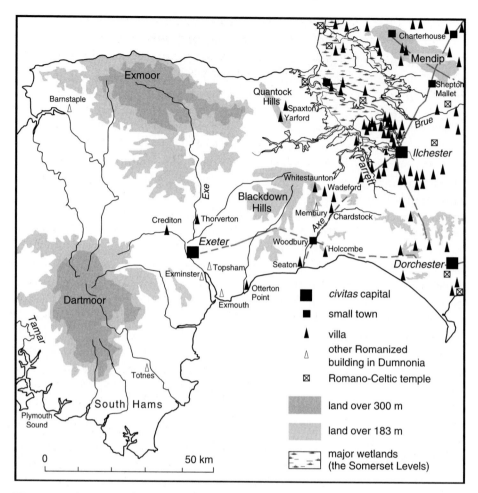

Fig. 4.5. Indications of Romanization in the countryside of south-west Britain (after Ordnance Survey 2001).

procurator's office overseeing tin production, rather than a normal agriculture-based villa. Large numbers of first- to second-century Romano-British artefacts have also been recovered from enclosures at St Mawgan-in-Pydar (Threipland 1956) and Carvossa (Carlyon 1987) that presumably represent communities or an elite who had a greater engagement with the rest of Roman Britain, and perhaps significantly the former site also shows evidence for tin working. Other signs of Romanization are few and far between, with fragments of Roman tile suggesting the presence of substantial buildings at a number of estuarine locations, and a kiln producing roof and hypocaust tile for a building of unknown character at Hatherleigh in west Devon (Griffith and Quinnell 1999; Wheeler and Laing-Trengrove 2006). Overall, however, it is the lack of artefacts that is so striking about first- to fourth-century AD sites in the South-West, a period when material culture is so abundant on even low-status settlements just across the Blackdown and Quantock Hills: while small amounts of imported Roman pottery and coins are found on most rural farmsteads, wheel-thrown, mass-produced pottery does not penetrate in significant amounts further west than Exeter (Fulford 1996, fig. 14; Holbrook 2001). Clearly, and in sharp contrast to neighbouring Somerset, communities living in the South-West during the Roman period had little desire to adopt the trappings of Roman life.

Agricultural intensification during the Roman period

This lack of Romanization should not, however, be taken to imply a low population or low intensity with which the landscape was exploited. The clearance of woodland and its replacement with pasture, representing a marked intensification of land-use seen during the Middle Iron Age, appears to have continued into the Late Iron Age and Romano-British periods. Near Exeter, at the very heart of the central lowlands of Devon, pollen from a mid-first-century AD well at the Pomeroy Wood shows an open pastoral landscape with very little woodland (Fitzpatrick *et al.* 1999, 342). The same is seen at Mosshayne in nearby Broadclyst, where a peat deposit within a palaeochannel reveals a very open pastoral landscape with the first appearance of cereal cultivation around the first to second centuries AD (Hawkins 2005b). Away from the lowlands there is also palaeoenvironmental evidence for continued agricultural expansion into the upland fringes. At Bywood, on the Blackdown Hills, cereal cultivation appears in the pollen record for the first time around the Late Iron Age to early Roman period, in what was largely a pastoral landscape where woodland was probably restricted to the steeper slopes (Hawkins 2005a). This woodland would have been an important resource as there was a nearby iron-smelting industry throughout the Roman and early medieval periods (Griffith and Weddell 1996; Wieken 2004).

At Hares Down, in mid Devon, there was a further decline in alder in the valley bottom during the Late Iron Age and a general episode of woodland clearance during the early Roman period, while on the fringes of Exmoor, at Moles Chamber, there was a dramatic woodland clearance at the same time (Fyfe 2000, 176–210; Fyfe *et al.* 2004). On Dartmoor the palaeoenvironmental record for this period is poor, but cultivation terraces on Wotter Common date to the Middle to Late Iron Age, when there was also some increase in the intensity of land-use at Tor Royal, and a phase of woodland clearance at Sourton Down (Smith *et al.* 1981, 228, 271; Gearey *et al.* 1997, 201; Straker 1997, 107). A similar replacement of woodland with pasture at Merrivale, on Dartmoor, is poorly dated, but may have occurred during the Roman period (Gearey *et al.* 1997, fig. 4). On Bodmin Moor there was further woodland clearance and an increase in herb-rich meadows during the Roman period at Rough Tor and Tresellern Marsh (Gearey *et al.* 2000b).

Though great care has to be taken with converting radiocarbon dates to calendar years, there appears to have been an increasing intensity of landscape exploitation in the later Romano-British period. On Exmoor there was a marked episode of woodland clearance and evidence for cultivation at Codsend Moor and Hoar Moor, while at Lobbs Bog to the south there was a decline in alder in the valley bottom (Francis and Slater 1990, 12–14; 1992, 23; and see Straker and Crabtree 1995, 47; Fyfe *et al.* 2004). In the lowlands of eastern Devon there was a marked phase of woodland clearance in the valley at Aller Farm in Stockland and an increase in the indicators of pastoralism around the third century AD (Hatton and Caseldine 1991, 112). This possible later Roman intensification in land-use in the South-West may be paralleled to the east, in modern Somerset and Dorset, where the third to fourth centuries saw considerable agricultural wealth and innovation as reflected in wetland reclamation, investment in villas, and urban prosperity (Pollard 1974; Rippon 2000c, 117–23; Scott 2000; Leach 2001).

The Romano-British fieldscape

The impression gained from palaeoenvironmental evidence in the South-West during the Iron Age and Roman periods is of an open, pastoral landscape with small areas of arable cultivation, and this is supported by the scarcity of evidence for field systems. This is in sharp contrast to the Middle Bronze Age when planned boundaries were laid out across many of the South-West's upland fringes (Fleming 1988; Johnson and Rose 1994; Riley and Wilson-North 2001), and similar, although less extensive (or well-preserved?) 'coaxial' field systems are also now being recognized in lowland areas across both Cornwall and Devon, although these appear to have been abandoned before the Iron Age (FitzPatrick *et al.* 1999; Herring forthcoming). In the far west of Cornwall they were replaced during the Iron Age by dense grids of smaller brick-shaped fields that saw the development of massive lynchets, suggestive of long periods of cultivation (Herring 1993; 1994; forthcoming). Elsewhere in the South-West, while some Iron Age and Romano-British settlement enclosures are associated with very localized field systems,[5] most are not.[6]

So is this lack of evidence for Iron Age and Romano-British field systems proof that they never existed? It is possible that although substantial enclosure ditches show up as cropmarks, lesser field boundary ditches do not, but in

---

[5] Published examples include Jarvis and Maxfield 1975; Jarvis 1976; Johnson *et al.* 1998–9; Fitzpatrick *et al.* 1999; Passmore 2005.

[6] For example Silvester and Balkwill 1977; Silvester 1978a; 1978b; Silvester 1980; Griffith 1984; Jones 1998–9a; Reed and Manning 2000; Simpson *et al.* 1989; CAT 2000; Weddell 2000; Wilkes 2004; Riley and Wilson-North 2001, 65–75; Riley 2006, 60–72.

an increasing number of cases extensive excavations and watching briefs have confirmed that the absence of Romano-British ditched field systems is real. One example is the Romano-British and early medieval ditched settlement enclosures at Hayes Farm near Exeter that lacked contemporary field systems even though a set of Middle Bronze Age coaxial boundary ditches did survive (CAT 2000). At several other sites near Exeter a similar picture is emerging. At Clyst Honiton, St Luke's College at Monkerton, and the former Royal Naval Stores Depot off Topsham Road, several Middle Bronze Age to Early Iron Age field systems have been recorded, while at Digby Clyst Heath School several boundary ditches have been excavated in association with an open settlement of Middle to Late Iron Age date, yet all these areas were devoid of Romano-British field systems, or undated features that could date to this period (Horner 2006; Peter Weddell pers. comm.). Watching briefs along linear developments such as the A30 Exeter to Honiton road, and the Kenn to Ashcombe pipeline, similarly failed to reveal Romano-British field systems, despite locating a variety of other archaeological sites (Fitzpatrick *et al.* 1999; Weddell 2000). The only other plausible explanation for the scarcity of Romano-British field systems is that rather than being ditched they consisted of banks or lynchets, such as those surviving on the limestone hills south of Newton Abbot (Phillips 1966, 12–16; Gallant *et al.* 1985; Quinn 1995) and at Beer Head (Griffith 1988b, 23), although on the softer geologies of lowland Devon and Cornwall this seems unlikely. Overall, the extremely limited evidence for Romano-British field systems in the South-West, in such stark contrast to the rest of southern Britain (e.g. East Anglia: see Chapter 5), remains striking and fits well with the palaeoenvironmental evidence for a predominantly open, pastoral landscape with just small-scale arable cultivation in the immediate vicinity of settlements. There was certainly nothing like the near continuous fieldscape that was created across the lowlands of the South-West in the medieval period (Fig. 4.6; see below).

THE FIFTH AND SIXTH CENTURIES AD: CONTINUITY IN THE RURAL LANDSCAPE AND RESOURCE EXPLOITATION

The lack of surviving artefacts and other material culture makes the early medieval landscape in the South-West extremely difficult to understand. The increasing use of radiocarbon dating, palaeoenvironmental analysis, and the distribution of Mediterranean imports, however, provide three indications of continuity between the Roman and earliest medieval periods (up until around the sixth century): first, that the tradition of enclosed settlement continues; second, that there was no significant change in the patterns of land-use in the lowlands and upland fringe; and third, that there was continuing external

Fig. 4.6. The South Hams, in south Devon, between the mineral-rich Dartmoor (foreground), and natural harbour of Plymouth Sound (in the far distance). Looking south-west from Hawks Tor, in Shaugh Prior parish, in south-west Dartmoor. Throughout the region's history (and prehistory) a wide range of its natural resources have been traded further afield, and the numerous natural harbours such as Plymouth Sound have played host to 'ports of trade' such as the Iron Age and Romano-British site at Mount Batten (Cunliffe 1988).

contact and exchange at coastal sites, involving traders from the Mediterranean and presumably tin. Continuity in burial practice also suggests that the South-West was 'a functioning, if distinctive, part of the Christian world of late antiquity' (Turner 2006b, 28; and see Weddell 2000; Petts 2004).

Relatively little is known about the landscape of south-west Britain immediately after the fourth century, although discontinuity here is less likely than elsewhere in Roman Britain as the collapse of the market-based economy will have had less impact in areas such as this that were not particularly Romanized. Pottery and radiocarbon dating certainly show that a number of enclosed rural settlements continued to be occupied into the fifth and even the sixth centuries (Guthrie 1969; Saunders 1972; Simpson *et al.* 1989; Appleton-Fox 1992; Quinnell 2004; S. Turner 2004, 29; 2006d, 72–5).[7] A number of hilltop sites were also reoccupied, although not on the same scale as the hillforts at South Cadbury and Cadbury Congresbury in Somerset (Pollard 1966; Grant 1995; Gent and Quinnell 1999a, 19, 24–6; 1999b, 82).

In past discussions of the South-West's landscape during the first millennium AD one potentially valuable source of information—palaeoenvironmental sequences—has seen relatively little attention (e.g. Dark 2000). Recent work has, however, led to a dramatic increase in the amount of data which strongly suggests broad continuity in land-use across large areas, with the continuous cultivation of cereals, albeit on a small scale, at Aller Farm in east Devon, Bow and Rackenford in mid Devon, Bywood and Greenway on the Blackdown Hills, Mosshayne near Exeter, and even on the southern fringes of Exmoor (Hatton and Caseldine 1991; Caseldine *et al.* 2000; Fyfe *et al.* 2004; Hawkins 2005a; Hawkins 2005b; Fyfe *et al.* 2003b). Only on the higher moors is there some evidence for a decrease in the intensity of human activity. On Exmoor there was a decline in arable and grassland, and increase in heather and possibly woodland, at Hoar Moor, the Chains, and possibly Codsend Moor (Moore *et al.* 1984; Francis and Slater 1990, 14). On Dartmoor there are hints at Merrivale and Tor Royal of a slight decrease in the intensity of human activity (Gearey *et al.* 1997, fig. 5), although Wotter Common and Blacka Brook, in contrast, appear to show continuity in land-use (Gearey *et al.* 2000b; Smith *et al.* 1981, 246). On Bodmin Moor the picture is similarly varied: there is continuity in land-use at Rough Tor North, but possibly a slight woodland regeneration at Tresellern Marsh and Rough Tor South (Gearey *et al.* 1997; 2000b, 501). These uplands, however, lay beyond the main areas of settlement, and as early medieval place names suggest they were used for transhumant grazing, a decrease in the intensity of their exploitation need not suggest a widespread dislocation in rural life (Padel 1985, 127–9; Herring 1996). The

---

[7] The growing importance of radiocarbon dating sites of this period is also illustrated by the aceramic 5th- to 6th-century coastal sites at Wembury Bay near Plymouth (Reed 2005).

overriding theme in the agrarian landscape between the late Roman period and the sixth century is, therefore, one of continuity.

It is during the late Roman and early medieval periods that we get the first evidence for ownership and control of land and resources with inscribed memorial stones occurring across Cornwall, west Devon, and Exmoor (Pearce 1978, 24; Okasha 1993; Thomas 1994). Perhaps the clearest reflection of a stratified society, however, is the distribution of late fifth- and sixth-century pottery imported from the Mediterranean from sites such as Tintagel, St Michael's Mount, Bantham, and Mothecombe, with Plymouth Sound another potential 'port of trade' (Fig. 4.6; Thomas 1981; 1993; Nowakowski and Thomas 1992; Herring 2000; Horner 2001; Fox 1995; Barrowman *et al.* 2007). The importation of this pottery suggests that communities in the South-West had something of value to exchange, and there are documentary references to English traders taking (presumably Cornish) tin to the continent from the seventh century (Penhallurick 1986, 240). A number of finds in Cornwall prove that tin was being worked in the early medieval period (Penhallurick 1986, fig. 121; Biek 1994; Ratcliffe 1995; Gerrard 2000, 23–4). Radiocarbon dates from both Exmoor and the Blackdown Hills have shown that iron production also continued into the post-Roman period, and a site at Carhampton in West Somerset has produced fifth- to sixth-century pottery imported from the Mediterranean (Griffith and Weddell 1996, 33; Riley and Wilson-North 2001, 112; Webster and Croft 1994, 177). Overall, therefore, it seems that the dominant theme in landscape exploitation during the fourth to the sixth centuries in the South-West was one of continuity: there were, no doubt, some changes, as landscape and society are never completely stable, but there do not appear to have been any major dislocations at this time. But what is the relationship between this fifth- and sixth-century landscape and the countryside of today?

BRIDGING AN ARCHAEOLOGICAL AND DOCUMENTARY GAP: THE ORIGINS OF THE HISTORIC LANDSCAPE

The survival of the late prehistoric to Romano-British/earliest medieval landscape?

In West Penwith, at the far western end of Cornwall, the present pattern of small, irregular, strongly lyncheted, stone-walled fields appears to perpetuate those of the late prehistoric and Romano-British periods, and at a number of locations this early origin for the present fieldscape was confirmed through survey and excavation (Fig. 4.7; Johnson and Rose 1982, 174; Quinnell 1986, 119–20; Herring 1993; 1994; Smith 1996). Both Romano-British courtyard houses and medieval farms are integrated into this field boundary pattern, with the former appearing to fill in gaps in the distribution of the latter,

extent of prehistoric fields surviving in use today ('Farmland Prehistoric' type in the Cornwall Historic Landscape Characterisation: Herring 1999)

Fig. 4.7. Rosemergy hamlet, in Morvah parish, and the Carn Galver mine, at West Penwith in Cornwall. Strongly lyncheted fields such as these appear to have been in use since the late prehistoric period (ground-level photo: the author).

suggesting that if we could excavate beneath one of these medieval farmsteads we might well find a Romano-British settlement (Rose and Preston-Jones 1995, 57–9): like the field systems with which they are so closely integrated, the present pattern of hamlets and farmsteads also appear to represent elements of the prehistoric countryside that have seen continuous occupation in what appears to have been a remarkably conservative landscape.

It has been claimed that there are potentially other examples of prehistoric field systems still surviving in use although the evidence is at present weak. In the South Hams, several areas of historic landscape have a seemingly planned, coaxial, layout, and at Decklers Cliffs in East Portlemouth, these appear to mark the continuation of a small relict field system that could be associated with two groups of roundhouses (although none of these features has been excavated: Waterhouse 2000, 9–10). Near Honiton, Weddell (1991, 31) suggests that a very fragmentary area of coaxially arranged historic landscape is on a different orientation from, and so pre-dates, a Roman road and the medieval borough, and a similar, highly speculative and fragmentary coaxial landscape around Axminster also requires testing through fieldwork in order to establish its date (Weddell *et al.* 1993, 72–3). At Sourton Down, to the north-west of Dartmoor, the historic landscape could contain fragments of a coaxial layout that may pre-date a Roman road, but a programme of excavations could not establish its date (Weddell and Reed 1997, 128–9). In and around Dartmoor several other areas of the historic landscape have a coaxial appearance (Fleming 1988, figs. 14, 15, 31, and 69) although nowhere can it be proved that this is due to the continuous use of prehistoric field systems. At Bittaford, for example, the coaxial layout of medieval fields and lanes may result from the continued use of a Middle Bronze Age reave system, or more probably derive their regularity from having been laid out between a series of medieval droveways extending from the South Hams up onto the moor (Fig. 4.8; Fox 1996; Lambourne 2004). Elsewhere, such examples of the historic landscape perpetuating the line of reaves are restricted to areas of later recolonization and the reuse of derelict boundaries.

The origins of today's historic landscape: the dispersed settlement pattern

Apart from West Penwith, there is little evidence for continuity between the Romano-British landscape and the countryside of today, and in order to examine the fate of the former, and understand the origins of the latter, we need to fast forward in time to see how far back the present pattern of settlements and fields can be traced. In the nineteenth century, when the historic landscape was first comprehensively mapped, the settlement pattern of the South-West was significantly more dispersed than in England's central zone, typically consisting of a mixture of small hamlets and isolated farmsteads (e.g. Combe, in Templeton, mid Devon: Fig. 4.9). Where there were larger

Fig. 4.8. Bittaford, in the South Hams, south of Dartmoor. The regularity in this landscape may result from an underlying extension of the Middle Bronze Age reave system into the lowlands surrounding Dartmoor, though it may be that the historic landscape is structured around a series of roughly parallel medieval droveways that allowed livestock to be driven from the South Hams up onto the open pastures of the moor.

settlements that might be compared to Midland villages, these were mostly failed small towns (e.g. South Zeal: Griffith 1988b, 83). Documentary and place-name research can trace the origins of many individual settlements in Devon back as far as the twelfth to thirteenth centuries, when it appears that the landscape was dominated by small clusters of farmsteads, with many of what are now isolated farms being small hamlets in the High Middle Ages (Hoskins 1952; Beresford 1964; Bonney 1971; Fox 1983; 1989b). The manors recorded in Domesday can be readily identified within the modern landscape, as can many of the places and landmarks recorded in a series of tenth- and eleventh-century charters (Finberg 1954; Hooke 1994; 1999). In Cornwall, Padel (1985; 1999) suggests that the common Cornish place-name elements *tre*, *bod*, and *ker* were coined sometime after the fifth century, certainly by the seventh century, and probably not after *c*.1100, although it is impossible to say when most of the English place names in Devon were created.

Tracing the origins of this settlement pattern back any further has, however, proved difficult. Unfortunately, many excavated medieval sites are in secondary locations such as the upland fringes, which may account for their lack of pre-thirteenth-century pottery (Allan 1994; Henderson and Weddell 1994; Weddell and Reed 1997). A number of modern farmsteads studied in advance

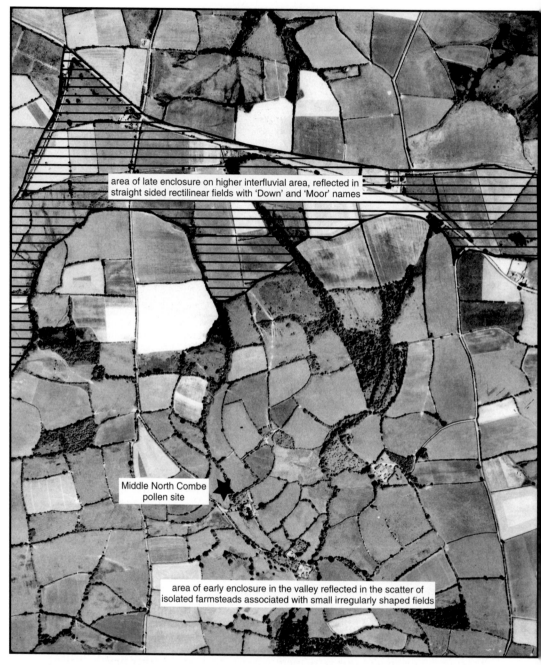

area of late enclosure on higher interfluvial area, reflected in straight sided rectilinear fields with 'Down' and 'Moor' names

Middle North Combe pollen site

area of early enclosure in the valley reflected in the scatter of isolated farmsteads associated with small irregularly shaped fields

Fig. 4.9. Middle North Combe, in Templeton parish, mid Devon. To the south the landscape of dispersed settlement and small enclosed fields is typical of lowland Devon. To the north, the larger, straight-sided fields on the higher ground, with characteristic 'Down' field names, are areas of former common pasture that may have been ploughed up occasionally (the 'outfield') (after Rippon *et al.* 2006a, fig. 8; aerial photo: NMR 3G/TUD/UK221 Part III 11 July 1946, frame 5303 © English Heritage (NMR) RAF Photography).

of the construction of the Roadford Reservoir in west Devon also appear to have been secondary settlements as eleventh-century pottery was absent. Five farmsteads were excavated and in each case there is documentary and archaeological evidence for them having originated in the twelfth or thirteenth centuries as small hamlets, of two or three tenements, on freehold land with little or no manorial control (Griffith 1988b, 124–7; Henderson and Weddell 1994, 131–2). At Okehampton Park it has been shown that what in the thirteenth century were small hamlets originated as isolated farmsteads (Austin 1978; 1985).

Even where excavations have been carried out within medieval settlements in the core lowland areas, it is impossible to trace their origins beyond the eleventh century, as Devon is aceramic before that date (Fox 1958; Jope and Threlfall, 1958; Allan 1994; Henderson and Weddell 1994; Weddell and Reed 1997; Allan and Langman 2002; Goodard and Todd 2005). It is possible to radiocarbon date the earliest stratigraphic horizons of a medieval settlement and, although recent work has shown that such deposits rarely survive the subsequent occupation of a site (Brown and Laithwaite 1993; Henderson and Weddell 1994; Brown 1998), excavations within Kingsteignton revealed a series of aceramic ditches that yielded radiocarbon-dated charcoal from the seventh to ninth centuries (Weddell 1987).[8]

THE SOUTH-WEST'S MEDIEVAL FIELDSCAPE

Our earliest maps, all dating to the post-medieval period, show that the medieval settlement pattern in the South-West was connected by a network of tracks and sunken lanes which wound their way through a near-continuous fieldscape, separated by relatively small areas of unenclosed common land on the higher ground used as rough grazing and occasionally cultivated as an 'outfield' (Fig. 4.9; Fox 1973; Herring 2006a). Traditionally, it has been assumed that the South-West always had a landscape of predominantly enclosed fields, which particularly in the case of Cornwall is associated with the romantic notion that the 'celtic' character was built upon individualism (Herring 2006a). There is now, however, a growing appreciation that open fields were found across the South-West. In today's landscape these are reflected in small blocks of long narrow fields, with curving boundaries, laid out between roughly parallel furlong-type alignments that are suggestive of the enclosure by agreement of open field strips (Fig. 4.10; Herring 1998; 2006a; 2006b). In a number of cases research into the patterns of nineteenth-century landholding within these blocks of long narrow fields shows that it was highly fragmented, supporting the idea that they represent enclosed former open fields

[8] 1350+/−80 BP (550–860 cal. AD), 1320+/−70 BP (600–880 cal. AD), and 1300+/−80 BP (600–890 cal. AD).

Fig. 4.10. The extant open field at Forrabury, Boscastle (© Steve Hartgroves, Historic Environment Service, Cornwall County Council).

(Fig. 4.11; Gillard 2002; Rippon 2004a, fig. 26; Herring 2006a; Ryder 2006). In a late eighteenth-century survey of Challacombe, on Dartmoor, for example, these strips were known as 'landscores' (i.e. 'land-shares'), which occurred in blocks referred to as 'wares' that were broadly similar to furlongs (Bonney 1971; Griffith 1988b, 97; Pattison 1999). Elsewhere across the South-West blocks of rectangular or square closes are found laid out in blocks between similar long, sinuous boundaries that may represent consolidated groups of strips in what have been termed 'cropping units', of which there were usually between eight and thirteen per field system (Herring 2006a, 69). Where not subject to recent intensive ploughing some of the 'cropping unit'-type fields contain the earthworks of low banks forming long, narrow, curving striplike subdivisions suggesting that they too may have formed parts of larger open fields (Fleming and Ralph 1982; Pattison 1999; Riley and Wilson-North 2001, figs. 4.12–13, 4.30, 5.6, 5.11–12; Riley 2006, 108–10). The origin of these field systems is unclear, although at Trerice, in St Dennis (Cornwall), the open fields were sufficiently mature by 1049 to have been divided in two, to have determined the line of a highway, and to be followed by a parish boundary (Herring and Hooke 1993).

While the presence of open fields in the South-West is clear, their extent is not. In Cornwall, it appears that a relatively large proportion—perhaps as much as 90 per cent—of the medieval cultivated land was arranged in fields

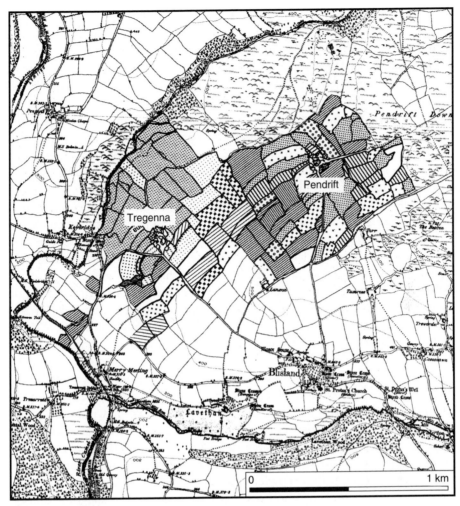

Fig. 4.11. Treganna and Pendrift, in Blisland parish on the western fringes of Bodmin Moor, Cornwall. The differently shaded fields represent the lands of tenements recorded on the Tithe map of 1839. The field boundary pattern and highly fragmented pattern of landholding reflects the fossilization of former open field strips (based on Herring 2006a, fig. 27, © Peter Herring) superimposed on the First Edition Ordnance Survey Six Inch Map).

consisting of unenclosed strips, this amounting to around 60 per cent of the whole of Cornwall (Herring 2007; Peter Herring pers. comm.). These open fields were, however, very different in character from the central zone, being individually very small, each related to its own hamlet, and associated with large areas of open pasture (e.g. Fig. 4.11). In Devon, a recent 'Historic Landscape Characterization' suggests that 43 per cent of the entire county was covered in strip-based fields (Turner 2007, fig. 45), whereas the traditional view is that they were of very limited extent, and were found mostly in the fertile lowlands of the south, east, and north-west (including Braunton: Fig. 4.10; Shorter *et al.*

1969, fig. 26). A closer examination of Turner's (2007) own evidence clearly shows, however, that what he sometimes regards as 'medieval enclosures from strip fields' are nothing of the sort, being highly irregular in shape. This scarcity of evidence for open field in parts of Devon is born out by the author's own work in mid Devon, such as at Middle North Combe in Templeton where strip-based fields are extremely rare (Fig. 4.9; Rippon *et al.* 2006a), and on the Blackdown Hills where evidence for open fields was absent from many parishes (Rippon *et al.* 2006b). The very limited extent of strip-based fields in Devon is also seen in the detailed research of Gillard (2002) on the greater Exmoor area, and Ryder's (2006) work on the Blackdown Hills, Hartland peninsula, and South Hams.

These various detailed local studies all conclude that while there were strip-based fields in medieval Devon, these were distributed very unevenly across the landscape and usually amounted to just 10 or 20 per cent of the cultivated ground within a parish. Although consisting of land that was subdivided into strips and furlongs, when first described in the early thirteenth century the management of these fields lacks many of the key characteristics of the 'Midland' system—such as comprehensive common pasturing of livestock on the post-harvest stubble and coordinated fallowing—because instead of two or three common fields that embraced all the land of a community, there was a multiplicity of smaller units, some called fields, some called furlongs, and some described as both (Fox 1981, 92). These small open field systems of around 0.2 to 0.5 km^2 were also on a completely different scale from the vast two- and three-field systems seen in England's champion countryside that covered up to *c.*90 per cent of a parish (around 5 to 10 km^2). Landholding within the South-West's strip fields was also more closely related to Welsh share-lands than the English common fields, with the strips belonging to individual tenements grouped together, close to the hamlet within which they were based, rather than scattered more widely (Fowler and Thomas 1962, 78).

Some of the documentary sources that have been used to suggest extensive open field farming also need to be interpreted with care. In the thirteenth century, for example, there is reference to the exchange of certain acres in *parva furlang de Churlebrooke* in the manor of Yarcombe, whereby the vicar of Yarcombe had 30 acres (12 ha) of land lying together, and not intermixed as some of the other holdings were (Finberg 1952, 274). This is suggestive of an open field, but an analysis of the historic landscape in Yarcombe quickly reveals a pattern of small irregularly shaped closes that cannot have been derived from open fields, and the scattered nature of nineteenth-century landholding in the parish is more suggestive of subdivided tenements than former open field. References to land that 'is tilled' and 'can be tilled', which Finberg (1952, 272–3) cites in support of open fields, simply show that there was a rotational system of cultivation, with only a proportion of land parcels being cultivated in any one year. This probably reflects a regionally distinctive system of mixed agriculture—known as convertible or ley husbandry—used across the

South-West in both enclosed and open fields. In this system of farming, the majority of fields (closes or parcels of open fields) were subject to alternating grain and grass crops, often with a short period of cultivation (*c.*2–3 years), followed by a long grass ley (*c.*6–8 years) producing a rotation of around ten years (Finberg 1951; Wood 1963; Hatcher 1970; Fox 1972; 1991; Alcock 1975; Fox and Padel 2000, pp. liii–xciv). This presumably accounts for the average of ten 'cropping units' per field system which would allow two or three to be cultivated in any one year while the rest were down to grass.

Overall, therefore, the medieval landscape of the South-West appears to have been characterized by a mixed pattern of settlements and field systems, with some areas having a mixture of hamlets and isolated farmsteads associated with closes held in severalty, and others small hamlets, associated with open fields. These open fields were, however, on a far smaller scale than those in England's champion countryside, and they were managed and cultivated in a different way. There is no reason to assume that they are a poorly developed version of the Midland system: along with the settlement pattern of small hamlets they appear to be a distinctive indigenous development. So where did this regionally distinctive landscape, only found to the west of the Blackdown and Quantock Hills, come from?

The relationship between the prehistoric and historic landscapes

From the discussion so far, it has been possible to trace the development of the prehistoric landscape through to the earliest medieval period (the fifth and sixth centuries), and trace the origins of the historic landscape back as far as the tenth and eleventh centuries in places. So what is the relationship between the two? What is clear is that apart from West Penwith, the medieval landscape of unenclosed farmsteads and hamlets was unrelated to the enclosed settlements of the late prehistoric, Roman, and earliest medieval periods. In and around Exmoor, for example, the deserted medieval hamlets immediately adjacent to (but not within) the hillslope enclosures at Bagley and Sweetworthy, first identified by Aston (1983) and cited then as possible examples of continuity, are in fact unique (Riley and Wilson-North 2001, 73–5). In Cornwall, while there are several examples of medieval settlements occurring just outside rounds (e.g. Crasken in Helston, and Tregear in Crowan), most medieval settlements are unrelated to these earlier enclosures, and there are no examples of rounds that continued in use past the sixth century (Preston-Jones and Rose 1986; Rose and Preston Jones 1995, figs. 3.1–2; Turner 2003, 176–8; 2005, 23; Herring forthcoming). Padel (1985, 223–5; 1999) has shown that habitative place names such as *tre-* (farmstead, hamlet, estate), which are so characteristic of the medieval landscape, were being created sometime after the fifth century, certainly by the seventh century, and probably not after *c.*1100, and none of these is located within a round, making it unlikely that these medieval farmsteads and hamlets represent prehistoric or Romano-British settlements that simply continued to be occupied. Turner (2006d) has shown that the distribution of *tre-* place names corresponds to those parts of the Cornish countryside whose present landscape character is one of 'ancient enclosure', in contrast to distribution of rounds that are found both here and in the lower parts of areas that until the past few centuries were unenclosed rough grazing. This suggests that the fieldscape of 'ancient enclosure' and *tre-* place names may have a common origin in the second half of the first millennium, and represents a slight contraction of the settled area.

Aerial photography, geophysical survey, and excavation are also revealing that Iron Age and Romano-British enclosed settlements, and the localized field systems that they are occasionally associated with, are on a different orientation from the medieval pattern, such as the late third- to fourth-century AD enclosure and possible field system at Teigngrace that underlies unconformably a small medieval strip field system (Gent 1997; and see Rose and Preston-Jones 1995, fig. 3.2; Herring 1998, fig. 42; S. Turner 2004; Herring forthcoming). Even at the level of vernacular architecture we see discontinuity: by the thirteenth century the dominant form of dwelling appears to have been the rectangular cross-passage houses, which can possibly be dated to the tenth and eleventh centuries at Mawgan Porth and Gwithian (Beacham 1990b; Child 1990; Taylor 1997; Pearce 2004, 304), and which stand in sharp contrast to the unicellular oval and sub-oval huts of the Romano-British and earliest medieval period (Preston-Jones and Rose 1986, fig. 6; Quinnell 1986, figs. 3–5; 2004). Other signs of change around the sixth and seventh centuries include hilltop sites such as Raddon and Haldon being abandoned (Gent and Quinnell 1999a, 19, 24–6; 1999b, 82), and pottery from the continent no longer reaching the South-West (despite it finding its way to sites around the rest of Britain's western seaboard: Thomas 1990). In another change to the repertoire of material culture, locally produced Romano-Cornish wares were replaced with Gwithian and grass-marked fabrics (Quinnell 2004, 243). Overall, there appears to have been a significant discontinuity in the landscape some time between the sixth century, when archaeological evidence for the continued use of what was essentially still the late prehistoric and Romano-British landscape ceases, and the tenth and eleventh centuries, being the date back to which we can trace the medieval landscape. Crucially, neither archaeological nor documentary sources can say whether this discontinuity was a sudden or a gradual process, or precisely when it occurred.

New palaeoenvironmental evidence for the origins of the historic landscape in south-west England

The origins of this convertible husbandry system of agriculture, and the landscape that supported it, may not be documented, but palaeoenvironmental research is increasingly pointing to a date around the seventh and eighth centuries. Previous palaeoenvironmental studies have done little to shed light on this crucial period as the sites examined were either located on the higher uplands that lay beyond the limits of contemporary settlement or failed to cover the mid first millennium AD (e.g. Codsend Moor, Hoar Moor, and the Chains on Exmoor; Merrivale and Wotter Common on Dartmoor: Fig. 4.4). Fortunately, recent work is now focusing on the lowlands.

In the south of Devon, a pollen sequence from the floodplain south of Slapton, which starts around the tenth century, shows that there was already cultivation in the vicinity of this location at the very margins of the parish, but unfortunately the earlier part of the peat sequence, precisely that which would indicate when this cultivation started, was not studied (Foster *et al.* 2000). A series of pollen sequences from around Rackenford (Middle North Combe, Hares Down, Lobbs Bog, and Windmill Rough) and the Clyst Valley (Broadclyst Moor, Hellings Park, and Mosshayne) in mid Devon, and the southern fringes of Exmoor (Ansteys Combe, Gourte Mires, and Long Breach), however, straddles the whole period from late prehistory through to the present day (Fig. 4.4). Between the fourth and sixth centuries AD there is very little significant change in any of these pollen records, suggesting continuity in an essentially pastoral landscape, with no evidence of woodland regeneration. Around the seventh to eighth centuries, however, many of these sequences do show significant changes in the local land-use. In the central lowlands of Devon near Exeter, for example, a small peat bog at Hellings Park in the Loxbrook Valley, Broadclyst, first saw the appearance of cereals and the weeds of disturbed ground, alongside an increase in grass and herbaceous species at this time (1320+/−50 BP, cal. AD 645–800: Hawkins 2005b), and although this change in land-use does not feature at nearby Mosshayne, or Bywood on the Blackdown Hills, this is because these peat sequences show the continuous presence of cereal cultivation in close proximity to the pollen sites ever since the Roman period (Hawkins 2005a). Other sites in the Blackdown Hills, however, do show significant changes in land-use. At Middleton, the stratigraphy within this valley-side mire changed from an organic clay to herbaceous peat very shortly before 1320+/−70 BP (cal. AD 620–880). This may have been the result of erosion caused by local deforestation (reflected in the pollen sequence by a marked decline in trees and influx of pine) that led to waterlogging of the site and the consequent growth of sedges and mosses; wheat/oats appear soon after. An increase in cereals and a decline in woodland at nearby Greenway may also have occurred at this time, although this date is interpolated from an earlier radiocarbon determination and must be treated with caution (Hawkins 2005a). At Aller Farm, on the eastern fringes of the Blackdown Hills, there was an increase in cereals somewhat later, perhaps around the ninth or tenth centuries (Hatton and Caseldine 1991, 112–13), and this may reflect the spread of common field agriculture at the very edge of the central zone (see Chapter 3).

Around Rackenford, in mid Devon, the evidence for a change in agricultural practice is especially clear, with an increase in cereals, herbaceous taxa associated with arable cultivation, and improved pasture. At Middle North Combe (Fig. 4.9; an interpolated date around 1350 BP, *c.* AD 600–800), Lobbs Bog (1240+/−50, cal. AD 670–890), and Windmill Rough (shortly after 1380+/−50, cal. AD 560–770) the change is characterized by the start of significant amounts of cereal pollen, notably oats/wheat and rye. At Lobbs Bog these taxa each reach levels of around 2 per cent total land pollen (TLP), while at Windmill Rough rye is recorded at levels up to 5 per cent TLP. At Middle North Combe wheat/oat type is recorded at up to 5 per cent TLP and rye up to 4 per cent TLP. These figures are very high, and as the pollen from cereals is poorly dispersed beyond the place of cultivation, the values recorded must represent arable cultivation in the immediate vicinity of the sites. At Windmill Rough and Lobbs Bog, there is also an increase in *Calluna* (heather) around the seventh to eighth centuries reaching up to around 10 per cent TLP, suggesting open rough grazing in the unenclosed land. At nearby Hares Down there is also an increase in heather alongside a further decline in *Alnus* (alder) around the seventh to eighth centuries, suggesting the removal of streamside wet woodland, although a constant cereal curve does not appear until around the tenth century (this decline in alder is not climatically induced, as these are groundwater fed mires, not rainfall-fed raised bogs). The later date for the appearance of cultivation in the vicinity of Hares Down is in keeping with evidence from the Romano-British period, when a slightly greater amount of woodland remained in what was a more steeply sided valley compared to Lobbs Bog and Windmill Rough.

The pollen 'signature' for convertible husbandry

One interpretation of this increase in cereal pollen around the seventh and eighth centuries is a classic 'push into the margins'. This would see arable cultivation, associated with settlements located in more favourable locations, expanding into these 'marginal' areas that were less suited to it, and that this process had now reached the catchments of these peat bogs. This may have been the case at Hares Down (where there was a decline in woodland at the same time as the rise in cereals), but such a 'push into the margins' is unlikely to have been the case elsewhere, particularly in the lowlands around Broadclyst and Rackenford. Middle North Combe (Fig. 4.9), for example, lies immediately adjacent to the Domesday settlement of Combe, but that the same levels of cereal pollen are also seen at Lobbs Bog, Hares Down, and Windmill Rough which all lie around 1 km from the nearest documented medieval settlement is significant. If permanent arable land had expanded from these farmsteads as far as the pollen sites, and if this intensity of cultivation is applied across the rest of the South-West, then virtually the whole of lowland Devon and Cornwall would have been under the plough! This cannot have been the case and there must have been another system of landscape management that led to such high cereal pollen values at these sites.

The palaeoenvironmental evidence itself similarly does not support a solely 'push into the margins' interpretation. If there had been a simple expansion of arable cultivation, then there should have been an equivalent decline in woodland and pasture, but this is not the case: virtually all the sites show the continuation of a rich pastoral flora, and woodland still present, with no reduction corresponding to the increase in arable. In addition, the pollen record shows not just a sharp increase in cereal, but also an expansion of heather at Hares Down, Lobbs Bog, and Windmill Rough (though not Middle North Combe), which is unlikely to have been growing on the peat bogs themselves, as macrofossil evidence suggests they were dominated by sedges. The presence of heather at these sites is most likely to represent rough grazing on the most marginal land outside the main agricultural holdings (whereas the lower-lying Middle North Combe lay in an area within which virtually all the land within its pollen catchment was agriculturally improved).

The appearance of such a strong cereal component in these pollen sequences, but without an equivalent significant decline in woodland or pasture, does not, therefore, represent a simple expansion of cereal cultivation, and as these valley mires were never themselves drained, it must reflect a new system of agriculture that brought arable farming close to the peat bogs, but within a regime that still included a strong pastoral component alongside areas of woodland and heath. This is precisely what 'convertible husbandry' consisted of (see above). Documentary sources suggest that this regionally distinctive system of rotational cropping was ubiquitous throughout the South-West by the fourteenth century as far east as the Blackdown and Quantock Hills, and so those sections of these peat bogs dating from the late medieval period reflect how convertible husbandry shows up in the pollen record. The 0.5 cm thick samples of peat used in the pollen analyses represent between five and ten years of pollen accumulation, during which period fields immediately adjacent to the mires are likely to have been cultivated for several years, leading to the high representation of cereals and other arable indicators, with the intervening ley periods resulting in the constant pasture signature in the pollen sequences (Rippon *et al.* 2006a, fig. 13). Crucially, having recognized the convertible husbandry signature from fourteenth century and later horizons, an examination of the earlier samples reveals no differences in landscape management between then and the onset of significant cultivation in the seventh to eighth centuries: it would appear, therefore, that convertible husbandry may have been introduced in the lowlands of Devon at this date, and several centuries later in the upland fringe.

DISCUSSION: THE EMERGENCE OF A REGIONALLY DISTINCTIVE LANDSCAPE IN SOUTH-WEST ENGLAND DURING THE 'LONG EIGHTH CENTURY'?

The fifth to tenth centuries are clearly a crucial, if ill-understood, period in the South-West, which saw the genesis of the historic landscape across most of the region (beyond the far west of Cornwall where late prehistoric landscapes appear to have remained in use). Landscapes are constantly evolving, and in the South-West the Late Iron Age and Roman periods were no exception, but the seventh to eighth centuries appear to have seen a particularly significant period of change. The fifth- to sixth-century landscape of hilltop settlements, lowland enclosures, and very localized field systems appears to have been abandoned, and the absence of seventh-century imported pottery from the continent, which is found elsewhere around Britain's western seaboard, suggests some disruption to socio-economic structures. By the eleventh century documentary sources suggest that the basic framework of today's countryside was in place, including its dispersed pattern of open settlements, with new styles of buildings, and a near continuous fieldscape that sits unconformably over the Romano-British landscape.

The recent palaeoenvironmental work is pointing to the seventh and eighth centuries as seeing a significant change in how the lowland landscape was managed, with the increase in cereal pollen at the same time as the continuation of extensive areas of improved pasture. The lack of a contemporary decline in woodland and rough grazing suggests that this was not simply an expansion of settlement and cultivation from primary to more secondary locations. These seventh- to eighth-century pollen assemblages are the same as those for the eleventh century, by which time we know the physical foundations of the historic landscape were laid. They are also the same as for the late medieval period, by which time we know that the regionally distinctive system of agriculture known as 'convertible husbandry' was in use. It seems likely, therefore, that it was the seventh to eighth centuries that saw the crucial transition from a Romano-British countryside to the historic landscape of today.

This was a turbulent period in the South-West, with the eastern part of the kingdom of Dumnonia (i.e. modern Devon) absorbed by the West Saxon kingdom of Wessex in the late seventh century. The exact chronology and nature of this 'conquest' is unclear, although Exeter was probably under West Saxon control by c.680 as the young Boniface is said to have received his education there, and Cenwalh (642–73) may indeed have founded its minster in c.670 as later traditions of the Wessex kingdom have claimed (Yorke 1990, 137; Pearce 2004, 181, 249). The 'West Welsh' of Cornwall retained their independence until the ninth century. The relationship between these political upheavals and the emergence of the historic landscape is, however, unclear.

There is no reason why this should have led to a sudden or synchronous replanning of the countryside, but these political changes could have started a period of economic expansion, innovation, and change, reflected in the cessation of trading contact with the Mediterranean world, the abandonment of hilltop settlements, and the granting of large tracts of land to both the Church and secular lords (e.g. King Æthelheard's grant of twenty hides of land at Crediton to Bishop Forthhere in 739: Finberg 1954, No. 2; Sawyer 1968, No. 255; and see Hooke 1994; 1999, 97). What may have been crucial was how land was owned, held, and organized, and Herring (2006a) suggests that the shift to open field agriculture did not simply reflect a change from land held in severalty to land held in common—as bricklike 'celtic' fields were also associated with hamlets and so may have been farmed in common—or the ability to accommodate a new form of plough, but was designed to give the new landowners closer control over land allotment and shareholding.

So was this change an insular development or another example of the far wider changes seen in southern England during the 'long eighth century'? And why did the approach towards the structuring of the landscape around villages and regularly arranged two- and three-field systems never spread to the west of the Blackdown and Quantock Hills around the tenth century? It is certainly not because the area was sparsely populated: Domesday population densities in the lowlands around Exeter and Torbay, for example, were the same as in central Somerset (Fig. 4.4). Antecedent landscape character may have been a significant factor: it seems clear that prehistoric and Romano-British society in the South-West showed some distinctive differences from the area to the east of the Blackdown and Quantock Hills (Fig. 4.1) and the developments seen around the eighth and tenth centuries may be further examples of the area's long-term distinctiveness. Landowners and their tenants may not have been receptive to the 'concept' of villages and common fields because they had already developed an efficient agricultural system that suited the region's climate and soils. But before we can decide why it was that the South-West's landscape developed in its own distinctive way, we need to compare its experience with another region beyond the edge of the central zone: East Anglia.

5

Champion and Woodland? Landscape
Evolution beyond the Central Zone
in Greater East Anglia

The preceding chapters examined the south-western limit of England's central zone and found that while the upland areas of the Blackdown and Quantock Hills appear to mark the limit to which villages and Midland-style common fields spread across Somerset, topography and soils do not explain all of the local and regional variation within that county's landscape character. Indeed, across the Blackdown and Quantock Hills, the countryside in Dumnonia appears to have undergone a profound period of change around the eighth century, several centuries before the creation of villages and common fields in Somerset. It also appears that the south-west peninsula had seen a significantly different cultural landscape compared to areas further east for many centuries and this deep-rooted distinctiveness may have been a significant factor in its divergent landscape development during the 'long eighth century'. We can now turn to another case study of regional variation in landscape development at the margins of England's central zone in what is referred to here as 'greater East Anglia' (Fig. 5.1).

This study area embraces the counties of Norfolk and Suffolk (which together form East Anglia in the modern sense), along with Essex and the eastern part of Cambridgeshire. It straddles the boundary between Roberts and Wrathmell's (2000, fig. 10) 'central' and 'south-eastern' provinces, Rackham's 'planned' and 'ancient' landscapes, and Leland's 'champion' and 'woodland' countryside. This region has benefited from a number of recent seminal studies including Christopher Taylor's (2002) examination of the eastern limit of villages and common fields in Cambridgeshire, Tom Williamson's (2003; 2006a; 2007) discussion of the development of the medieval countryside across East Anglia and the East Midlands, and the results of Edward Martin and Max Satchell's (forthcoming; Martin 2007) East Anglian Fields Project. The region benefits from a virtually continuous and relatively well-dated ceramic sequence, and has a long history of fieldwalking (made possible

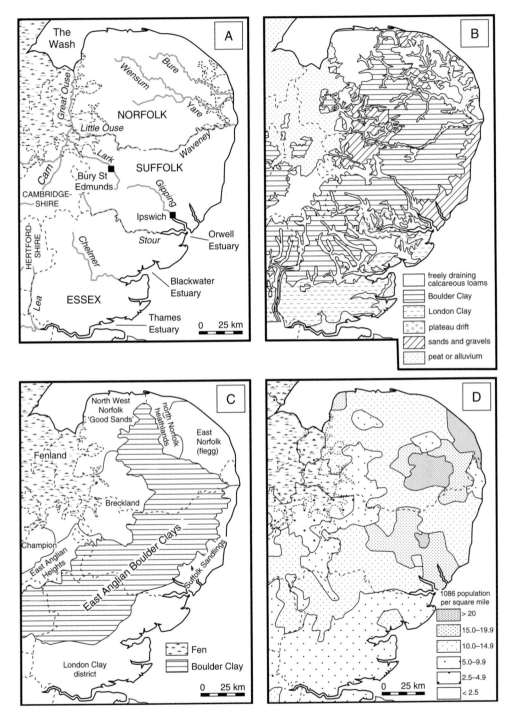

Fig. 5.1. Aspects of the East Anglian landscape. (A) major rivers; (B) soils (after Williamson 2003, fig. 8); (C) major physical *pays* (after Williamson 2003, fig. 22); (D) Domesday population density (after Darby 1977, fig. 34). Drawing by Adam Wainwright.

by the extensive areas of modern arable), and a large number of development-led excavations that allow the evolution of settlement patterns and field systems to be studied in far greater detail than is possible in many other areas. The attention paid to field systems in this chapter is a deliberate attempt to adopt a more holistic approach towards studying the early medieval landscape and to move on from the very settlement-focused studies that have characterized previous work in this region and beyond (e.g. Dark 2000; Baker 2006b). The picture that is emerging suggests that landscape development in this region also occurred within some deep-rooted boundaries and that in the north of the area there was, once again, a profound change in the structure of the landscape during the 'long eighth century'.

THE PHYSICAL AND CULTURAL REGIONS OF 'GREATER EAST ANGLIA'

In contrast to the dramatic variations in topography seen across Somerset and the south-west of England, greater East Anglia is a region of more subtle—although nonetheless significant—differences in relief, geology, and soils (Fig. 5.1). The region is dominated by a Boulder Clay plateau that extends from the northern coast of Norfolk, through Suffolk, and into central Essex. To the west there is a chalk escarpment that forms the northern extension of the Chiltern Hills and underlies the 'East Anglian Heights', beyond which lies the lowlands of Hertfordshire, Cambridgeshire, and the vast wetland expanse of Fenland. The chalk itself only outcrops on the scarp-face and in valley sides, elsewhere being capped by superficial drift deposits, notably clay with flints and brickearths on the Chilterns themselves, extensive areas of sand known as Breckland on the Suffolk–Norfolk border, and Arthur Young's (1804, 10–12) 'Good Sand' region to the north. To the south of the Boulder Clay, in southern Essex, there are extensive areas of heavy London Clay, while the eastern, coastal, districts of Norfolk, Suffolk, and Essex are dominated by a series of estuaries that dissect areas of lighter loams and sandy gravels. Across the whole of greater East Anglia the topography is relatively flat, although the extensive Boulder Clay plateau is dissected by river valleys that have lighter, better-drained soils compared to the interfluvial areas and watersheds.

Culturally, the north-west corner of modern Essex around Great Chester-ford—beyond the chalk escarpment—appears to have looked towards north-ern Hertfordshire and Cambridgeshire. Artefact distributions suggest that in the Iron Age and Roman periods it lay within the Catuvellaunian tribal area/*civitas*, and in the fifth to seventh centuries the Early Saxon cemeteries around Great Chesterford share their greatest affinities with the Cambridge region (Fig. 5.2; Evison 1994, 46–518, fig. 10; Baker 2006b, fig. 3). To the east, the Gipping and Lark valleys—or the interfluvial area to the south that

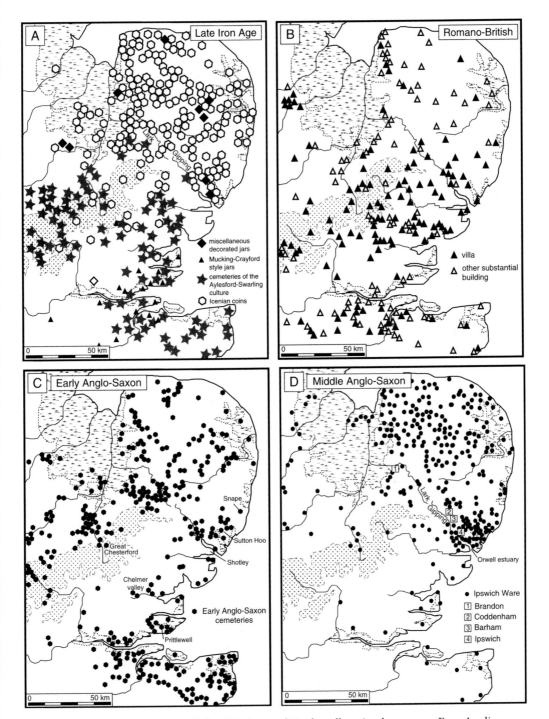

Fig. 5.2. The significance of the Gipping and Lark valleys in the greater East Anglian landscape. (A) selected Late Iron Age pottery, coins, and burials (Cunliffe 2005, figs. 5.9 and 7.6); (B) Roman villas and other substantial buildings (Ordnance Survey 2001; Going 1996, fig. 1; Plouviez 1999, 43); (C) Early Anglo-Saxon cemeteries (Penn 1994, 37; Tyler 1996, fig. 1; West 1999, 45; Riddler 2004, 27; Morris 2005, fig. 9.39); (D) the distribution of Ipswich Ware (Blinkhorn 1999, fig. 2; Suffolk Historic Environment Record).

marks a continuation of the East Anglian Heights—appear to have marked
a boundary zone of similar long-term cultural significance, dividing modern
Suffolk in half along a line between Bury St Edmunds in the north-west and
Ipswich in the south-east. Perhaps because of the long tradition within this
region of county-based research, and an assumption that the border between
the kingdoms of East Anglia and the East Saxons was along the river Stour
which marks the present boundary between Suffolk and Essex (e.g. Pewsey
and Brooks 1993, p. x), the importance of this division has only recently
been recognized (e.g. Brown *et al.* 2002; Williamson 2005; 2006a, 28; Rippon
2007a; Martin 2007): it hardly features in earlier work such as Warner's
(1996) study of Suffolk. The distributions of burials, pottery, coins, and other
metalwork suggest that the Iron Age people known as the Iceni occupied the
area north of this boundary, while the Trinovantes occupied the area to the
south (Fig. 5.2; Moore *et al.* 1988, 13–15, fig. 9; and see Davies 1999, 16–17;
Martin 1999a, 82–91; Cunliffe 2005; Rippon 2007a). The distribution of
Roman amphorae imported into Late Iron Age Britain noticeably does not
extend into northern East Anglia, suggesting that the Iceni did not embrace
contacts with the continent in the same way as the Trinovantes to the south. In
the Roman period the Icenian *civitas* also has noticeably fewer villas.

There is also a marked difference in the landscapes of northern and southern
East Anglia in the early medieval period, with far greater evidence for Anglian
settlement in the north than there is for actual Saxon immigration in the
south, which is largely restricted to coastal districts of Essex and the Chelmer
valley (Brown 1981; Evison 1981; Hines 1984; West 1998). Although Parker
Pearson *et al.* (1993) suggest that the famous early seventh-century cemetery
at Sutton Hoo, in south-east Suffolk, may have been the burial ground of
an East Saxon king, and the material culture both there and at the nearby
cemetery of Snape shows some affinities with that in Essex (Filmer-Sankey
and Pestel 2001, 265), Bede states that Rendlesham between the two was the
East Anglian king's country seat (Farmer 1990, 180; although Blair (2005,
66–90) has argued that such *villae regialis* may not have been such permanent
features of the landscape as has often been assumed). Other evidence also firmly
points to the Gipping–Lark boundary as marking the division between East
Anglia and the East Saxons. Series S *sceattas*, for example, were probably the
royal coinage of the East Saxons produced as an expression of independence
from their political overlords in Mercia: coins of Mercia were copied, but
the king's head was replaced by a sphinx, perhaps recalling the past classical
glories of Colchester (Metcalf 1993, 21; 2001, 46; Rippon 1996b, 117; Morris
2005, figs. 9.5–6). Their occurrence is largely restricted to modern Essex,
Hertfordshire, and London, a distribution that is almost mutually exclusive
to that of Ipswich Ware, whose widespread use was restricted to East Anglia
(Fig. 5.2D: Blinkhorn 1999). Despite the proximity of Essex and south-west
Suffolk to the production site at Ipswich, very little of this material moved

south. Only two sites—Wicken Bonhunt (Wade 1980) and Barking (Redknap 1991)—have produced more than a handful of sherds, and of the remaining sites there is a strong coastal relationship, a pattern that the recent find of a near complete vessel from Althorne Creek, on the Crouch estuary, reinforces (Rippon 1996b, 117; Cotter 2000, 26; Walker 2001).

This distribution of Ipswich Ware suggests that the Gipping–Lark line was therefore the boundary between the 'East Sexena' and 'East Engle' of the Tribal Hidage: whilst in other periods the distribution of pottery is largely a reflection of trading links, this was a period before a money-based market economy when exchange would have been more socially embedded. The distribution of eighth-century 'productive sites' in East Anglia could also be significant. These possible centres for trade and exchange occur across south-east England, often in coastal and estuarine locations, particularly around the fringes of East Anglia: with the exception of Caistor St Edmunds, most of these sites occur around the margins of the main area of Ipswich Ware, and the location of Brandon in the Lark Valley, and Barham and Coddenham in the Gipping Valley, upstream from the emporium at Ipswich, reinforces the impression of these valleys being a zone of liminal interaction. It was only around the tenth century, when the English shires were created, that the boundary between Essex and Suffolk was established along the Stour valley to the south.

A NOTE ON TERMINOLOGY

Across East Anglia the traditional terminology of 'Early Saxon' (AD 410–700), 'Middle Saxon' (AD 700–850), and 'Late Saxon' (AD 850–1066) is used for both periods and material culture (i.e. we read of 'Early Saxon pottery' and the 'Early Saxon period'). This confusion of cultural identity and period terminology is unfortunate and potentially misleading as an 'Early Saxon' site (in terms of a settlement occupied during the fifth to seventh centuries) may actually have been inhabited by the direct descendants of the native Romano-British population rather than immigrants of 'Germanic' origin. The arguments over who is buried in fifth- to seventh-century Anglo-Saxon cemeteries is now well rehearsed, but whether one takes a minimalist or maximalist view of the extent of the Anglo-Saxon migration, it is clear that there was at least some settlement of people of continental origin in fifth-century greater East Anglia, and that they brought with them new forms of burial rite (cremation and the deposition of grave goods), buildings (sunken-featured buildings or *Grubenhäuser*), and material culture (e.g. *Schlickung*-treated pottery with a distinctive surface treatment involving the application of a coarse slip, and which is largely restricted to the fifth century: Hamerow 1993, 31–5). In other cases, however, 'Germanic' material culture could easily have been used by descendants of the native Romano-British population. For example, assertions such as 'excavated evidence shows that the first wave of Saxons settled on Roman villa sites at Little Oakley … and at Rivenhall' (Tyler 1996, 110) are not necessarily true: both sites have indeed produced sherds of fifth- to sixth-century pottery with clear continental affinities but there are no distinctively 'Germanic' *Grubenhäuser* or burials with grave goods. It is impossible to say whether this pottery was used by first-generation immigrants from the continent and their descendants, or the native British occupants of the site who no longer had access to pottery produced in the Romano-British tradition. Unfortunately, the terms 'Early Saxon', 'Middle Saxon', and 'Late Saxon' are so well embedded within the literature of Norfolk, Suffolk, and Essex it is impossible to avoid their use here, but the terminology must be used with great care.

A CHARACTERIZATION OF THE HISTORIC LANDSCAPE

Based on Roberts and Wrathmell's (2002, fig. 1.4) analysis of nineteenth-century settlement, it would appear at first sight that the regionally significant difference in landscape character either side of the Gipping–Lark valleys had disappeared over the course of the medieval period (Fig. 5.3A). Their characterization divides the historic landscape of greater East Anglia along a roughly north-east to south-west line with predominantly dispersed settlement patterns to the east (their 'Anglia' sub-province) and more nucleated patterns in the west (their 'Wash' sub-province). They suggest, however, that the latter lay outside their central zone that extended only as far as western/central Cambridgeshire and north-west Essex (the 'East Midlands' sub-province). This boundary of the central zone broadly concurs with Gray's (1915, frontispiece) mapping of the two- and three-field systems (Fig. 5.3B), and more recent work has confirmed that the scale, structure, and management of the common field systems in Norfolk and Suffolk were indeed different from those of the Midlands (see below). There was, however, also a significant difference in the character of the field systems within northern East Anglia. To the east, the open fields were enclosed earlier and in a piecemeal fashion compared to the west, with very little common field surviving into the era of Parliamentary Enclosure. By the sixteenth century these central and eastern districts of Norfolk and Suffolk were predominantly pastoral, used mostly for dairying and pig rearing, while the western areas, with their light sandy soils, were characterized by mixed sheep-corn farming (Thirsk 1967, 40–9).

   This east–west difference in the character of the medieval landscape of northern East Anglia is evident in the work of Roberts and Wrathmell (Fig. 5.3A), although Rackham (1986a, fig. 1.3) is wrong to place western Norfolk and Suffolk in the region of England's champion landscape (his area of 'planned countryside': Fig. 5.3C) as this was not a landscape of Midland-style villages and two- and three-field systems. It is certainly true, however, that the boundary of the central zone in northern East Anglia is not as clear as it is to the south, where the edge of landscapes characterized by strongly nucleated settlement and regularly arranged common fields corresponds with the Chiltern escarpment, to the east of which settlement patterns were highly dispersed and common fields were of more limited extent (Roden 1973, 345–55; Lewis *et al.* 1997). This difference in the clarity of the central province's eastern boundary—the south being clearer than the north—suggests that there may have been a significant difference in landscape character within greater East Anglia, and this can be seen in Williamson's (2006a, fig. 3.12) simple but effective division of nineteenth-century field boundary patterns into those indicative of planned enclosure, earlier piecemeal enclosure, and irregular field boundary patterns suggestive of direct enclosure from 'waste' (Fig. 5.3D): the boundary between the last two types runs along the Gipping–Lark valleys.

Another indication of a significant north–south variation in medieval landscape character is the distribution of deserted medieval villages (DMVs). The correlation between known DMVs—as mapped by Beresford and Hurst (1971, fig. 13)—and Roberts and Wrathmell's (2000, fig. 21) 'central province' is generally strong but with the exception of two main areas. The first is eastern Wessex, where a large number of DMVs lie outside their 'central province', although here a strong case can be made for its inclusion as it had a pattern of predominantly nucleated (albeit linear) villages in the nineteenth century, very low levels of dispersed settlement also reflected in the scarcity of place names with the element 'green', and extensive regularly arranged two- and three-field systems in the medieval period (e.g. Roberts and Wrathmell 2000, fig. 23; 2002, figs. 2.10–11; Dyer 2001, 118; Hinton 2005). This is significant as the second area that has an abundance of deserted medieval villages outside the 'central province' is Norfolk and northern Suffolk. We have to take great care in assuming that Beresford and Hurst's database of 'deserted medieval villages' is an accurate reflection of the degree of settlement nucleation in the medieval period as, for example, some of what are called 'villages' may have been no more than hamlets, while other abandoned villages may lie undiscovered, but as it stands it is another indication that the northern part of East Anglia had a significantly different landscape character in the medieval period compared to the area to the south. Indeed, an overview of the results from fieldwalking and large-scale development-led excavations suggests that the southern part of East Anglia never did have nucleated villages (see below).

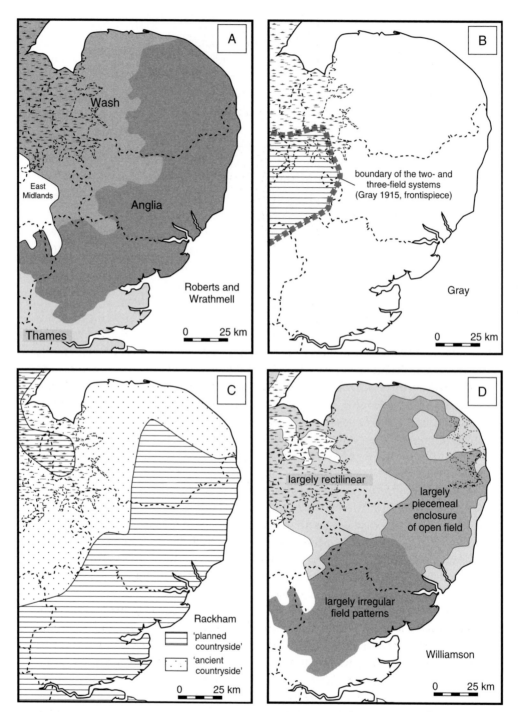

Fig. 5.3. Mappings of landscape character in greater East Anglia. (A) 19th-century settlement patterns (after Roberts and Wrathmell 2002, fig. 1.4); (B) two- and three-field systems (Gray 1915, frontispiece); (C) 'planned' and 'ancient' countryside (Rackham 1986a, fig. 1.3); (D) rapid characterization of 19th-century field shape (after Williamson 2006b, fig. 3.12). Drawing by Adam Wainwright.

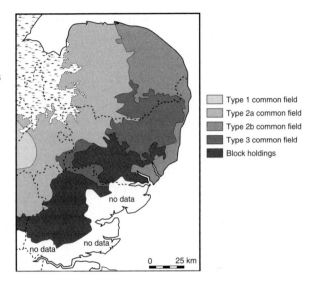

Fig. 5.4. Mapping landscape character in greater East Anglia: the East Anglian Fields Project (after Martin 2007; Martin and Satchell forthcoming). Drawing by Adam Wainwright.

Type 1 common field
Type 2a common field
Type 2b common field
Type 3 common field
Block holdings

no data

no data   no data

0   25 km

The most comprehensive analysis of landscape character in this region has been the East Anglian Fields Project that studied both the physical fabric of the historic landscape and documentary sources that describe how the fieldscapes were managed (Fig. 5.4; Martin 2007; Martin and Satchell forthcoming). In the south and west of Cambridgeshire they have confirmed that Midland-style, regularly arranged two- and three-field systems predominated ('Type 1 common field'). In the east of Cambridgeshire, along with north-west Suffolk and western Norfolk, common fields on a similar scale to those of the Midlands frequently survived into the period of Parliamentary Enclosure, although they were managed in a less regular way ('Type 2a common field'). There were some communal cropping and folding arrangements, and the strips of individual tenements were spread fairly evenly across the fields, but there was little ridge and furrow and larger numbers of smaller fields than seen in the Midlands. In eastern Norfolk and coastal districts of Suffolk the open fields tended to be even more numerous but less extensive (i.e. covering a smaller percentage of the agricultural land within a community), the remaining areas being held in severalty, as closes ('Type 2b common field'). These small open fields were subject to earlier enclosure, complex/flexible cropping arrangements (the 'shift' system), have less evidence for communal cropping and folding, and a marked tendency for the strips of individual tenements to be concentrated close to the homestead of the tenement rather than right across two or three great fields (and see Postgate 1973; Hesse 1997; Amor 2006). In the far south of Norfolk and north-eastern Suffolk the evidence for open fields is less and they were mostly enclosed by the sixteenth century ('Type 3 common field'; and see Dyer 2007). They covered less than half the agricultural land in a parish, and there is little evidence for communal cropping and folding. Landholdings were concentrated in those fields nearest to the farmstead to which they belonged rather than being evenly distributed across all the fields.

To the south of the Gipping–Lark valleys the medieval field systems were very different from Martin's 'block holdings'. Gray (1915, 387) suggested that 'the early field system of few English counties is so difficult to describe as that of Essex'. The fieldscape of this area, and indeed south-west Suffolk, is actually fairly simple in that it appears to have been dominated by what were always enclosed fields or closes. There were some open fields but they were very limited in extent, and were subdivided between just a few tenements that were located in the numerous hamlets that characterized the dispersed settlement patterns. Roden (1973, 355–63) could find no explanation for this difference in field systems within greater East Anglia in terms of the strength of manorial authority, inheritance patterns, or the extent of woodland and pasture. Martin (2007) suggests two possible causes. The first relates to topography: south of the Gipping–Lark valleys the landscape is more undulating and so has more sloping ground, whereas to the north there are greater areas of flatter, more poorly drained, land and he argues that common fields in the north were a way of sharing out the more limited areas of good land. This accords with Williamson's (2003; 2006a, 28) contention that the character of different field systems is primarily a function of the way in which the natural environment determines what farming practices are most effective, with the nature of settlement patterns following on from that (nucleated villages being appropriate for strongly communal forms of landscape management, and more dispersed patterns for smaller-scale open field farming and tenements held in severalty). He therefore suggests that the differences in field systems seen either side of the Gipping–Lark line reflect 'in large measure, aspects of soils and topography, for north of the Gipping the clay plateau was only infrequently cut by major valleys, whereas to the south it was much more dissected' (Williamson 2002, 84). Rather than a long-term cultural boundary between peoples, Williamson (2006a) also suggests that the sustained differences in material culture in these two regions are due to the ways in which topography has influenced the orientation of economic systems.

Martin also argues, however, for a significant cultural factor, in that the area of common fields in the north appears to correspond with the area of greater Scandinavian influence reflected in place names, language, and the proportion of the rural population that were freemen. The majority of Anglo-Scandinavian metalwork is also concentrated to the north of the Gipping and Lark valleys. He therefore suggests that the 'block' field systems of Essex and southern Suffolk are the oldest in our greater East Anglian region and that to the north landscapes such as these were restructured following the Scandinavian settlement, when land was redistributed amongst peasant farmers. The antiquity of these 'block field' systems of southern greater East Anglia is also inherent in the traditional views of how Midland-style villages and common fields impinged upon the region, spreading from the Midlands but stopping short of the South-East, leaving its existing landscape to develop in its own way (Fig. 1.3). In explaining this long-term boundary in landscape character, we therefore have a fascinating set of opposing hypotheses that include the rival of some very traditional views, and as such make this an exciting time to be placing this area in a wider context.

It would appear, therefore, that in the context of this case study there are three crucial issues that we must address. First, does the landscape of southern East Anglia represent a slowly evolving, but essentially Romano-British countryside, unaffected by the later transformations seen in areas such as the Midlands? Secondly, when did the distinctive landscape character of northern East Anglia emerge? And thirdly, what is the date when villages and common fields were created at the eastern edge of the central zone in Cambridgeshire, and why did this transformation of the landscape not spread any further into East Anglia? The approach to answering questions such as these in the South-West—which is aceramic and poorly documented in the early medieval period—was to see how far the late prehistoric/Romano-British landscape continued in use during the early medieval period, and how far back we can trace the origins of the historic landscape of today. In greater East Anglia the same approach is adopted, although in this case a near continuous ceramic sequence gives us far better chronological definition.

THE ORIGINS OF THE HISTORIC LANDSCAPE IN SOUTHERN EAST ANGLIA

'Persistence, continuity and change': The Trinovantian civitas *and the kingdom of the East Saxons*

The extensive surveys and excavations that have been carried out particularly in Essex make this an ideal region within which to study the Roman to medieval transition, and Morris (2005; 2006) has recently reviewed 'persistence, continuity and change' in the Essex landscape. The story that is emerging is that while a number of sites appear to have been abandoned during the third century, around 70 per cent of first-century AD settlements were still occupied in the fourth century. This mid Roman period of change included the replacement of small fields with larger enclosures at a number of sites, and may have been due to the emergence of larger agricultural estates or a change in the emphasis of agricultural production from sheep to cattle, seen in the food consumed in towns such as Colchester, Chelmsford, Great Dunmow, and Kelvedon, and at rural sites such as the villa at Wendens Ambo (Luff 1993, 128–38; Going 1996, 104). In the most recent overview of the Essex landscape in the Romano-British period, Going (1996, 104) suggests the fourth century was one of decline, although the circulation of albeit small amounts of both late fourth-century pottery (including shell-tempered ware and late Oxford-shire colour-coat types) and coins (up to Honorius and Arcadius) does suggest that many settlements were still occupied at least until the last decade of the fourth century (Drury and Rodwell 1980, 71; Lavender 1997; Garwood 1998; Germany 2003a; Baker 2006b, 61–8, 78–80; Morris 2006, fig. 7.37). There is also a surprising amount of evidence for the demolition of major buildings in the late fourth century, suggesting that the material was being reused elsewhere (Morris 2005, 38–9; 2006, 164–8).

Bryn Morris (2005; 2006) has also found that across Essex 34 per cent of Romano-British settlements occupied in the fourth century have produced small amounts of what in Essex is called 'Early Saxon' (i.e. fifth- to seventh-century) pottery. Crucially, these Romano-British sites with fifth- to seventh-century pottery are distributed right across Essex, having a far broader distribution than distinctively Germanic sites associated with burials with grave goods, *Grubenhäuser*, and *Schlickung*-treated pottery that are largely restricted to the far south and east of the county, and around Great Chesterford in the far north-east (Fig. 5.5: Jones 1980; updated in Morris 2006, figs. 9.13–14, 9.19). Drawing conclusions from such distributional patterns is fraught with danger, although it is noticeable that recent finds (e.g. Lavender 1998b; Reidy and Maynard 2000) confirm this pattern: the lack of distinctively 'Germanic' settlement in central Essex, first noted by Wheeler (1935), still holds true. Morris (2005, fig. 14) has similarly shown that this coastal bias is genuine by plotting the location of Early Saxon *Grubenhäuser* and burials against a background showing the density of archaeological activity between 1990 and 2001 (Fig. 5.5). The results are startling, as while concentrations of Early Saxon sites in the Thurrock, Southend, and Blackwater estuary areas do correspond to areas that have seen large amounts of archaeological investigation, other areas that have seen as much or even more survey and excavation such as Chelmsford, Greater London, and the Lea Valley have little or no evidence for these distinctively Germanic sites (with the exception of a small cluster of findspots at Harlow: Tyler 1996, 108, fig. 1; Germany 2008). 'Early Saxon' burials also concentrate in the far north-west of Essex, and in the far south and east, a pattern confirmed by recent discoveries (Tyler 1996; Ennis 2005; Baker 2006b). Baker (2006a) also notes the broadly coastal distribution of *hām* place names, which are thought to relate to the earlier phases of Anglo-Saxon migration and colonization.

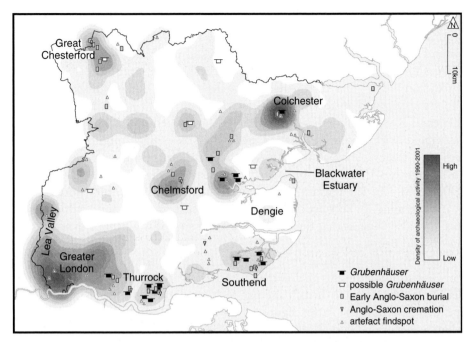

Fig. 5.5. The distribution of distinctively 'Germanic' sites and material culture, mapped against a background of the density of archaeological activity in Essex between 1990 and 2001 (after Morris 2005, fig. 14; © Bryn Morris).

Beyond the edge of the excavation: fieldwalking in the wider landscape

The results of excavations on settlement and burial sites have been summarized very briefly above, as this material is relatively well known (e.g. Tyers 1996; Baker 2006b; Morris 2006). What has received less attention is the wider landscape, which forms the core of this study. The analysis of the results of fieldwalking surveys allows the trends seen in these county-wide distribution maps to be explored in far greater detail. On the Boulder Clay plateau of north-west Essex, near Saffron Walden, Williamson (1984; 1986) found 1.3 late Romano-British settlements per square kilometre. These were mostly located on the lighter soils of the valley sides but also on the heavier soils of the interfluvial areas, although pottery assemblages from the latter suggest that they were of lower status or shorter-lived. Relatively dense manure scatters around settlements on the interfluvial areas, however, suggest extensive cultivation, with more lightly manured 'outfields' beyond, and relatively little woodland. In the early medieval period settlement was restricted to the lighter soils of the valley sides, with many Romano-British sites there still occupied into the tenth to twelfth centuries, when Saxon-Norman pottery was in use, suggesting there was no major dislocation of the settlement pattern in the first millennium AD (as described later, this is a crucial difference from northern East Anglia where around the eighth century there was a marked nucleation of settlement into villages that went on to acquire parish churches). Other large-scale fieldwalking surveys on the Boulder Clay plateau have been carried out at Stanstead Airport and its associated infrastructure (including the A120 trunk road). A light scatter of Romano-British settlements was uncovered and although none was associated with extensive ditched field systems—suggesting large areas of pasture—the evidence of a corn drier and crop-processing debris at Duckend Farm indicates there was some arable cultivation (Havis and Brooks 2004a; 2004b, 536–7). Far fewer sites yielded fifth- to seventh-century pottery, and bearing in mind the scarcity and very friable nature of the pottery in this period, this may also suggest that the heavier clayland soils saw a decline in settlement (Havis and Brooks 2004b, 341, 346–7).

A review of fieldwalking projects by the Essex County Council Archaeological Unit in Essex reveals that across 1,865 ha examined there was an average density of one Romano-British site per 38 ha, compared to one 'Saxon' period site per 266 ha. The latter figure in part reflects the poor preservation of what is generally very friable early medieval pottery: in some cases sites that when fieldwalked produced a single sherd were found to have clear evidence for occupation when excavated (Medlycott and Germany 1994, 17; Medlycott 2005). Subsequent fieldwalking projects have done little to change this picture, with fairly widespread Romano-British settlement and manuring, and a reduction in the number of sites producing early medieval material (e.g. Lavender 1997; 2004; Guttman 2000; Medlycott 2000; Brown and Germany 2002; Foreman and Maynard 2002). At Crondon Park near Stock, for example, of three Romano-British settlements within the survey area just one produced 'Early Saxon' sherds (Germany 2001).

Excavations are also increasingly confirming that many Romano-British settlements were still occupied into the fifth and sixth centuries. In many cases the evidence is ephemeral, such as occasional features containing 'Early Saxon' pottery (e.g. Coggeshall: Isserlin 1995, 96; Great Waltham: Tyler and Wickenden 1996; Ship Lane, Aveley: Foreman and Mynard 2002), or simply a scatter of residual artefacts (e.g. New Source Works in Castle Hedingham: Lavender 1996, 22). At North Shoebury (Fig. 5.6) and Buildings Farm in Great Dunmow, a small number of fifth-century sherds were recovered from the upper fills of late Romano-British ditches suggesting that they remained open and were still being manured (Wymer and Brown 1995, 46; Lavender 1997, 81). In other cases it is less clear-cut whether there was actually continuity in occupation, such as the *Grubenhaus* at Chadwell St Mary which lies close to a Roman villa but was associated with only sixth-century pottery (Lavender 1998b). While some Romano-British and early medieval settlements were long-lived, others were occupied relatively briefly, suggesting a landscape that was constantly evolving (the same is true of the evidence from field systems: see below). At Frog Hall Farm in Fingringhoe, for example, a scatter of sixth- to seventh-century pottery was unrelated to any Romano-British or later settlement (Brooks 2002).

The evolution of fieldscapes in southern East Anglia

So far the discussion has been largely about settlement, with a picture emerging of a dispersed Romano-British pattern that focused on the river valleys but extended up onto the interfluvial areas, with a contraction of the areas occupied in the early medieval period but no widespread landscape desertion. Another aspect of the countryside that is crucial to our understanding of the origins of the historic landscape is that of the field systems, although this has to date been a rather neglected topic. The lighter soils (ideal for cropmarks) and extensive development-led excavations particularly in the east and south of Essex mean, however, that there is now a large corpus of data, although unfortunately there has been less work on the Boulder Clays of south-west Suffolk (Carr 1991: a trawl through the annual 'Archaeology in Suffolk' summaries in the *Proceedings of the Suffolk Institute of Archaeology and History* shows that the bias in fieldwork in favour of the north and east of the county remains). A review of this evidence across Essex is, for the first time, showing some fascinating trends.

The fluidity of Iron Age/Romano-British field systems

One consistent picture that is emerging from large-scale excavations is that late prehistoric and Romano-British field systems in southern East Anglia were usually relatively localized and short-lived, being maintained for a few centuries, abandoned, and then replaced by a new enclosure system often on a different orientation. One of the clearest examples is at North Shoebury (Fig. 5.6) where a rectangular enclosure and fragmentary traces of a ditched field system were laid out on a NNW–SSE orientation in the Middle Bronze Age (*c*.1500–1000 BC), being replaced in the Late Bronze Age (*c*.1000–600 BC) by a field system oriented NW–SE that continued in use into the Early Iron Age (until *c*.300 BC). This area was then abandoned and a new north–south oriented field system laid out to the west in what had presumably been an area of open pasture. The orientation of this Middle–Late Iron Age system was maintained into the Roman period when the area of fields expanded eastwards, although in the third century there was a further remodelling. Several late Roman ditches must have remained open for a while, as they contained sherds of 'Early Saxon' pottery, while a small fifth-century cremation and inhumation cemetery also indicates occupation in the area. Other examples of field systems in Essex that underwent frequent remodelling include Buildings Farm near Great Dunmow (Lavender 1997), Chigborough (Wallis and Waughman 1998, 76–98),

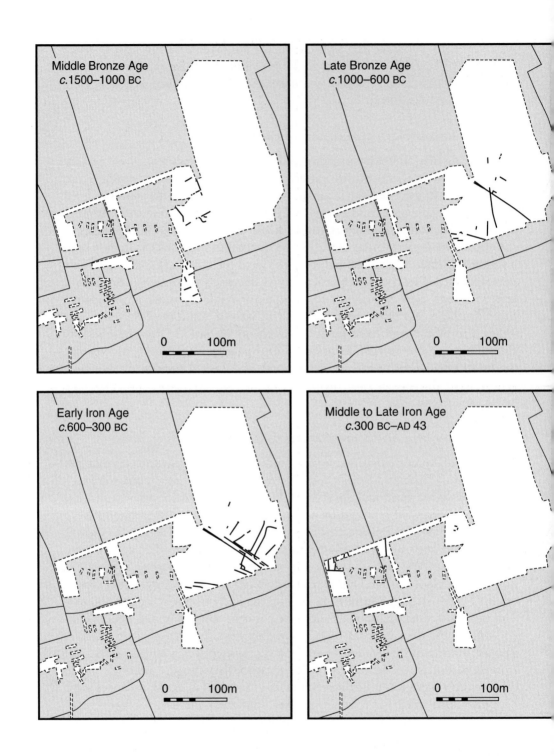

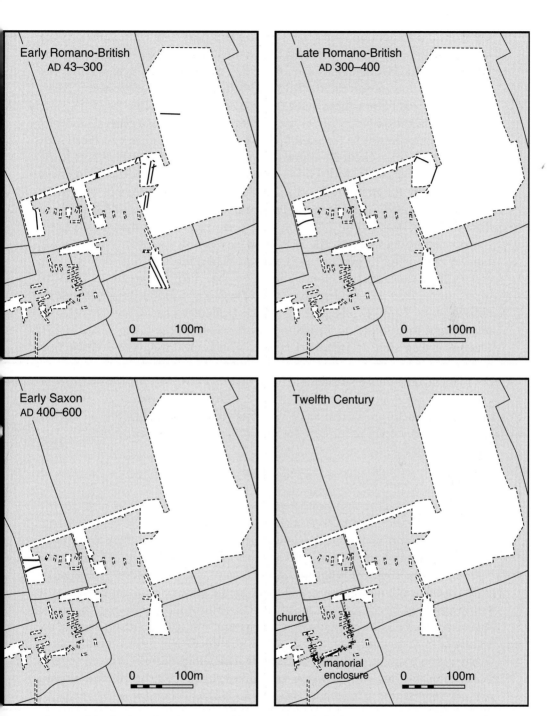

Fig. 5.6. The fluidity of prehistoric and Romano-British field systems at North Shoebury in south-east Essex (after Wymer and Brown 1995, figs. 14, 19, 22, 25, 31, and 36). Drawing by Adam Wainwright.

Curry Hill in Rettendon, and Downhouse Farm near East Hanningfield (Dale *et al.* 2005), Lodge Farm in St Osyth (Germany 2007, 10), the New Source Works in Castle Hedingham (Lavender 1996), and the Rayne Bypass (Smoothy 1989). In south-west Suffolk, the Romano-British landscape at Preston St Mary was reorganized two or three times (Martin *et al.* 1996, 482).

Around the third century AD, Going (1996, 101) has noted a general tendency for small enclosures to be replaced by larger fields, and this has since been seen at Buildings Farm in Great Dunmow (Lavender 1997), Founton Hall near Little Oakley (Barford 2002), Mill Hill in Braintree (Humphrey 2002), Monument Borrow Pit in Rawreth (Dale *et al.* 2005), Ship Lane in Aveley (Foreman and Maynard 2002), and Strood Hall (near Great Dunmow) and the Rayne Roundabout (Timby *et al.* 2007). It is also worth stressing that there clearly was not a continuous fieldscape in Roman Essex, with a number of large-scale excavations failing to produce evidence for field ditches of this date (e.g. the eastern area excavated at North Shoebury: Fig. 5.6). Along the new A130, for example, Iron Age field systems were present at Sandon Brook, Windmill Hill, Shotgate Farm, Doublegate Lane, and Dollymans Farm, but all went out of use, and there were no Romano-British replacements (Dale *et al.* 2005). The same was seen at Stifford Clays in Thurrock during the construction of the new A13 (Wilkinson 1988, 23), Slough House Farm to the north of the Blackwater estuary (Wallis and Waughman 1998, 41), and St Osyth near Clacton-on-Sea (Germany 2003b). At Great Holts Farm, part of an extensive mid Roman enclosure system has a very clear boundary (ditch 198) with what was presumably open pasture to the south (Fig. 5.7; Germany 2003a).

Fieldscapes of continuity

There is, however, a less consistent picture emerging with regard to the relationship between Romano-British field systems and the historic landscape. Great Holts Farm in Boreham typifies the situation, in that there appears to be both continuity and discontinuity within the same site (Fig. 5.7; Germany 2003a). To the south of what was an extensive area excavation, the Roman field system was presumably abandoned, as the historic landscape overlies it unconformably. In contrast, to the north, elements of the late Roman enclosure system are on the same orientation as the historic landscape, with one boundary having been re-dug in the medieval period (ditches 63 and 59). A few sherds of 'Early Saxon' pottery, including some with *Schlickung*-treated surfaces, suggest occupation into the fifth century, and although the sixth to ninth centuries are not represented within the excavation, the tendency for early medieval settlements to shift around means that occupation of this period could easily lie in adjacent fields. Building 440 is dated to the tenth to thirteenth centuries while Great Holts Farm immediately to the east is documented from the late thirteenth century (Reaney 1935, 241).

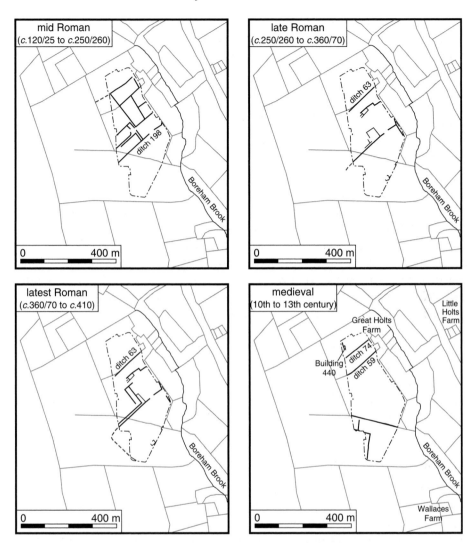

Fig. 5.7. Excavations to the south-west of Great Holts Farm in Boreham. The northern part of the Romano-British enclosure complex is clearly on the same orientation as the historic landscape, though to the south field systems have been reorganized since (after Germany 2003a, figs. 4, 12, 13, 17, 48, 49, and 50).

Potential continuity in field systems is also seen elsewhere. At the New Source Works in Castle Hedingham and Buildings Farm near Great Dunmow the latest Roman-period field systems are on the same orientation as the historic landscape (Lavender 1996; 1997). The same similarity in orientation between late Romano-British and medieval features is also seen at East View Close in Radwinter (Havis 2001), Palmer's School in Grays (Rodwell 1983), Shillingstone Field in Great Sampford (Garwood 1998), William Edwards School in Grays (Lavender 1998a), Stebbing Green (Bedwin and Bedwin 1999), and Wendens Ambo (Hodder 1982). A mid Roman ditch at Stebbingford must have survived as an earthwork into the twelfth century, as it was incorporated into the layout of a farmstead (Medlycott 1996, 100). At Bishops Park College in Clacton-on-Sea the Roman field system was re-excavated in the medieval period, implying either continuity in its use, or, if abandoned, that it survived as a set of earthworks (Letch 2005). At Founton Hall near Little Oakley a late Roman field system was on the same orientation as the historic landscape, with fourth-century ditches containing fifth- to sixth-century pottery in their upper fills; significantly, the underlying Iron Age/early Romano-British landscape was on a different orientation, giving a date around the third century for the creation of the framework of today's historic landscape (Barford 2002). At Chignall St James, the enclosure surrounding a palatial Roman villa must have survived into the medieval period in order to influence the course taken by a trackway, while a Roman or later field system to the south perpetuated the line of a late Roman enclosure system (Clarke 1998, 65). In south-west Suffolk, the latest Romano-British landscape at Preston St Mary appears to share alignments with the historic landscape (Martin *et al.* 1996, 482).

The 'coaxial' landscapes

There have been various claims that planned landscapes of Roman or pre-Roman date survived in the landscape of 'greater East Anglia'. Some have tried to identify Roman centuriation, although the modest ideas of Haverfield (1920), based on two straight, parallel roads west of Colchester, and the more ambitious claims of Coles (1939) that such planning can be identified across north and west Essex, have been rightly rejected (Dilke 1971, 191–5). In a number of places across East Anglia it has been suggested that the historic landscape has a 'coaxial' layout based around a series of sinuous but roughly parallel boundaries that appear to be prehistoric in origin as they are overlain by Roman roads (e.g. Little Waltham in central Essex: Fig. 5.8; for general discussions see Williamson 1987; 1998; Rippon 1991; Hinton 1997; Martin 1999a, 52–8). There has been much discussion of the date and character of these landscapes, with Wilkinson (1988) and Rippon (1991) suggesting that some of the southern Essex examples are medieval in date, and Hinton (1997) questioning the date and character of the East Anglian examples (and see Williamson 1998 for a response). In the most recent review, Martin and Satchell (forthcoming) suggest that rather than extensive, planned landscapes, these coaxial systems actually consist of a series of smaller blocks, and that while those around Scole do indeed appear to incorporate late prehistoric boundaries, those around South Elmham St Michael are probably early medieval in date.

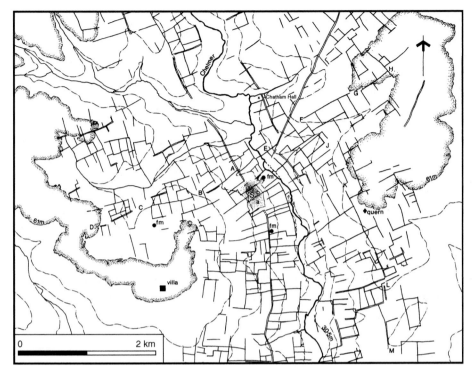

Fig. 5.8. The coaxial landscape at Little Waltham, preserved within the fabric of the historic landscape and apparently cut by Roman roads (Drury 1978, fig. 74).

Although just outside this region, work at Broxbourne and Wormley, in eastern Hertfordshire, has used survey and excavation to establish a Romano-British date for a very similar coaxial landscape (Bryant *et al.* 2005), but unfortunately the dating evidence from Essex is at best fragmentary. In the Slade Valley, at Saffron Walden, in the far north-west of the county, Bassett (1982, 7–9, 14, 30) suggests that a Late Iron Age ditch was on the same orientation as the coaxial landscape there, and that a minor Roman settlement was laid around one of its major elements. The place name Walden (*Waela-denu*) means 'valley of the Britons/serfs', which implies the survival of a native population in the area which lends support to the possibility that a Romano-British landscape of fields and roads could have remained in use throughout the early medieval period (Reaney 1935, 537; Bassett 1982, 10). A cemetery of perhaps 200 inhumations excavated in 1830 and 1876 appears to date from the Romano-British and early medieval periods (Bassett 1982, 9–12). Some burials were associated with third- to fourth-century grave goods and oriented north to south, although a majority were unaccompanied and oriented east to west. None was associated with Anglo-Saxon artefacts although there was a scatter of sand and grass-tempered pottery (broadly fifth to ninth century) from the site; distinctively 'Anglo-Saxon' decorated pottery was noticeably absent. A Scandinavian necklace from one of the graves probably dates from the ninth century (Bassett 1982, 9–15, 80). Overall, although based on antiquarian excavations, Saffron Walden suggests the survival of a native Romano-British community at the very margins of the area around Great Chesterford and southern Cambridgeshire that saw extensive Anglo-Saxon immigration, supporting the evidence for continuity from Williamson's nearby fieldwalking surveys on the Boulder Clays to the south (see above).

Around Braintree, Chelmsford, and Witham other coaxial landscapes appear to be cut by Roman roads (Drury 1976; Drury and Rodwell 1980, 62; Rodwell 1993, 58–9), as is also the case at Little Waltham in the Chelmer Valley to the north (Fig. 5.8; Drury 1978, 134–6). Here, along with the rather more fragmentary and less convincing system at Rivenhall in the Cressing Brook Valley, excavations have established that elements of the historic landscape date back to the Late Iron Age (Rodwell and Rodwell 1986, 68, figs. 8, 10, and 50). Further tentative support for the hypothesis that these coaxial landscapes are Late Iron Age in origin is the way that they are best preserved on the lighter soils of river valleys, which surveys and excavations across Essex have shown were the most intensively occupied, including in the early medieval period, as opposed to the heavier soils of the interfluvial areas that tended to have been less densely populated or even abandoned in the early medieval period.

In the south of Essex there are also areas of historic landscape with apparently planned layouts but which differ significantly from the long, sinuous, coaxial systems in having a more rectilinear layout (Rippon 1991; Short 2006, 113, fig. 5.6). To the south of Wickford, the historic landscape is structured around a series of long, straight boundaries that appear to have been laid out according to Roman surveying methods (Fig. 5.9). One of these boundaries proved to be a Roman road upon excavation (Rodwell 1966), although Rippon (1991, 57) was cautious in ascribing a date to the landscape suggesting that 'maybe this is very fragmented centuriation, or more likely, an example of "a land assignation made in multiples of *actus* by someone with at least a vague notion of Roman surveying" (Dilke 1971:193, discussing Ripe in Sussex)'. Recent excavations within this landscape at Monument Borrow Pit, along the line of the new A130 to the east of Great Fanton Hall in North Benfleet, however, have revealed a field system dating to the Late Iron Age to early Roman period, which included a trackway whose line was perpetuated in the mid to late Roman period when a ditch was dug along its length: all of these excavated features conform to the orientation of the historic landscape, suggesting a late pre-Roman date for its origin (Fig. 5.10; Dale *et al.* 2005).

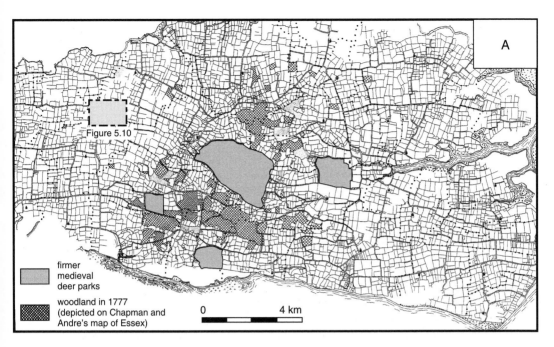

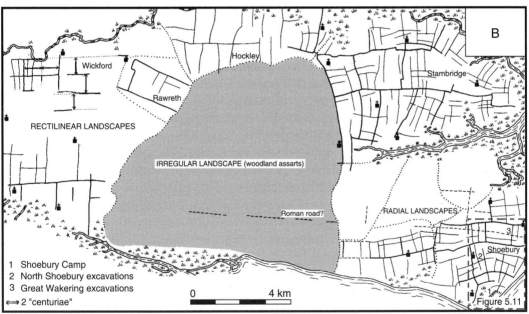

Fig. 5.9. The historic landscape of south-east Essex. (A) the field boundary pattern *c.*1840 (based on Tithe maps), excluding areas of wetland reclamation and the enclosure of medieval deer parks. Woodland depicted on the 1777 map of Chapman and Andre is also shown. (B) an analysis of this historic landscape, showing the area characterized by woodland assarting, the rectilinear planned landscape south of Wickford (part of which has been excavated at Great Fanton Hall: Fig. 5.10), and the radial landscapes around Stambridge and Shoebury (see Figs. 5.6 and 5.11) (after Rippon 1991, figs. 5 and 6).

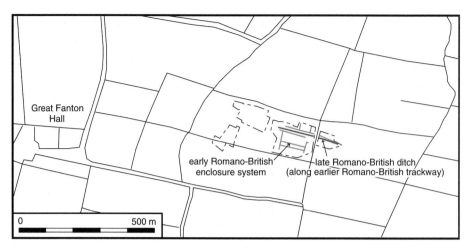

Fig. 5.10. Excavations at the Monument Borrow Pit, east of Great Fanton Hall, showing a Romano-British enclosure system on the same alignment as a clearly planned area of historic landscape (see Fig. 5.9A for location).

Further west, but also on the London Clay, the historic landscape also has a rectilinear layout, but rather than a single planned network of roads and fields, this landscape can be broken down into a series of discrete blocks laid out around roughly parallel boundaries that may have originated as trackways linking coastal districts with the interior (Rippon 1991), the same process that may have occurred south of Dartmoor at Bittaford (Fig. 4.8). In various locations these areas of landscape are clearly medieval in date, as they overlie Romano-British enclosure systems that are on a different alignment. To the east, in the Rochford Hundred near Southend-on-Sea, another carefully planned landscape has a radial pattern that is on a different orientation from, and so clearly post-dates, the late Romano-British field system, with 'Early Saxon' pottery in its upper fills, excavated at North Shoebury (Figs. 5.6, 5.9, and 5.11). Further Roman-British ditches on a different orientation from the historic landscape have been excavated at Great Wakering, to the north (Rippon 1991), and South Shoebury to the south (Mattinson 2005).[1]

A third area of planned landscape in southern Essex covers the Dengie peninsula (Drury and Rodwell 1978). This is a remarkable system of almost square blocks of fields and roads that clearly pre-dates the late eleventh- or early twelfth-century church at Asheldham which overlay one of the major axial elements of the landscape. A ditch perpendicular to this axial boundary had a series of ten recuts, most of which were aceramic but the last containing

---

[1] Note that contrary to an earlier assumption (Rippon 1991) that the D-shaped enclosure towards the apex of this radially planned landscape was a Danish fort that the Anglo-Saxon Chronicle records was constructed at Shoebury in 894 (Swanton 1996, 87), subsequent excavations have shown that this earthwork is Middle Iron Age in date (Gifford and Partners 1999; Mattinson 2005).

Fig. 5.11. The radial planned landscape at Shoebury in south-east
Essex, as depicted on the Tithe
maps of 1840 (for location see
Fig. 5.9B). A *terminus post quem*
is provided by the excavated late
Romano-British field systems at
North Shoebury and Great Wakering.

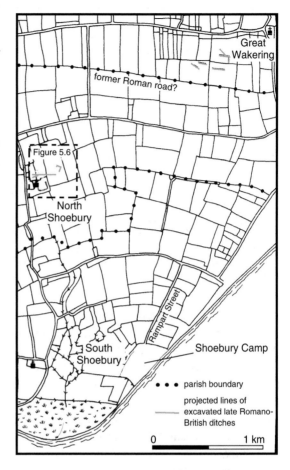

grass-tempered pottery originally dated to the seventh century. More recent
work on grass-tempered pottery in Essex suggests that it was used in very
small amounts during the fifth century, but only became common in the sixth
century; it was contemporary with the use of Ipswich Ware and was certainly
still in use in the ninth century (giving a *terminus ante quem* of this date for
the planned landscape), but not the tenth.[2] The other dating evidence for the
Dengie landscape is its relationship to parish boundaries. Although it is clear
that some boundaries follow major axial elements—notably roads—others do
not, zigzagging through, and clearly post-dating, the field systems. In an elegant
piece of analysis, Morris (2006, figs. 7.10–7.13) has identified some of these
parishes as being relatively recent creations, being carved out of what were once
larger territories, and when these are removed the relationship between the

---

[2] Based on its associations at sites such as Othona (Bradwell-on-Sea), Nazingbury, Wicken Bonhunt,
Heybridge, Waltham Abbey, Mucking, Barking Abbey, London, and Colchester (Rodwell 1976;
Huggins 1978; Wade 1980; Drury and Wickenden 1982; Huggins 1988; Hamerow 1993; Redknap
1991; Vince and Jenner 1991, 48; Cotter 2000, 23–6).

older parish boundaries and major axial elements within the Dengie landscape becomes even clearer. Along with the excavations at Asheldham, this suggests that the planned landscape of Dengie is earlier than tenth century. It is tempting to suggest that this major planned landscape is Roman, and associated with the shore fort at Bradwell, although there is little other evidence that the shore forts impacted on their hinterlands in this way. Bearing in mind the extensive landscape changes seen across southern and eastern England around the eighth century that are the focus of this book, a similar date for the Dengie landscape is not implausible.

Fieldscapes of discontinuity

In contrast to this evidence for the survival of Romano-British field systems in some places, in other cases they appear to have been abandoned and were on a different orientation from the medieval landscape. At Gun Hill in West Tilbury, Woodham Walter, Woodside Industrial Park in Birchanger, How-ells Farm near Heybridge, and Elm Park in Ardleigh, the Romano-British field systems were abandoned in the second century (Drury and Rodwell 1973; Buckley and Hedges 1987; Medlycott 1994; Wallis and Waughman 1998, 117; Brooks 2001). At Lofts Farm, Slough House Farm, and Chig-borough, all to the north of the Blackwater estuary, an extensive cropmark complex of trackways and field systems, dated through excavation to the Roman period, was on a different orientation from a historic landscape that certainly existed by the twelfth century, when an enclosure was dug con-forming to the latter's orientation (Maldon Archaeological Group n.d.; Wallis and Waughman 1998, 41–53, 76–98). These sites are all on light sands and gravel, but the same is seen on heavier clay soils. At Coggeshall (Isser-lin 1995), Curry Hill in Rettendon (Dale *et al.* 2005), Downhouse Farm (Dale *et al.* 2005), Rayne Roundabout and Strood Hall along the A120 between Stanstead Airport and Braintree (Timby *et al.* 2007), Ivy Chimneys in Witham (Turner 1999), and Newman's End in Matching (Guttman 2000), late Roman ditches were similarly on a different orientation from the historic landscape. At Preston St Mary, in southern Suffolk, the medieval field sys-tem also lies unconformably over the late Romano-British landscape (Martin *et al.* 1996).

At the Rayne Bypass (Smoothy 1989) late Roman ditches were also on a different orientation from the overlying medieval field systems, and these late Roman ditches had sherds of 'Early Saxon' pottery in their upper fills. This was also seen at North Shoebury (see above) where there was no evidence from the sixth to tenth centuries, although around the eleventh or twelfth centuries a rectangular enclosure was constructed to the east of the parish church (the present structure of which dates from the early thirteenth century: RCHME 1923, 101). This enclosure, and a number of other nearby features,

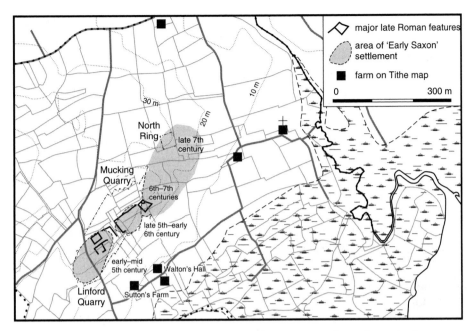

Fig. 5.12. The migration of the 'Early Saxon' settlement at Mucking, Essex, in the context of the later historic landscape (based on the Tithe map of 1846: ERO D/P 108/27/2).

were on the same orientation as the rectilinear pattern of fields that make up the historic landscape of today and were first mapped in 1703 (ERO TS/M5). The character of the North Shoebury field system is suggestive of closes held in severalty, not open field. At Mucking, in contrast, the late Roman field system appears to have gone out of use around the mid fourth century, and it was in this landscape of 'agri deserti' that the Germanic immigrants established their settlement in the fifth century. A number of the Romano-British boundaries must have survived as earthworks, as they affected the plan of the fifth- to seventh-century settlement, although the medieval landscape—including what appears to have been a small open field system—was laid out on a different orientation sometime after the early eighth century (the date of the latest pottery from the excavated 'Early Saxon' settlement (Fig. 5.12: Clark 1993, 21–2; Hamerow 1993, fig. 51)).

   A number of key conclusions have emerged from this overview of the development of late prehistoric and Romano-British field systems in southern East Anglia, and their relationship to those of the medieval period. First, field systems in many areas were relatively discrete and surrounded by areas of unenclosed land, especially by the fourth century: there was no continuous fieldscape until the creation of today's historic landscape. Secondly, in the later prehistoric and Roman periods field systems were relatively unstable, with cycles of creation, abandonment, and re-creation every few hundred years: the roughly ten centuries of comparative stability since the creation of the framework of today's historic landscape is quite unprecedented. Thirdly, there are many examples of Romano-British field systems that went out of use (although often after the fifth century) and are unrelated to the medieval landscape that lies unconformably on top, implying a discontinuity in landscape exploitation, although these tend to occur in what can be regarded as physically marginal areas in terms of arable-based agriculture, notably very light soils of the Thames and Blackwater gravel terraces, and heavy soils of the Boulder Clay interfluvial plateaux (confirming the evidence from fieldwalking surveys that these areas were abandoned: Williamson 1986). Even here, however, palaeoenvironmental evidence does not indicate a woodland regeneration, suggesting at least continued grazing (Havis and Brooks 2004a; 2004b). Fourthly, however, there are also many cases of Romano-British and medieval field systems that appear to show continuity. Sometimes elements of both continuity and discontinuity are seen within a single site such as Great Holts (see above) as well as cropmark complexes such as Ardleigh (Fig. 5.13; Brown 1999, 180–4, fig. 4) and Lofts Farm, near Maldon (Wallis and Waughman 1998, fig. 130). Both on individual sites, and across Essex as a whole, the overall picture appears to be one of partial survival of Romano-British landscapes into the medieval period, and partial discontinuity that suggests a decrease in the intensity with which the landscape was exploited, but not its abandonment. There is also some patterning in the topographical location of these landscapes of discontinuity which tends to occur most frequently in areas of soil that were less favourable for arable-based farming, although this was not always the case: the early medieval site at Mucking, for example, is on a gravel terrace some distance from areas of medieval settlement, whereas North Shoebury lies on the fertile brickearths of south-east Essex that are amongst the most fertile soils in the county. What both these examples of discontinuity have in common, however, is that the Romano-British/early medieval landscapes were replaced by planned field systems: the open fields of Mucking (laid out sometime after the early eighth century), and radial block fields, apparently always held in severalty, of the Rochford Hundred (datable to the sixth to tenth centuries).

This leaves one crucial question: does the close relationship between some Romano-British and medieval field systems imply that they have remained in constant use, or might the earlier fields have been abandoned but preserved as earthworks that were then reused? Observations by the author, and a sequence of cartographic sources showing modern field systems that have gone out of use on the Benfleet Downs in south-east Essex, show that previously cleared land is enveloped with brambles within a few years, closely followed by the invasion of hawthorn scrub, making the area impassable within around ten years. After about thirty years the area is covered in light woodland. The question is, if medieval farmers had then cleared such woodland and scrub, would significant earthworks from the earlier field systems have survived, and if so

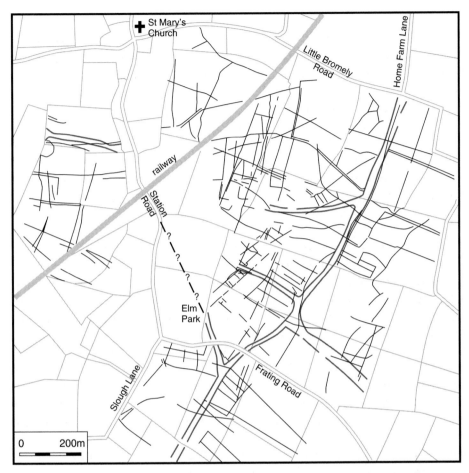

Fig. 5.13. Relationship between the historic landscape (taken from the First Edition Ordnance Survey Six Inch maps) and cropmark complex at Ardleigh in Essex showing partial continuity/survival of the major structural elements (after Brown 1999, figs. 3 and 4). Drawing by Adam Wainwright.

could they have been reused? Again, observations from the Benfleet Downs are instructive. In bramble- and scrub-infested, recently abandoned fields the dense undergrowth makes former field boundaries practically invisible. The process of clearance—cutting and clearing vegetation, pulling out stumps, and ploughing the ground—is also likely to destroy simple earthen banks and ditches (as is the tradition in this county where suitable stone for building field boundaries is lacking). Earthworks are in fact more visible in mature woodland, as the tree canopy restricts the growth of ground vegetation, although the process of clearing mature woodland is likely to cause as much disturbance if not more. Overall, therefore, if a field system is abandoned for more than a decade or so, then it is unlikely that its boundaries will survive the subsequent woodland clearance.

The palaeoenvironmental evidence

So far discussion has focused on the sometimes close physical relationship between the Romano-British and medieval landscapes, but a crucial question that has emerged is whether this necessarily means that the landscape was occupied and used continuously. Even into the 1990s, the traditional view that the early medieval period saw an extensive woodland regeneration can be found in the literature for the history and archaeology of this region (e.g. Brooks 1992, 49), while Oliver Rackham (1976, 57) even suggested that 'village and hamlet names ending in -ley are strikingly concentrated on the Huntingdon and Suffolk borders [of Cambridgeshire], suggesting that here the early Anglo-Saxons found and colonized tracts of wildwood that the Romans had left'; his figure 9 shows a similar cluster of -ley names on the Cambridgeshire/Hertfordshire/Essex border which by implication were similarly carved out of wildwood. Archaeological surveys in a number of places have also revealed cases of Roman material from areas that in the medieval period were wooded, but these tend to be on areas of poorly drained clays on the interfluvial plateaux (e.g. the Boulder Clays of north-west Essex: Williamson 1984, 228; the Rayleigh Hills in south-east Essex: Rippon 1999, 23).

Fortunately there is now increasing palaeoenvironmental evidence with which to explore the extent of any post-Roman woodland regeneration. A national overview of tree ring dating does suggest that a number of timbers used in medieval structures started to grow around the fifth century and several examples are from Essex (Barking Abbey, Mersea Island, and Slough House Farm: Tyers *et al.* 1994, 18–21, fig. 3.5). This does not, however, necessarily suggest the widespread regeneration of woodland over what had been agricultural land, as these timbers may simply be from hedgerows that were no longer being laid, or from former coppiced woodland that was left unmanaged. Palaeoenvironmental sequences provide a better indication of land-use history. The only possible evidence for post-Roman woodland regeneration is from the Mar Dyke in Thurrock, where there is a slight increase in tree pollen at the very top of a sequence that, although not radiocarbon dated, may be early medieval (Wilkinson 1988, 109–14, fig. 98).

The majority of the evidence, however, suggests that the early medieval landscape in Essex remained largely open with no woodland regeneration. In the Crouch estuary, a peat layer with radiocarbon dates from its upper and lower surfaces of 1610+/−70 BP (cal. AD 380–540) and 1380+/−80 BP (cal. AD 604–81) produced very low levels of tree pollen, suggesting an open landscape (Crouch site 9: Wilkinson and Murphy 1995, 49). At Chigborough and Slough House Farm, north of the Blackwater estuary, samples from a series of seventh-century features show a less wooded (in fact almost treeless) landscape compared to the Late Iron Age/early Roman period, and with far greater cereal cultivation (Wallis and Waughman 1998, 172–204). At Stanstead Airport, on the Boulder Clay plateau in north-west Essex, pollen and plant macrofossils from the 'BRS' palaeochannel suggest a largely open landscape in the fifth to sixth centuries with some cereal cultivation in the vicinity; the levels of microscopic charcoal similarly indicate human activity. Around the late sixth or seventh centuries the palaeochannel started to dry out and there was an increase in cereal cultivation (Havis and Brooks 2004b, 350–4). At the Sandon Culvert site, in the mid Essex Chelmer Valley, plant macrofossils from a sequence of channel fill that accumulated between the Roman period (1770+/–70 BP, cal. AD 117–413) and around the twelfth century (869+/–70BP, cal. AD 1029–1265) suggests an open landscape throughout, with relatively little woodland (Murphy 1994, 25–6). None of these sequences shows a significant change in land-use around the eighth century.

Historians have often regarded Essex as a relatively well-wooded county in the eleventh century, contributing to a view that its landscape of dispersed settlement was the result of relatively late colonization (e.g. Roden 1973). Oliver Rackham (1980) suggests that 20 per cent of Essex was wooded in 1086, compared to 15 per cent in the rest of England, although he acknowledges that the measure used in the Domesday survey of Essex—'woodland for x swine'—is rather imprecise. Locating this woodland is also especially difficult due to the practice of enclaving, whereby some of a manor's resources was held in detached parcels some distance away. Round (1903) has shown how this explains another curiosity of the Essex Domesday—the 'pasture for x sheep', which is recorded for some inland manors but actually lay in the coastal marshes—while Rackham (1986b, fig. 14) and Rippon (2000a, fig. 69) have shown the extent to which medieval woodland was similarly enclaved. Bryn Morris's (2005, fig. 16; 2006, figs. 9.8–10) careful mapping of woodland-indicative place names against the topography also shows that it was not evenly distributed across the landscape as some earlier, often smaller-scale, distribution maps suggest (Fig. 5.14; cf. Darby 1952, fig. 61; Roberts and Wrathmell 2000, fig. 24).

The value of place-name evidence

Baker (2006b) has recently reviewed the place-name evidence in Essex, Hertfordshire, Middlesex, Buckinghamshire, and southern Cambridgeshire for the survival of a native British population, and the extent of immigration from the continent. It is claimed that there are place names containing pre-English elements, although they occur both in central Essex and Hertfordshire, where archaeological evidence suggests little fifth- or sixth-century Germanic settlement, and in the far south and east of Essex where the opposite is true (Baker 2006b, fig. 4.1). The interpretation of these place names also seems far from

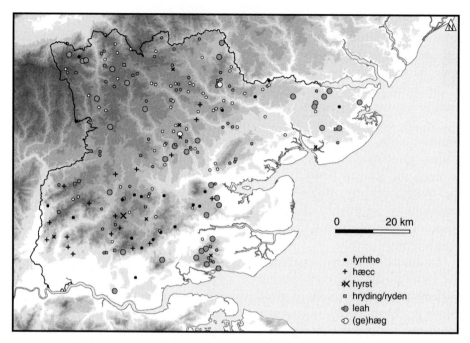

Fig. 5.14. The distribution of woodland-indicative place names in Essex mapped against a background of topography showing its uneven distribution across the landscape (Morris 2005, fig. 16, © Bryn Morris).

clear: Childerditch, in southern Essex, for example, clearly contains the Old English *dīc*, 'ditch', while the first element may be related to the river names Chelt (as in Cheltenham) and Chilt (in Sussex), a pre-English hill name cognate with Chiltern, an Old English word related to the Norwegian *Kult*, meaning 'lump' or 'hillock', or an Old English personal name: quite why it is therefore regarded as a 'certain or probable' pre-English name element (Baker 2006b, 141, fig. 4.1), when we clearly have little idea what it means, is a mystery to this author. The distribution of pre-English river names similarly shows little spatial patterning. Certain Old English place-name elements—such as *dūn* and *ford* (Baker 2006b, figs. 5.4–5)—might show a tendency to occur in areas with archaeological evidence for fifth- to sixth-century Germanic settlement, although most do not. Overall, it is difficult to disagree with Baker's (2006b, 216) own conclusion that 'having looked in detail at Old English topographical place names it is difficult to draw firm conclusions about their worth as indicators of early Old English influence in the Essex and Chiltern regions', or that 'it may be doubted whether place names can really be used as a guide to Germanic cultural movement' (Baker 2006b, 240).

Where are the 'Middle Saxon' settlements?

So far the picture that is emerging is one of gradual change and evolution in the Essex landscape in the Roman and earliest medieval (fifth to seventh centuries) periods, with continuity in some areas, discontinuity in others, but no widespread transformation of the landscape and certainly no widespread woodland regeneration. Throughout this period settlements and field systems were established, modified, and abandoned, with some being longer lasting than others. The landscape appears to have been in a constant but gradual state of evolution, albeit with certain periods that may have experienced greater change than others, such as the mid Roman period when some landscapes may have been restructured, and the late fourth or fifth century, when there appears to have been a contraction of settlement from areas such as the heavy interfluvial clays of the Boulder Clay plateau.

It has been suggested that across southern England significant numbers of excavated 'Early Saxon' settlements were abandoned around the seventh century (e.g. Mucking in Essex, West Stow in Suffolk, Bishopstone in Sussex, Chalton in Hampshire), which led to the model of a 'Middle Saxon shuffle' whereby Early Saxon sites on lighter soils were abandoned in favour of richer soils in the valleys around the late seventh century (Arnold and Wardle 1981; Moreland 2000, 86–7). One problem with this idea is that most of the major excavations of 'Early Saxon' settlements are in locations that extensive field survey is suggesting are not typical of that period, such as the high gravel terrace at Mucking. Hamerow (1991; 2002, 121–4) has also argued that, as many settlements have not been completely investigated, their final phases may lie beyond the edge of the excavations, and Mucking can also be reinterpreted in this way (Fig. 5.12). The eastwards migration of the settlement was clearly demonstrated by Hamerow (1993), and if we place Mucking in an even wider context we see that from the fifth to the seventh centuries the focus of occupation shifted at least 1.2 km south-west to north-east, this distance being calculated from the centre of fifth-century occupation that includes the Linford Quarry site to the west of the main Mucking excavation (Barton 1962), as far north as the 'North Ring' site excavated in 1978 separately from the main Mucking campaign where the occupation is dated to the late seventh century (Bond 1988, 20, 45–51). Just *c.*900 m further west lies the parish church, the earliest fabric of which is (?)twelfth or thirteenth century (RCHME 1923, 94). This raises the possibility that rather than there being a sudden dislocation of settlement, whereby it shifted from the gravel terrace to the lower-lying site occupied by the parish church—the 'Middle Saxon shuffle' model—it actually ended up there by continued, gradual, migration. Also significant is that a few sherds of Ipswich Ware were found from the far east of the site which if

Blinkhorn's (1999) redating is correct takes the occupation of the settlement into the eighth century (and see Hamerow 1993, 22). The discovery of two early eighth-century *sceattas* from the area immediately beyond the edge of the excavations (the precise location is not known) supports the idea that the settlement at Mucking continued to be occupied until at least that date but continued to shift its location (Helena Hamerow and Michael Metcalf pers. comm.). Another significant feature of this site is that the early medieval settlement appears to have been replaced by an open field system whose strips and furlong boundaries were still preserved within the historic landscape when it was first mapped in 1846 (Fig. 5.12; ERO D/P 108/27/2; Clark 1993, 22). After several centuries of migration, maybe there was a transformation of the landscape associated with the creation of the open fields sometime after the early eighth century. The open fields did not last long, however, as Walton's Hall and Sutton's Farm, which appear to lie in the southern part of the now enclosed open field, are recorded as early as 1199 and 1220 respectively (Reaney 1935, 164).

So where are the eighth-century settlements in Essex? There have been a number of important excavations of what in this region are called 'Middle Saxon' sites, although these mostly relate to the higher echelons of society, notably the high-status site at Wicken Bonhunt (Wade 1980) that Rippon (1996b, 121) has suggested was a probable *villa regalis*, Christian communities at Barking (MacGowan 1987; Redknap 1991; Hull 2002), Nazingbury (Huggins 1978; Bascombe 1987), and Waltham Abbey (Huggins 1988), and a possible eighth- to early ninth-century coastal trading site near Barking Abbey (Hull 2002). Unfortunately, these sites tell us little about the wider rural landscape. A re-examination of a number of 'Early Saxon' sites, however, suggests that there may have been a closer relationship between the Romano-British and medieval landscapes than was previously thought.

In a number of cases, 'Early Saxon' settlements and cemeteries have been discovered during the excavation of earlier enclosures that were visible as cropmarks.[3] Understandably, these mostly rescue excavations focused on major cropmark complexes, but, if the early medieval settlements had migrated to the extent of that at Mucking, then they would soon have drifted beyond the areas that were later to be excavated. At the Orsett Cock, for example, three *Grubenhäuser* to the east of the cropmark enclosure were associated with mid-fifth- to mid-sixth-century pottery, including distinctively early *Schlickung*-treated ware (Milton 1987, 30–1), whereas three *Grubenhäuser* to the west, within the old enclosure, were sixth century in date (Carter 1998, 102). Did the settlement continue to drift further west, beyond the edge of the excavations?

---

[3] e.g. Ardale School (Wilkinson 1988, 42–57); Gun Hill in Tilbury (Drury and Rodwell 1973); Frog Hall Farm in Fingringhoe (Brooks 2002); Orsett Cock (Carter 1998); Orsett Causewayed Enclosure (Hedges and Buckley 1985); Springfield Lyons (Tyler and Major 2005).

And what are the origins of Barrington's Farm immediately to the north, first documented in 1548, and possibly named after the Barrington family recorded in Orsett in 1482 (Reaney 1935, 166)? Another example of early medieval settlement migration potentially ending up at an extant farmstead could be Little Oakley, where small amounts of eighth- or ninth-century 'Middle Saxon' pottery were found halfway between a Romano-British to late fifth-century settlement and the Domesday manor of Founton Hall (Barford 2002, 164).

The problem that 'Middle Saxon' settlements may have drifted away from archaeologically very visible sites, such as enclosures and villas, and so have simply not been identified, is compounded by the very limited material culture that appears to have been used on most lower-status sites in this period and the ephemeral traces that the timber buildings have left. On the gravel terraces north of the Blackwater estuary, for example, what has been described as a 'boat-shaped' building (structure 38) constructed with earth-fast posts was not associated with any material culture, although parallels for the building are most common from the eighth to tenth centuries (Wallis and Waughman 1998, 98, 106–8). A group of eight seventh- to eighth-century loom weights have been found as packing in a post hole of a rectangular building just 110 m to the north (Tyler 1986). Another aceramic rectangular timber building built from earth-fast posts has been excavated at Takeley, but here a radiocarbon date of 1245+/−35 BP (cal. AD 670–880) establishes a date around the eighth century (Timby *et al.* 2007, 152–6). It lies 100 m to the north of the parish church and on a different orientation from the historic landscape. At Bishops Park College in Clacton-on-Sea, midden deposits containing mostly seventh- to eighth-century grass-tempered pottery and a single sherd of Ipswich Ware were found in the slumped upper fill of a largely silted-up Late Bronze Age ditch, but the only other features certainly dating to this period were a small number of pits. A series of post holes, however, formed the plan of what is described as a 'bow-sided' building for which the only dating was a single fragment of (? residual) Roman brick but the plan is in keeping with an early medieval date (Letch 2005). Another 'bow-sided' building constructed of earth-fast posts has also been excavated at Downhouse Farm in West Hanningfield where the few sherds of fifth- to sixth-century pottery were 'insufficient to provide conclusive dating' (Dale *et al.* 2005). Early to Middle Saxon pottery has also been recovered from Roxwell Quarry, 1.5 km south of the Chignall St James villa (Bennett 2000, 220). Along with the early eighth-century occupation now recognized at Mucking it appears that, unlike in northern East Anglia (see below), 'Middle Saxon' occupation in the south of our region was found scattered across the landscape rather than nucleated into villages that went on to become parish centres.

The origins of the later medieval settlement pattern

So how old is the historic landscape in southern East Anglia? Documentary sources, place-name evidence, and dendrochronological dating of standing structures all show that the highly characteristic dispersed settlement pattern of later medieval Essex and south-west Suffolk was in existence by the thirteenth to fourteenth centuries: just as we have seen on the National Trust's Holnicote Estate near Porlock in West Somerset (Fig. 2.7), standing medieval buildings in Essex are spread across the landscape rather than only being found in a small number of discrete villages (e.g. Stenning 1996; 2003; Ryan 2000; Andrews 2004). Fieldwalking and major development-led excavations are also confirming that there are no deserted medieval villages hidden in this landscape: the medieval settlements being found are all isolated farmsteads scattered throughout ditched field systems. At Roxwell Quarry in Chignall St James, for example, on the Boulder Clay of central Essex, excavations have revealed a small farmstead of the tenth to twelfth centuries whose enclosure ditches conformed to the historic landscape (Brooks 1992). At Stebbingford and Blatches, in the Stebbing Valley also on the Boulder Clay, isolated farmsteads have similarly been excavated dating to the mid twelfth to mid fourteenth and mid thirteenth to fourteenth centuries respectively (Medlycott 1996; Timby *et al.* 2007, 161–6). At Slough House Farm and Chigborough, on the gravel terraces north of the Blackwater estuary, two small farmsteads date from the twelfth to early thirteenth and twelfth to fourteenth centuries respectively (Wallis and Waughman 1998, 53, 98). On the London Clays in southern Essex work along the line of the new A130 revealed small areas of medieval occupation at Ashdale Bridge near Battlesbridge (eleventh to sixteenth century), Downhouse Farm near East Hanningfield (eleventh to thirteenth century), Old Barn Lane near West Hanningfield (mid thirteenth to mid fourteenth century), and Dollymans Farm near Rawreth (eleventh to fourteenth century) (Dale *et al.* 2005). None of these developments—which have revealed large numbers of deserted isolated farmsteads—has revealed a deserted medieval village.

So how far back can we trace the origins of this later medieval settlement pattern? While it is not uncommon to find 'Late Saxon' material from still-occupied medieval settlements (Rippon 1996b, 124) there is growing evidence, often from small-scale work, that at least some were also occupied before the tenth century. The 'Middle Saxon' occupation at Asheldham is well known (Drury and Rodwell 1978, 137). At Great Wakering, late Roman and early medieval occupation associated with 'Early Saxon' and 'Middle Saxon' pottery has been recorded immediately east of the medieval parish church (Bennett 2001, 260; Medlycott 2003). At Chadwell St Mary a sixth-century *Grubenhaus* has been excavated just 120 m from the church (Lavender 1998), while in Chipping Ongar 'Saxon' pottery was found the same distance from its parish church (Gilman and Bennett 1995, 242). 'Early Saxon' sherds have been found next to the church in Tollesbury (Bennett 2002, 410). At Great Waltham late Roman, 'Early, (?)Middle and Late Saxon' pottery has been found 300 m from the church (Tyler and Wickenden 1996), while 'Saxon' pottery has been found adjacent to St Peter and St Paul's churchyard in St Osyth (Bennett 2000, 214). It is not just parish churches that have evidence for early medieval occupation in their vicinity. Mid Roman to 'early/mid Saxon' material was recorded at Thorpe Hall in Thorpe le Soken, while 'Early Saxon' sherds have been found at Cuton Hall in Chelmsford close to the excavated Late Saxon settlement at Springfield Lyons (Bennett 2002, 393). Limited excavations adjacent to Heybridge Hall revealed Late Iron Age to early Roman occupation along with 'Early-Middle and Late Saxon' pottery (Bennett 1999, 220). Late Roman and 'Early Saxon' occupation has also been recorded immediately south of Downhouse Farm in West Hanningfield (Dale *et al.* 2005). In south-west Suffolk, small amounts of residual Iron Age, Romano-British, and 'Early and Late Saxon' pottery from excavations at St Botolph's church in Burton suggest broad continuity in the occupation of that site (Murray 2005).

The overall theme that is emerging from this overview of settlement history is the same as that for field systems: some continuity, some discontinuity, but an overall picture of gradual evolution rather than sudden transformation. As population grew, and more and more land was taken into field systems, there must have been an increasing number of fixed elements within the landscape: the roads that linked settlements, the boundaries around increasingly scarce resources such as woodland and common grazing, and indeed parish churches that emerged around the tenth or eleventh centuries (which in some places did form a—but never the only—focus of settlement within a parish). There is no evidence of a major transformation of the countryside in the tenth century, as appears to have been seen in central Somerset (see Chapters 2 and 3), or around the eighth century as we will soon discover happened in the northern part of East Anglia: in Essex and south-west Suffolk landscape evolution happened at a far slower pace.

Churches and burial in the landscape

A further aspect of the origins of the historic landscape is that of its churches. Essex has numerous examples of medieval churches lying on or close to Roman villas, a relationship that has seen much discussion nationally (e.g. Morris and Roxan 1980; Morris 1989; Bell 1998; 2005). Of the 88 certain, probable, and possible villas in Essex, 21 (23 per cent) are overlain by or adjacent to a manorial hall, church, or church–hall complex, and of the nine of these villas that have good dating evidence all were still occupied in the late fourth century (Morris 2006, 242, appendix 9.3). It is possible that this relationship simply represents the desire of the church builders to be close to a source of stone, as in Essex, at least, the evidence for timber phases pre-dating the present stone churches is slim (see below). While it is also possible that the location of these churches may simply have been due to the 'sense of history' of these places (Morris and Roxan 1980, 82), we cannot rule out some form of continuity of these locations as central places for the surrounding territories.

So what of the origin of Essex's churches? Archaeological and documentary evidence from across England suggests that burials within minster churches started in the eighth century, as the earlier trend for kings to be buried within churches trickled down to the lower levels of society (Blair 2005, 228–9). It is generally thought, however, that churchyard burial for the whole population started several centuries later, perhaps around the tenth century when the new phenomenon of manorial churches forced people to bring their dead to these central locations, leading to the abandonment of scattered rural cemeteries (Blair 1994, 72–3; Hadley 2000; 2002; Hamerow 2002, 123): 'the tenth century may have been the first time when English people at large were told where they had to be buried' (Blair 2005, 463). This timescale for churchyard burial is based largely on documentary sources, such as a law code of Æthelstan of *c*.930 that refers to burial within 'a hallowed graveyard', although it receives some support from archaeological evidence. At well-known sites such as Wharram Percy, in Yorkshire (Bell and Beresford 1987), and Raunds Furnells in Northamptonshire (Boddington 1996), excavations have shown that churchyard burial did indeed begin around the tenth century, but at Yarnton in Oxfordshire, it appears that people started burying their dead in small family groups near to their homes in the Middle Saxon period before the creation of centralized, communal, churchyards (Hey 2004).

So what of the situation in Essex? There are only nineteen parish churches in Essex with some pre-Conquest fabric (Taylor and Taylor 1965; Taylor 1978, 1076), and the county's Domesday survey contains just 36 places with churches and/or priests, compared to 345 in Suffolk (Darby 1952, 249–51). Along with other documentary and archaeological evidence, Rodwell and Rodwell (1977, 92) suggest that there is some evidence for 86 pre-Conquest churches in the county. There is, however, almost no evidence for churches before the tenth or eleventh centuries.[4] Rodwell and Rodwell (1986) have claimed that 'Structure 1' adjacent to the Roman villa at Rivenhall was a Middle Saxon church, although only the corner of an undiagnostic rectilinear foundation trench was actually excavated (see Reece 1986, Millett 1987, and the discussion of

---

[4] It has been suggested that two possibly abutting structures within the rural settlement at Springfield Lyons near Chelmsford may have formed the nave/chancel and tower of a church (Tyler and Major 2005, 127–8, 193), although the evidence is not convincing. The two structures, while aligned approximately east–west, are slightly offset, and although the 'nave' appears to have contained an inhumation without grave goods abutting its north wall the stratigraphic relationship is unclear and this burial may equally relate to an earlier 5th- to 6th-century cemetery of which several inhumations with grave goods in the vicinity are on the same orientation (Tyler and Major 2005, 18). Pottery from the Springfield building(s) also dates to the 10th/11th centuries, not the Middle Saxon period.

Asheldham below, for similar over-interpretations of much the same evidence; the Rodwells' putative eastern boundary ditch of their 'Middle Saxon' cemetery, F.58, also failed to show up in the recent excavations: Clarke 2004, 70, fig. 22). The attribution of 'Structure 1' to the 'Middle Saxon period' was on the basis that it cut a number of graves, one of which (G.326) is radiocarbon dated to cal. AD 789–980,[5] while another grave (G.298) dated cal. AD 1166–1265 cut through it (Rodwell and Rodwell 1993, 104). Further excavations and radiocarbon dating, however, overwhelmingly point to a tenth-century and later date for this cemetery, while 'Structure 1' has been redated to the eleventh or twelfth century (Clarke 2004, 69–70). The Rodwells' 'Structure 1' lay 30 m to the north-west of the medieval parish church, excavations at the east end of which revealed a series of fragmentary traces of east–west oriented gullies that they interpret as a timber church ('Building 7'). Quite how a church can be reconstructed from this disparate series of gullies, not all of which are parallel, and several of which have butt ends, must be regarded as questionable, and the dating evidence is simply that they post-date Roman features and pre-date the fourteenth-century extension to the chancel. The dating for the first phase of the stone church at Rivenhall is a little firmer, as it post-dates robbed-out footings of the Roman villa, containing pottery of the ninth to eleventh century, and is associated with radiocarbon-dated burials of cal. AD 998–1153 and cal. AD 990–1163 (Rodwell and Rodwell 1986, 90–1; 1993, 104).

Other archaeological evidence for pre-Conquest churches in southern East Anglia suggests that there is sometimes evidence for structures and/or burials that pre-date the often twelfth-century standing structures, although none can be pushed back further than the tenth century. Drury and Rodwell (1978) claimed that excavations around the medieval parish church at Asheldham church revealed a timber church that pre-dated the present stone structure, although this 'church' was in fact simply a gully (F.151) that formed the corner of a rectangular building, adjacent to which were two graves that were sealed by a buried soil containing tenth- to eleventh-century pottery. The gully appeared to date to the tenth or eleventh century but failed to show up in later work (Andrews and Smoothy 1990). At Little Oakley, two post holes and a grave that stratigraphically pre-dated the twelfth-century stone church could relate to some timber predecessor, although there is no evidence for their date (Corbishley 1984, 21). At All Saints Cressing, excavations show that the present structure had a stone predecessor, with a possible timber structure beneath that (Hope 1984), while St Mary's West Bergholt also has a range of ephemeral features interpreted as an early timber church but which are of unknown date or character (Turner 1984). Work over the past decade by the Essex County Council Archaeology Section has failed to reveal any other

---

[5] Note that the suggested date of the late 8th century in volume i of the Rivenhall report is clearly wrong (Rodwell and Rodwell 1993, 83).

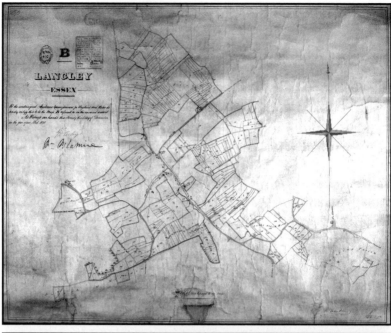

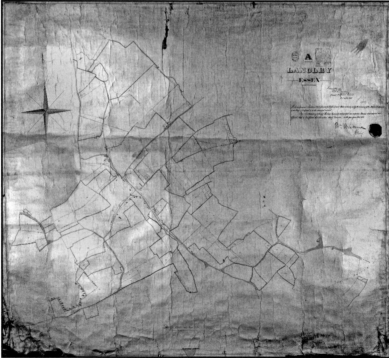

Fig. 5.15. Langley, in north-west Essex. Pre- and post-enclosure maps showing an extensive open field system, key features of which are still evident within the historic landscape following enclosure by agreement (ERO Q/RDc41B–C, © Essex Records Office).

evidence for burials or timber phases that pre-date the present stone structures, and just one site—Broomfield—has revealed pre-Conquest pottery (David Andrews pers. comm.). Overall, the evidence from southern East Anglia seems to support the traditional view that parish churches appeared around the tenth century.

The later medieval field systems of southern East Anglia

Finally, we must consider the character of the medieval field systems in Essex. The far north-west of the county had the greatest amount of open field, much of which survived until the era of Parliamentary Enclosure (e.g. Thaxted: Newton 1960; Saffron Walden: Cromarty 1966). At Langley, for example, a relatively rare pre-enclosure map of 1851 shows the strips and furlongs within an extensive open field system, although aspects of its management distinguish it from the Midland-style common fields, such as the clustered, as opposed to scattered, distribution of strips belonging to individual tenements (Fig. 5.15: ERO Q/RDc 41B; Williamson 1986; Hunter 1999, 40). Langley also had relatively large areas of anciently enclosed land and woodland, and lacked a single compact village, having a more dispersed settlement pattern of scattered hamlets. In western Essex (and Hertfordshire) open fields also appear to have been quite numerous, although they were similarly less extensive than in true 'champion' countryside, and not organized in such a regular fashion (Roden 1973). Each of the several hamlets within a parish would have its own open field, and the holdings of individual tenants were in relatively close proximity rather than spread across the whole field system (e.g. Roydon: Fig. 5.16; Medlycott 2004). Although mostly enclosed before the eighteenth century, some small parcels of open field in the west of Essex survived to be recorded on Tithe maps (e.g. Buckhurst Hill in Chigwell: Erith 1948).

Beyond the far north and west of the county, open fields appear to have been very limited in both their frequency and individual extent. The historic landscape, as mapped in the nineteenth century, contains very few traces of former open field, and the relatively large numbers of sixteenth-century and later estate maps are equally devoid of strip fields. In Cressing, for example, the northern part of the parish was occupied by a series of isolated farmsteads that in the nineteenth century were associated with compact blocks of land and with a predominance of 'croft' field names and nothing in the field boundary patterns to suggest the former existence of open field. In the south of the parish, occupied by the Knights Templar, there were a series of large documented 'fields' (e.g. North Field, covering *c.*200 m by 500 m), although their single ownership precludes them having been communal open fields (cf. Hunter 1993a; 1995; 2003, 15–19).

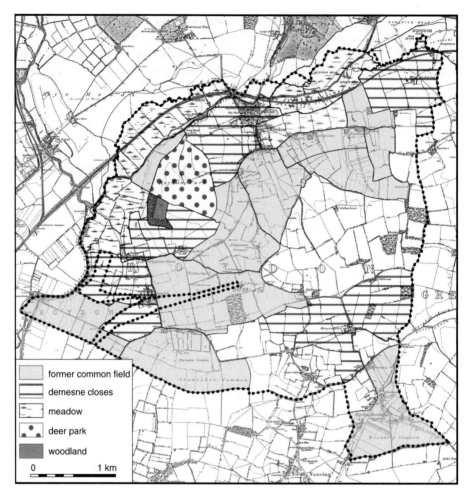

Fig. 5.16. Roydon, in west Essex. Historic landscape characterization and documentary research by Maria Medlycot (2004) has identified a series of small open fields within a landscape otherwise dominated by closes held in severalty and meadow on the floodplain of the river Lea. Drawing by Adam Wainwright.

But what if there had been common fields in Essex that were enclosed far earlier than in areas such as the Midlands, with the longer period of time between enclosure and the earliest cartographic sources meaning that there was more opportunity for continued evolution to alter the form of the immediate post-enclosure closes making their origins as former common field more difficult to recognize? While this possibility cannot be ruled out, medieval documentary sources also fail to reveal evidence for anything other than a scatter of small-scale and highly irregular open fields within a landscape dominated by closes. In the large Thames-side parish of Havering, for example, there is 'no clear indication of open-field agriculture...prior to 1251 and none at all thereafter' (McIntosh 1986, 93). Around Colchester and in the Lexden Hundred there was 'an unsystematic arrangement of fields large and small, some subdivided and some not, in which holdings were usually made up of compact blocks of land rather than strips' and weakly developed rights of common pasturage on uncropped arable (Britnell 1988, 159; Cooper 2001). In Witham, Rivenhall, Great Waltham, and High Easter the twelfth- to fifteenth-century landscape was largely enclosed, and although there are references to some parcels within subdivided fields, 'newly enclosed' land, and widespread use of a three-course rotation of crops, there is no evidence for communal cropping or pasturing in common on uncropped arable land. The land of individual tenements was in compact blocks, and nineteenth-century field names give no indication of extensive former common field (Poos 1983, 191–2; 1991, 51–6; Britnell 1983; Rodwell and Rodwell 1993, 134–73; Pitchforth 2001).

Discussion

In contrast to areas such as the East Midlands and the northern part of East Anglia (see below), the landscape history of Essex and south-west Suffolk has been relatively neglected. It is a landscape of dispersed medieval settlement and predominantly enclosed fields. In places there appears to be a degree of continuity from Roman to medieval, while elsewhere landscapes of the two periods bear little relationship to each other. This appears to have been a countryside of gradual evolution, with periods of expansion and contraction, and occasional local reorganizations of settlement patterns and field systems, against a backdrop of long-term continuous exploitation. Around the fifth century there may have been a decline in occupation on the heavier clays of the interfluvial areas, while settlements may have shifted away from some of the gravel terraces around the eighth century, but even in these areas the landscape may not have been abandoned entirely as there is no palaeoenvironmental evidence for the widespread woodland regeneration that would have happened if grazing had ceased entirely. There are several carefully planned landscapes that do suggest localized replanning of the landscape—most notably in the Dengie and Rochford hundreds—and in the case of the latter at least, this can be dated to between the sixth and tenth centuries. There are some open fields, but they were not widespread. The landscape of southern East Anglia clearly did not experience a major transformation like that seen in England's central zone, which led to the creation of villages and common fields: of the regions we have looked at so far, this one sits alongside the far west of Cornwall in being characterized by gradual evolution rather than sudden transformation.

THE ORIGINS OF THE HISTORIC LANDSCAPE IN NORTHERN
EAST ANGLIA

The landscape of northern East Anglia—Norfolk and the north and east of Suffolk—is a particularly interesting one to study, as it has seen a series of extensive and well-published parish-based fieldwalking surveys,[6] and a long history of metal detectorists reporting their finds. Compared to Essex there have, however, been fewer large-scale excavations, and this affects any discussion of how the landscape of this region developed: we have a clear picture about how settlement patterns developed across the landscape, but less information on the detailed evolution of individual sites.

The Icenian civitas *and kingdom of the East Angles*

In the Roman period this region became the *civitas* centred on *Venta Icenorum* (Caistor-by-Norwich), but compared to other parts of lowland Roman Britain the area saw the development of relatively few villas (Fig. 5.2B; Gurney 1994; Plouviez 1999). This is not just a product of differential visibility, as extensive fieldwalking across the region, such as in the Deben Valley in south-east Suffolk, has failed to reveal any new villa-type settlements (Newman 1992, 29). The distribution of other known rural settlements shows a consistent pattern across the region, with Romano-British sites concentrating in the river valleys but also spread across the flatter interfluvial areas.[7] The size of pottery scatters suggests a predominance of farmsteads and small hamlets. In Barton Bendish, for example, there was an average of 0.74 sites per square kilometre with each site associated with what appear to have been extensively manured areas (Fig. 5.17); in Hales, Heckingham, and Lodden the figure is 0.89 sites per square kilometre, and Fransham 0.85 (Rogerson *et al.* 1997, 13–17). In the clay districts of the Deben Valley in Suffolk, fieldwalking revealed nearly one site per square kilometre, although the density on the lighter soils of the Sandlings was half this (Newman 1992, 30).

The analysis of coin finds from eastern Suffolk suggests that a marked decline in circulation had set in by the third or fourth quarter of the fourth century, although whether this reflects depopulation or simply a decline in the

---

[6] Fieldwalking surveys: Norfolk: Barton Bendish and Caldecot: Rogerson *et al.* 1997; Egmere and Roundham: Cushion *et al.* 1982; Godwick: Davison 2003b; Hales, Heckingham, and Lodden: Davison 1990; Hargham: Davison 1995; Illington: Davison *et al.* 1993; Kilverstone and Rougham: Davison 1988; Langford: Davison 2001; Launditch Hundred: Wade-Martins 1980; West Acre: Davison 1996; 2003a; Witton: Lawson 1983. Suffolk: Deben Valley: Newman 1992; East Suffolk Claylands: Warner 1987; Menham, Metfield, and South Elmham: Moore *et al.* 1988, 58–9; Walsham le Willows: West and McLaughlin 1998.

[7] Examples of distribution maps of known settlements include the Burn and Stiffkey valleys (Gregory and Gurney 1986, fig. 10), the Blackwater and Wensum valleys (Rickett 1995, fig. 139), the Black Bourn and Lark valleys (West 1985, fig. 304), and the Little Ouse Valley (Mudd 2002, fig. 2).

market economy is unclear (Newman 1992, 31; Plouviez 1995, 74): there is a desperate need for more radiocarbon dating of the latest phases of occupation on all Romano-British sites in this region to see when their occupation really did cease. In the fifth century there was continuity in some areas, notably in the sandy regions and the lighter soils of the valley sides, and discontinuity elsewhere, especially the flatter and more poorly drained interfluvial areas. In Norfolk, Witton is typical. An extensive Romano-British settlement on the high ground near Whitton Hall produced no 'Early Saxon' pottery, while on the lower slopes near Common Farm to the east large amounts of residual third- to fourth-century pottery were recovered from the excavated fifth- to sixth-century settlement associated with several *Grubenhäuser*, suggesting late Romano-British occupation in the vicinity. The site was abandoned before the use of Ipswich Ware, whose distribution is concentrated around the parish church (Lawson 1983, 44–5). Surveys in Hales, Heckingham, and Lodden, as well as Barton Bendish, similarly show that the scattered late Romano-British settlements were mostly deserted in the fifth century, apart from a small number of sites associated with 'Early Saxon' pottery on the lighter soils of the valley sides; none of these fifth- to seventh-century sites is associated with Ipswich Ware (Davison 1990, 16, 66; Rogerson *et al.* 1997). In Mannington, Wickmere, and Wolterton there was similarly a marked decrease in the density of settlement, with one 'early Saxon' site compared to seven of the Romano-British period, while in the Fransham and the Wymondham parishes, where extensive metal detecting has complemented fieldwalking, the heavier interfluvial areas were similarly deserted, although settlement continued in the valleys (Williamson 1993, 58; Rogerson 2005). A similar picture is emerging in Suffolk where the heavy clays were abandoned, while settlements continued in use on the lighter sandy soils into the sixth or seventh centuries. Only a few of these sites have a few Ipswich Ware sherds, suggesting a dislocation of the settlement pattern perhaps towards the end of the seventh or early eighth century (Warner 1987, 9; Newman 1992, 32; 2005b, 481–3; Martin *et al.* 1986, 232–4; 1992, 378; 1994, 206–7; 1995, 344).

Palaeoenvironmental evidence suggests a very similar picture. A series of pollen sequences all show broad continuity in land-use from the late Roman through to the early medieval period, with a largely open, pastoral landscape and some arable on the lighter soils: there may have been some contraction in the extent of cultivation, but this was replaced by grassland, and there was very limited or no woodland regeneration.[8] An indication that the heavier soils of

---

[8] Caudle Heath (Wiltshire 1999), Diss Mere (Peglar *et al.* 1989), Hockham Mere (Godwin and Tall-antire 1951; Bennett 1983a; 1983b; Sims 1978), Micklemere (Murphy 1996, 29–31), Old Buckingham Mere (Godwin 1968), Scole (Wiltshire forthcoming), and Seamere (Sims 1978). In such a flat landscape, the catchment of these meres is likely to have been from a radius of about 10–20 km (Jacobson and Bradshaw 1981).

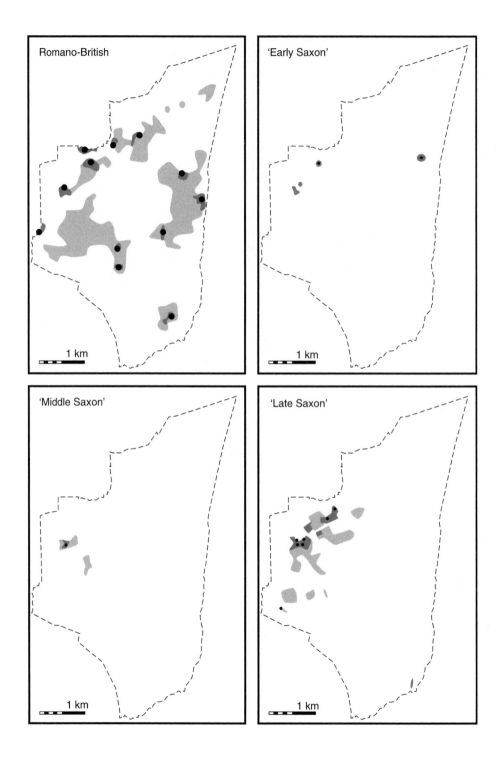

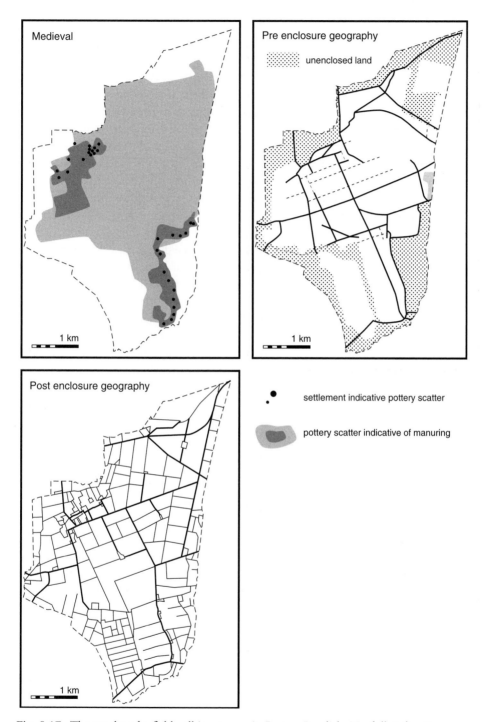

Fig. 5.17. The results of a fieldwalking survey in Barton Bendish, Norfolk (after Rogerson *et al.* 1997). Drawing by Adam Wainwright.

the interfluvial areas may not have been entirely abandoned is that seeds of a distinctive species of weed (*Anthemis cotula*, stinking mayweed) from amongst the cereals at the Early Saxon settlement at West Stow suggest some arable cultivation was on the Boulder Clay (Murphy 1985, 105).

As was discussed for southern East Anglia, the results of such surveys enable us to discuss the development of settlement patterns in broad spatial terms, but not who was actually living in those settlements: we have to remember that some of the fourth-century settlements that lack fifth- to seventh-century 'Early Anglo-Saxon' pottery could have been occupied by the aceramic descendants of the native British population. In contrast to southern East Anglia, however, the area north of the Gipping–Lark valleys does have a large number of fifth- to seventh-century cemeteries (Fig. 5.2C), suggesting a substantial Anglian settlement from the second or third quarters of the fifth century (Scull 1992, 8). The extent to which a native population survived and how they interacted with the newcomers is unclear, but in a number of cases it is noticeable how 'Early Saxon' settlements were located at the periphery of late Romano-British sites, as seen in the relative locations of West Stow and Icklingham, and also at Burgh Castle, Hacheston, Long Melford, Pakenham, and *Venta Icenorum* (Williamson 1993, 67; Plouviez 1995, 78–9; Blagg *et al.* 2004). It may have been either that the immigrants were drawn to these agriculturally productive areas but wanted to avoid living amongst the ruins of abandoned Roman sites, or that an aceramic native British population survived and the newcomers were forced to settle at the periphery of what were still functioning territorial centres.

A 'Middle Saxon shuffle'? Reorganization and intensification in the settlement patterns of northern East Anglia during the long eighth century

Across northern East Anglia, fieldwalking and metal detecting surveys show a major dislocation in the settlement pattern around the eighth century, with the dispersed scatter of Romano-British and 'Early Saxon' settlements being abandoned in favour of a series of nucleated villages that were later associated with parish churches. Archaeological work in what is now farmland (i.e. outside deserted and still-occupied medieval settlements) is also consistently revealing a dispersed settlement pattern in the Roman and earliest medieval periods (the fifth to seventh or eighth centuries),[9] while work within deserted medieval villages and still-occupied medieval settlements is increasingly

---

[9] Archaeological work outside extant villages: the A12 roundabout in Hopton-on-Sea (Gurney and Penn 2000, 528), Bowthorpe in Cotessey (Trimble 2001; Gurney and Penn 2005, 753), Broome (Robertson 2003), Flixton Park Quarry in Flixton (Boulter 2003), Gallows Hill in Barking (Boulter 2002a; 2002b), Grange Farm and Wash Lane in Snetterton (Gurney and Penn 2001, 175; Robertson 2004), Melford Meadows in Brettenham (Mudd 2002), Priory Farm in Aldeby (Gurney and Penn 2000, 522), RAF Lakenheath (Caruth 2002a; 2002b), and Yarmouth Road in Broome (Gurney and Penn 2002, 164).

producing evidence for occupation associated with 'Middle and Late Saxon' pottery.[10] Although the fieldwalking surveys suggest that most of the dispersed settlement pattern associated with 'Early Saxon' pottery was abandoned before Ipswich Ware came into circulation, which is now dated by Blinkhorn (1999) to the early eighth century, a number of earlier sites in northern Suffolk have produced small amounts of this 'Middle Saxon' pottery such as Lakenheath (Jo Caruth pers. comm.) and Bloodmoor Hill in Carlton Colville (Tipper *et al.* forthcoming). West Stow has also produced Ipswich Ware (West 1985, 137), and although the excavated areas of the nearby site at Lackford Bridge and Melford Meadows near Thetford (Dallas 1993; Mudd 2002) lacked Ipswich Ware, considering the shifting nature of early medieval settlement, occupation of this period could lie in adjacent unexcavated areas. In the Deben Valley some, but not all, of the 'Early Saxon' sites produced a few sherds of Ipswich Ware, once again suggesting a dislocation of the settlement pattern around the early eighth century (Newman 1992, 32; 2005b, 481–3). The abandonment of the excavated areas of settlement at Kilverstone also gives us a *terminus post quem* for the laying out of the common fields over the same area (Fig. 5.18; Davison 1988, 18–32; Garrow *et al.* 2006).

The nucleation of settlement in the 'Middle Saxon' period is also clearly evident in the major published fieldwalking surveys of Norfolk parishes such as Barton Bendish (Fig. 5.17), and in northern and eastern Suffolk (e.g. Deben Valley: Martin *et al.* 1995, 344; Newman 1992; 2005; the South Elmhams: Martin *et al.* 2002, 213; Sudbourne: Martin *et al.* 1992, 378; Westleton: Martin *et al.* 1994, 208). These pottery scatters are sometimes relatively extensive and are suggestive of more than single farmsteads. Occupation associated with Ipswich Ware has also been confirmed by excavations at now isolated churches such as Iken and Barham in Suffolk (West and Scarfe 1984; Martin *et al.* 1982, 159). Across northern East Anglia a high proportion of these settlements associated with 'Middle Saxon' pottery are associated with *hām* place names which is in keeping with the view that this was the habitative name most favoured in the earliest years of English name giving (Gelling 1992, 55): in Launditch Hundred, for example, six out of eleven villages producing Ipswich Ware have *hām* names, and all but one of the *hām* names that have been surveyed have produced Ipswich Ware (Wade-Martins 1980, 84–5). In contrast, of the six -ton place names none has produced Middle Saxon pottery (Wade-Martins 1980, 85; Gelling 1992, 56–7). It is noticeable that there are relatively few *hām* names in South-West Suffolk, providing yet another

---

[10] Archaeological work within extant Norfolk villages: Mileham: Gurney and Penn 1998, 201; Burnham Market: Gurney and Penn 1999, 370; 2000, 524; Sedgeford: Faulkner 2000, 126; Cabot *et al.* 2004; South Walsham: Albone 2000, 27; Gurney and Penn 2001, 724; Brettenham: Gurney and Penn 2005, 752, 762; Whissonsett: Mellor 2004; Gurney and Penn 2005, 752, 762; Trimble 2006. Archaeological work within extant Suffolk villages: Grundisburgh: Martin *et al.* 1993, 95–6; 1994, 213; Haughley: Martin *et al.* 2000, 523; South Elmham St Margaret: Martin *et al.* 2002, 213.

example of how this region has more in common with Essex than the rest of Suffolk and Norfolk (Martin 1999b). It is also during the period when Ipswich Ware was in use that the heavier claylands of northern East Anglia started to be recolonized (Newman 1992, 34).

It is likely that the locations chosen for these 'Middle Saxon' villages were among the many isolated farmsteads that were spread across the landscape in what were to become medieval parishes. Some deserted medieval villages that have been fieldwalked have produced significant amounts of late Roman pottery suggestive of settlements in the vicinity (e.g. Kilverstone), although the very small amounts of material from other sites are more difficult to interpret, and could simply have been from manure scatters (e.g. Beachamwell, Egmere, Rougham, Roundham, and Whissonsett: Cushion *et al.* 1982, 50, 86; Davison 1988, 10–11, 34, 63; Mellor 2004, 6; Trimble 2006). This was certainly the case at the hamlet of Cotes in Great Palgrave as documentary sources and fieldwalking both suggest that this hamlet was only established in the thirteenth century (Davison 1982). In the Launditch Hundred Survey, on the relatively high Boulder Clay plateau of Norfolk's central watershed, only four out of the twelve villages associated with Ipswich Ware scatters have produced Roman material, although 'Early Saxon' pottery was entirely absent (Wade-Martins 1980, 82–4; Rogerson *et al.* 1997, 44). This lack of pre-'Middle Saxon' material is also seen elsewhere: relatively extensive excavations at Barton Bendish, for example, produced just a single sherd of first-century AD pottery (Rogerson *et al.* 1997, 59).

Across northern East Anglia there are just a few Ipswich Ware scatters away from the village cores and these are probably secondary 'daughter settlements', in peripheral areas of parishes, in that they are just a few sherds amongst what are predominantly 'Late Saxon' scatters (Newman 2005b, 483). The formation of these secondary settlements marks the beginning of a trend towards the dispersion of settlement with the migration of farmsteads to the edges of the large commons that occupied areas of heavier soil in the interfluvial areas (Warner 1987, 17–18; Newman 2005b, 483). From around the eleventh century the migration of settlement away from the 'Middle to Late Saxon' villages towards nearby commons and greens became widespread, and many parish churches were eventually left isolated: for much of northern East Anglia, the era of villages was short-lived.

Interestingly, this same pattern—of a small number of relatively compact villages associated with 'Middle and Late Saxon' pottery, followed by the expansion and migration of settlement along droveways towards areas of common land—is also seen in the extensive reclaimed wetlands of the Norfolk Marshland, in the far west of the county. As a reclaimed wetland that saw extensive post-Roman flooding, this was a 'cleaned slate' upon which the medieval landscape was created without an antecedent cultural landscape to affect its character (as was also seen in Somerset: see Chapters 2 and 3), and the similarity of landscape development here compared to the dryland areas of Norfolk suggests that nucleated villages were the way that Norfolk society chose to structure its landscapes in the 'long eighth century' (Silvester 1988; 1993; Rippon 2000a, 208–11; Crowson *et al.* 2004).

The Romano-British and early medieval field systems of northern East Anglia

Another issue to consider is the relationship of the Romano-British fieldscape to the historic landscape. As in southern East Anglia, excavations are suggesting that some Romano-British field systems remained in use into the fifth century, although they invariably go out of use sometime before the creation of the historic landscape of today. At Lakenheath, Spong Hill, Barking, Melford Meadows, and Broome, for example, late Romano-British ditches were still open in the fifth century, as they contained sherds of 'Early Saxon' pottery; in many cases these ditches were respected during the construction of mid- to late fifth-century *Grubenhäuser*, but they were then abandoned and an entirely new pattern of medieval fields created at some unknown date (Martin *et al.* 1993, 217–18; Rickett 1995; Boulter 2002a; 2002b; Mudd 2002, 52–69; Robertson 2003). At Kilverstone, in the Norfolk Breckland, in contrast, the Romano-British landscape appears to have been deserted before the area was reoccupied in the sixth century although this settlement was in turn abandoned in the seventh century, being replaced at an unknown date by the common fields of Kilverstone village (Fig. 5.18; Garrow *et al.* 2006). At Bloodmoor Hill in Carlton Colville, near Lowestoft in Suffolk, an extensive first- to second-century Romano-British field system was similarly abandoned before the site was reoccupied in the fifth century, and this settlement was in turn deserted in the early eighth century, with the medieval pattern of fields lying unconformably over these earlier landscapes (Dickens *et al.* 2006). One site where a Romano-British field system is on a similar orientation to the historic landscape is Grange Farm, Snetterton, in the Norfolk Breckland, although this may be a coincidence: the way in which a *Grubenhaus* cuts one of the Romano-British ditches suggests that the earlier field system had all but disappeared, while a ditch associated with tenth- to eleventh-century pottery was on a completely different orientation from both that and the overlying medieval landscape (Robertson 2004).

This review of the relationship between excavated Romano-British field systems and the historic landscape suggests that there is far less evidence for continuity than in southern East Anglia (see above), and this appears to be confirmed by the evidence from cropmarks (although these are mostly restricted to the lighter soils in the east of Norfolk and Suffolk). Here, in places such as Witton, a fairly extensive series of cropmarks that excavation has dated to the Romano-British and 'Early Saxon' periods are on a different orientation from the medieval field system that evolved into the historic landscape

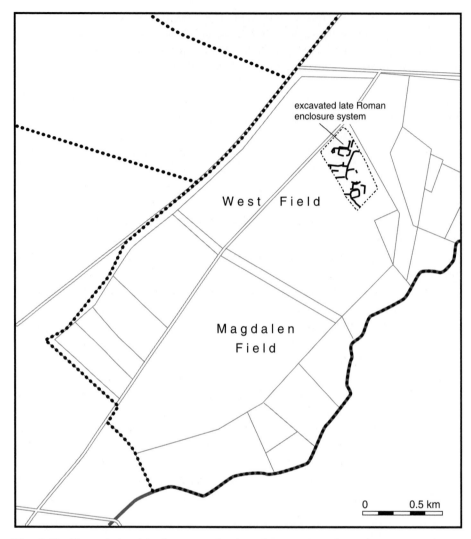

Fig. 5.18. The relationship between the late Romano-British enclosure complex at Kilverston and the historic landscape based on the Tithe map of 1839 (redrawn based on the Ordnance Survey First Edition Six Inch map) (after Davison 1988, fig. 8 and Garrow *et al.* 2006, fig. 4.13). Drawing by Adam Wainwright.

of today (Lawson 1983, 92–3). The National Mapping Programme in Norfolk is producing a similar picture, with extensive areas of cropmarks being pieced together that are on a different orientation from those of the medieval period (*Norfolk Archaeology and Environment Annual Review* 2005–6, 4–5).

One argument in favour of the survival of Romano-British field systems was put forward by Williamson (1987; 1993) and Warner (1996, 45–53), who have identified a series of apparently planned coaxial landscapes across the heavier claylands of northern East Anglia that they suggest ignore the natural topography (being 'terrain oblivious'), and must date to the late prehistoric period as they appear to be cut by Roman roads (as at Little Waltham in Essex: Fig. 5.8). Such an extensive survival of field systems would imply a significant degree of continuity in land-use (for which there is some palaeoenvironmental evidence: see above), and the maintenance of field boundaries. Although the late prehistoric date for these coaxial landscapes was rejected by Hinton (1997), and reiterated by Williamson (1998; 2003, 40–3), unfortunately there is still no undisputed dating evidence, although at North Creake, in Burnham Sutton (north Norfolk), it appears that a common field system was created within a framework of roughly parallel boundaries inherited from the Roman period (Percival and Williamson 2005).

In common with southern greater East Anglia, a final characteristic of the Romano-British and 'Early Saxon' landscapes in the north is their fluidity, with sites being periodically occupied, abandoned, and reoccupied (e.g. Thornham and Wighton: Gregory and Gurney 1986). Romano-British field systems were equally transitory, with localized ditched enclosure systems created, left to silt up, and recreated, often on slightly different orientations and alignments (e.g. Melford Meadows in Brettenham: Mudd 2002, figs. 7, 13, and 14; Spong Hill: Rickett 1995, figs. 38, 44, and 47). The mobility of 'Early Saxon' settlement has long been recognized with West Stow a classic example (West 1985), to which fieldwalked settlements such as Illington and recently excavated sites at Melford Meadows, Bloodmoor Hill, and Lakenheath can be added (Davison *et al.* 1993; Mudd 2002; Tipper *et al.* forthcoming; Jo Caruth pers. comm.). The overall impression is that away from the major Roman roads there was little in the way of a fixed physical framework within the landscape, and that many settlements and field systems had a lifespan of just a few generations before being abandoned: the stability of some medieval villages in northern East Anglia, occupied from around the eighth century to the present day, is a real change from earlier times.

Changing land-use around the eighth century

Palaeoenvironmental sequences are also suggesting that the period around the eighth century was one of change, most notably an expansion in agricultural production. The well-dated pollen sequence from the Oakley palaeochannel at Scole suggests that there was a marked intensification in cereal cultivation in the fifth century and no change in the extent of woodland or scrub in the post-Roman period; the area of pasture either contracted or was grazed more heavily. Around the eighth century (based on a calibrated radiocarbon date of AD 670–820) there was then a further agricultural intensification, with an increase in cereal pollen, the emergence of viticulture, and the cultivation of hemp, which was also seen at Diss and Old Buckenham (see below) (Wiltshire forthcoming). At Micklemere there was also a marked increase in cereal pollen dated 1290+/−100 BP (cal. AD 588–972) at the same time as there was a high influx of mineral sediment, implying increased soil erosion in the catchment (Murphy 1994, 29). It is possible that other pollen sequences from northern East Anglia that show a period of agricultural intensification in the early medieval period date to this 'long eighth century', although the dating evidence is not as good: at Old Buckenham Mere there is a decline in oak woodland dated '*c.*800 AD' (Godwin 1968, 102), while at Diss Mere (Peglar *et al.* 1989), Old Buckenham Mere (Godwin 1968), and Sea Mere (Sims 1978) there is a marked increase in the pollen of *Secale cereale* (rye), *Avena/Triticum* type (wheat), *Hordeum* type (barley), and *Cannabis* type (hemp) at around '1500 BP' (around the sixth century). At Hockham Mere a similar expansion in cultivation is dated to 'around 1300 BP' (around the ninth century) (Sims 1978, 57; Bennett 1983a; 1983b).

Burials and churches in the landscape

One view of these changes in the rural landscape, including the expansion of settlement onto heavier soils, is that it reflects the need to increase agricultural production to support the population of newly emerging coastal trading settlements such as Ipswich (Moreland 2000; Hamerow 2002, 123). Indeed, the recent identification of large numbers of 'productive sites'—a term used by numismatists to describe locations yielding relatively large numbers of early medieval coins—suggests that there was a growing non-agriculturally productive sector of society, as trade and exchange increased across the region, reflected in the widespread distribution of manufactured goods such as Ipswich Ware. So was the nucleation of settlement into villages simply a product of the need to increase agricultural efficiency?

The 'long eighth century' was also the period when there was a profound change in burial practice, with the abandonment of 'early Anglo-Saxon' cemeteries and the cessation of burial with (datable) grave goods (Geake 1997). While many fifth- to seventh-century cemeteries were close to settlements but not within them (e.g. West Stow, Suffolk: West 1985; Flixton, Suffolk: Boulter 2003), others such as Spong Hill were so large that they must have served a considerable area, and it has been argued that they were replaced by small, Christian 'final-phase' cemeteries associated with individual settlements (e.g. Faull 1976). Although Boddington (1990) has questioned this model, suggesting that these eighth-century burial grounds were part of the constant process of the creation and desertion of cemeteries (and see Geake 1997), we are still left with the problem of where people were buried, between the demise of the 'early Anglo-Saxon' cemeteries in the seventh or early eighth centuries, and the appearance of large numbers of parish churches in the landscape, which is traditionally dated to around the tenth century (see above): so when did burial grounds change from being located beyond the edges of settlements to being situated within them? In the context of this study, this is crucial to understanding the relationship between parish churches and the villages associated with Ipswich Ware that occur around them in northern East Anglia: did settlement nucleate around a church, or were churches added to existing villages?

North Elmham shows how ecclesiastical sites became a focus for 'Middle Saxon' settlement, although as an episcopal centre it is hardly typical (Wade-Martins 1980). There is, however, growing evidence that some eighth- and ninth-century settlements, in East Anglia at least, had churches. Rik Hoggett (pers. comm.) has observed that where a scatter of pottery around a medieval church contains only Ipswich Ware and no 'Late Saxon' material (the settlement having shifted its location to a nearby green), it suggests that the church was contemporary with the 'Middle Saxon' settlement (e.g. Mileham: Wade-Martins 1980, 47–8). Unfortunately, we will never be able to excavate large numbers of churchyards, as the majority are still in use, although at All Saints in Barton Bendish a cemetery that was stratigraphically beneath the first stone church itself cut a buried soil containing tenth-century pottery (Rogerson *et al.* 1987). At Iken and Framingham, burials have also been recorded that pre-date the stone church (West and Scarfe 1984; Rogerson *et al.* 1987, 81), while at Whissonsett a series of graves are associated with Middle Saxon pottery (Mellor 2004; Trimble 2006). Burial also appears to have occurred within eighth-century settlements at Ipswich (Scull and Bayliss 1999; Scull 2001) and Bloodmoor Hill in Carlton Colville (Tipper *et al.* forthcoming), both in the east of Suffolk, along with Gamlingay in Cambridgeshire (Murray and McDonald 2005). A 'Middle to Late Saxon' cemetery has also recently been excavated close to the parish church at Caister-on-Sea in Norfolk (Albone 2001). At Sedgeford, in north-west Norfolk, a cemetery of 184 east–west oriented graves without grave goods *c.*350 m to the south-east of the medieval parish church was sealed by an eighth- to ninth-century occupation horizon, and one of the graves was radiocarbon dated to cal. AD 600–760. It is unclear, however, whether this was an 'ordinary' rural settlement, as there have been a number of finds including two styli that suggest this may be a 'productive site' of a type that some have claimed have monastic associations, such as Brandon and Burrow Hill in Suffolk (Fenwick 1984; Faulkner 2000, 125; Cabot *et al.* 2004; Pestel 2005, 31–64).

Discussion

The Romano-British and earliest medieval (fifth- to seventh-century) landscape in northern East Anglia appears to have been of broadly the same character as that to the south (with the exception of there having been fewer villas): there was a predominantly dispersed settlement pattern, with isolated farmsteads and small hamlets associated with localized field systems. Settlement was concentrated on the lighter soils of the valleys but also spread up onto the heavier clays of the interfluvial areas. There was considerable fluidity in a countryside that was constantly evolving, and the fifth century appears to have seen a period of settlement contraction from the heavier soils, but around the eighth century there was a more profound change. The dispersed settlement pattern and localized field systems were replaced by a series of nucleated villages that were presumably associated with the open field systems that survived into the late medieval period or later. These open fields, along with the network of roads that linked the villages and the churches that were added to them around the tenth century, provided a degree of stability to the landscape that it had not previously experienced, although in some areas the migration of settlement to the greens and commons left the churches to stand in splendid isolation. Around the eighth century palaeoenvironmental sequences also show a period of agricultural intensification, also not seen in southern East Anglia.

THE ORIGINS OF VILLAGES AND COMMON FIELDS AT THE EASTERN EDGE OF THE CENTRAL ZONE IN CAMBRIDGESHIRE

To complete this overview we should turn to Cambridgeshire, which sees the eastern limit of the central zone as defined by Roberts and Wrathmell (2000) and discussed by Taylor (2002). Fieldwalking in Cambridgeshire has confirmed that a dispersed Romano-British settlement pattern continued into the early medieval period (e.g. Caxton: Oosthuizen 2005, 169; Whittlesford: Taylor 1989, 217–18). At Cardinal Distribution Park, in Godmanchester, for example, a Romano-British settlement was occupied throughout the fifth to seventh centuries, with just six sherds of Ipswich Ware and the absence of Maxey Ware suggesting it was abandoned by the early eighth century (Gibson and Murray 2003). In common with areas such as Northamptonshire, this scatter of farmsteads was at some stage swept away and replaced with nucleated villages, and excavations at Gamlingay show that the common fields there were laid out over a settlement associated with 'Early to Middle Saxon' pottery (including Maxey and Ipswich wares) that was abandoned by the mid ninth century ('Late Saxon' pottery being absent: Murray and McDonald 2005). At Haslingfield, there was a scatter of settlements associated with 'Early and Middle Saxon' pottery, some of which were deserted when a large oval-shaped green was created to the north of a possibly planned village next to the church (Oosthuizen 2002, 75–6). Research by Oosthuizen (2005; 2006) in the Bourne Valley has revealed an extensive common field system whose long furlongs cut across several parishes, a hundred boundary, and the boundary between Comberton and Toft that is recorded in a charter of 975, suggesting they were in place before the early tenth century. They also cut unconformably across several Romano-British settlements, and as such large-scale landscape planning is regarded as unlikely in the fifth to seventh centuries, Oosthuizen suggests they were laid out in the eighth or ninth centuries in order to increase agricultural production.

Roberts (1987, 49–51) and Taylor (1989; 2002) have provided us with a series of fascinating discussions of village plans and the possible ways that they may have evolved over time, but perhaps the most significant advance has been recent archaeological work within the historic cores of still-occupied villages. In Taylor's (1989) discussion of Whittlesford, for example, the crucial piece of evidence in the context of this study is that the village has produced 'Late Saxon' Thetford Ware, as has also been the case at Houghton and Wyton (Lewis 2005; forthcoming). Several excavations within extant villages, however, are suggesting an origin in the eighth century. One of the most extensively excavated sites is at West Fen Road in Ely where an extensive village-like settlement—extending some 500 m north to south—was laid out in the early eighth century (Mortimer *et al.* 2005, 4, 144–8). The orientation of the tenement boundaries is the same as the furlong boundaries within the common field system that covered Ely in the medieval period (Hall 1996, 40), suggesting that the whole landscape was laid out at the same time. Even if this was a somewhat untypical settlement, associated with the nearby monastery founded in *c.*673, it still shows that the concept of planned, nucleated settlements existed in this region at that time. In Cottenham, a cluster of settlement enclosures developed during the eighth century which were then abandoned as the focus of occupation shifted to the south where a radially arranged series of tenement plots developed (Mortimer 2000). At Hinxton, a small settlement, probably a single farmstead, was occupied between the late sixth/early seventh and eighth centuries after which it was replaced by a series of timber halls set within enclosures suggestive of a series of adjacent farmsteads which also appear to represent the beginnings of the village; in the eleventh century they were replaced by the present planned settlement (Taylor *et al.* 1994; Taylor 2002, 55–6). At Cherry Hinton, extensive excavations have revealed a spread of 'Middle Saxon' pottery and several ditches, which were replaced in the late ninth or early tenth century by a large, possibly manorial, enclosure associated with a church and cemetery containing 670 east to west oriented inhumations (Cessford 2005). Various excavations within Chesterton have similarly revealed residual 'Middle Saxon' pottery, with stratified occupation deposits from the 'Late Saxon' period associated with a series of ditched enclosures (Cessford 2004). 'Middle Saxon' pottery has also been recovered from the villages at Fordham, Whaddon, and Willingham (Oosthuizen 1993; Mortimer 2000, 20; Taylor 2002, 63).

Taken altogether, this recent evidence from Cambridgeshire is suggesting that the 'Middle Saxon' period saw a crucial change in the landscape with the start of settlement nucleation. Often, the earliest 'Middle Saxon' occupation is simply represented by a scatter of residual pottery and just a handful of features, suggesting either small-scale occupation or that the focus of activity lay outside the excavated area: indeed, a degree of settlement mobility is seen at both Cherry Hinton and Cottenham. As Mortimer (2000) suggests, this putative eighth-century date for the origins of villages is a departure from the prevailing view that nucleation happened around the mid ninth century at the interface between the periods when 'Middle Saxon' and 'Late Saxon' pottery was in use, although some villages were undoubtedly created at this later date. Indeed, all of these recent excavations within still-occupied medieval villages show how the settlements continued to evolve with expansion, reorganization, and desertion of certain areas (and see Oosthuizen 1993; 2002; Taylor 2004).

DISCUSSION: REGIONAL VARIATION IN CONTINUITY, REORGANIZATION, AND DIVERGENT DEVELOPMENT

This discussion of the landscape in greater East Anglia has confirmed that it lay outside England's central zone of champion countryside: this was not a region of compact nucleated villages surrounded by large common fields. It is also clear, however, that this was not a landscape carved out of woodland in the later first millennium AD: palaeoenvironmental sequences consistently show there was an extensively cleared landscape by the Roman period and that there was no significant woodland regeneration in the post-Roman period. There was, however, a significant difference within this region along the line of the Gipping–Lark valleys or watersheds that corresponds to a long-lasting socio-political division between the tribal area and *civitas* of the Iceni and kingdom of the East Angles to the north (in Norfolk and northern/eastern Suffolk), and the tribal area and *civitas* of the Trinovantes and the kingdom of the East Saxons to the south.

Williamson (2002, 84; 2006a, 42) suggests that the long-term division of this region along the Gipping–Lark line is probably due to continuity in the systems of contact and exchange that were determined by the configuration of coast and rivers, rather than by any direct survival of political entities. This is, however, a rather physically deterministic explanation, and if it was the case then one would surely expect a far stronger east–west division within the landscape of greater East Anglia, along the lines of the East Anglian Heights and the central watershed in Norfolk, with society to the east focused on the estuaries flowing into the North Sea, and society to the west looking towards the Fenland Basin. Such a boundary is evident in landscape character to a certain extent—with more nucleated settlement and regularly arranged two- and three-field systems to the west, and more dispersed settlement and smaller-scale open fields in the east (cf. Figs. 5.1 and 5.3)—but it was the north and south divide, along the

Gipping–Lark valleys, that was far more significant. It is suggested here that, as we have seen in the South-West, there are certain places within the British landscape where different societies have taken certain natural features as the boundaries between themselves, of which the Blackdown and Quantock Hills in the South-West and the Gipping and Lark valleys in East Anglia are two examples.

This boundary was particularly important during the 'long eighth century', when many of the character-defining features of the historic landscape were created. Before that time, settlement patterns across the region were predominantly dispersed, with a scatter of farmsteads and hamlet-sized settlements spread right across the landscape, although with greater densities in the river valleys. There was greater Romanization in the south, as reflected in the higher density of villas, but society in the north was still clearly stratified as reflected in the accumulation of wealth deposited in hoards. This dispersed settlement pattern was associated with relatively discrete and unstable fieldscapes that were periodically deserted and then reordered. In the fourth and fifth centuries there are some signs of economic decline and a decrease in the intensity with which some areas were exploited, although few if any areas appear to have been completely abandoned: if grazing had ceased across large areas there would very soon have been a woodland regeneration and this is not evident in the palaeoenvironmental record. During the earliest medieval period (the fifth to seventh centuries), settlement certainly appears to have retreated from the heavier interfluvial areas, although once again some form of agriculture must have continued to prevent the spread of scrub and woodland.

Fluidity and mobility were still key characteristics of this period, and in southern East Anglia this remained the case throughout the medieval period, albeit within an increasingly fixed framework of roads and field boundaries in what was becoming a crowded landscape. There is growing evidence here for a scatter of 'Middle Saxon' and later settlements spread across the landscape, both beneath still-occupied places and what are now agricultural fields. Palaeoenvironmental sequences point to broad continuity in land-use as a backdrop for the localized creation and desertion of settlement. There were some open fields, perhaps an innovation brought in from the northern part of East Anglia or the Midlands, but the field systems were predominantly enclosed: this remained a physical landscape designed by and for the individual rather than the community.

Until there is a major programme of excavation to test the date of the coaxial and other planned landscapes, their real significance cannot be appreciated. Small-scale work at sites such as Little Waltham and Saffron Walden appears to support an Iron Age date for at least some of the coaxial patterns, although in Dengie all we can say is that its rectilinear layout is pre-tenth century. The radial landscape in Rochford Hundred is clearly post-fifth century and pre-tenth century in date. The different dates of these planned landscapes make an important general point about the landscape in southern East Anglia: it is a complex palimpsest that has been constantly evolving.

In northern East Anglia, however, there was a profound change in landscape character around the eighth century. The dispersed settlement pattern was abandoned as farmsteads coalesced into a series of nucleated settlements that were in essence villages, and also provides the most obvious context for the emergence of common fields. By the eleventh century these settlements had parish churches, most of which probably originated before the tenth century. This transformation of the landscape during the 'long eighth century' does not appear to be much different from that seen in the East Midlands, although in East Anglia it was much shorter-lived. Even within the period when Ipswich Ware was in use, we start to see secondary settlements being created, and by the eleventh century fieldwalking and excavation show a widespread tendency for settlement to drift away from the early villages, and their parish churches, towards greens and commons that so characterized the interfluvial areas.

So how can we explain this marked difference in landscape character between northern and southern East Anglia? Williamson (2003) and Martin (2007) both note differences in topography and soils, with the clayland in the south, for example, being more frequently dissected by river valleys. What to modern farmers might seem relatively minor differences in the properties of soil may indeed have been more significant in the past, given the nature of medieval technology and farming practices. Williamson (2006a, 56) has also argued that the greater abundance of meadow in the Midlands, compared to East Anglia, promoted a more communal approach to managing the landscape as hay making requires good weather, abundant labour, and careful timing of its collection. This, he argues, means that large areas of meadow encourage the growth of large nucleated villages 'in which the workforce could be quickly assembled', whereas in places where meadow occurred in smaller, more scattered areas, settlement would be more dispersed. Williamson argues that southern greater East Anglia (to the south of the Gipping–Lark valleys) had less meadow than the Midlands, and this is certainly in keeping with the former having more dispersed settlement than the latter, but the hypothesis falls down when it comes to northern East Anglia. This region has more nucleated settlement compared to southern East Anglia yet it has less meadow, as the more widely spaced valleys tend to be filled with peaty soils. In fact, it is very difficult to see any difference in the physical environment that can explain why landscape and society in the north and south of East Anglia were so different, or why the Gipping–Lark valleys were such a persistent boundary between peoples and the ways that they structured and managed the landscape.

Instead of being dictated by the natural environment, is it not possible that the landscape of northern East Anglia was different from that of the south because of deep-rooted differences in society that are clearly evidenced in the

Iron Age, Roman, and earliest medieval periods, and which appear to have persisted as social and economic networks (though it must be acknowledged that these could have been influenced by topography)? Just a few examples must suffice. One regionally distinctive aspect of the ecclesiastical landscape in the north was the large numbers of circular church towers: there were 185 to the north of the Gipping–Lark valleys, and just six in Essex (Williamson 2006a, 91). It has been argued that this design was adopted due to the lack of good freestone in the county necessary for building corners, but this cannot have been the reason (Heywood 1988). First, Essex and southern Suffolk are similarly deficient in this material yet have overwhelmingly square church towers, and secondly there were several sources of freestone in the west of Norfolk used in church building including both circular and square towers (Allen 2004a). Clearly, the decision of these communities to build circular church towers had nothing to do with the nature of local building supplies. Another oddity of the ecclesiastical landscape to the north of the Gipping–Lark line is that there are seventeen examples of two or three churches being located in the same churchyard; there is just one in Essex (Williamson 2006a, fig. 4.12). This cannot, in any way, be due to regional variation in the physical landscape and must be due to differences in the structure of society, such as the relatively large proportions of freemen in the north who may have collectively founded a new church next to an existing one as an expression of their independence from lordly control (Williamson 2006a, 89): in the Domesday survey this area certainly had a very high proportion of freemen in the population compared to the rest of the country (Darby 1977, fig. 20).

There are even differences either side of the Gipping–Lark line in vernacular architecture, for example in how roofs were supported, and in the presence of 'Wealden' styles houses in both towns and the countryside in southern greater East Anglia but not the north (Alston 1999; Colman 1999; Colman and Barnard 1999; Haward and Aitkins 1999). During the sixteenth century, when open halls were floored over and chimneystacks replaced hearths, in south-west Suffolk and Essex they tended to be inserted against the cross-passage, while in north-east Suffolk and Norfolk they were usually placed between the hall and the inner room (Williamson 2006a, 100). And one last example: north of the Gipping–Lark line ceramic pantile roofs were found on over 30 per cent of post-medieval buildings (in Norfolk and north-west Suffolk the figure is over 60 per cent), whereas in Essex and southern Suffolk they occurred on less than 5 per cent of buildings (Williamson 2006a, 104). It is remarkable how persistent and ever present the Gipping–Lark boundary is in so many facets of the landscape of greater East Anglia: soils will have affected farming practice, which may indeed account for some of the differences in how the countryside was structured, but they did not determine how house plans and roof structures were designed. In an interesting revisiting of old ethnic and migration-based explanations for landscape change, Martin (2007) has also noted that place-name and linguistic evidence suggests a greater Scandinavian influence in northern East Anglia compared to the south, but this may simply have been another layer added to a pattern of regional difference that was already firmly established. The nucleation of settlement around the future site of parish churches—or perhaps the early churches themselves—clearly happened around the eighth century, before any Scandinavian influence, and in seeking possible causal factors we may have to look no further than the wider economic and social changes of the 'long eighth century' that will be discussed in Chapter 6.

6

Marching On? The Development of Villages
and Common Fields in South Wales

By the eleventh century, it is clear that landscapes characterized by nucleated villages and common fields had been created across large areas of central England, as far south-west as central Somerset. Key character-defining features of this agrarian system were that the vast majority of a community's cultivated land was arranged in two or three common fields, which were exploited from a single nucleated settlement, with relatively small areas of meadow, permanent pasture, and/or woodland usually located in the peripheral parts of the parish. This approach to social organization and managing the countryside was relatively consistent across large areas of the 'champion' countryside, and the villages and common fields that appear to have been created on Glastonbury Abbey's central Somerset estates during the tenth century, for example, would have been quite at home in the East Midlands. It would appear, therefore, that part of medieval society had a very well-developed idea of how the landscape might be physically constructed and communally exploited, and this chapter explores whether this concept was exported when new areas of land were acquired whether by conquest or colonization, using southern Wales as a case study.

Two areas—southern Monmouthshire and Pembrokeshire—have been selected as case studies through which to examine the character of landscapes created under English influence beyond the central zone (Fig. 6.1). Southern Monmouthshire, in south-east Wales, was conquered in the late eleventh century and then divided between two lordships—Netherwent and Caerleon—that fell into Anglo-Norman and Welsh hands respectively (the latter receiving protection from the English crown). Of particular significance for this study is the way in which the landscapes of these two areas developed so differently following the Norman Conquest, most notably on the extensive area of marshland that fringed the coast and were reclaimed and settled in the late eleventh and twelfth centuries. The second case study is Pembrokeshire, in south-west Wales, where documentary sources tell us that the Norman Conquest was followed by extensive Anglo-Norman and Flemish colonization, and the south of which

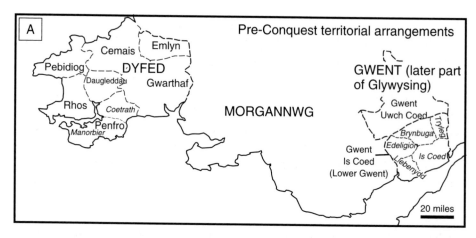

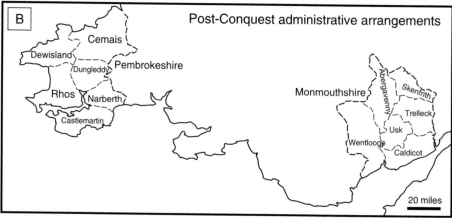

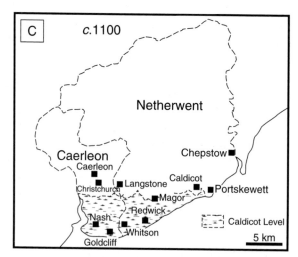

Fig. 6.1. The major pre- and post-Norman Conquest political and administrative divisions of south-east and south-west Wales (Monmouthshire and Pembrokeshire respectively) (after Rees 1951, plates 29–30, 38, and 40; Richards 1969).

was described in the sixteenth century as 'England beyond Wales' due to its strongly Anglicized culture. Austin (2005) has recently questioned whether the Anglo-Norman marcher lords really had a significant impact on this landscape, or whether the English character of the region was simply a sixteenth-century myth written by an aspirant gentry in the context of the Tudor policy of amalgamation that culminated in the Acts of Union. It is certainly true that by the sixteenth century the south of Pembrokeshire was strongly Anglicized in terms of its language, architecture, and self-perception, but does this explain the very real differences in the physical structure of the countryside compared to the north? Taken together these two case studies hopefully shed further light on the processes that contributed to local and regional variation in medieval landscape character.

There is, however, one drawback to studying these areas that needs to be acknowledged: the early medieval period is virtually aceramic apart from a handful of sites producing pottery imported from the Mediterranean during the fifth to seventh centuries (as is also the case for much of south-west England), and there is almost a complete dearth of palaeoenvironmental sequences covering the past two millennia (Caseldine 2006, map 7.2).

THE ENGLISH AND WELSH LANDSCAPES OF SOUTH-EAST MONMOUTHSHIRE

Hills and marshes: the physical topography of south-east Monmouthshire

The physical topography of south-east Monmouthshire is one of dramatic variations, with a broad coastal plain comprising reclaimed marshland known as the Gwent Levels, lying between the Severn estuary to the south and a range of hills to the north (Fig. 6.2). The largest area of former marshland is the Caldicot Level between Sudbrook Point in Portskewett and the river Usk, which was extensively settled in the Roman period but then suffered a period of flooding as it reverted to an intertidal saltmarsh. Although there may have been some earlier medieval settlement, the area was substantially reclaimed after the Norman Conquest and as such provided a 'cleaned sheet' upon which the new Marcher lords and their communities created an entirely new cultural landscape (a process also seen in Somerset and the Norfolk Marshland: see Chapters 3 and 5). So how far did this colonization reflect the concept of villages and common fields that was now so prevalent just across the Severn estuary in England's central zone?

The Anglo-Norman lordships in south-east Wales

During the first half of the eleventh century, southern Wales was divided between a series of kingdoms with Gwent in the south-east (approximating to

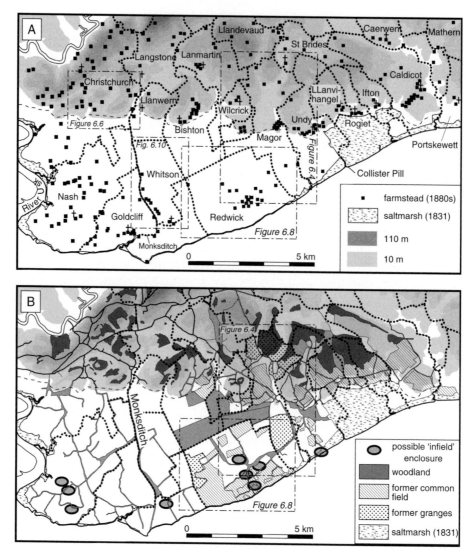

Fig. 6.2. South-east Monmouthshire (the Caldicot Level and adjacent dryland areas). (A) variation in the 19th-century settlement pattern (based on the Ordnance Survey First Edition Six Inch maps). (B) distribution of selected historic landscape character types (based on 18th- and 19th-century maps listed in Rippon 1996a, 129–32), and possible early 'infield' enclosures (after Rippon 2000b, fig. 4).

the pre-1974 county of Monmouthshire), Morgannwg to the west (in the area later covered by Glamorgan), and Dyfed in the south-west (in what became Pembrokeshire and Carmarthenshire) (Fig. 6.1). The border with England was marked by the mighty river Wye, across which there were a number of English incursions during the 1040s and 1050s. The Anglo-Saxon Chronicle describes these as culminating in 1065 when Earl Harold constructed some form of building, perhaps used as a hunting lodge, at Portskewett on the strategically important Sudbrook headland, which looks out across the Severn estuary towards Bristol (Swanton 1996, 190–1). The English victory was, however, brief, as later that year, Caradog, son of Gruffydd, raided Portskewett, killing most of the people there. Shortly after 1066, however, the Norman William fitz Osbern, earl of Hereford, founded a castle at Striguil (now known as Chepstow), marking the start of the Anglo-Norman conquest of South Wales (Davies 1987, 27–9; Williams 1993; R. Turner 2004).

English and Welsh control of the lordships of Netherwent and Caerleon

In order to explain the divergent ways in which the landscape of south-east Monmouthshire developed, it is necessary to understand some of its political history. In 1071 William fitz Osbern died and was succeeded by his son Roger de Breteuil who was involved in a conspiracy against the king and so forfeited his estates to the crown in 1075. Under William II (1087–1100) much of southern Gwent was incorporated into the royal lordship of Netherwent (Lower Gwent), based at Chepstow Castle, which Henry I granted to Walter fitz Richard around 1115, and on whose death in 1138 it descended to his nephew Gilbert de Clare (R. Turner 2004, 225). In 1189 the lordship passed to William Marshall following his marriage to Isabel de Clare, and upon the death of the last male in the Marshall line in 1245 the lordship was divided, with Chepstow being granted to the Bigod family. The lordship of Netherwent extended as far west as Langstone, which included a sub-manor of Whitson on the Caldicot Level to the south (CIPM v. 335–6; see below), and the demesne manor of Magor, which included its own subsidiaries down on the reclaimed marshes (Redwick and Porton). Following the death of William Marshall in 1245, Magor was retained by the crown, although it was subsequently divided between two manors based in Magor itself and Redwick (Courtney forthcoming). To the south-west of Chepstow lay the small lordship of Caldicot which in 1086 was held by Durand, sheriff of Gloucestershire (DB fo. 162; *DB Gloucs.* W15), and which subsequently was divided between various family lines (see below; Bradney 1932, 110; Courtney forthcoming).

To the west of Chepstow lay the lordship of Caerleon, a symbolic reoccupation of the former Roman legionary fortress that would have helped secure the strategically important Usk estuary, and was presumably intended as a base for further expansion (Howell 2001). The Herefordshire Domesday survey refers to William of Ecouis as holding eight carucates of land in the castlery of Caerleon that Thurstan held from him (DB fo. 185ᵛ; *DB Herefs.* 14,1). During the reign of William II Thurstan's lands were granted by the crown to Winebald de Ballon, who lost Caerleon to Morgan ap Owain around 1136. Caerleon lordship at this time must have included extensive areas of coastal marshland to the east of the Usk, as Morgan and his brother Iorwerth granted land there, in Nash and Goldcliff, to the newly founded Goldcliff Priory (CChR ii. 360–1; Williams 1970–1, 39; Davies 1987, 96; Courtney forthcoming). In 1157/8 Morgan was slain and the lordship passed to Iorwerth (*Brut y Ty*, 60, 66, 70; Davies 1987, 275; Courtney forthcoming). Caerleon remained in Welsh hands until 1217 when it was captured by William Marshall from Morgan ap Howel, although the latter, and his successor Maredudd ap Gruffydd, continued to hold the commote or manor of Llebenydd (which became the parish of Christchurch, to the east of the Usk). The partition of the Marshall inheritance in 1247 gave Caerleon and the westernmost lands of the lordship of Chepstow to Richard de Clare, whose successor Gilbert de Clare dispossessed Maredudd of Llebenydd in *c.*1270 (*Brut y Ty*, 96; Davies 1987; Courtney forthcoming). This meant that English supremacy was finally established over the whole region, including all parts of the Caldicot Level, although not before the historic landscape had developed in very different ways in those areas which, during the late eleventh and twelfth centuries, had been under English and Welsh control, and this forms the focus of this case study.

The impact of lordship on the historic landscape: the fen-edge villages of Netherwent

The eastern part of our study area lies in the parish of Caldicot, whose landscape is dominated by a castle and adjacent village, surrounded by extensive common meadows and open fields that physically at least bear strong similarities to the central zone of England (Fig. 6.2). In Domesday it was a single manor held by Durand the sheriff (DB fo. 162; *DB Gloucs.* W15), although by the early thirteenth century it was divided between the Bohun manor of Caldicot East End, based at the castle, and the fitz Herbert manor of Caldicot Westend (also known as Caldicot by Caerwent: see above). By 1613 it was further divided between four manors—Caldicot (Eastend) (with [Shire]Newton),[1] Dewstow, Westend, and Priory—whose lands were so intermingled that their bounds could not be described (Bradney 1932, 110); Priory represents the former lands of Llanthony-by-Gloucester Priory based at Church Farm (Birbeck 1970, 14; Rhodes 2002, p. xiv). Dewstow is an isolated farm beyond the northern edge of the open fields which is probably the '1 carucate of land at St Deweys' which remained an episcopal estate until 1650 (Moore 1982, note W6), and as such appears to be a survivor from the pre-Anglo-Norman dispersed settlement pattern that the village and open fields appear to have replaced to the south. Large areas of these dryland common fields are documented from the thirteenth century (e.g. GwRO D.43/5557, 5559, 6166), and they survived into the eighteenth and nineteenth centuries when maps show that West (or

---

[1] Shirenewton was a detached block of land (the 'sheriff's new farm') carved out of the forest of Wentwood *c.*5 km to the north, presumably as his hunting ground (Courtney forthcoming).

Great) Field and Elm (or Church) Field lay to the north of the village, and South (or Mill) Field to the south (GwRO D.501/1332; D.1670/0069). The wetland areas also appear to have been managed communally as a series of common meadows. In contrast, there is nothing in the structure of the historic landscape, or surviving as earthworks, to suggest that the land around Dewstow was ever laid out as open fields.

To the west of Caldicot lay three strip parishes (Ifton, Rogiet, and Llanfihangel) whose landscape was also typical of Midland England. In the nineteenth century each consisted of wooded hills to the north, and large rectangular or polygonal fields suggestive of enclosed common fields on the lower slopes that surrounded small but compact villages adjacent to a church and manor house close to the fen-edge. Ifton was held by the Pycott family and in 1306 was also known as Picotsfield (Bradney 1932, 124), and a perambulation of the manorial bounds in 1677 includes reference to 'a stile called Temple Stile lying in the west field of Yfton' (Bradney 1932, 124). The former existence of common fields in neighbouring Rogiet is suggested by the Ifton perambulation, which refers to 'Rogiatt's Field', an area that a map of *c*.1760 shows as still having several small patches of unenclosed strips (NLW Tredegar Maps, vol. viii; Bradney 1932, 124). Llanfihangel Rogiet is first recorded in *c*.905 when Brochfael, king of Gwent, granted Cyfeilliog, bishop of Llandaff, six *modii* of land at *Uilla Tref Peren id est Lannmihaegel maur* (Davies 1979, No. 233). By 1777 the settlement consisted of just two farmhouses and four cottages, although in 1651 there were nineteen farms and seven cottages along with an alehouse, bakehouse, and a forge, all built around a substantial village green: this rapid depopulation was due to engrossment by the lord of the manor (Stopgate 1986), which may also account for the small size of Ifton and Rogiet. The field boundary pattern in Llanfihangel is suggestive of enclosure by agreement of former common fields, small fragments of which survived to the east of the village to be mapped in the eighteenth century and described in the perambulation of 1710 (GwRO D.668/25). The parishes of Ifton and Rogiet extended all the way to the coast, although there was very limited reclamation, with the majority of the area forming the large intertidal saltmarsh of Caldicot Moor. The western side of the Moor was marked by Collister Pill, down which a sea wall ran from the fen-edge to the coast at which point it turned west to embrace the rest of the Caldicot Level, thereby protecting that area from tidal inundation. Why the marshes south of Ifton, Rogiet, and Llanfihangel were left mostly unreclaimed is unclear.

Undy, to the west of Llanfihangel is a more substantial strip parish, but follows a similar pattern to those to the east, extending from a fen-edge village up onto the wooded hills to the north, and across the marshes to the coast in the south (Figs. 6.2–4). Immediately north of the village lay at least two common fields that survived into the mid seventeenth century (Great Common Field and West Field: NLW Tred. 87/164). The lowest-lying backfen was occupied by a

Fig. 6.3. Aerial view of the fen-edge villages of Magor and Undy, and the reclaimed marshland of the Caldicot Level to the south, looking north-east from above the Severn estuary.

substantial common, while the slightly higher marshes towards the coast were covered by an area of irregularly shaped fields and small common meadows that survived into the eighteenth and nineteenth centuries (NLW Lockwood, vol. i, fo. 12; Tredegar, vol. viii).

Magor is the last of these strip parishes to run from the hills that rise above the Caldicot Level all the way to the coast, and its historic landscape is of broadly similar character to Undy, with woodland in the north, a substantial nucleated village surrounded by common fields on the lower hills, common land in the lowest-lying backfen, and reclaimed marshes towards the coast (Figs. 6.2–4). The common fields survived substantially unenclosed until the mid nineteenth century (and are mapped on the Tithe Survey: Rippon 1996a, fig. 36), and a series of eighteenth-century leases record their subdivisions as 'Beedumwat Field', 'Knowl Field', 'Marle Pitt Field', 'Middle Field', 'Uppermost Field', and 'Skiviocke' (e.g. GwRO D.25/0489, 0564; NLW Tredegar 58/95). There is some documentary evidence that the village may have had an unusual status, as there are references to 'burgages' (e.g. Bradney 1932, 229), and Magor may have been a small rural borough, perhaps similar to those in Pembrokeshire where tenants had burghal status but an agricultural means of subsistence, and performed agrarian labour services such as ploughing, harrowing, and reaping on the lord's demesne (see below: Kissock 1990, 230). Unlike the parishes to the east, the settlement pattern in Magor was not wholly nucleated, since on the northern hills, beyond the common fields, there was a series of isolated farmsteads. Of these Red Castle (later renamed in Welsh as Castell Coch) is documented in 1270 and 1314, when it was held as half a knight's fee by Roger Seymour, while another separate 'manor' at Salisbury was held in 1314 by the heir of John ap Adam (Bradney 1932, 228, 230). These may have been Welsh

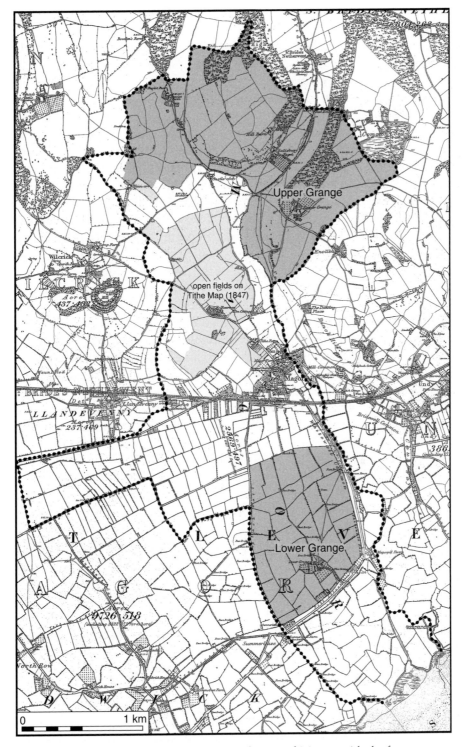

Fig. 6.4. Ordnance Survey First Edition Six Inch map of Magor, with the former granges of Tintern Abbey, and common field extant on the 1831 Commissioners of Sewers map highlighted. For the location see Fig. 6.2.

survivors from the pre-Anglo-Norman landscape that escaped the restructuring of the landscape across the southern part of the parish, or they may have originated as secondary settlements, perhaps woodland assarts, founded after the village and common fields were laid out. A third isolated farmstead hints at the former: Upper Grange first appears in the documentary record as *Merthyr Geryn* (the church of Geryn the martyr), a road to which is referred to in the pre-Conquest bounds of the Llanfihangel Rogiet charter of *c*.905 (see above). In 1133–48 it was granted to Tintern Abbey, becoming their 'Upper Grange' in order to distinguish it from Lower Grange down on the marshes (CChR iii. 96–100; LPFD Hen. VIII xii (i). 350–1; Bradney 1932, 231; Williams 1965, 2; 1990, 63; Parkes and Webster 1974). Ninety acres (36 ha) at Skeviot was granted to Tintern Abbey in the mid twelfth century (Williams 1965, 3), and Hill Barn, which clearly occupies a woodland assart, is also on tithe-free land that probably reflects the former extent of the monastic estate.

The series of compact nucleated villages on the fen-edge continues to the west of Magor. Llandevenny was a detached hamlet of St Bride's parish (Fig. 6.5), and in 1766 still had the remains of a small open field to the east: its limited size, and small percentage of the agricultural land within the parish that it covered, is such that it cannot really be regarded as a common field system in the Midland sense (NLW Lockwood, vol. i, fos. 9 and 10; Bradney 1932, 227). The manor and parish of Bishton can be traced back to an estate called *Lann Catgualatyr* granted to Bishop Berthwyn of Llandaff in the early eighth century (Davies 1979, No. 180b). At this stage the estate extended as far south

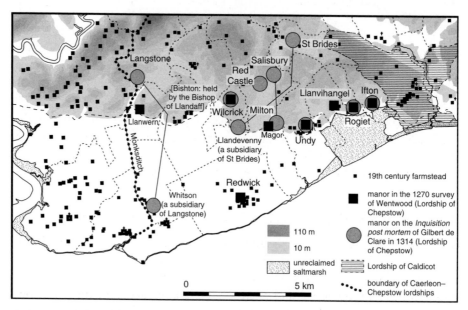

Fig. 6.5. English manors in the 1270 Survey of Wentwood, and manors in the *Inquisition post mortem* of Gilbert de Clare in 1314 (Bradney 1932).

as the coast, although following the Anglo-Norman Conquest the separate manor/parish of Redwick was created on these marshes. Bishton has a compact village with what appears to be a small, planned block of tenements at its core. This lies 1 km along the fen-edge from the pre-Conquest church, a difference in location that may reflect a desire on the part of its inhabitants to be closer to the tract of relatively flat agricultural land in this area, which an estate map of 1758 shows had been laid out as an open field, with extensive common meadows along the fen-edge (NLW x.M00/912). Llanwern is first recorded in *c*.970 when King Morgan of Glamorgan returned a series of estates to Bishop Gwgon of Llandaff, including *Lann Guern Tiuauc* (Davies 1979, 125). By the nineteenth century the parish church stood in splendid isolation due to the creation of a substantial landscape park, although an engraving of *c*.1700 shows a large number of houses nearby, suggesting another compact village (Bradney 1932, 251). The creation of the park has swept away all trace of the earlier field system.

The dryland landscape in the lordship of Caerleon

To the east of Llanwern lies the extensive parish of Christchurch, which corresponds to the medieval commote or manor of Llebenydd based at Liswerry on the fen-edge (Welsh *Llys* = court). Llebenydd was under Welsh control from 1136, when the lordship of Caerleon was seized by Morgan ap Owain, until *c*.1270 when it was seized by Gilbert de Clare (see above), and this different political history may account for some of the marked differences in the structure of the historic landscape compared to Bishton, Magor, and the other parishes within the lordships of Chepstow and Caldicot to the east. In the nineteenth century the settlement pattern was almost wholly dispersed, with a series of isolated farmsteads and small hamlets, surrounded by closes that bear none of the tell-tale signs of former common fields that are found further east (Fig. 6.6). A farm called Hendre ('winter dwelling'), lies on the hills overlooking the fen-edge at Pwll-Pan, which may reflect the seasonal way that this landscape was exploited before permanent settlement was possible on the marshes. This landscape of dispersed settlement is presumably what the areas further east looked like before the creation of villages and common fields.

Discussion: contrasting landscapes of English and Welsh character

Overall, the fen-edge parishes/manors in Netherwent (the later lordship of Chepstow) all show a striking similarity, reminiscent of England's central zone, with wooded hills restricted to the periphery of the parishes to the north, arable common fields on the lower slopes surrounding compact, sometimes planned, villages with common meadows along the fen-edge. We know very little about the landscape that these villages and common fields replaced, although the

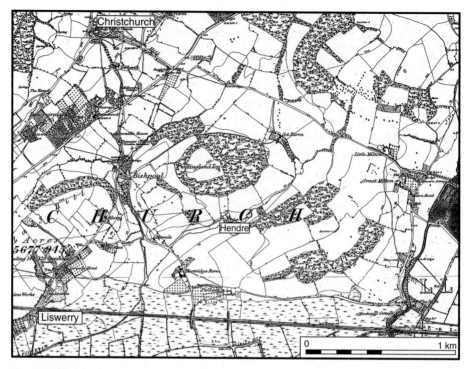

Fig. 6.6. The distinctive pattern of dispersed settlement and fields always held in severalty in Christchurch parish (based on the First Edition Ordnance Survey Six Inch sheets for Monmouthshire XXIX and XXXIV surveyed in 1881–2, with additional shading for wetlands of the Caldicot Level). For the location see Fig. 6.2.

Llandaff charters show that by the eighth to tenth centuries this was settled countryside divided up into a series of estates. Analogy with Christchurch and other areas to the west, within the Welsh lordship of Caerleon, suggests that in the pre-Conquest period there would have been a dispersed settlement pattern, of which the scattered farmsteads in the northern part of Magor including Merthyr Geryn, along with Dewstow in Caldicot, may be the last survivors that escaped the nucleation of settlement and creation of common fields.

The Caldicot Level: a landscape created on a 'cleaned slate'

The boundary between the English lordship of Chepstow and the Welsh lordship of Caerleon, as it crosses the Caldicot Level, is marked by the Monksditch Stream which flows between the fen-edge parishes of Llanwern to the east and Christchurch to the' west (Fig. 6.2). As the stream crosses the Caldicot Level it has been straightened and embanked and few traces survive of its former, naturally meandering, course. Until the area's reclamation this was a vast coastal saltmarsh, with the Romano-British landscape sealed by a layer of alluvium (Bell 1994; Locock and Walker 1998; Locock 2000;

Meddens and Beasley 2001; Allen 2002). During the early medieval period this was, therefore, a physically relatively uniform environment traversed by a network of naturally meandering tidal creeks, some of which carried the waters of freshwater streams flowing off the adjacent uplands, and due to this uniform antecedent landscape any local variation in landscape character emphatically cannot be due to differences in soils or topography. The historic landscape of today was created through a long process of reclamation that has been described elsewhere in some detail (Rippon 1996a; 2000a; 2001). In summary, it appears that the earliest phase of colonization involved the construction of low embankments that encircled roughly oval-shaped areas that acted as 'summer dykes', designed to keep unseasonally high summer tides off a small area of agricultural land, but which made no attempt to protect the area all year round (Fig. 6.2). Examples of these 'infield' enclosures are preserved within the later field boundary patterns,[2] and such features are found on the marshes all around the Severn estuary, suggesting that we are seeing a common (but very simple and logical) approach towards the initial stages of marshland colonization in both English and Welsh areas. Excavation and palaeoenvironmental analysis at one such 'infield' enclosure on the North Somerset Levels at Puxton has shown that the encircling bank was constructed on the surface of what was still an intertidal saltmarsh, although by the later eleventh century conditions had changed as the entire wetland area was protected from tidal inundation and a wholly freshwater ecology was established (Rippon 2006a).

East of Monksditch: the creation of reclaimed landscapes in the English lordships

Thus far the landscape across most of the Caldicot Level appears to have developed in the same way, but once protected by a sea wall, and once the work of converting this former saltmarsh into productive agricultural land began, the areas either side of Monksditch developed very differently. Once protected by a sea wall, the earliest areas to be settled and enclosed lay on the naturally higher areas beside the coast (which are around 6 m OD (Ordnance datum)), leading to the earlier 'infield' enclosures being incorporated into the post-reclamation landscape, with the lower-lying inland areas (the 'backfens', around 5.5 m OD) being enclosed later. To the east of the Monksditch there were two wholly marshland communities—Whitson and Redwick—while large areas of reclaimed marshland also fell within the parishes of Magor and Undy. The settlement pattern in this area was almost wholly nucleated, with villages at Redwick and Whitson and a small number of dispersed settlements,

---

[2] Chapel Tump in Undy (Allen 2004b), Church Farm, Brick House, and Broadmead Farm in Redwick, Great Porton in Whitson, and Farmfield, Ashtree Farm, and Burnt House in Nash.

of which Lower Grange in Magor and Grangefield ('New Grange') in Redwick were monastic granges of Tintern Abbey (Fig. 6.7). Little Porton may be a coastal fishing settlement established after the sea wall was set back to its present location in the late medieval period (see above) as it is clearly inserted into the earlier field boundary pattern. The remaining isolated farmstead, Chapel Tump in Undy, lies adjacent to an 'infield' enclosure (Allen 2004b). As only Chapel Tump can therefore be regarded as a normal farmstead, the settlement pattern in this area of reclaimed marshland was almost wholly nucleated.

Redwick: a nucleated village in Wales

The landscape in Redwick was focused on the village, which in the nineteenth century was an agglomeration of farmsteads and cottages, some of which held a few acres of land, located next to the church (Figs. 6.7–9). That there was a more sizeable settlement here in medieval times is shown by several areas of shrunken settlement earthworks, and recent excavations that have revealed evidence for twelfth- or thirteenth-century occupation in plots that were later abandoned (Rippon 1996a, fig. 5; Gaimster and Bradley 2001; 2002). A series of broad droveways radiated from the village centre, passing through field systems whose irregular patterns at first defy explanation. A closer examination, however, reveals evidence for extensive former common fields, with some subtly different characteristics to the north and south of the village. The earliest map of Redwick, drawn up by the Commissioners of Sewers in 1831, shows that to the south of Redwick the small, irregularly shaped closes also contained some areas of surviving common field, and the similarly highly fragmented pattern of landownership in the adjacent enclosed areas suggests that these were also once managed in this way (Fig. 6.8). Several of the farms on the southern side of the village appear to occupy former strips within this common field system, suggesting that they migrated there following enclosure. These former common fields are first documented in 1361, when John Durant leased certain lands in Redwick to Richard Hobelow including 'a furlong called *Colyslonde*' adjacent to land called *Robartslond* (GwRO D.43/542), which also abutted *Cheleshalfacre* (GwRO D.501/80); later sources place these to the east of Sea Street and south of South Row Street (GwRO D.368/25; NLW Tredegar 149/55). To the north of Redwick village the landscape is subtly different, with slightly larger, more irregularly shaped fields and a less fragmented pattern of landholding whose character is more in keeping with closes held in severalty than common fields. Several farms (North Row, Brick House, Greenmoor Farm, and Longlands) lie beside the two droveways that head north from the village and, in addition to holding relatively compact blocks of adjacent fields (what can be regarded as 'home grounds'), they also held detached parcels in the extant and former common fields south of the village. An analysis of the pattern of landholding in 1831 shows that tenements typically included strips scattered right across the common fields of Redwick, as was the case in England's central zone, rather than clustered close to the farmstead, as was seen in areas such as East Anglia.

To the west of the village, from Windmill Reen to the parish boundary at Elver Pill Reen, the map of 1831 shows an extensive common field called Broad-mead within which virtually all the farms in Redwick held strips. The northern (inland) limit of Broadmead was marked by a long sinuous watercourse known as Mere (= OE *boundary*) Reen that continues around the northern edge of the village 'home grounds' where it becomes Cocks Street Wall (recorded in 1430: GwRO D.43/4002), Long Land Reen, and finally Ynis Wall Reen. The 'wall' names gives us a clue as to the origin of this important landscape feature: as these backfens were progressively enclosed there would have been a growing problem with flooding which led to the construction of fen-banks or 'walls' that were designed to prevent the freshwater run-off from encroaching into the enclosed lands further south. This Mere Wall Reen–Ynis Wall Reen boundary was the first of a series of such embankments, the second being Rush Wall which marks the northern edge of Redwick parish. These fen-banks, and their adjacent drainage ditches, would have taken considerable human effort to construct, and their considerable length suggests a strong degree of either central control or community cooperation. Between the Long Land Reen and Rush Wall, the pattern of fields has a clearly planned layout, with several long, straight parallel boundaries between which were a series of long narrow fields. In three areas (Cocks Furlong, Ready Mead, and Toad Mead)[3] there are common meadows that survived into the nineteenth century, while the similarly highly fragmented pattern of landownership in the adjacent enclosed areas suggests that these were also once held in common. Most farmsteads in Redwick held detached parcels in Broadmead and the former common fields to the north and south of the village.

In the north-west corner of the parish, between Mere Reen and Rush Wall, there is a series of large rectangular closes laid out between a series of straight, parallel boundaries in an area known as the 'Black Moores' from at least the fifteenth century (Bradney 1932, 238). A large part of this area can be identified as Tintern Abbey's New Grange, and a survey of two, concentric, moated enclosures there suggests that the 'Black Moores' were enclosed after the earliest moat was dug, but before it was extended (CPR Edw. VI iv. 31–2; LPFD Hen. VIII ii (i). 724; NLW Tredegar No. 254; Williams 1990, 31, 63; Rippon 1996a, 80–1). Landownership within those closes that were not part

---

[3] Although Rush Wall itself is first documented in 1656 (NLW Bad. D. 1397), 'Little Cox Furlong' is first recorded in 1503 abutting 'Brownslands' (Bradney 1932, 238), while small parcels of one and a half acres in 'Great Cox Furlong' are recorded from 1605/6 to the north of Cox Street and abutting Black Moor (GwRO D.43/3994; D.501/109; Bradney 1932, 238). One and a half acres in Toad Mead are recorded in 1520 (GwRO D.501/81).

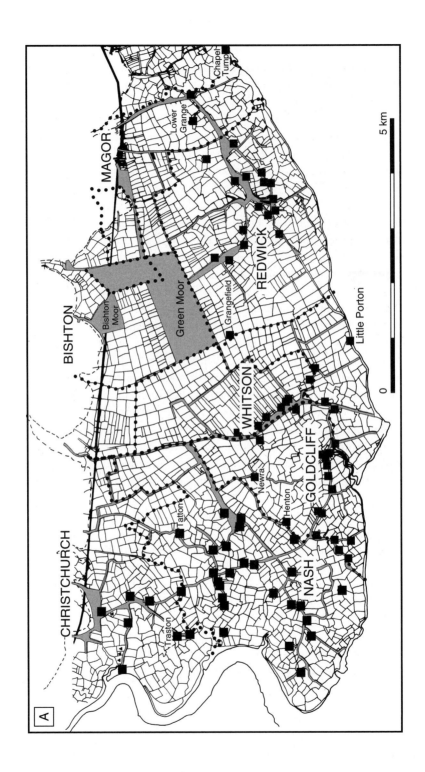

A

CHRISTCHURCH

BISHTON

MAGOR

Chapel Tump

Lower Grange

Bishton Moor

Green Moor

Grangefield

REDWICK

WHITSON

Little Porton

Tatton

Newra

Henton

GOLDCLIFF

Traston

NASH

5 km

0

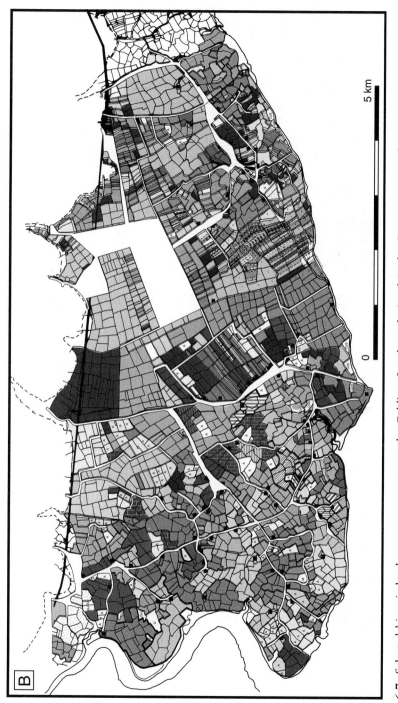

Fig. 6.7. Selected historic landscape components on the Caldicot Level, as depicted in the Commissioners of Sewers maps of 1831 (GwRO D.1365.1). (A) the patterns of fields, roads, commons, and settlements; (B) the pattern of landholding (with each tenement shaded differently). For greater detail on Redwick see Fig. 6.8 and for Whitson Fig. 6.10.

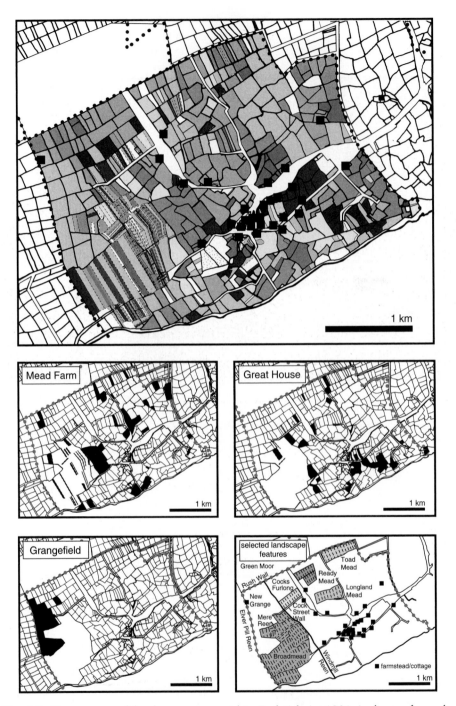

Fig. 6.8. The pattern of land occupancy within Redwick in 1831 (redrawn from the Commissioners of Sewers map: GwRO D.1365.1). Most tenements held highly fragmented landholdings (as illustrated individually for Mead Farm and Great House), reflecting the former extent of arable common fields and common meadows. The great common meadow at Broadmead was unenclosed when the Commissioners of Sewers survey was undertaken in 1831. The large block of rectangular fields to the north-west of Broadmead represents Tintern Abbey's former 'New Grange', now Grangefield Farm. For the location see Fig. 6.2.

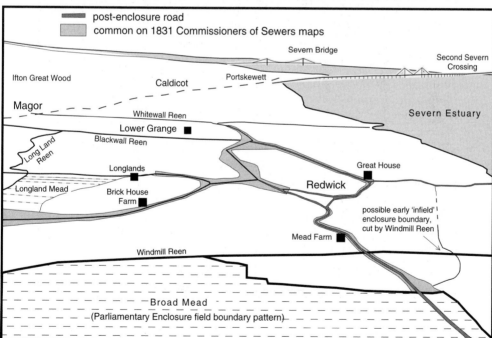

Fig. 6.9. Aerial view of Redwick and the eastern end of the Caldicot Level, looking east towards the Severn estuary.

of the New Grange estate was extremely fragmented, and the place name 'Black Moores', along with the field boundary morphology which is not suggestive of a former open field, indicates that this was once an area of common pasture, with parcels having been distributed amongst those tenements that had held rights there. The area to the north of Rush Wall, known as Green Moor, remained unenclosed until the mid nineteenth century. This was a large extra-parochial common, first recorded in 1327, that formed part of the medieval manors of Magor and Redwick, although a custumal of *c.*1596 records that the tenants of nearby Bishton, Llandevenny, Porton, Wilcrick, and Whitson all had rights of pasture there in return for the payment of an annual rent (CIPM vii. 46; NLW Tredegar 149/54).

The planned village of Whitson

To the west of Redwick is Whitson, where the parish church, with a fine Norman doorway, lies next to a possible infield 'enclosure', suggesting that the earliest phase of this area's colonization was the same as that seen in Redwick (see above). The place name Whitson appears as Wytteston in 1291 and is of English origin, possibly a 'personal name + -ton' type (Charles 1938, 256). Whitson was the most westerly knight's fee in the lordship of Gilbert de Clare in 1314, being part of the upland manor of Langstone, and the lower-lying backfens beyond the village at Whitson were known as Langstone Moor into the post-medieval period (Fig. 6.5; CIPM v. 336; GwRO D.501/918; NLW Bad.D.885–6). Langstone is first recorded in the late twelfth century when its lord, Nicholas fitz Robert (de Berkeley), granted the advowson of its church to St Augustine's Abbey in Bristol (Smyth 1883, 45), although it is unclear whether the Berkeley family held Whitson at this time. The village in Whitson was not around the church, but a short distance to the north. It initially consisted of a series of long narrow tenements, *c.*200 to 220 feet (60–7 m) wide, laid out along the edge of a funnel-shaped common (Fig. 6.10 and 6.11). At first sight these have the appearance of an open field, but there is no documentary evidence for this. In fact, the pattern of landownership and occupancy recorded on the Commissioners of Sewers map of 1831 suggests something very different. All the farmsteads in Whitson lay down the eastern side of the funnel-shaped common. Each has a block of land to the east. These first-phase tenements ended at two closely spaced ditches which were probably dug either side of a fen-bank, but which later became the narrow lane known as Middleway (Fig. 6.11). Over time these tenements were extended several times, the last of which terminated at the Keywall, resulting in a series of long, narrow landholdings (GwRO D.501/353; Rippon 1996a, 84–7; 2000b, 152–8). This sequential extension of the tenements created a distinctive planned landscape that is unique not just in the Caldicot Level but in all of the wetlands around the Severn estuary. So where did this remarkable planned village come from?

The closest parallels are to be found in the Low Countries where planned landscapes, with a single-row-plan village strung out along a linear feature with a series of tenements that were sequentially extended, are found where a great landowner appropriated the 'regality', or rights of exploitation, of wilderness areas, and leased them to colonists for a minimal rent in exchange for them undertaking reclamation (e.g. Besteman 1986, 338). There is no direct evidence for Dutch or Flemish involvement in the reclamation of Whitson, although Hassal (1815, 282) records a local tradition, regarded by him as superstition, that the Gwent Levels were drained by the Dutch, and on the neighbouring Wentlooge Level there is manor of Cogan Fleming recorded from the late seventeenth century (GwRO D.43/5397). This Flemish link is intriguing—there is also a place called Flemingston further west in Glamorgan—as it is well documented that the new Anglo-Norman lords employed Flemings to colonize their newly acquired estates in both Pembrokeshire (see below) and Scotland (Toorians 1990; 1996). Interestingly, Ralph Bluet (III; d. 1198 × 1199), steward of Chepstow Castle when it was held by the king as guardian of Isabel de Clare and then William Marshall after he married Isabel, held both Langstone and Whitson, along with Wiston in Pembrokeshire (Crouch 1990, 198–9). The latter is named after one of a series of Flemish colonists, Wizo, documented in the twelfth century, whose potential impact on the landscape of Pembrokeshire is discussed later in the chapter. The possibility of these Flemish colonists having been involved in the foundation of Whitson cannot be ruled out.

The impact of lordship on the historic landscape west of Monksditch: Goldcliff and Nash

The landscapes of Redwick and the fen-edge parishes east of Monksditch all bear the mark of English lordship and/or their colonists, and this fact that villages and common fields, so characteristic of England's central zone, were created in this area of newly colonized land suggests that this was a well-established approach towards managing the countryside. The landscape to the west of Monksditch, in the Welsh lordship of Caerleon, was, however, of a very different character (Fig. 6.7).

There were two wholly marshland parishes, at Goldcliff and Nash, while the largely dryland parish of Christchurch also extended from the hills overlooking the Usk down onto the wetlands. The primary area of settlement probably lay on the higher coastal marshes where a number of 'summer dykes' can be identified, including that west of the chapel at Nash where recent excavations have yielded twelfth- to thirteenth-century pottery (Bradley and Gaimster 2003, 337). When the surrounding areas were embanked and reclaimed, however, a very different landscape was created compared to Redwick and Whitson just the other side of Monksditch, with a dispersed settlement pattern of isolated farmsteads and small hamlets linked by a network of sinuous, meandering droveways that

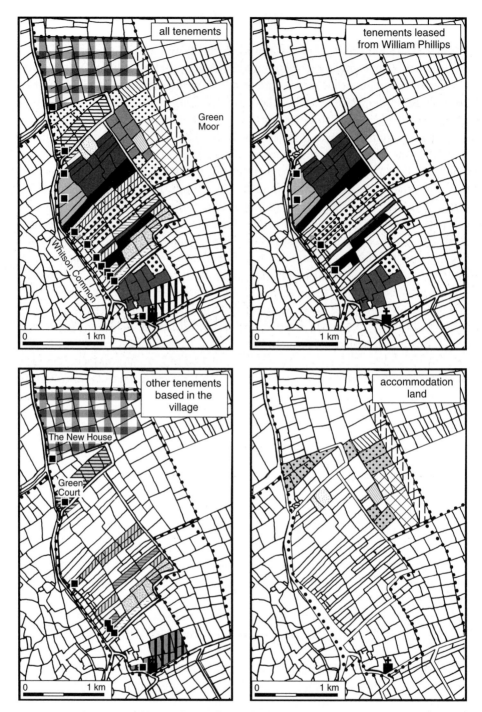

Fig. 6.10. Whitson in 1831 (redrawn from the Commissioners of Sewers map: GwRO D.1365.1). The superficially fragmented pattern of landholding can be disaggregated to reveal a series of discrete tenements that run back from the row of farmsteads along the edge of Whitson Common. Areas of 'accommodation land' (i.e. land held by farms outside the parish as summer grazing for fattening livestock) concentrate to the north and east of the medieval village, in areas of moorland that were only enclosed in the post-medieval period.

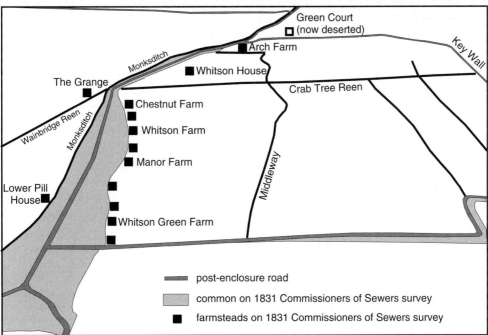

Fig. 6.11. Whitson, looking north. Note how the row of farmsteads is set back from the post-enclosure road as they lay along the edge of the funnel-shaped Whitson Common. For the location see Fig. 6.2.

show no sign of planning. The excellent survival of earthworks on the RAF air photography of the late 1940s reveals a number of deserted farmsteads and shrunken hamlets scattered across the area, but no deserted medieval villages like either Redwick or Whitson. This area also lacked an English manorial structure, as by the time the area was under the control of the de Clares in the early fourteenth century there were no knights' fees (CIPM v. 335–6), reflecting the impact of Welsh control during the twelfth century when most sub-infeudation occurred further east in the English lordship of Chepstow (Fig. 6.5).

The pattern of landownership and occupancy, as mapped in the eighteenth–nineteenth centuries, was also markedly different from that further east, being characterized by moderately compact but often interlocking landholdings suggestive of larger tenements that had been subdivided in a way that gave each new tenement a share of land in different areas (Fig. 6.7B). There is none of the highly fragmented landholding that appears to reflect the former existence of open fields, and there is only very slight documentary evidence for a single, small, open meadow known as Broadmead.[4] Otherwise, there is nothing in the field boundary pattern, a large collection of eighteenth-century estate maps, earlier documents, or the patterns of landholding to suggest the presence of open fields in the marshlands west of Monksditch. By the sixteenth century a number of other farms are recorded further from the coast, such as Henton, Newra, Tatton, and Traston (Bradney 1932, 283, 287–8, 309; Charles 1938, 245), and it is noteworthy that these larger and more compact landholdings were located towards the lower-lying backfens where secondary colonization of former open moorland is to be expected.

The language of a landscape: field and place names

In addition to the physical structure of the landscape there is marked spatial variation in the character of place and field names.[5] Most of the evidence is, unfortunately, post-medieval, although significant amounts of late medieval material survives for Magor, Redwick, and Rogiet, along with good sixteenth-century collections for Bishton and Undy, a series of sixteenth- to seventeenth-century leases and surveys of Caldicot (GwRO D.668/25; NLW Tredegar 147/31, 37, 169), and manorial bounds for Bishton (1552: GwRO D.43/4547), Caldicot (1613: NLW Tredegar 147/31; Bradney 1932, 110–11; Rees 1953, 135), Ifton (1677: Bradney 1932, 124), Llanfihangel (1650: GwRO D.668/25), Rogiet (1677: Bradney 1932, 267).

[4] In 1655 Edward, Lord Herbert, who held the demesne of Liswerry, had 'two small parcels in Broad Meade called the two Free Meares' (Bradney 1932, 291), and 'two pieces in Broadmead' are shown on an estate map of Pill Farm dated 1788 as two closes (NLW Lockwood dep. vol. i).
[5] This analysis is based on the 1st edn. One and Six Inch maps, field names on the Commissioners of Sewers maps of 1831, a wide range of 18th-century estate maps, and the calendared late medieval and post-medieval documents for each of the parishes in the study area in the National Library of Wales and Gwent Records Office (listed in Rippon 1996a, 129–32).

The strongest trend is north to south, with the almost universal use of English on the Levels, but significantly more Welsh on the adjacent drylands. In Redwick, for example, just 1 per cent of the field and place names were Welsh, and there is no Welsh name recorded for Redwick itself (Bradney 1932, 242–4). This can be contrasted with the fen-edge parish/manor of Bishton, immediately to the north, which was called *Lann Catgualatyr* in the early eighth century when it was granted to Bishop Berthwyn of Llandaff (Davies 1979, No. 180b), becoming known as Llangadwaladr or Tref Esgob in later years (Bradney 1932, 257). A perambulation of 1552 (GwRO D.43/431) provides a sample of twenty-six place names of which 65 per cent are Welsh, including the two streams that formed the eastern and western boundaries of the manor of which the latter, 'Nant Halen', is probably the 'Aber nant Alun' recorded in the bounds of the early eighth-century charter. All of these Welsh names in the perambulation, however, were on the dryland part of the manor, and all the landscape features recorded on the Levels in a series of sixteenth-century deeds are English (Alwarrsmeade, Bystonys mede, Chortmede, Lords Mead, Great Mead, Green Moor, Ryding, Short Meadow: NLW Bad. 109, 113, 115, 912–14). Even the Nant Halen stream was renamed the 'Earls Reen' (now the 'Elver Pill Reen') as it crosses the Levels (NLW Mad. Man. 2198). Overall, 44 per cent of the recorded place and field names in Bishton are Welsh, both in the sixteenth and nineteenth centuries.

There is also a significant east–west variation in the proportions of English and Welsh names within this study area. On the Caldicot Level, around a fifth of documented names in Christchurch and Nash are Welsh, with examples of watercourses (*Caepill* and *Ffynon Efa*), roads (*Hewl y Pont Ddy*), farms (*Pont Faen, Ty-Du, Ty-Pondra, Ty-Pontref*), and fields (*Dwy Erow Pen Y Wall, Gwain Glan Y Nant, Hewl Y Pont, Wayne Vawr*, and *Y Kae Mawr*). In Goldcliff and Whitson there are no recorded Welsh names, while in the backfen of Redwick there is just one hybrid name (*Ynis* Wall). On the drylands this marked east–west difference is also apparent with just two Welsh names (both watercourses) in Caldicot, a composite name (*Pwll* Rock) in the 1677 perambulation of Ifton, a single meadow (*Ffrith*) in Rogiet, and a single Welsh field name (*Erow Vain*) and *Monydd Hylen* Common in Llanfihangel. In Undy the landscape appears to have become entirely English in its language, while in Magor a handful of Welsh place names are found on the uplands (*Mertyr Geryn*), and on the Levels (the small port at *Abergwaitha* and *Pull-Y-Ffern* Reen). In Christchurch, in contrast, around half the place and field names on the uplands were Welsh.

It would appear, therefore, that the language of field and place names reflects the east to west, English–Welsh, division already identified in the physical fabric of the landscape. One conclusion of this analysis is that following the Conquest, the eastern part of Chepstow lordship (certainly as far west as Magor), saw an almost complete renaming of the landscape, presumably associated with its physical restructuring that led to the creation of villages and common fields, while Welsh remained strong in the west (the lordship of Caerleon). The field and place names that were created following the reclamation of the Caldicot Level follow the same pattern, with an almost wholly English nomenclature to the east of Monksditch, and significantly greater use of Welsh to the west.

Language is, however, fluid and it is conceivable that the greater use of Welsh to the west of Monksditch may be due to changes in society that post-date the initial creation of the fields, roads, and settlements that make up the physical fabric of the historic landscape. This is, however, a relatively small study area, and it is noticeable that there is not just east–west variation in the extent to which Welsh was used, but also significant north–south differences. If, for example, there was a general resurgence in the use of Welsh that spread from east to west, this cannot explain why there are also so few Welsh names on the Levels, compared to the adjacent drylands (the north–south variation), and it is tempting to suggest that this reflects the chronology of these landscapes. It would appear that the language of landscape is confirming the other indications of far greater Welsh influence in the west of the study area.

Discussion

The initial stage of colonization on the Caldicot Level was uniform across the whole area, with a series of 'summer dykes' constructed on the surface of what remained an intertidal marsh. None of these 'summer dykes' on the Caldicot Level has been excavated, although at Puxton, on the North Somerset Levels, an example has been dated to the late tenth or eleventh century, and palaeoenvironmental analysis shows that it was built on the surface of a saltmarsh. It would appear, therefore, that there was a common approach towards the early stages of marshland exploitation and modification all around the Severn estuary at this time, including all of the coastal fringes of the Caldicot Level (Rippon 2000a; 2000b; 2006a).

As the use of the Caldicot Level intensified over time, however, landscapes of very different character emerged, with villages (Redwick and Whitson) in the east, and a highly dispersed settlement pattern in the west (Goldcliff and Nash). The field systems in the east are dominated by common fields (with the exception of Tintern Abbey's granges at Lower Grange and New Grange), while in the west closes were almost all held in severalty. The landscapes in the east display clear evidence for planning, with a series of fen-banks stretching across Redwick, and the remarkable planned village of Whitson. The landscapes in Goldcliff, Nash, and Christchurch, in contrast, appear to have developed in a piecemeal fashion. A similar east to west contrast is also seen on the adjacent drylands with nucleated villages and common fields in the east (as far west as Bishton and possibly Llanwern), and dispersed settlement and fields held in severalty in the west that are far more in keeping with landscape character seen elsewhere in south-east Wales. This east to west variation in the physical character of the countryside is also reflected in the language of the landscape, with English field and place names dominating in the east, and Welsh being far more significant in the west. The boundary between these landscapes of different character would appear to be Monksditch, between Llanwern and Whitson in the east, and Goldcliff and Christchurch to the west.

There is no reason to believe that these physical differences within the fabric of the historic landscape do not reflect the medieval situation. In the post-medieval period at least there was a predominance of pastoral farming on the Levels, and the preservation of earthworks on the RAF aerial photography on the late 1940s is superb (Rippon 1996a, fig. 5, table 5). All these earthworks, however, are consistent with local variations in the character of the extant historic landscape: spade-dug gullies (known as gripes) that drained the surface of fields, occasional field boundaries that have been removed, and several areas of shrunken settlement earthworks. There is no evidence, however, for earthworks of earlier, relict, landscapes that would indicate a significant change in the character of the historic landscape: there never were villages in Goldcliff, Nash, or Christchurch, for example, or significantly dispersed settlement in Redwick, Magor, and Undy.

It seems clear, therefore, that on the drylands east of Monksditch the traditional Welsh landscape of dispersed settlement and fields predominantly held in severalty, as seen in the hills of Christchurch, was replaced with a landscape of nucleated villages and common fields similar to that of the central zone of England. This landscape contained a mixture of English and Welsh names, in contrast to the adjacent marshes which, following their reclamation, were named almost entirely in English. The physical fabric of the landscape, and the communal way in which it was managed, was also distinctive in its character, in sharp contrast to Nash and Goldcliff to the west whose landscape characteristics mirror those of Christchurch to the north. This case study has demonstrated how the reorganization (on the dryland areas) and creation (on the reclaimed wetlands) of landscapes in the Anglo-Norman lordship of Netherwent was clearly inspired by recent trends in the central zone of England, including Gloucestershire and Somerset which lay just across the Severn estuary. In the Welsh lordship of Christchurch, in contrast, there was no major change in the character of the dryland landscape, and this tradition of dispersed settlements surrounded by fields held in severalty was perpetuated when the adjacent marshes were reclaimed and colonized.

THE ENGLISH, WELSH, AND FLEMISH LANDSCAPES OF SOUTH-WEST WALES

The example of south-east Wales clearly shows the impact that conquest and lordship could have on the landscape, and the same appears to be true in the Pembrokeshire peninsula, in south-west Wales, which became known as 'Anglia Transwallia' ('England beyond Wales': Miles 1994, 36) because of the degree to which the countryside became Anglicized. By the sixteenth century there was a marked regional difference in the character of Pembrokeshire society, reflected in the dominance of the English language in the south and Welsh in the north. This has traditionally been attributed to Anglo-Norman colonization in the south, and as such provides an ideal region within which to examine how far the concept of managing a landscape through the creation of villages and common field was transplanted into newly colonized regions.

The southern half of Pembrokeshire is a predominantly lowland region of gently rolling hills bounded by the uplands around Narberth to the east and the Preseli (Prescelly) Hills to the north (Fig. 6.12). The vast majority of the area south of the Preseli Hills is drained by a series of rivers that flow south into the estuary of Milford Haven, while to the north a further area of gently undulating land is drained by a number of rivers that flow into Cardigan Bay. Across Pembrokeshire the soils are largely grade 3 in terms of their modern agricultural productivity, with most areas put down to pasture, and Williams (1988, 30) suggests that this was always a region of 'limited agrarian productivity', with the climate and soils 'mostly suited to pastoralism'. He goes on to suggest that 'similar conditions of limited productivity presumably obtained in the 1st millennium BC' (ibid.), although this very modern perspective can be questioned. The soils are, in fact, inherently fertile, particularly in the south, and apart from in upland areas the climate is characterized by very mild winters with little frost and warm, wet summers that are ideal for the growth of grass, root crops, and oats, with wheat and barley growing well in the lower-lying coastal areas to the south (Davies 1939, 98–102; Dicks 1967–8, 221). Early accounts of the region support the idea that this was far from being environmentally marginal. In the twelfth century, for example, Gerald of Wales suggested that 'of all the different parts of Wales, Dyfed … is at once the most beautiful and the most productive. Of all Dyfed, the province of Pembroke is the most attractive' (Giraldus Camb. 151). In the sixteenth century Leland described Dewisland on the west coast as 'bare of wood and meatily plentiful of barley corn, and reasonably of all other corn' (Toulmin Smith 1906, 63).

The antecedent landscape: Pembrokeshire before the Norman Conquest

In reclaimed coastal wetlands, such as the Somerset and Caldicot Levels, the prehistoric and Romano-British landscape cannot have influenced how the medieval countryside evolved: there were no antecedent landscapes that could have affected local and regional variation in historic landscape character. In dryland areas, however, this was not the case, and so for Pembrokeshire we must consider the landscape that existed before the Norman Conquest.

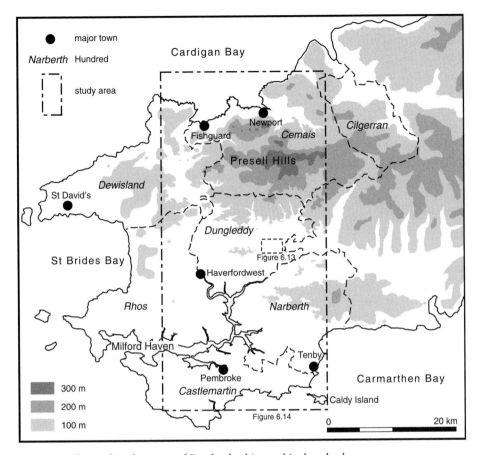

Fig. 6.12. The medieval county of Pembrokeshire and its hundreds.

Unfortunately, we know relatively little about the early medieval landscape in this region, although in the late prehistoric and Romano-British period the settlement pattern was characterized by both multivallate hilltop forts and smaller, more weakly defended univallate farmsteads, usually on hillside locations, some possibly associated with localized field systems (Spurgeon 1963; Crossley 1963; 1965a; 1965b; Wainwright 1971a; 1971b; James and Williams 1982; Vyner 1982; 1986; Williams 1988; Williams and Mytum 1998). As far as we can see this pre-Anglo-Norman landscape was of uniform character across Pembrokeshire. There are, in fact, strong similarities between the character of this landscape and that of the south-west peninsula (Fox 1952). This landscape of small, scattered enclosures is certainly evident until at least the third–fourth centuries with some sites occupied into the early medieval period (e.g. Drim camp and Dan-y-Coed in Llawhaden: Edwards and Lane 1988, 68–9; Williams and Mytum 1998, 30–65). Dating has been problematic at some sites which have failed to reveal datable artefacts (e.g. Wainwright 1971a; James 1987), and the true extent of this early medieval occupation is only now being revealed through radiocarbon dating of the aceramic latest phases of settlements, an advance also now seen in the south-west of England (see Chapters 2, 3, and 4). There were also open settlements (e.g. Stackpole Warren: Benson *et al.* 1990), although their frequency across the landscape is unclear.

At Stackpole there are fragmentary traces of a field system within which ploughmarks and cattle hoofprints suggest both arable cultivation and animal husbandry, and similar field systems are known at a number of other coastal locations. Elsewhere, however, the extent to which settlements were associated with enclosed fields is unclear. A number of sites are known to have been associated with concentric outworks linked to the inner enclosure by an embanked trackway, and these structures may have allowed the movement of livestock through a small area of arable cultivation. Otherwise there is only limited evidence for relict field systems at a number of sites, and many appear to have lain in an open landscape (e.g. Fig. 6.13), another parallel with the south-west of England in this period. Although the density of settlements is often fairly high, one of the greatest concentrations being the eleven sites spread across the *c.*4 km² plateau of northern Llawhaden, it appears that not all of these sites were occupied at the same time. Although small amounts of Romano-British

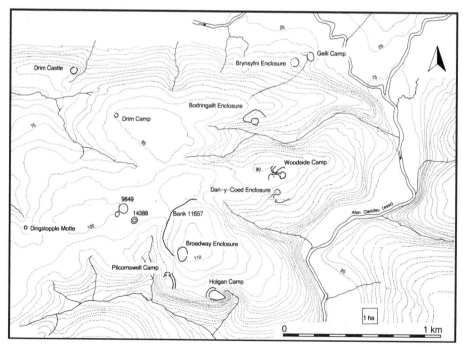

Fig. 6.13. A landscape of small, enclosed settlement at Llawhaden. Apart from outworks associated with a number of the settlements (e.g. Broadway and Bodringalt), there is almost no evidence for field systems (source: Williams and Mytum 1998, fig. 1).

material culture are found on some sites, and there is a trend towards rectilinear structures replacing roundhouses, there are no villas, suggesting that this region saw significantly less Romanization compared to the Vale of Glamorgan and the lowlands of Gwent further to the east (Wainwright 1971a; Robinson 1988; James and Williams 1982, 297–302; Williams and Mytum 1998, 134).

Unfortunately relatively little can be said about the economic development of this region, although there appears to have been an open, largely pastoral landscape with limited arable cultivation. Pembrokeshire is lacking in well-dated palaeoenvironmental sequences that cover the late prehistoric and historic periods (Edwards 1999, 531), and a recent programme of work on the Preseli Hills revealed that peat cutting has removed all but the early prehistoric parts of the sequences in a number of small peat bogs (Ralph Fyfe, pers. comm.). There is, however, some evidence from excavated contexts. James and Williams (1982, 291–2) are at pains to emphasize that along with four-post structures at a number of sites that may be interpreted as granaries, there is some pollen and macrofossil evidence for arable cultivation. A similar picture has emerged from more recent work at Llawhaden (Caseldine and Holden 1998; Williams and Mytum 1998, 145). The presence of some arable cultivation is not surprising—subsistence communities in all but the most inhospitable locations will have cultivated some crops—and the key issue is the relative significance of arable and pastoral farming. This will always be difficult to determine, although at the most extensively excavated sites, the relatively low density of crop remains, along with the suggestion that several sites were consuming crops grown elsewhere, and the lack of evidence for extensive relict field systems, indicates a largely pastoral landscape (Caseldine 1990, 69). A number of pollen sites in the Preseli Hills show some post-Roman woodland regeneration, although others do not (Caseldine 1990, 94), and analogy with the south-west of England suggests that these upland sequences may not reflect the situation in lowland areas that show a far greater degree of continuity (Fyfe and Rippon 2004; Rippon *et al.* 2006a).

During the immediate post-Roman period it is possible that there was some Irish immigration into south-west Wales, and a number of distinctive place names suggest some Scandinavian colonization, notably in the far south-west of Pembrokeshire. Early biological research on blood groups (notably the high proportion of 'A' type) suggests that this Scandinavian immigration is still reflected in the genetic make-up of the local population, although this is disputed by Kissock (1990, 132).

The Norman Conquest and its impact on the landscape: 'England beyond Wales'

Administratively, south-west Wales lay within the pre-Norman kingdom of Dyfed, which was divided between a series of districts ('cantrefi': Fig. 6.1).

Penfro lay to the south and east of Milford Haven, and was divided between the commotes of Manorbier and Coetrath, which broadly correspond to the post-Conquest hundreds of Castlemartin and Narberth. The Welsh cantrefs of Rhos and Daugleddau lay between Milford Haven and the foothills of the Preseli Mountains, and became the Anglo-Norman hundreds of Rhos and Dungleddy. Pebidiog and Cemais embraced the Preseli Hills and the coastal lowland areas to the north, and were transformed into the post-Conquest hundreds of Dewisland (St David's) and Cemais (Figs. 6.1 and 6.12; Miles 1994, 50; Richards 1969, 306–7).

The Norman expansion into south-west Wales began in 1093 by Roger of Montgomery, earl of Shrewsbury, and William fitz Baldwin, sheriff of Devon, but, following the establishment of the earldom of Pembroke (in the southern part of what was to become Pembrokeshire), the task of consolidation was left to a series of lesser magnates such as Arnulf of Montgomery (who also held land in Holderness, in eastern Yorkshire), and local Marcher families who actually lived in the area, such as the castellans at Pembroke and Haverfordwest. Periodic Welsh offensives, however, soon restricted the area of Anglo-Norman control to the southern coastal fringes, notably the Castlemartin peninsula, but in 1102 the earldom was forfeited to the crown, and Henry I then pursued an active policy of subjugation and colonization (Rowlands 1980; Kissock 1992, 39; 1997).

It has been suggested that it was this early twelfth-century conquest that led to the distinctive landscape of southern Pembrokeshire. By the sixteenth century, Pembrokeshire was divided in two, with an essentially Welsh region to the north (the 'Welshry'), and an area of distinctly English character to the south (the 'Englishry') (Miles 1994, 41). The crucial divide—described by the sixteenth-century writer George Owen as the 'Landsker'—lay along a line between Narberth in the east, through Clarbeston, Spital, Treffgarne, and Roch, to Newgale in the west (on the coast at St Brides Bay: Fig. 6.14). Although Austin (2005) has stressed that this specific term 'Landsker' was first used in the sixteenth century, it had a physical reality that can be traced back to the twelfth century. This was a frontier zone—*stricto sensu* a march—initially marked by a zone of timber castles (thirteen of the seventeen mottes in Pembrokeshire lay across this border zone) and later a line of major stone fortresses (Llanstephen, Laugharne, Narberth, Llawhaden, Wiston, and Roch: Davies 1939; Bowen 1957, 339–43, fig. 72; Dicks 1967–8; Kissock 1990, 96, 218). The parishes along this frontier (Lampeter Velfrey, Llawhaden, Wiston, Rudbaxton, Camrose, and Roch) were also of far greater size than those around them, and this was not because they covered large areas of unoccupied upland, but because they were border communities in a socio-political sense, which contained a number of planted villages and knights' fees whose tenants were required to perform military service in addition to their agricultural services. The 'Englishness' of southern Pembrokeshire is seen in a wide variety of forms,

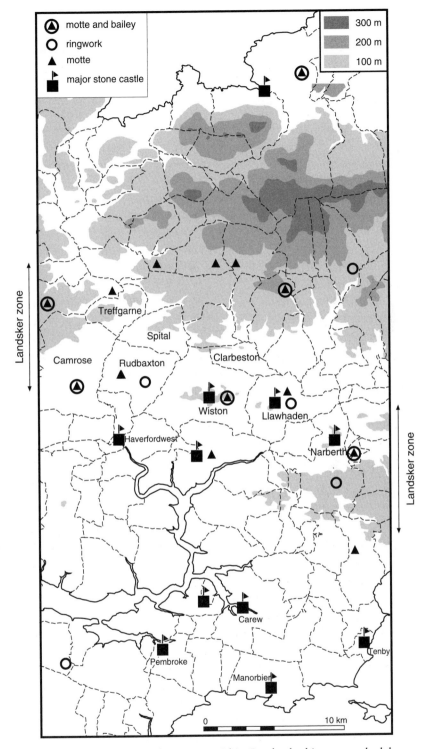

Fig. 6.14. The 'Landsker' boundary zone within Pembrokeshire as marked by a series of Norman earthen castles (Kissock 1990, fig. 5.1), the later stone fortresses at Wiston, Llawhaden, and Narberth, and relatively large parishes of Camrose, Rudbaxton, Wiston, and Narberth (parish boundaries taken from the Tithe maps: Kain and Oliver 2001).

including the large numbers of '-ton' place names, the distribution of Norman manorial tenure, and the language spoken (Fig. 6.15).

The Welshry of northern Pembrokeshire

In the north of Pembrokeshire (the cantrefs Pebidiog and Cemais, and hundreds of Dewisland and Cemais), the landscape is characteristic of large parts of Wales. The churches are typically small structures of Gothic design but without towers or transepts, and usually with just a simple bellcote surmounting the western gable (Fig. 6.16). They are usually in valley bottoms or on hillsides next to springs. The place names in northern Pembrokeshire are predominantly Welsh, and Welsh was the dominant language in 1603 (Fig. 6.15; based on the account of George Owen: see Kissock 1990, fig. 5.5): even into the twentieth century the people were either bilingual or solely Welsh speakers. Although, following the Conquest, a Norman bishop was appointed at St David's in the cantref (hundred) of Dewisland, and a castle and lordship established in Kemes on the north coast at Trefdreath (now known as Newport), there was little wholesale or lasting change in the character of the landscape or the people.

The lowland areas of northern Pembrokeshire had fertile soils that in 1603 George Owen described as 'very fruitful for corn ... for I have not seen better or finer land nor greater store of corn that I have seen growing about St Davids' (Miles 1994, 58). Oats predominated, along with barley and a spring-sown wheat ('holy wheat'), and in 1603 George Owen observed that this tillage of oats, as opposed to winter-sown crops, could not be accounted for in terms of the quality of the land as this was 'good and apt enough to bear wheat and rye' (see Miles 1994, 64). Instead he suggests it was due to the customary Welsh preference for these crops, and the use of gavelkind inheritance that had led to such fragmented landholdings that 'in every five or six acres you shall have ten or twelve owners': as it was customary to graze livestock on these subdivided fields following the harvest, winter-sown crops could not be planted. By the sixteenth century much of the cultivated areas were said to be arranged in open strip-based fields that survived well into the post-medieval period (Dicks 1967–8, 218; and see Howells 1987, 10). These open fields were, however, small scale and localized in their extent, being associated with the numerous individual hamlets within a township, and so were quite unlike the extensive two- and three-field systems in the central zone of England or indeed south-east Monmouthshire described above. The cropping systems were also totally different, as instead of one or two years' cultivation followed by a fallow year, as seen in the English central zone, in northern Pembrokeshire the spring-sown oats and barley were grown in the same fields for between seven and ten years in succession, after which the land was put down to pasture for the same length of time. Following this long fallow period the turf was ploughed up and left to dry before being burnt and the ashes spread across the

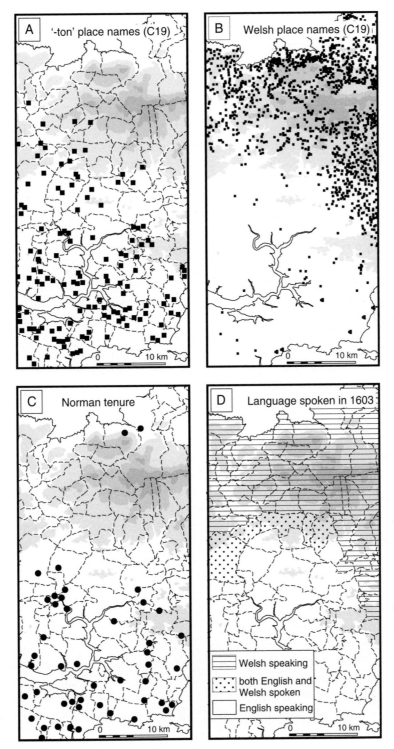

Fig. 6.15. The English and Welsh regions of Pembrokeshire. (A) '-ton' place names in the 19th century (Rees 1951, plate 47); (B) Welsh place names in the 19th century; (C) Norman tenures (Dicks 1967–8, fig. 1); (D) linguistic divisions in 1603 according to George Owen (Kissock 1990, fig. 5.5).

Fig. 6.16. The church at Llanstinan, which is typical of the Welsh churches of northern Pembrokeshire in both (A) its valley-bottom location close to water, and (B) its simple architecture with a bellcote at the west end.

field. During the years of cultivation the land was manured during the autumn by constructing temporary folds for cattle and sheep that were shifted every third or fourth night, and also by spreading sea sand (Miles 1994, 65). Overall, this was a landscape not unlike that of south-west England both physically—in terms of its dispersed settlement pattern and small-scale open fields—and how the land was managed.

The Englishry of southern Pembrokeshire

In southern Pembrokeshire (the cantrefs of Rhos, Daugleddau, and Penfro, and hundreds of Rhos, Dungleddy, and Castlemartin), the landscape was very different. The Norman Conquest saw the imposition of a new 'elite landscape package' of castles, boroughs, and monasteries, mirroring that seen in south-east Wales, and although Kissock (1990, 93) argues that at the opposite end of the social scale little changed, this can be questioned. The parish churches in southern Pembrokeshire are almost all of an English style, with towers, naves and chancels with different roof lines, one or more transepts, and a porch (e.g. Fig. 6.17). Many occupy conspicuous hilltop locations, and some contain Norman fabric, establishing that this difference compared to northern Pembrokeshire dates to shortly after the Conquest. The place names are predominantly English, and from at least the late sixteenth century English was the only language of the vast majority of the people (Fig. 6.15; Miles 1994, 33; Davies 1939, fig. 7; Kissock 1990, fig. 5.5). Southern Pembrokeshire also had very English forms of land tenure, with knights' fees, freeholders, and customary tenants who owed labour services such as mowing in the lord's meadows (e.g. Manorbier: Walker 1991, 134). Another impact that lordship had on the landscape was in the local measures that were used. A customary acre based on a nine-foot perch (5,760 square yards; 4,800 square metres), used widely in the south-west of England and therefore known as the Devon acre or Cornish acre, was used widely across southern Pembrokeshire in peasant holdings that were termed bovates (Howells 1967–8, 227–9).

Narberth was a lordship that contrasted with those areas to the south, in that no knights' fees were carved out of it, possibly because it was settled permanently by Englishmen at such a late date that the creation of knights' fees was by then regarded as an obsolete way of securing military service. Narberth also differed from adjacent lordships, in that peasant holdings were known as burgages and had very light customary services, which may also represent a relatively late attempt to attract colonists to what was politically and physically a relatively marginal frontier area. This approach was also used elsewhere along the 'Landsker' where a number of 'rural boroughs' were created within which the tenants held burgage status, yet had an agricultural means of subsistence, performed agrarian labour services (such as ploughing,

Fig. 6.17. Churches of English character in the south of Pembrokeshire. (A) the hilltop location of Robeston Wathen church, looking north-west from Coxhill in Narberth; (B) the church at Wiston, which is typical of the English-style churches of southern Pembrokeshire in having a hilltop location and a substantial tower at the west end. Round-headed doors on both the north and south sides of the nave, and a Norman font, suggest a 12th-century date.

harrowing, and reaping on the lord's demesne), and lacked markets (e.g. Little Newcastle, Llawhaden, New Moat, Templeton: Kissock 1990, 232).

The settlement pattern in southern Pembrokeshire, when first mapped in the nineteenth century, shows a far greater degree of nucleation compared to the north, and, bearing in mind the post-medieval trend towards settlement dispersion as common fields were enclosed (see below), and the shrinkage of some medieval settlements due to population decline, this difference would probably have been even greater in the twelfth century (Kissock 1990, 58). St Florence, for example, was a demesne manor within the lordship of Pembroke that may have been one of the *tir bwrdd* (demesne lands) within the commote of Coetrath, having been seized by the Anglo-Normans from the Welsh kings (Davies 1978, 109; Kissock 1993b, 4). The village is clearly planned, with a ladder-like arrangement of boundaries to the south of the church and a triangular-shaped green, lying at the centre of what was clearly an extensive common field system structured around a series of sinuous furlong boundaries that radiate from the village, and partly incorporate what may have been earlier landscape features. In places, the nineteenth-century field boundary pattern still included blocks of long, narrow, but curvilinear fields that probably fossilize strips within extensive open fields that have the appearance of the common fields of England's central zone. By the nineteenth century most farmsteads lay within the village, although there was a scatter of isolated farmsteads in the more remote parts of the parish, including Flemington in the far west whose morphology is suggestive of a severely shrunken planned settlement (Roberts 1987, 199, fig. 10.4) and which may have been associated with its own field system. In the small parish of Redberth just to the north, settlement was wholly restricted to a small planned village similarly surrounded by extensive open fields within areas of common land beyond.

An analysis of the historic landscape gives some impression of the extent of these open fields. Around a number of settlements in southern Pembrokeshire, the pattern of furlong boundaries and former strips is clearly preserved through enclosure by agreement (e.g. Fig. 6.18). Documentary sources confirm that the landscape of southern Pembrokeshire was dominated by common fields, with the flatter and gently undulating areas of Roose and Castlemartin being described in 1603 as 'the chiefest corn land in Pembrokeshire ... which yields the best and finest grain ... being a country of itself naturally fit and apt for corn ... a champion and plain country without much wood or enclosure' (Miles 1994, 58). Owen also describes how 'the lands of these tenements do lie divided among the tenants in small parcels lying intermixedly', although areas around the seats of the gentry and the old several/consolidated freehold farms were predominantly enclosed (Miles 1994, 58). The manor of Manorbier is particularly well documented. The main village is on the best land with two secondary hamlets—Newton and Jameston—founded on areas of poorer soils towards the edge of the parish during the twelfth and thirteenth centuries. On

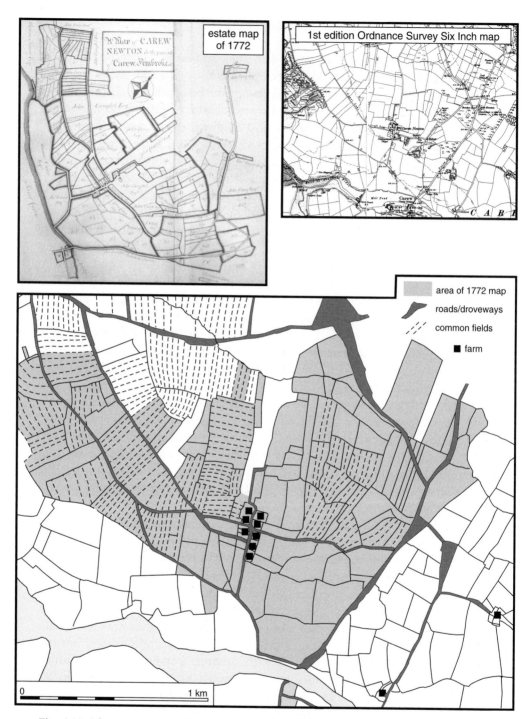

Fig. 6.18. The estate map of Carew Newton, dated 1772, and covering 370 acres (PemRO D/BUSH/6/26; © Pembrokeshire Records Office), alongside the Ordnance Survey First Edition Six Inch map for the same area. The combination of these sources allows a landscape to be reconstructed that contained an almost wholly nucleated settlement pattern with a double-row planned village and extensive common fields to the north, with areas of closes held in severalty and several isolated farms to the south-east.

the eastern edge of the parish/manor lay several freehold tenements, the largest of which was the compact farm of Norchard, whose closes have clearly been enclosed from former common fields. The manor was surveyed in 1609, which gives us a detailed description of a south Pembrokeshire community albeit five hundred years after it was established, and the landscape has a very English feel. Alongside the demesne and freeholders, the majority of tenants were described as *coloni vocati husbandryholders* with tenements made up of 12-acre (5-ha) landholdings (bovates) or multiples thereof, representing the consolidation of tenements in the late medieval period.

Across southern Pembrokeshire the majority of customary tenants lived in 'township farms', located in the nucleated villages and hamlets, and had small to medium-sized landholdings consisting of scattered strips, arranged within furlongs in the common fields (*campi*) with appurtenant meadow and pastures. The 'several farms' were usually freeholds and were located between the perimeter of the old township fields and the parish boundary, with a series of arable closes around the farmhouse with larger fields beyond that were used as rough pasture and temporary cultivation. The way that land was cultivated in southern Pembrokeshire differed significantly from that in the north and included many English practices. In contrast to the north of the county, where oats and other spring-sown crops predominated, to the south of Pembrokeshire both winter- ('bearded' and 'knotted' wheat, and rye) and spring-sown crops (barley) were grown, suggesting a three-field system, which is specifically documented at Llangwm (Owen 1911–18; and see Miles 1994, 62–3). At Lamphey a two-field system is described in a survey of 1326, while in 1609 St Florence had four fields (Davies 1973, 516–19). Across southern Pembrokeshire strips were grouped together in furlongs that were manured from dung collected in the farmyards, along with regular marling and the spreading of lime, while peas and beans were grown after several years of cereal cultivation (Dicks 1967–8, 222; Davies 1973; Miles 1994, 63).

The origins of the settlers in Pembrokeshire are not clear, although there are intriguing links with the south-west of England. The initial push into what became Pembrokeshire was led by Baldwin, sheriff of Devon (see above), and a number of the local Marcher lords also held estates in Devon and Somerset, including the de Brian family whose name is still preserved in the Pembrokeshire place name Tor Bryan (Rowlands 1980, 148). Other place names with Devonian parallels include Puncheston (from Punchardon?) and Morvil (from Morville, tenants in the honour of Okehampton) just to the south of the 'Landsker'. Even the customary acre in the lordship of Pembrokeshire was identical to that in Devon and Cornwall (Howells 1967–8). Some of the church architecture shows links with Somerset, although this is most obvious from the early thirteenth century, as seen at St Mary's in Haverfordwest where the complex piers in the nave and chancel arcades closely resemble those at Wells. Early fourteenth-century monuments in St David's cathedral have very close parallels with Berkeley and Bristol, and the late fourteenth- and fifteenth-century nave arcade and spire at St Mary's, Tenby, are very close in design to that at St Mary's in Bridgwater (Lloyd *et al.* 2004, 41, 45, 469–70). Rather than indicating a possible origin of the early twelfth-century colonists and their continued links with their homeland this may, however, simply represent trading contacts with Bristol and its hinterland: in 1603, for example, George Owen described how 'The lower part of the shire send and sell their wool to Bristol men, Barnstaple [in North Devon] and Somerset, which come twice every year to the county to buy the wool' (Miles 1994, 60).

The 'Landsker' frontier and Flemish colonization

To the north of the lordship of Pembroke and to the south of the 'Landsker', in the former cantrefs of Rhos and Daugleddau that were forfeited to the crown by Arnulf de Montgomery following his disgrace, it is well documented that during the early twelfth century Henry I established a series of Flemish settlements: the *Brut y Tywysogyon*, for example, records that in 1105–8, 'a folk of strange origin and custom ... were sent by king Henry to Dyfed. And they occupied the whole cantref called Rhos, near the estuary of the river called Cleddyf [Milford Haven], and drove all the inhabitants from the land. And that folk had come from Flanders ... because the sea had overwhelmed the land and its bounds and had thrown sand all over the ground' (Jones 1952, 27). During the Middle Ages the term 'Fleming' was used as loosely as 'Holland' is today, referring to people from the Low Countries as a whole, including modern Flanders and Holland. During the eleventh and twelfth centuries these areas saw a considerable expansion in population which was probably a major contributory factor to the expansion of wetland reclamation at this time, with the counts of Flanders being instrumental in bringing new lands into cultivation. 'Flemings' had already been settled in Northumbria, where they acquired a reputation for populating towns in newly conquered areas. They are also recorded in Cumbria and Yorkshire, including in the newly created lordship of Holderness in east Yorkshire which from 1096 until 1102 was held by Arnulf de Montgomery, who also held the earldom of Pembrokeshire (Harvey 1982, 65–6; Kissock 1990, 56; Creighton 2002, 104).

Gerald of Wales described the Flemings in Pembrokeshire as 'a brave and robust people but very hostile to the Welsh and in a perpetual state of conflict with them. They are highly skilled in the wool trade, ready to work hard and to face danger by land or sea in the pursuit of gain, and ... prompt to turn their hand to the sword or the ploughshare' (Giraldus Camb. 141). Even the names of their leaders—such as Wizo 'princeps of the Flemings' (who acquired a compact group of estates in Daugleddau), Tancard (castellan of Haverfordwest), and Letard the 'Little King'—are known, and they appear to have acted as *locators* ('allocators'): middlemen between the crown and the colonists, and who were also responsible for planning new villages (Kissock 1990, 59; 1997; Toorians 1990; 1996, 1; 2000). The names of these Flemings are still preserved in the region's place names, such as Letterston (named after Letard), Tankredston (named after Tancard), and Wiston (named after Wizo) (Figs. 6.19–21; Toorians 1990, 113–14; Charles 1992, 203, 217, 456; Weeks 2002, 27). Each of these settlements lay on the northern border of the Anglo-Norman lordship and they were clearly frontier communities. What became the borough of Wiston, for example, grew up in the shadow of a substantial motte and bailey castle whose bailey, of just over one hectare, is exceptionally large and comparable in size to other small towns in south-west Wales (Fig. 6.20; Murphy 1997a; 1997b). This was very much a border area, with a series of Welsh raids recorded throughout the twelfth century, including in 1147 when the castle at Wiston was taken by Hywel ap Owain (Jones 1952, 221), and it is possible that the original settlement lay within the 'bailey', only expanding into the adjacent planned settlement in the thirteenth century.

Contemporary sources describe the main area of Flemish settlement as being in the former cantrefs of Rhos and Daugleddau, that is the middle part of modern Pembrokeshire in the hinterland of Haverfordwest, although by the sixteenth century writers could identify no trace of its language or culture (e.g. George Owen writing in 1603: Miles 1994, 19). There are, however, a number of place names that refer to Flemings, although they mostly lie around the edges of this area (e.g. Fleming Castle in the far north of Ambleston parish), or beyond Rhos and Dungleddy hundreds (e.g. Flimston in Narberth North, Flimstone in Martletwy, and Flemingston in St Florence): in a wholly or predominantly Flemish community such names would not make sense, so this distribution is, perhaps, suggestive of where outlying (minority) communities were located (Fig. 6.19). There are, however, a series of other probably Flemish place names, many of which are personal names combined with '-ton' (Charles 1938; Toorians 1990, 113–14), and these show a remarkably even distribution across Rhos, Dungleddy, Narberth, and Castlemartin hundreds.

So did this Flemish settlement have any physical effect on the landscape? It is noticeable that in several places along the 'Landsker' there are landscapes remarkably similar to Whitson, on the Caldicot Level, and indeed medieval reclamations in the Low Countries (Fig. 6.21). In places such as Letterston (note the Flemish place-name villa referred to as *villa Letard* in 1291: Roberts 1987, 199–200), and Wallis in the parish of Henry's Moat, along with Angle in south-west Pembrokeshire outside our study area, linear villages are laid out along a street, perpendicular to which were a series of long, narrow tenements that are carefully planned and contained within discrete blocks. Austin (1988; 2005, 44–9) and Kissock (1993a; 1997) have argued that these are in fact earlier, coaxial field boundary patterns that have been absorbed within the historic landscape, although there are several problems with this interpretation. These planned landscapes occur in coherent, rectilinear blocks that, even where they

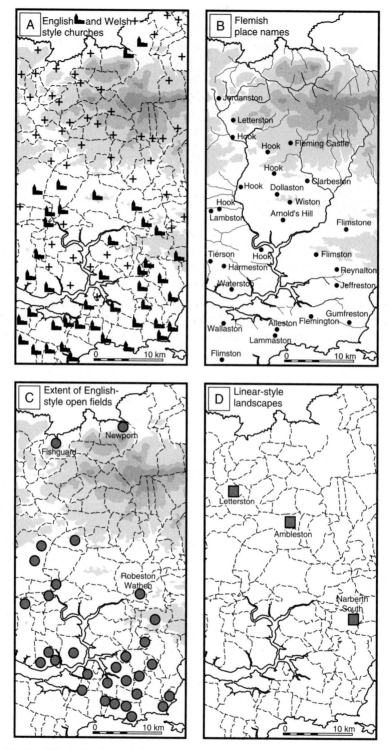

Fig. 6.19. Possible indication of the extent of Anglo-Norman and Flemish colonization. (A) church architecture; (B) Flemish place names (after Toorians 1990; 1996; 2000); (C) English-style common fields; (D) linear-style landscapes based on planned villages.

Fig. 6.20. Wiston Castle, established by 1112, looking north from the main entrance, across the substantial bailey, towards the early 13th-century stone shell keep added to the earlier earthen motte.

are in close proximity, are not all coaxial. The vast majority of the surviving examples are associated with medieval villages: had they been survivors from the prehistoric period then we would have expected them to occur more widely. Is it that these morphologically distinctive landscapes are actually Flemish? Some support for this comes in a simple metrical analysis that reveals that many of the plots to the north and south of the village at Letterston are either 55 or 110 m wide: in Holland, and areas where Dutchmen were employed as colonists, for example by the archbishops of Bremen and Hamburg, tenements were 30 *roeden* wide (110 m) (Linden 1982, 47, 53).

Survival of the native population and landscape?

It is not clear from the twelfth-century documentary sources whether the native population of what became southern Pembrokeshire was entirely expelled, or whether the English and Flemish colonists lived alongside them. George Owen, writing in 1603, claims that 'the countries of Roose [Rhos], Castle-martin, Narberth and most of Daugleddau hundred (the bishop's lordship excepted) were wholly put to fire and sword by the Normans, Flemings and Englishmen, and utterly expelled the inhabitants thereof and peopled the country themselves' (Miles 1994, 42). It might be expected, for example, that the Anglo-Norman lords seized much of the better land and granted this to their colonists, while new settlements were also planted in some of the

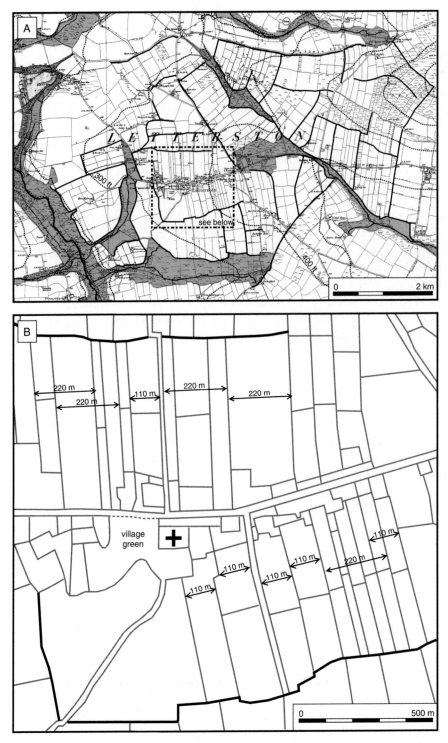

Fig. 6.21. The planned village of Letterston. (A) an interpretation of the Ordnance Survey First Edition Six Inch Map with areas of probable recent enclosure shaded, and major elements of the field boundary pattern highlighted. (B) detailed analysis of the village area, with examples where units of 30 Dutch *roede* (rods, 110 m), or multiples thereof, appear to have been used.

more marginal 'frontier' locations. Within these areas of English and Welsh settlement there are a handful of Welsh place names, although it is unclear whether these represent the survival of native settlements from the eleventh century, the later renaming of settlements, or foundation of new settlements at a later date. There are, however, a number of distinctive settlements with a radial plan that Kissock (1997, 133–5) suggests are native Welsh villages.

English colonization: A Tudor fiction?

In a stimulating paper, David Austin (2005) has recently reconsidered the traditional views of southern Pembrokeshire as being 'little England beyond Wales'. He shows quite clearly how the aspirations of the emerging gentry class were partly responsible for the perception of this region as being strongly Anglicized, and correctly observes that the pre-Norman landscape was not entirely swept away and replaced by nucleated villages and common fields. It is certainly true that some facets of any landscape and society are very fluid, and can change over time, of which language—including field and place names—is one example. What he does not give adequate consideration to, however, is the physical fabric of the landscape of southern Pembrokeshire: the medieval villages and field systems that had far more in common with 'champion' countryside than the area north of the Preseli Hills, the almost universally English design of medieval parish churches which in some cases contain twelfth-century fabric, and their predominantly hilltop location (Fig. 6.17). These were not a myth created by the Tudor gentry, but a physical reality derived from a period of profound landscape change following the Norman Conquest. The 'Landsker' frontier zone, for example, may only have been called this from the sixteenth century, and was meant by Owen to mean the linguistic divide, but it was a physical reality in the twelfth century when it was marked by a line of earthen mottes, stone castles, and planned villages set within unusually large parishes. Austin (2005, 44) also plays down the difference in the structure of the field systems in the north and south of Pembrokeshire, based on documentary references to the use of open fields in both areas and rotational agriculture. This superficial similarity, however, hides fundamental differences in the agricultural practices, such as the northern Pembrokeshire practice of growing spring-sown oats and barley in the same fields for between seven and ten years in succession, after which the land was put down to pasture for the same length of time, which were completely different from the two- or three-course rotations found in the south. The physical extent of the field systems, as revealed through an analysis of the historic landscape itself, was also completely different, with small open fields in the north, and large common fields that covered a large proportion of the parish in some parts of the south. While it is clear that earlier writers may have exaggerated the extent of these English-style fields, their presence in some areas cannot be denied.

It is argued here, therefore, that there was indeed a significant reorganization of the landscape in southern Pembrokeshire following the Norman Conquest, and that this is reflected in the creation of villages and common fields that were very different in character from the dispersed settlement patterns and small open fields in the Welsh areas of northern Pembrokeshire. While the impact of lordship on the landscape appears clear, the extent of peasant colonization is not. The design of church architecture could reflect the preferences of the landed elite, while the popular language and place names could have changed through time without there having been large-scale population movement (just as English was adopted in the West Country without Anglo-Saxons replacing the native Britons). It is noticeable, however, that while '-ton' names occur across the whole area with predominantly English place names in central and southern Pembrokeshire, they are mostly found in Castlemartin, Narberth, and the southern part of Rhos, which also corresponds to the area in which manors with Norman tenure were located (Fig. 6.15). There is a much lower density in northern Rhos and Dungleddy, and the fact that the change in place names was not evenly spread across southern Pembrokeshire might suggest that there was a genuine difference in the extent of Anglo-Norman influence.

DISCUSSION: LANDSCAPE CHANGE IN THE MARCHER LORDSHIPS

In both south-east Monmouthshire and Pembrokeshire the historic landscape, as first systematically mapped in the nineteenth century, shows marked local variation in its character. In the case of the reclaimed wetlands of the Caldicot Level this cannot be attributed to either the natural environment or an antecedent landscape, as the distinctive 'English' and 'Welsh' landscapes either side of Monksditch were created on the same reclaimed alluvial soils that seal the Romano-British and early medieval ground surfaces. On the adjacent drylands there is similarly no difference in the physical characteristics of the topography or soils to account for the different settlement patterns and field systems seen in the lordships of Chepstow and Caerleon. The same is true in Pembrokeshire, as although the far south generally has rather better soils, is lower lying, and so has a more favourable climate, apart from the Preseli Hills, the differences in soils, topography, and climate between the north and the south are moderate. In the sixteenth century, for example, the south had marginally higher population levels but the density of ploughteams and dairies was the same (Dicks 1967–8). Instead, the difference in historic landscape character between northern and southern Pembrokeshire can be attributed to changes that took place following the Norman Conquest.

There are several clear parallels between these two sample areas. In both cases dryland landscapes were clearly reorganized following the Norman Conquest, and this included the introduction of nucleated and occasionally planned villages, regularly arranged common fields, and a communal approach towards managing agrarian resources. This very 'English' approach towards landscape organization and management was also used when areas of newly reclaimed wetland were settled in that part of the Caldicot Level which fell within the Anglo-Norman lordship of Netherwent (Chepstow). The landscape here is of a different character from the parishes of Goldcliff, Nash, and Christchurch in the Welsh lordship of Caerleon, even though the initial stages of marshland colonization had been so similar, being based around the creation of 'summer dykes', which are found all around the Severn estuary. The emergence of this local variation in landscape character seen on the Caldicot Level must be due to the different approaches to landscape organization and management on the part of the Anglo-Norman and Welsh lords, and whether or not a Flemish *locator* was involved in the foundation of Whitson, the creation of this planned village, and the systematic development of this marshland, can be seen alongside the construction of castles, towns, and markets on the adjacent dryland areas, and in Pembrokeshire, as examples of the Anglo-Norman lords' desire to develop their newly acquired estates.

7

Discussion and Conclusions

This book has sought to explore some of the reasons why the landscape of southern Britain varies so dramatically in its character. It has used a series of study areas on the fringes of England's central zone, whose landscape was characterized by villages and common fields, to explore why this approach towards managing the countryside did not spread into areas such as southern East Anglia and the south-west peninsula. Where the data allows, the same questions have been asked of each area: how late did the Romano-British landscape survive, and how far back can we trace the origins of our present countryside? In addition to traditional archaeological work, on abandoned sites, the cumulative effect of PPG16 (Planning Policy Guidance Note 16) related work within still-occupied settlements is starting to have a significant effect on our understanding of the origins of the historic landscape. In a period when previous discussion was based on the results of a handful of large-scale excavations, particular attention has been paid to the wider landscape, notably the results of fieldwalking surveys, field systems, and palaeoenvironmental sequences. A wide range of possible explanations for local and regional variation in landscape character have been explored, and in a number of places it has been possible to use reclaimed coastal wetlands—where factors such as variations in soils and antecedent landscape character cannot have been significant as they were uniform across the whole area—as a means of exploring social factors such as the role of lordship.

In recent decades there was a strong reaction against environmental determinism, although we must remember that factors such as topography and soils do have a very real impact on how human communities manage the countryside: communities on the chalk downland of Wessex will obviously have created landscapes of different character from those of the high uplands of the Brecon Beacons, or the extensive peat bogs of Fenland. These are all areas where the physical character of the landscape will have placed significant constraints on how human communities could manage them, but such environments have not been the focus of this study. Instead, discussion has concentrated on a series of case studies where large areas had muted relief and good soils that offered fewer constraints to medieval farmers, and as such it is remarkable just how different the settlement patterns and field systems were. While focusing on the specific issue of regional variation in landscape character in southern Britain, this study has, therefore, tried to address the far wider issue of how human society interacts with the natural environment within a complex and dynamic socio-economic context.

In recent years there have been a series of discussions of regional variation in landscape character both at a national (Rackham 1986a; Roberts and Wrathmell 2000; 2002) and a regional scale, most notably in East Anglia and the East Midlands (Lewis *et al.* 1997; Williamson 2003; Jones and Page 2006; Oosthuizen 2006). There is, however, no agreement on the chronology of when villages and common fields emerged, with Brown and Foard (1998) arguing for a two-staged process starting before the mid ninth century, when what had been a dispersed settlement pattern was replaced by nucleated villages, followed by a later phase of settlement restructuring, whereas Lewis *et al.* (1997) see village formation as occurring after the mid ninth century. There has also been much discussion as to why 'champion' countryside came to dominate England's central zone. While the attribution of villages and common fields to the Early Anglo-Saxon immigrants can now be dismissed, the contribution of Scandinavian colonization or overlordship is still being discussed (e.g. Martin 2007). A consensus, however, has emerged that structuring the landscape in this way occurred within the context of a reorganization of landed estates, and was a response to various pressures that called for increased efficiency in how land was managed whether it be through rising population leading to increased demand for food, or the growing power of the state and its demands for greater taxation and military service. Conversely, there was a more or less explicit view that those areas that did not see the creation of villages and common fields, notably the south-east, south-west, and west of England, did not experience these pressures and therefore experienced some form of arrested development:

the areas where the nucleated village was the dominant form of settlement in the middle ages, appear to have had consistently higher proportions of arable land in cultivation in 1086, which is likely to reflect a long standing bias towards cereal cultivation ... In other regions, however, this adaptive evolution of field boundaries and settlements was not followed. Where the arable contribution to the economy was less dominant, the pressure on the land never reached the point at which a transformation of the landscape seemed either necessary or desirable. Although the areas of continued dispersed settlement were subject to the same factors, such as increased population or the emergence of markets, nonetheless the availability of additional land for cultivation, their pastoral interests, or opportunities to make a living from the woods and wastes, insulated them from radical change.

(Lewis *et al.* 1997, 198–200)

This study, however, takes issue with this view, not least because the correlation between England's central zone and high densities of population and ploughteams in Domesday is weak—as has been shown here in Somerset and the South-West (e.g. Figs. 2.13 and 4.4)—and so this book has set out to challenge this rather Midland-centric view. While trying to take discussion beyond England into southern Wales the author does acknowledge that from a continental perspective this study is still very 'Anglo-centric', as settlement nucleation and the creation of common fields was also going on in mainland Europe. While there is, therefore, a desperate need for a wider synthesis, such a work can only be based on thorough local studies and it is hoped that this example contributes to that wide understanding of landscape change in the later first millennium AD.

It has also been argued that the idea of managing land and people through villages and common fields may have spread through emulation, and while this does indeed appear to have been the case in some instances (e.g. southern Wales during the twelfth century: see Chapter 6) it does not explain why the concept did not spread to other areas, such as East Anglia and parts of the South-West, whose population densities were similar to those in the central zone. It has been suggested that the champion landscape was significantly different from that around it even before villages and common fields were created and that it was this 'antecedent landscape character' that led to it continuing to evolve in its own way. The relative power of lordship versus community may also have been a factor, although this is more difficult to map. Williamson (2003) has recently widened the debate by suggesting that certain physical characteristics of the landscape led to people living together in villages, notably where there were large areas of meadow to harvest and soils that offered a relatively short window of opportunity for their ploughing.

There are merits to all these suggestions, but a problem that has emerged is a tendency to seek a monocausal explanation, for example population pressure *or* the natural environment. Another problem is that when mapped at a small, national scale there are indeed superficial correlations between England's central zone and a number of these variables. This book has attempted to bring some scientific method to this debate by using the landscape as a laboratory in order to try and examine the significance of some of these possible causal factors under 'controlled conditions' (i.e. where the contribution of other potential variables can be ruled out). The examination of several reclaimed wetland landscapes has been particularly instructive in this respect, as all of these areas were intertidal mudflats and saltmarshes in the early medieval period, giving them uniform soils and antecedent landscape character: the very different settlement patterns and field systems that were created following their reclamation cannot, therefore, be attributed to these factors. In the same way, the diversity of settlement patterns and field systems that emerged on the estates of a single major landowner on one of these reclaimed wetlands—the bishops of Wells's manors on the North Somerset Levels (see Chapter 3, and Rippon 2006a)—shows that in this particular case it was not lordship but subtenants and/or local communities that must have taken the leading role in shaping landscape character.

Somerset: a county of contrasts

In Somerset, there is considerable variation in the character of the nineteenth-century historic landscape, making it an ideal case study with which to start our discussion. In central and south-east Somerset there was a relatively nuc-leated settlement pattern, with many of the isolated farmsteads lying within what were clearly enclosed former common fields. To the west lay a land-scape of very different character, with scattered farmsteads and small hamlets mostly associated with field systems that always appear to have consisted of closes, and only occasional small-scale open fields that, although comprising blocks of unenclosed strips, lacked the scale or management practices of the Midland common field system. When these settlement patterns and field sys-tems are characterized within the context of their contemporary territorial units—parishes and tithings—then a remarkably clear division emerges just to the east of the Blackdown and Quantock Hills, which is only broadly similar to the edge of Roberts and Wrathmell's (2000) 'central province'. A wide range of evidence shows that this difference in landscape character can be traced back to the medieval period, including documentary evidence for the extent of common fields, and vernacular architecture that confirms that the standing late medieval buildings to the east of this boundary lay in villages, while to the west they were scattered across the landscape.

Within Somerset the area that had villages and common fields shares many characteristics with the Midlands: gentle relief, heavy soils that present a relat-ively short window of opportunity for ploughing, an abundance of meadow but scarcity of woodland, and a relatively high Domesday population. Crucially, however, the Vale of Taunton Deane, to the west, shared most of these physical characteristics yet had a very different cultural landscape of dispersed settle-ment and enclosed fields. The similarly varied landscapes that were created on the nearby reclaimed wetlands confirm that factors related to the natural environment and antecedent landscape character were not solely responsible for this local variation in settlement patterns and field systems. A large part of Somerset that did see the development of villages and common fields was held by Glastonbury Abbey by the time of the Domesday survey, and increasingly, archaeological survey and excavation within extant villages such as Meare (Rippon 2004b) and Shapwick (Aston and Gerrard 1999; Gerrard with Aston 2007) shows that they existed by that time. As Glastonbury acquired the *core* of its central Somerset estates by the early eighth century it is highly likely that villages and common fields were created during its period of ownership, and while it must be remembered that many areas never held by the Abbey also saw this transformation of the landscape, it is tempting to suggest that the monks and abbots must have been involved in this process on their estates in some way.

In the case of Shapwick, the tenth-century date for the dispersed settlement pattern being swept away and the nucleated village and common fields being created has led to the suggestion that it may have been the reforming Abbot Dunstan who was responsible (Costen 1992b). This period of investment and reform is indeed a very logical context for a reordering of the agrarian landscape, and several other villages on Glastonbury's central Somerset estates have very similar plans, notably nearby Edington and Middlezoy. What is more striking, however, is that other villages within adjacent parishes have very different plans, as does nearby Meare. Clearly, there was no single 'Glastonbury' way of restructuring a landscape. It is possible that this morphological variation reflects changing fashions over time, or that the Abbey was not centrally responsible for planning these landscapes. That was certainly the case on the estates of the bishops of Wells, where it must have been subtenants and the local communities who were left to create their own landscapes. In the case of Glastonbury there are hints that it somehow encouraged nucleation and the creation of common fields, as one of its outlying estates in western Somerset, at West Monkton, appears to have had a landscape of this character that was quite different from that which prevailed in the region. The extent of the open field at Braunton in north Devon is also on a scale not otherwise seen in the South-West, and this too may represent the exporting of this approach to managing agricultural land from the central zone to one of Glastonbury's outlying estates.

Another feature of Glastonbury Abbey's *outlying* estates is the way that many were clearly acquired *after* villages and common fields had been created. The study of the relationship between parish boundaries and the physical fabric of the landscape, along with place names and ecclesiastical relationships, suggests that the landscape had been replanned within the context of estates that were larger than post-Conquest manors and parishes but smaller than a series of large *regiones* that can be reconstructed across Somerset. These estates, of perhaps 20 to 60 hides, appear to have been created through the fragmentation of the *regiones*, and were often themselves further subdivided into units of just a few hides that became the manors recorded in Domesday. This, then, provides the immediate context for the restructuring of the landscape in Somerset, while factors such as the desire to increase agricultural production and support newly created thegns required to perform military service for the emerging English state may also have been important factors (Abels 1988). In part, the reason why only some parts of Somerset saw this transformation of the landscape may relate to the estate management policies of individual estate owners, but to a considerable extent it appears to have been decision making at a lower level of society—minor, local lords, subtenants of the great landowners, and local communities—that was most important, with the 'concept' of villages and common fields probably spreading through emulation.

Landscape change through emulation

At this point one would like to move beyond general and somewhat abstract concepts of landscape development to the actual people who were responsible: the agents of change. How were landscapes modified through emulation? What was the actual process whereby a pattern of dispersed settlements, each associated with their own field systems, was replaced by a single nucleated village and set of common fields? This takes us back to the discussions of 'power and conflict in the medieval village' (Dyer 1985) and 'initiative and authority in settlement change' (Harvey 1989). These papers raise a number of important issues but are essentially discussions of society—and notably the relationship between landlords and their tenants—in the post-Conquest period, for which we have good documentary sources. The emphasis of Dyer and Harvey on the power of the community to manage the landscape is certainly relevant here, but the regulation of institutions that already exist, such as the communal organization of common fields, is one thing whereas their initial creation through the sweeping away of an existing landscape is an altogether different scale of undertaking. Dyer and Harvey were also writing at a time when it was assumed that settlement nucleation was a relatively late phenomenon—of the tenth to twelfth centuries—whereas it is argued here that this process began significantly earlier in the East Midlands and East Anglia, around the eighth century, when the structure of society would have been very different.

In the case studies presented here the conclusion has been that there is no simple answer as to whether it was lords or their communities who were responsible for landscape change. Different landowners appear to have adopted different strategies towards managing their estates. In southern Wales we have seen the clear impact that Anglo-Norman lordship had on the landscape in the twelfth century, and the replanning of settlement patterns and field systems may have been part of the same strategy towards developing their newly acquired estates that also saw the building of castles, the foundation of towns, and the creation of markets. This was, however, a very different time and place from eighth-century England where our story began. In Somerset, we have seen that Glastonbury Abbey was responsible for subdividing the estates whose landscapes were subsequently transformed, but was it the Abbey or its subtenants, who were given these newly created small parcels of land, who were responsible for creating the villages and common fields? The lack of uniformity in how the landscapes of individual Glastonbury Abbey manors were physically arranged certainly suggests that it had little central control on how these subtenants structured their landscapes. We simply do not have the documentary sources to tell us who these thegns were, although perhaps their names are preserved in the villages that they created: Catcott (Cada's *cot*), Cossington (Cosa's *tūn*), Edington (Eadwine's *tūn*), and Woolavington (Hunlaf's *tūn*). Costen (2007, 73) has come to a similar conclusion, and his reconstruction of a series of estates in Dorset, where 'landscapes created on a large scale, perhaps by the kings of Wessex after the seventh century, were first divided into large estates and then subdivided and tiny holdings created for dependents at a late date in the old English period', is a very similar process to that which we have seen in Somerset.

In areas such as central and eastern Somerset there clearly was a concept of how the landscape should be managed in the late first millennium AD, and similarity between the compact, sometimes planned, villages and common fields here and those as far north as the East Midlands suggest that the concept had indeed spread through emulation (and see Lewis *et al.* 1997, 200; Taylor 2002). How would this have worked in practice? We know that there was plenty of social contact on the part of the higher echelons of society, and perhaps ideas of agricultural practice spread in the same way as ecclesiastical reform. At the more local scale, we may not need any more complex social theory than copying one's neighbour.

Across the watershed in the South-West

So why did the concept of villages and common fields not spread beyond the Blackdown and Quantock Hills into the South-West? Was this a less well-developed region that simply did not experience the same socio-economic pressures as those in Somerset and the rest of the central zone? Clearly not. By the tenth and eleventh centuries the South-West was part of the English kingdom, and some areas had population densities comparable to those of Somerset. If the South-West had been a region of 'arrested development' we would also expect to see an essentially late prehistoric/Romano-British landscape surviving into the medieval period, but with the exception of the far west of Cornwall this is not the case. Sometime between the seventh and ninth centuries, the landscape of small, enclosed settlements ('rounds') that does not appear to have been associated with particularly extensive field systems was replaced with one of scattered, unenclosed small hamlets and isolated farmsteads associated with a near continuous fieldscape. Palaeoenvironmental sequences show that around the eighth century there was a significant change in agricultural practice that might be associated with the emergence of 'convertible husbandry'. This increasing intensity of landscape exploitation may have been associated with the region's assimilation into Wessex and any associated changes in landownership, although the view that landscape change has to be the result of lordship has of course just been questioned. Could the reason why the landscape of the South-West developed in this way be due to the more deeply rooted 'differentness' of that region?

The people of the South-West failed to Romanize to the same extent as in areas to the east of the Blackdown Hills, where the late Romano-British landed elite invested considerable resources in building palatial villas, and the market economy and manufactured goods reached all levels of society. In the South-West, by contrast, there were just a handful of small-scale villas, and excavation of a typical rural settlement produces a meagre haul of artefacts. This distinctive character is also seen in the Iron Age, with the massive developed hillforts of the Durotriges having no parallel in Dumnonia. Rather than being a remote region, whose landscape suffered arrested development, the South-West may actually have been occupied by a society who chose to manage their landscape in a different way, and were responsible for transforming the countryside several centuries earlier than in neighbouring Wessex.

On the claylands of greater East Anglia

On the other side of the central zone we see a not dissimilar set of circumstances in 'greater East Anglia'. In part, the boundary of medieval landscapes characterized by villages and common fields was marked by a distinct topographical feature: the Chiltern Hills and East Anglian Heights. There was also a boundary of great long-term cultural significance—roughly along the Gipping and Lark valleys—that appears to have divided the Iceni from the Trinovantes in the Iron Age and Roman periods, and the East Angles from the East Saxons in the early medieval period. Though losing its political significance when the shires of Essex and Suffolk were created around the tenth century, the Gipping–Lark line remained of great significance in marking the boundary between a region within which common fields embraced a significant proportion of the agricultural land to the north, and a landscape of predominantly enclosed fields to the south.

Although differing from the classic villages and common fields of the East Midlands in a number of respects, a case can be made for the landscape in northern East Anglia showing some links with those of the central zone, notably the nucleation of settlement around the eighth century and formation of extensive common fields. In contrast, as an area that never saw these developments, southern East Anglia may well have been a region that really did see 'arrested development'. The huge amount of archaeological survey and excavation here means that a relatively clear picture is emerging with regard to how the landscape evolved from the Roman through to the medieval periods. In the Roman period the landscape was quite densely settled, particularly in the river valleys, with a dispersed pattern of rural settlement alongside a series of small towns (and the major urban centre at *Camulodunum*, modern Colchester). Field systems were not particularly extensive, and relatively fluid in their structure, being periodically reorganized: there was nothing like the relatively stable and continuous fieldscape of the medieval period. In the earliest medieval period (the fifth to seventh centuries) there is growing evidence for continuity in terms of the numbers of Romano-British sites that are producing 'Early Saxon' pottery and/or lie beneath later medieval settlements. At least some Romano-British field ditches remained open into the early medieval period, as they contain sherds of 'Early Saxon' pottery, while in many places the relationship between excavated Romano-British field systems and the medieval landscape suggests that the latter has gradually evolved from the former. The palaeoenvironmental evidence we have similarly suggests broad continuity within a landscape that remained open: there was no widespread woodland regeneration, which means there must have been at least continued grazing by livestock if not arable cultivation.

Against this background a few observations can be made about the much debated coaxial landscapes first identified by Drury and Rodwell (1980), some of which are of a similar type to those identified by Williamson (1987) further north and whose date has recently been called into question (Hinton 1997; and see Williamson 1998). The extent of these coaxial systems which appear to form a continuous fieldscape over large areas is not particularly in keeping with the excavated evidence elsewhere that seems to show relatively localized field systems with open areas in between (e.g. North Shoebury and Great Holts: Chapter 5, Figs. 5.6 and 5.7); however, there remains some excavated evidence from within these landscapes that does support their late prehistoric date. The palaeoenvironmental evidence for broad continuity in land-use and the lack of woodland regeneration also make it perfectly plausible for Romano-British field systems to have survived, as appears to have happened in a number of places (e.g. Ardleigh and Great Holts Farm). In contrast, a number of other, morphologically different, planned landscapes, such as the radial pattern in south-east Essex, cannot be firmly dated to the early medieval period, and the curious pattern in the Dengie peninsula remains frustratingly undated.

Actual evidence for 'Germanic' settlement in southern East Anglia is relatively limited and concentrated in coastal and estuarine districts. This fits very well with the other evidence for a strong degree of continuity in the landscape, with the survival of a substantial native British population. A re-examination of the landscape context of one of the most important Early Saxon sites in the country, Mucking, suggests that while it may have gradually migrated east towards the parish church, the settlement may have been abandoned around the eighth century when a small open field system was laid out, perhaps echoing what was going on elsewhere in southern England. There is growing evidence, however, that the settlement pattern across southern East Anglia remained predominantly dispersed throughout the medieval period. A number of settlements have now been excavated that can be dated to the 'Middle Saxon' period and these are scattered across the landscape as well as being located beneath later medieval settlements that similarly form a dispersed pattern. Neither the extensive fieldwalking surveys, nor the large-scale development-led excavations that this region has seen, have revealed evidence for villages of any period. There is similarly no evidence for extensive common fields: an analysis of the historic landscape and documentary sources both point to a fieldscape that has always been predominantly enclosed, albeit with some small areas of open field shared between a few farmsteads. In its detail the medieval landscape of, say, the eleventh century was different from that of the late Roman period, but the intervening years appear to have seen gradual evolution rather than a sudden transformation.

There was a very different story in the northern part of East Anglia. In the Roman period there was a similarly dispersed settlement pattern: while the greatest numbers of farmsteads were in the valleys there was some occupation of the heavier soils of the interfluvial areas. Once again, survey, excavation, and palaeoenvironmental sequences all point to continuity and gradual evolution in the earliest medieval period, whereas around the eighth century there was a dramatic transformation. The dispersed settlement pattern was abandoned just as Ipswich Ware came into use, to be replaced by a series of nucleated settlements at locations where parish churches later stood. Indeed, there is some evidence that these churches and cemeteries may in fact have their origins in the 'Middle Saxon' period, and if we postulate that the surrounding common fields were laid out at the same time, then these nucleated settlements may have had many of the characteristics of villages (i.e. nucleated settlements, with some service provision, and whose communities exploited most of the land within their territory). Excavated field systems also show far greater discontinuity in northern East Anglia compared to the south, with little or no evidence that Romano-British systems continued in use beyond the earliest medieval period (a worrying observation for those who believe the coaxial landscapes of this area represent the survival of late prehistoric landscapes). The palaeoenvironmental sequences from this area do, however, suggest broad continuity in land-use from the Roman through to the earliest medieval period, although a marked intensification in arable cultivation around the eighth century is in keeping with the archaeological evidence for a dramatic transformation of the landscape at that time.

In many respects, therefore, northern East Anglia shows many similarities with the East Midlands, with a dispersed settlement pattern being replaced by nucleated villages at a time when 'Middle Saxon' pottery was in use and before the circulation of 'Late Saxon' wares. Indeed, the colonization of the extensive wetlands of the Norfolk Marshland at this time also shows that it was nucleated settlements that were the fashion of the day. In nearby Cambridgeshire, within what was to become the champion countryside of England's central zone, recent survey, and particularly a series of large-scale excavations within extant settlements, are all showing that the creation of villages similarly occurred around the eighth century, with some evidence for later restructuring of villages that fits the model presented by Brown and Foard

(1998) for the East Midlands of two broad phases in village development (initial nucleation and then replanning). The reason why northern East Anglia does not fall into the central zone when we try and map the later medieval landscape is not because of events in this early medieval period, but because its landscape then diverged from that of Cambridgeshire and the East Midlands as settlement became more dispersed and the common fields failed to develop into the sophisticated structures that are so characteristic of champion countryside.

The East Midlands

Whilst this study has tried to steer clear of the well-trodden fields of the East Midlands, it is now appropriate to briefly reconsider what was happening in this region at this time, most notably the chronology of settlement nucleation and in particular the two-stage process, starting in the 'Middle Saxon' period, advocated by Brown and Foard (1998), and the tenth- to twelfth-century 'village moment' put forward by Lewis *et al.* (1997). In part, this discrepancy may be down to archaeologists and historians talking at cross-purposes: recent excavations within extant villages in Cambridgeshire, for example, have shown that while the initial settlement nucleation happened in the eighth century, the present settlement form was created a century or so later through a further replanning. In Northamptonshire fieldwalking certainly suggests that numerous scattered farmsteads associated with 'Early to Middle Saxon' pottery (around a quarter of which are located on or adjacent to Romano-British sites) were replaced by far fewer but larger nucleated settlements that evolved into our modern villages, some of which have produced Late Saxon material (e.g. Foard 1978; Hall and Martin 1979; Taylor 1983, 116; Hall 1988; Shaw 1993/4; Brown and Foard 2004; Parry 2006). We know little about the field systems associated with this dispersed settlement, but manure scatters found during fieldwalking surveys suggest an infield/outfield system (Parry 2006, 95).

   This process of village creation is now seen as a two-phase process with the initial nucleation of settlement around a single existing focus sometime before the mid ninth century (and perhaps associated with the fragmentation of large estates into smaller manorial holdings), followed by a reorganization/replanning of these villages and the laying out of their common fields around the tenth century as seen at Raunds (Cadman and Foard 1984; Brown and Foard 1998; 2004, 96; Parry 2006, 275). Unfortunately this first phase is poorly dated, but it must have been after the early eighth century, as the scattered farmsteads that were abandoned are associated with 'Middle Saxon' Ipswich Ware pottery (whose use extended from *c.*720 to *c.*850: Blinkhorn 1999), but before the mid ninth century as they lack 'Late Saxon' pottery. There is also growing evidence for 'Middle Saxon' occupation within extant and deserted villages, such as beneath the manorial complex at Goltho (Beresford 1987, 22–8; and see Everson 1993, 91). The palaeoeconomic evidence from Raunds and West Cotton also suggests broad continuity in agriculture during the 'Early and Middle Saxon' periods, with an increase in alluviation on the floodplain around the eighth or ninth centuries (Brown 2006, 25). Preserved cereal remains suggest that open field farming was introduced by the Late Saxon period when there was a further increase in alluviation (Keevill 1992; Campbell 1994; Brown 2006, 35; in press). There is scattered evidence for the origin of open fields in the 'Late Saxon' period, including the abandonment of sites such as Catholme (Losco-Bradley and Kinsley 2002).

A similar pattern of dispersed 'Early to Middle Saxon' settlement being replaced by the 'Late Saxon' period by nucleated settlements is also discernible elsewhere in the East Midlands, for example in parts of Buckinghamshire (e.g. the desertion of Pennylands and origins of Great Linford: Williams 1993, 95), while in Leicestershire and Rutland a dispersed scatter of small farmstead-size sites, recorded as 'Early Saxon' pottery scatters and occasional finds of 'Early to Middle Saxon' metalwork, were similarly abandoned before the use of 'Late Saxon' pottery whose distribution is restricted to medieval villages (Bowman 2004; Liddle 1996; Cooper 2000, 152; Cooper and Priest 2003; Knox 2004). In Lincolnshire, fieldwalking along the Fenland edge suggests that the scatter of 'Early Saxon' sites was abandoned before the use of 'Middle Saxon' pottery and in the north of the county (Lane and Hayes 1993, 69), at Rigby Crossroads, west of Grimsby, a dispersed settlement pattern similarly appears to have undergone nucleation around the late seventh century (Steedman 1994). The deserted medieval village of Sempringham has produced 'Middle Saxon' pottery (Hayes and Lane 1992, 48), as has the still-occupied settlement at Sleaford (Taylor 2003, 233). At nearby Quarrington, a settlement associated with 'Early to Middle Saxon' pottery, including Ipswich Ware, was abandoned before the use of 'Late Saxon' wares, and was replaced by common fields that were being manured by the eleventh to twelfth centuries (Taylor 2003). On the Lincolnshire Fens settlement nucleation appears to have been a little later, as the dispersed scatter of settlements are associated with 'Middle Saxon' pottery, although around the eighth century these were abandoned (they lack 'Late Saxon' pottery), in favour of a series of nucleated villages on the higher coastal marshes many of which have produced 'Middle Saxon', but not 'Early Saxon' pottery (Hayes 1988, 323; Hayes and Lane 1992; Lane and Hayes 1993, 69). The colonization of the nearby Norfolk Marshland also suggests that the idea of structuring landscapes around nucleated settlements was prevalent in that region by the 'Middle Saxon' period. Just a single 'Early Saxon' site has been found on this extensive wetland, at the margins of the intertidal saltmarshes and the freshwater backfen, which was abandoned by the eighth century (it lacked 'Middle Saxon' pottery) when a line of substantial regularly spaced settlements that were associated with Ipswich Ware, around 1–3 km apart, was established on the higher coastal saltmarshes in what was clearly a planned/coordinated act of colonization based on the idea of structuring landscape around nucleated villages, rather than isolated farmsteads (Silvester 1988; 1993; Rippon 2000a, 174).

A similar process of dispersed settlement patterns being replaced by more nucleated forms around the eighth century is also seen in the South Midlands and central southern England. In Oxfordshire, extensive survey and excavations within the former common fields of Cassington and Yarnton have revealed an unstructured 'Early Saxon' landscape of dispersed settlement that was joined in the 'Middle Saxon' period by a more compact and structured settlement—one that starts to have the characteristics of a village—immediately to the south of what became the church/manor complex. This period also saw significant agricultural intensification with increased arable production, the introduction of new crops, the more intensive use of the floodplain for pasture and meadow, and the manuring of common fields that certainly existed by the tenth century when all the earlier dispersed settlements were abandoned (Hey, 2004), while a restructuring of the settlement at Yarnton in the 'Late Saxon' period mirrors that seen in Cambridgeshire (Chapter 5) and Northamptonshire (see above). In the Thames Valley generally there was an increase in alluviation from around the eighth and ninth centuries (Robinson 1992, 201), and the pollen sequence at Snelsmore on the nearby Berkshire Downs shows an increase in cereal cultivation around the ninth century (Waton 1982, 83, fig. 3). In Gloucestershire, at Sherbourne House and Kent Place, there is evidence for nucleated settlement from the eighth century (Bateman *et al.* 2003; cf. Reynolds 2006, 152; Kenyon and Collard 2004), while at Lower Slaughter a possibly manorial enclosure next to the parish church dates from the eighth century (Kenyon and Watts 2006). At Chalton, in Hampshire, 'Middle Saxon' pottery, similar to that found in small quantities at the nearby Church Down site (occupied during the fifth to eighth centuries), has also been found at Manor Farm in the medieval village (Cunliffe 1972; Hughes 1984, 72–6). In Wiltshire, Draper (2006) has drawn together the fragmentary evidence for that county, showing a number of dispersed settlements associated with early medieval grass-tempered pottery but nothing later, while several villages have evidence for 'Middle Saxon' occupation including Avebury whose plan was restructured in the 'Late Saxon', a phenomenon we have seen in the Midlands (Pollard and Reynolds 2002, 183–238).

The phenomenon of ninth- and tenth-century manorial enclosures is well known—such as Faccombe Netherton in Hampshire (Fairbrother 1990), Trowbridge and Yatesbury in Wiltshire (Graham and Davies 1993; Reynolds 2000, 116), and Goltho in Lincolnshire (Beresford 1987)—but Draper has highlighted the importance of settlements with '-bury' place names, suggesting many were 'Middle Saxon' manorial and ecclesiastical enclosures that have been the catalyst for settlement nucleation, as may have been the case in Gloucestershire (e.g. the enclosures at Lechlade and Lower Slaughter: see above). Indeed, Gelling (1997, 143) suggests that '-bury' place names initially meant an 'enclosed place', with a secondary usage referring to a minster church, while Blair (2005, 250) suggests that its dominant meaning before the mid eighth century was in the sense of 'minster'. Draper (2006, 103–6) suggests that the '-bury' at Avebury may actually refer to a manorial enclosure rather than the 'Late Saxon' burh postulated by Pollard and Reynolds (2002, 204). Other 'Middle Saxon' enclosures include Bramford in Suffolk (Reynolds 1999, 141–4), Raunds, in Northamptonshire, (Boddington 1996), and possibly Wicken Bonhunt, in Essex (the plan of which is unfortunately incomplete: Wade 1980).

Overall, it would appear, therefore, that there was a marked trend towards a stratification of the settlement pattern around the eighth century which involved the construction of high-status enclosures, which probably continued the trend towards enclosure seen in some seventh-century settlements that were then abandoned such as Cowdery's Down (Millet and James 1983). The period around the eighth century was, however, one of more widespread landscape change, including settlement nucleation and agricultural intensification, seen across the East and South Midlands, northern East Anglia, the South-West, and possibly central southern England, but this was part of a prolonged process that continued into the tenth century when many settlements appear to have been restructured and ditched boundaries start to become a common feature. We must no longer see village origins as a single event—a moment or a great replanning—but part of a long process.

Exporting villages and common fields into the Welsh marches

By the eleventh century, the idea of organizing the rural landscape through nucleated villages and communally managed common fields dominated a broad swathe of central England. We have seen that initially this approach may have been even more common, for example being used in northern East Anglia, while in other areas such as the South-West local communities had developed their own very different approaches to managing the landscape. The last question to be asked in this study is whether any of these approaches to structuring the countryside were exported from England to the Anglo-Norman Marcher lordships in Wales.

South-east Monmouthshire was divided between two lordships, one—Netherwent—in English hands and the other—Caerleon—remaining under Welsh control. The extensive area of coastal marshland now known as the Caldicot Level was similarly divided between the two, and the earliest phase of its reclamation—when a series of oval-shaped 'infields' were created—was the same right across the area. Thereafter, however, the landscapes of the Caldicot Level within the lordships of Netherwent and Caerleon developed along very different lines, and this is also seen on the adjacent dryland areas. The fen-edge parishes within Netherwent saw the creation of very English-style villages and common fields, whereas in Caerleon the traditional Welsh landscape of dispersed settlement and enclosed fields survived. On the reclaimed wetlands of the Caldicot Level—a 'cleaned sheet' upon which twelfth-century landscapes were created unencumbered by variations in soil or antecedent landscape character—there was a similarly marked difference. Within Netherwent settlement was nucleated and associated with extensive common fields, along with the planned settlement at Whitson whose inspiration may have been further afield. The field and place names were almost wholly English, in contrast to the western part of the Caldicot Level where a significant number were Welsh; this area also had a dispersed settlement pattern and almost no open field. Very clearly, the dryland landscape of south-east Monmouthshire was transformed along central English lines, while the settlements and field systems created on the newly reclaimed marshes were similarly inspired by such arrangements. In contrast, to the west, the newly created wetland landscape mirrors those on the adjacent dryland areas within the lordship of Caerleon in having a traditional Welsh character.

It has long been thought that another area of Anglo-Norman lordship that saw the introduction of very English-style landscape was in southern Pembrokeshire: 'England beyond Wales'. Austin (2005) has recently questioned the extent to which this was the case, but the analysis of the physical fabric of the historic landscape presented here firmly points to a significant English, and possibly Flemish, impact on the landscape in the twelfth century. There is a very real difference in the character of the settlement patterns and field systems of southern and northern Pembrokeshire, the dividing line being known as the 'Landsker' (a frontier zone rather than a linear boundary). This is reflected, for example, in both the architecture and the location of parish churches, which along with a series of other facets of the countryside clearly distinguish between the 'Englishry' in the south and the 'Welshry' to the north. The 'concept' of villages and common fields did indeed spread as far as south-west Wales.

Conclusions

The aim of this study has been to show that once we look beyond the 'village zone' of England's central zone there was important regional variation in landscape character right across southern Britain. Whilst not setting out to write definitive landscape histories, an attempt has been made to show the benefits of reflecting on a long time period, from late prehistory through to the medieval period, and using a wide range of sources: in the spirit of inherently interdisciplinary 'historic landscape analysis' (Rippon 2004a) the various case studies have made use of archaeological surveys and excavations, palaeoenvironmental evidence, cartographic and documentary sources, studies of standing buildings, and field- and place-name evidence. Inevitably, much use has been made of characterizations of the historic landscape as portrayed on nineteenth-century maps, but care was taken to use other evidence to confirm the antiquity of the key character-defining features of different areas. For the areas studied, an attempt has been made to ask a common set of questions—how far into the early medieval period did the Romano-British landscape survive, how far back can we trace the origins of the historic landscape, and what is the relationship between the two—although the discontinuous ceramic sequences, lack of large-scale fieldwalking surveys and excavations, and work within still-occupied medieval settlements in western areas make these issues more difficult to address. There are, however, some fairly clear patterns emerging.

In a number of areas we have seen that there was a significant period of change and innovation in the countryside during a period that historians have called the 'long eighth century' (the late seventh to early ninth centuries: Hanson and Wickham 2000) when there was an expansion of the European economy. In this study, we have seen that in various regions of southern England this period may also have seen changing agricultural practices, settlement nucleation, and possibly changes to the layout of field systems. Even within southern East Anglia, whose landscape does not appear to have been profoundly changed at this time, the creation of discrete planned landscapes such as that around Shoebury—which dates to between the sixth and ninth centuries—may also have occurred during this period of innovation. Overall, the suggestion that 'archaeological evidence shows that the date at which nucleated villages were created can be narrowed down to the period 850–1200' (Lewis *et al.* 1997, 191) can be challenged on two grounds with regard to this start date: first, the initial act of settlement nucleation does not necessarily equate to the formation of villages in what was to become their later medieval form, and secondly, this initial act of nucleation across the East and South Midlands, northern East Anglia and Fenland, and possibly parts of central southern England can now be dated to around the eighth century. The increasing intensity with which the landscape was being exploited is even reflected in the appearance of fixed fishtraps around the coasts and estuaries of south-east England at this time (Cohen 2003; Peter Murphy, pers. comm.).[1] Although the focus of this study was on southern Britain, the intensification and innovation seen here around the eighth century was in the context of similar trends seen elsewhere, for example northern Gaul (Hanson and Wickham 2000; Wickham 2005, 301).

This was also, however, a period of growing stability in the landscape. The appearance of the Christian Church led to the creation of fixed, focal

---

[1] The fishtrap at Collins Creek, in Essex, has radiocarbon dates of 1300+/−45 BP (cal. AD 650–797), 1286+/−45 BP (cal. AD 654–858), and 1261+/−45 BP (cal. AD 664–862). The Nass, in Tollesbury, also in Essex, has dates of 1268+/−39 BP (cal. AD 664–862) and 1227+/−24 BP (cal AD 690–882), and Sales Point, also in the Blackwater Estuary, dates of 1277+/−43 BP (cal. AD 659–860), 1251+/−21 BP (cal. AD 682–800), 1214+/−16 BP (cal. AD 772–881), and 1144+/−16 BP (cal. AD 873–957).

points within the landscape, and an associated territorial structure (Blair 2005, 204, 260). From around the eighth century the folk territories started to be replaced by smaller and more stable estates of perhaps 100 to 300 hides that were granted to the Church and leading individuals in Anglo-Saxon society (Faith 1997; Dyer 2005; Wickham 2005, 320–1): it is important to remember that although the Church became a significant landowner, and is relatively well documented, the vast majority of land at this time was in secular hands and the emergence of a landed elite was in itself another aspect of the greater stability of this period (Wickham 2005, 303). The centres of these estates also became stable points within the landscape—often also acquiring minster churches—that would become the focus for settlement, while their boundaries also started to become fixed, some being recorded in the boundary clauses of charters. The period around the eighth century also saw increasing administrative stability, with a system of shires emerging in Wessex by the time of King Ine (688–726) whose laws described how a man should pay a fine of 60 shillings to his lord if he 'steals into another shire' (Reynolds 1999, 72; Draper 2006, 59). One context of this administrative stability was the increased formalization of royal power and social obligations that are documented by the late seventh century, reflected for example in the military services laid out in the same Laws of King Ine, the writing of Bede about Mercia and Northumbria to the north, and eighth-century charters referring to the 'common burdens' of military service, bridge building, and the maintenance of fortifications (Abels 1988, 13, 25–37, 52). By the tenth century shires were divided into smaller administrative districts called hundreds, and while the first explicit reference to them is under King Edgar (957–75), it 'appears likely that earlier social and political institutions were reshuffled at this time' (Reynolds 1999, 65). Indeed, Reynolds (forthcoming) has shown that from the late seventh or eighth centuries there is increasing evidence for 'execution cemeteries' that show a very strong relationship to hundred boundaries (and see Draper 2004). Control of land meant control of people and the means of agricultural production, and this was also the period of increasingly stable political structures that saw the writing of law codes and the imposition/formalization of rents, renders, and dues (Whitelock 1955, 368–9, clause 42).

There was a tendency in past research to focus on the origins and development of villages and common fields, but this was clearly not a single process and did not occur at the same time in different places: this book has focused on that period of transition from the Romano-British through to the medieval landscape and it is important to stress that the story does not stop here. We must not confuse the initial stage of settlement nucleation—which across large parts of the Midlands and northern East Anglia appears to date to around the eighth century—and the date when our medieval villages finally crystallized which appears to have been several centuries later. Indeed, we have seen how later changes in landscape character in places such as northern East Anglia led to the landscape character of that region diverging from the Midlands, and it could be argued that rather than the central zone being the innovative and dynamic region with areas on either side being somewhat remote and backward, it was actually the Midlands that saw 'arrested development' once the villages and common fields had been created.

This study has also sought to explore the possible causes of this regional variation in landscape character, and has attempted to move away from monocausal explanations (though it is not the first to try this: e.g. Dodgshon 1981, 138). In recent years we may have seen the first signs of a reaction against the prevailing emphasis on social agency as the sole cause of variation in landscape character, and change over time, with Williamson's (2002, 21) championing of the 'natural environment in moulding social, economic and agrarian arrangements'. The debate is becoming very polarized, but at the risk of sounding like a recently ex-Prime Minister, is there a middle way? General factors such as the properties of soils, population density, economic development, and the impositions upon landowners of the growing English state will all have affected people's view of the landscape, but they do not individually explain why some areas saw the development of villages and common fields and others did not. The example of medieval landscapes created on the 'cleaned slate' of coastal wetlands shows that major differences in landscape character could come about without differences in antecedent landscape character (but see below), population density, or soils being significant although this is not to say that these factors were not important elsewhere. Similarly, the diversity of landscape character found on the estates of the same landowner shows that lordship was not an overriding factor, which is in agreement with Williamson's (2003; 2007) observation that the central zone shows no correlation with the density of freemen recorded in Domesday and Lewis *et al.*'s (1997, 175–6) assertion that the form taken by settlement was often in keeping with those prevailing in the locality rather than being dictated by the policy of individual lords: it was local communities that were the main force behind shaping landscape character.

Whilst it has been shown that significant variation in landscape character can arise without antecedent landscape character being a significant factor, we have also seen two examples where a long-standing boundary within the physical environment had a profound effect on the cultural landscape: the Blackdown–Quantock Hills and the Gipping–Lark valleys in the South-West. This is not to say that they formed fixed political boundaries such as those that emerged from the Roman period onwards—Hadrian's Wall and the other fixed frontiers of the empire—but simply that, for some reason, the peoples living on either side maintained a separate identity for over a millennium, reflected most obviously in the degree of Romanization and extent of landscapes characterized by villages and common fields. Everitt (1977) and Phythian Adams (1987) have argued that until relatively recent times upland areas and watersheds often formed important cultural boundaries, being zones of reduced contact between neighbouring societies. In this respect the Gipping–Lark boundary is a little anomalous, and further research at a more detailed scale may show that at certain times at least it was the interfluvial areas either side that were the real boundary. Either way, there is little to challenge the traveller in the muted relief of East Anglia, and even the Blackdown and Quantock Hills only reach *c.*250 m OD and are dissected by a number of valleys: they were a landmark that marked a boundary but were not in themselves a barrier to communication that caused this boundary between peoples to be perpetuated. Instead, we appear to be looking at two peoples—the Durotriges who were conquered by the West Saxons, and the Dumnonians, who chose to manage their landscapes in different ways, which is probably why the concept of villages and common fields, which appears to have spread, perhaps through emulation, across the central zone of England, failed to take root in areas such as the South-West.

To conclude, it is time to move away from the Midland-centric debate about the origins of the villages and common fields in England's central zone, and take a far wider view of regional variation in landscape character that appears to have been changing across southern Britain between the seventh and ninth centuries, and which was a prelude to the further restructuring of landscapes in some Midland areas around the tenth century. These developments can be seen in the context of wider changes in society that reflect greater stability, the emergence and subdivision of well-defined estates, and increasingly sophisticated social and economic structures. Yes, this was the period that saw the development of stable kingdoms that started to exert their increasing power but change and innovation in the countryside was not restricted to one particular kingdom. Indeed, while authorities such as the Church and the other great landowners may have had a role in shaping how the landscape was managed—some more than others—it was ultimately the different practices of local farming communities that shaped the way that the countryside was structured.

References

ASChr	Anglo-Saxon Chronicle (Swanton 1996)
BRO	Bristol Records Office
Brut y Ty	*Brut y Tywysogyon, or The Chronicle of the Princes* (Jones 1952)
CChR	Calendar of Charter Rolls
CIPM	Calendars of the Inquisitions Post Mortem
CPR	Calendars of Patent Rolls
DB fo. 90	Domesday Book folio 90
DB Dev.	*Domesday Book Devon* (Phillimore edition, Thorn and Thorn 1985)
DB Dor.	*Domesday Book Dorset* (Phillimore edition, Morris 1983)
DB Gloucs.	*Domesday Book Gloucestershire* (Phillimore edition, Moore 1982)
DB Herefs.	*Domesday Book Herefordshire* (Phillimore edition, Thorn and Thorn 1983)
DB Som.	*Domesday Book Somerset* (Phillimore edition, Thorn and Thorn 1980)
ECR	Eton College Records (transcribed by Felicity Strong)
ERO	Essex Records Office
Giraldus Camb.	Gerald of Wales, *The Journey through Wales/Description of Wales* (Thorpe 1978)
GwRO	Gwent Records Office
LPFD	Calendars of Letters and Papers, Foreign and Domestic
NLW	National Library of Wales
PemRO	Pembrokeshire Records Office
SRO	Somerset Records Office
SSAVBRG	Somerset and South Avon Vernacular Buildings Research Group
SVBRG	Somerset Vernacular Buildings Research Group

AALBERSBERG, G. 1999, 'The alluvial fringes of the Somerset Levels'. Unpublished Ph.D. thesis, University of Exeter.

ABELS, R. P. 1988, *Lordship and Military Obligation in Anglo-Saxon England*. London: British Museum Publications.

ABRAMS, L. 1994, 'The early surveys of Shapwick including the Polden estate', in M. A. Aston and M. D. Costen (eds.), *The Shapwick Project: A Topographical and Historical Study*. Bristol: University of Bristol, Department of Continuing Education, 72–5.

—— 1996, *Anglo-Saxon Glastonbury: Church and Endowment*. Woodbridge: Boydell Press.

Albone, J. 2000, 'South Waltham, St Lawrence's church', *Medieval Settlement Research Group Annual Report*, 15: 27.

——2001, 'Caister-on-Sea, Norwich Road', *Medieval Settlement Research Group Annual Report*, 16: 51.

Alcock, N. W. 1975, 'Fields and farms in an East Devon parish', *Rep. Trans. Devonshire Ass.* 107: 93–107.

Allan, J. 1994, 'Medieval pottery and the dating of deserted settlements on Dartmoor', *Proc. Devon Archaeol. Soc.* 52: 141–7.

——and Langman, G. 2002, 'A group of medieval pottery from Haycroft Farm, Membury', *Proc. Devon Archaeol. Soc.* 60: 59–74.

Allen, J. R. L. 2002, 'The context and meaning of the Roman Goldcliff Stone, Caldicot Level', *Archaeology in the Severn Estuary*, 13: 147–54.

——2004a, *Carrstone in Norfolk Buildings: Distribution, Use, Associates and Influences*. BAR British Series 371, Oxford: British Archaeological Reports.

——2004b, 'Chapel (Tump) Farm, Undy, Caldicot Level: an intertidal secondary medieval site and its implications', *Archaeology in the Severn Estuary*, 15: 71–80.

Alston, L. 1999, 'Wealden houses', in Dymond and Martin (1999, 182–3).

Amor, N. R. 2006, 'Late medieval enclosure: a study of Thorney, near Stowmarket, Suffolk', *Proc. Suffolk Institute of Archaeol. Hist.* 41 (2): 175–97.

Andrews, D. D. 2004, 'Historic buildings notes and surveys', *Essex Archaeol. Hist.* 34: 272–82.

——and Smoothy, M. 1990, 'Asheldham church revisited', *Essex Archaeol. Hist.* 21: 146–51.

Andrews, P. 1995, *Excavations at Redcastle Furze, Thetford, 1988–9*. East Anglian Archaeology 72.

Appleton-Fox, N. 1992, 'Excavations at a Romano-British round: Reawla, Gwinear, Cornwall', *Cornish Archaeol.* 31: 69–123.

Arnold, C. 1988, *An Archaeology of the Early Anglo-Saxon Kingdoms*. London: Routledge.

——and Wardle, P. 1981, 'Early medieval settlement patterns in England', *Med. Archaeol.* 25: 145–9.

Aston, M. 1982, 'The medieval pattern 1000–1500 AD', in Aston and Burrow (1982, 123–33).

——1983, 'Deserted farmsteads on Exmoor and the Lay Subsidy of 1327 in West Somerset', *Proc. Somerset Archaeol. Natur. Hist. Soc.* 127: 71–104.

——1986, 'Post Roman central places in Somerset', in E. Grant (ed.), *Central Places, Archaeology and History*. Sheffield: University of Sheffield Dept. of Archaeology, 49–78.

——1988a, *Aspects of the Medieval Landscape of Somerset*. Taunton: Somerset County Council.

——1988b, 'Settlement patterns and form', in Aston (1988a, 67–82).

——1988c, 'Landuse and fields systems', in Aston (1988a, 83–8).

——and Burrow, I. C. G. (eds.) 1982, *The Archaeology of Somerset*. Taunton: Somerset County Council.

——and Gerrard, C. 1999, ' "Unique, traditional and charming": the Shapwick Project, Somerset', *Antiq. J.* 79: 1–58.

——and MURLESS, B. 1978, 'Somerset archaeology 1977', *Proc. Somerset Archaeol. Natur. Hist. Soc.* 122: 117–52.

——AUSTIN, D., and DYER, C. (eds.) 1989, *The Rural Settlements of Medieval England*. Oxford: Blackwell.

AULT, W. O. 1972, *Open-Field Farming in Medieval England*. London: George Allen and Unwin.

AUSTIN, D. 1978, 'Excavations in Okehampton Park, Devon, 1976–78', *Proc. Devon Archaeol. Soc.* 36: 191–240.

——1985, 'Dartmoor and the upland village of the South-West of England', in Hooke (1985, 71–80).

——1988, 'Review "The making of the English village"', *J. Hist. Geogr.* 11: 201–2.

——2005, 'Little England beyond Wales: re-defining the myth', *Landscapes*, 6 (2): 30–62.

BAGWELL, S., and WEBSTER, C. J. 2005, 'Somerset archaeology 2004', *Proc. Somerset Archaeol. Natur. Hist. Soc.* 148: 103–37.

————2006, 'Somerset archaeology, 2006', *Proc. Somerset Archaeol. Natur. Hist. Soc.* 149: 159–90.

BAILEY, K. 1989, 'The Middle Saxons', in S. Bassett (ed.), *The Origins of Anglo-Saxon Kingdoms*. Leicester: Leicester University Press, 108–22.

BAKER, A. R. H., and BUTLIN, R. A. 1973a, *Studies of Field Systems in the British Isles*. Cambridge: Cambridge University Press.

————1973b, 'Conclusion: problems and perspectives', in Baker and Butlin (1973a, 619–56).

BAKER, J. T. 2006a, 'Topographical place-names and the distribution of *tūn* and *hām* in the Chilterns and Essex region', *Anglo-Saxon Studies in Archaeol. Hist.* 13: 50–62.

——2006b, *Cultural Transition in the Chiltern and Essex Region, 350 AD to 650 AD*. Studies in Regional and Local History 4, Hatfield: University of Hertfordshire Press.

BALAAM, N. D., BELL, M. G., DAVID, A. E. U., LEVITAN, B., MACPHAIL, R. I., and SCAIFE, R. G. 1987, 'Prehistoric and Romano-British sites at Westward Ho!, Devon: archaeological and palaeoenvironmental surveys 1983 and 1984', in N. H. Balaam, B. Levitan, and V. Straker (eds.), *Studies in Palaeoeconomy and Environment in South West England*. Oxford: British Archaeological Report 181, 163–264.

BALKWILL, C. J. 1976, 'A Roman site at Okehampton', *Proc. Devon Archaeol. Soc.* 34: 89–92.

BARFORD, P. M. 2002, *Excavations at Little Oakley, Essex, 1951–78: Roman Villa and Saxon Settlement*. East Anglian Archaeology 98.

BARROWMAN, R. C., BATEY, C. E., and MORRIS, C. D. 2007, *Excavations at Tintagel Castle, Cornwall, 1990–1999*. London: Society of Antiquaries.

BARTON, K. 1962, 'Settlements of the Iron Age and pagan Saxon burials at Linford, Essex', *Trans. Essex Archaeol. Soc.* 3rd Series, 1 (2): 57–102.

BASCOMBE, K. 1987, 'Two charters of King Suedred of Essex', in K. Neale (ed.), *An Essex Tribute to F. G. Emmison*. London: Leopard Head Press, 85–96.

BASSETT, S. R. 1982, *Saffron Walden: Excavation and Research 1972–80*. London: Council for British Archaeology Research Report 45/Chelmsford Archaeological Trust Report 2.

BASSETT, S. R. 1989, 'In search of the origins of the Anglo-Saxon kingdoms', in S. Bassett (ed.), *The Origins of Anglo-Saxon Kingdoms*. Leicester: Leicester University Press, 3–27.

——1997, 'Continuity and fission in the Anglo-Saxon landscape: the origins of the Rodings (Essex)', *Landscape Hist.* 19: 25–42.

BATEMAN, C., ENRIGHT, D., and OAKLEY, N. 2003, 'Prehistoric and Anglo-Saxon settlements to the rear of Sherbourne House, Lechlade: excavations in 1997', *Transactions of the Bristol and Gloucestershire Archaeological Society*, 121: 23–96.

BAXTER, S. 2007, *The Earls of Mercia: Lordship and Power in Late Anglo-Saxon England*. Oxford: Oxford University Press.

BAYLEY, J. 2001, 'Precious metal refining in Roman Exeter', *Proc. Devon Archaeol. Soc.* 59: 141–7.

BEACHAM, P. (ed.) 1990a, *Devon Buildings: An Introduction to Local Traditions*. Exeter: Devon Books.

——1990b, 'The longhouse', in Beacham (1990a, 47–60).

BEAGRIE, N. 1989, 'The Romano-British pewter industry', *Britannia*, 20: 169–92.

BECKETT, S. C., and HIBBERT, F. A. 1979, 'Vegetational change and the influence of prehistoric man in the Somerset Levels', *New Phytologist*, 83: 577–600.

BEDWIN, O. 1996, *The Archaeology of Essex: Proceedings of the Writtle Conference*. Chelmsford: Essex County Council.

——and BEDWIN, M. 1999, *A Roman Malt-House: Excavations at Stebbing Green, Essex 1988*. East Anglian Archaeology Occasional Papers 6.

BELL, M, 1994, 'Field survey and excavation at Goldcliff, Gwent 1994', *Archaeol. in the Severn Estuary 1994*, 115–55.

BELL, R. D., and BERESFORD, M. 1987, *Wharram Percy: The Church of St Martin*. London: Society for Medieval Archaeology Monogr. 11.

BELL, T. 1998, 'Churches on Roman buildings: Christian associations and Roman masonry in Anglo-Saxon buildings', *Medieval Archaeol.* 42: 1–18.

——2005, *The Religious Reuse of Roman Structures in Early Medieval England*. BAR British Series 390, Oxford: British Archaeological Reports.

BENNETT, A. 1998, 'Archaeology in Essex 1997', *Essex Archaeol. Hist.* 29: 194–215.

——1999, 'Archaeology in Essex 1998', *Essex Archaeol. Hist.* 30: 210–31.

——2000, 'Archaeology in Essex 1999', *Essex Archaeol. Hist.* 31: 210–32.

——2001, 'Archaeology in Essex 2000', *Essex Archaeology and History*, 32: 250–66.

——2002, 'Archaeology in Essex 2001', *Essex Archaeol. Hist.* 33: 390–413.

BENNETT, K. 1983a, 'Devensian late-glacial and Flandrian vegetational history at Hockham Mere, Norfolk, England I: pollen percentages and concentrations', *New Phytologist*, 95: 457–87.

——1983b, 'Devensian late-glacial and Flandrian vegetational history at Hockham Mere, Norfolk, England II: pollen accumulation rates', *New Phytologist*, 95: 489–504.

BENSON, D. G., EVANS, J. G., WILLIAMS, G. H., and DARVILL, T. 1990, 'Excavations at Stackpole Warren, Dyfed', *Proc. Prehist. Soc.* 56: 179–245.

BERESFORD, G. 1987, *Goltho: The Development of an Early Medieval Manor c.850–1150*. London: English Heritage Archaeological Report 4.

BERESFORD, M. W. 1964, 'Dispersed and grouped settlement in medieval Cornwall', *Agric. Hist. Rev.* 12 (1): 13–27.

—— and HURST, J. G. 1971, *Deserted Medieval Villages Studies*. London: Lutterworth Press.

———— 1990, *The English Heritage Book of Wharram*. London: English Heritage.

BESTEMAN, J. 1986, 'The history of medieval settlement in North Holland and the reclamation of peat areas in archaeological perspectives', in P. Murphy and C. A. French (eds.), *The Exploitation of Wetlands*. BAR British Series 186, Oxford: British Archaeological Reports, 327–69.

BIDWELL, P. 1979, *The Legionary Bath-house and Basilica and Forum at Exeter*. Exeter: Exeter Archaeol. Rep. 1.

—— 1980, *Roman Exeter: Fortress and Town*. Exeter: Devon Books.

BIEK, L. 1994, 'Tin ingot found at Praa Sands, Breage, in 1974', *Cornish Archaeol.* 33: 57–70.

BIRBECK, T. T. 1970, 'Medieval Caldicot', *Severn and Wye Review*, 1 (1): 11–16.

BISHOP, T. A. M. 1935, 'Assarting and the growth of the open fields', *Econ. Hist. Rev.* 6: 26–40.

BLAGG, T., PLOUVIEZ, J., and TESTER, A. 2004, *Excavations at a Large Romano-British Settlement at Hacheston, Suffolk, 1973–74*. East Anglian Archaeology 106.

BLAIR, J. 1991, *Early Medieval Surrey*. Stroud: Alan Sutton.

—— 1994, *Anglo-Saxon Oxfordshire*. Stroud: Alan Sutton Publishing.

—— 2005, *The Church in Anglo-Saxon Society*. Oxford: Oxford University Press.

BLINKHORN, P. 1999, ' "Of cabbages and kings": production, trade and consumption in middle Saxon England', in M. Anderton (ed.), *Anglo-Saxon Trading Centres: Beyond the Emporia*. Glasgow: Cruithne Press, 4–23.

BODDINGTON, A. 1990, 'Models of burial, settlement and worship: the final phase reviewed', in E. Southwood (ed.), *Anglo-Saxon cemeteries: a reappraisal*. Stroud: Alan Sutton, 177–99.

—— 1996, *Raunds Furnells: The Anglo-Saxon Church and Churchyard*. London: English Heritage.

BOND, D. 1988, *Excavation at the North Ring, Mucking, Essex: A Late Bronze Age Enclosure*. East Anglian Archaeology 43.

BONNEY, D. J. 1971, 'Former farms and fields at Challacombe, Manaton, Dartmoor', in K. J. Gregory and W. L. D. Ravenhill (eds.), *Exeter Essays in Geography in Honour of Arthur Davies*. Exeter: University of Exeter Press, 83–91.

BOULTER, S. 2002a, 'Archaeological trench evaluation: land at Gallows Hill, Barking, Suffolk'. Unpublished report, Suffolk County Council Archaeological Service.

—— 2002b, 'Barking, Gallows Hill', *Medieval Settlement Research Group Annual Report*, 17: 59.

—— 2003, 'Flixton Park Quarry: a royal estate of the first Anglo-Saxon kings?', *Current Archaeology*, 187: 180–5.

BOWEN, E. G. 1957, 'The South-West', in E. G. Bowen (ed.), *Wales: A Physical, Historical and Regional Geography*. London: Methuen and Co., 329–52.

BOWMAN, P. 2004, 'Villages and their territories: parts I and II', in P. Bowman and P. Liddle (eds.), *Leicestershire Landscapes*. Leicester: Leicestershire Museums Archaeological Fieldwork Group Monograph 1, 105–36.

BRADLEY, J., and GAIMSTER, M. 2003, 'Medieval Britain and Ireland', *Medieval Archaeol.* 47: 199–339.

BRADNEY, J. 1932, *History of Monmouthshire*, iv/2: *The Hundred of Caldicot Part 2*. London: Mitchell, Hughes and Clarke (repr. Cardiff: Merton Press, 1994).

BRIGERS, J. L. 2006, 'Report on archaeological investigation: "Little Haven", Church Road, Edington, Somerset'. Unpublished report in Somerset Historic Environment Record, PRN 14452.

BRITNELL, R. H. 1983, 'Agriculture in a region of ancient enclosure, 1185–1500', *Nottingham Medieval Studies*, 27: 37–55.

——1988, 'The fields and pastures of Colchester, 1280–1350', *Essex Archaeol. Hist.* 19: 159–65.

BROOKS, H. 1992, 'Two rural medieval sites in Chignall St James', *Essex Archaeol. Hist.* 23: 39–50.

——2001, 'A beaker burial, Late Iron Age and Roman features: observation and excavation at Elm Park, Ardleigh, 1994–1996', *Essex Archaeol. Hist.* 32: 75–91.

——2002, 'A Bronze Age and Saxon occupation site at Frog Hall Farm, Fingringhoe', *Essex Archaeol. Hist.* 33: 54–62.

BROOKS, N. 1989, 'The creation and early structure of the kingdom of Kent', in S. Bassett (ed.), *The Origins of Anglo-Saxon Kingdoms*. Leicester: Leicester University Press, 55–74.

BROWN, A. G. 2006, 'The environment of the Raunds area', in Parry (2006, 19–30).

——in press, 'Colluvial and alluvial response to land use change in Midland England: an integrated geoarchaeological approach', *Geoarchaeology*.

BROWN, C. G., and HUGO, T. E. 1983, 'Prehistoric and Romano-British finds from Mount Batten, Devon, 1979–1983', *Proc. Devon Archaeol. Soc.* 41: 69–75.

BROWN, D. 1981, 'Swastika patterns', in V. I. Evison (ed.), *Angles, Saxons and Jutes*. Oxford: Clarendon Press, 227–40.

BROWN, N. 1999, *The Archaeology of Ardleigh, Essex: Excavations 1955–1980*. East Anglian Archaeology 90.

——and GERMANY, M. 2002, 'Jousting at windmills: the Essex Cropmark Enclosures Project', *Essex Archaeol. Hist.* 33: 8–53.

——KNOPP, D., and STRACHAN, D. 2002, 'The archaeology of Constable Country: the crop-marks of the Stour Valley', *Landscape History*, 24: 5–28.

BROWN, S. 1998, 'Recent building recording and excavations at Leigh Barton, Churchstow, Devon', *Proc. Devon Archaeol. Soc.* 56: 5–108.

——and HOLBROOK, N. 1989, 'A Roman site at Otterton Point', *Proc. Devon Archaeol. Soc.* 47: 29–42.

——and LAITHWAITE, M. 1993, 'Northwood Farm, Christow: an abandoned farmstead on the eastern fringes of Dartmoor', *Proc. Devon. Archaeol. Soc.* 51: 161–84.

BROWN, T., and FOARD, G. 1998, 'The Saxon landscape: a regional perspective', in Everson and Williamson (1998, 67–94).

————2004, 'The Anglo-Saxon period', in M. Tingle (ed.), *The Archaeology of Northamptonshire*. Northampton: Northamptonshire Archaeological Society, 78–101.

BRYANT, S., PERRY, B., and WILLIAMSON, T. 2005, 'A "relict landscape" in south-east Hertfordshire; archaeological and topographic investigations in the Wormley area', *Landscape Hist.* 27: 5–16.

BUCKLEY, D. G. 1980, *The Archaeology of Essex to* AD *1500*. CBA Research Report 34, London: Council for British Archaeology.

—— and HEDGES, J. D. 1987, 'Excavation of a cropmark enclosure complex at Woodham Walter, Essex, 1976', *East Anglian Archaeology*, 33: 1–47.

BURGESS, C. 1985, 'Population, climate and upland settlement', in D. Spratt and C. Burgess (eds.), *Upland Settlement in Britain: The 2nd Millennium* BC *and After*. BAR British Series 143, Oxford: British Archaeological Reports, 195–219.

BURROW, I. 1981, *Hillfort and Hill-top Settlement in Somerset in the First to Eighth Centuries* AD. Oxford: British Archaeological Reports.

BUTLER, L., and WADE-MARTINS, P. 1989, *The Deserted Medieval Village of Thuxton, Norfolk*. East Anglian Archaeology 46.

CABOT, S., DAVIES, G., and HOGGETT, R. 2004, 'Sedgeford: excavations of a rural settlement in Norfolk', in J. Hines, A. Lane, and M. Redknap (eds.), *Land, Sea and Home*. Leeds: Society for Medieval Archaeology Monogr. 20, 313–24.

CADMAN, G., and FOARD, G. 1984, 'Raunds: manorial and village origins', in M. Faull (ed.), *Studies in Late Anglo-Saxon Settlement*. Oxford: Oxford University Department for External Studies.

CAHN, W. 1991, 'Medieval landscape and the encyclopedic tradition', *Yale French Studies*, 80: 11–24.

CAMPBELL, B. M. S. 1981, 'Commonfield origins: the regional dimension', in Rowley (1981, 112–29).

—— 2000, *English Seigniorial Agriculture 1250–1450*. Cambridge: Cambridge University Press.

CAMPBELL, G. 1994, 'The preliminary archaeobotanical results from Anglo-Saxon West Cotton and Raunds', in Rackham (1994, 65–82).

CANNELL, J. 2005, 'The archaeology of woodland exploitation in the Greater Exmoor area in the historic period'. Unpublished Ph.D. thesis, University of Exeter.

CARLEY, J. 1988, *Glastonbury Abbey*. London: Guild Publishing.

CARLYON, P. M. 1987, 'Finds from the earthworks at Carvossa, Probus', *Cornish Archaeology*, 26: 103–41.

—— 1998–9, 'Killhallon: an update', *Cornish Archaeol*. 37–8, 132–6.

CARR, J. 1991, 'The Suffolk excavation index', *Proc. Suffolk Institute Archaeol. Hist.* 37 (3): 179–85.

CARTER, G. A. 1998, *Excavations at the Orsett 'Cock' Enclosure, Essex, 1976*. East Anglian Archaeology 86.

CARUTH, J. 2002a, 'Lakenheath, recycling centre, RAF Lakenheath', *Medieval Settlement Research Group Annual Report*, 17: 62.

—— 2002b, 'Lakenheath, Wells Road, RAF Lakenheath', *Medieval Settlement Research Group Annual Report*, 17: 62–3.

CARVER, M. 1992, *The Age of Sutton Hoo*. Woodbridge: Boydell Press.

—— 2005, *Sutton Hoo: A Seventh-Century Princely Burial Ground and its Context*. London: British Museum Press.

CASELDINE, A. 1990, *Environmental Archaeology in Wales*. Lampeter: Archaeology Department, St David's University College.

—— 2006, 'The environment and deserted medieval settlement in Wales: potential and possibilities for palaeoenvironmental studies', in K. Roberts (ed.), *Lost Farmsteads:*

Deserted Rural Settlements in Wales. York: Council for British Archaeology Research Report 148.

—— and HOLDEN, T. G. 1998, 'The carbonized plant remains', in G. Williams and H. Mytum (eds.), *Llawhaden, Dyfed: Excavations on a Group of Small Defended Enclosures, 1980–4.* BAR British Series 275, Oxford: British Archaeological Reports, 105–18.

CASELDINE, C. 1980, 'Environmental change in Cornwall during the last 13,000 years', *Cornish Archaeol.* 19: 3–16.

—— 1999a, 'Environmental setting', in Kain and Ravenhill (1999, 25–34).

—— 1999b, 'Archaeological and environmental change on prehistoric Dartmoor: current understanding and future directions', in K. J. Edwards and J. P. Sadler (eds.), *Holocene Environments of Prehistoric Britain, J. Quat. Sc.* 14 (6)/*Quat. Proc.* 7, 575–85.

—— and HATTON, J. 1993, 'The development of high moorland on Dartmoor: fire and the influence of Mesolithic activity on vegetation change', in F. M. Chambers (ed.), *Climate Change and Human Impact on the Landscape.* London: Chapman & Hall, 119–31.

—— —— 1994, 'Into the mists? Thoughts on the prehistoric and historic environmental history of Dartmoor', *Proc. Devon Archaeol. Soc.* 52: 35–48.

—— —— 1996, 'Vegetational history of Dartmoor: Holocene development and the impact of human activity', in D. J. Charman, R. M. Newnham, and D. G. Croot (eds.), *Devon and East Cornwall Field Guide.* London: Quaternary Res. Ass., 48–62.

—— and MAGUIRE, D. J. 1986, 'Late-glacial/early Flandrian vegetation change on northern Dartmoor, south west England', *J. of Biogeography,* 13: 255–64.

—— JUGGINS, S., and STRAKER, V. 1988, 'Preliminary palaeoenvironmental analyses of floodplain deposits from a section near the river Exe in Exeter, Devon', in P. Murphy and C. French (eds.), *The Exploitation of Wetlands.* BAR British Series 186, Oxford: British Archaeological Reports, 145–62.

—— COLES, B. J., GRIFFITH, F. M., and HATTON, J. M. 2000, 'Conservation or change? Human influence on the mid-Devon landscape', in R. A. Nicholson and T. P. O'Connor (eds.), *People as Agents of Environmental Change.* Oxford: Oxbow, 60–9.

CAT 2000, *Hayes Farm, Clyst Honiton, Nr. Exeter, Devon: Archaeological Evaluation Phase 1 (1999).* Cotswold Archaeological Trust Report 001127, Cirencester.

CESSFORD, C. 2004, 'The origins and early development of Chesterton', *Proc. Cambridgeshire Antiq. Soc.* 93: 125–42.

—— 2005, 'The manor of Hintona: the origins and development of Church End, Cherry Hinton', *Proc. Cambridgeshire Antiq. Soc.* 94: 51–72.

CHARLES, B. G. 1938, *Non-Celtic Place-Names in Wales.* London: London Medieval Studies, University College London.

—— 1992, *The Place-Names of Pembrokeshire.* Aberystwyth: National Library of Wales.

CHILD, P. 1990, 'Farmhouse building tradition', in Beacham (1990a, 33–46).

CLARK, A. 1993, *Excavations at Mucking, i: The Site Atlas.* London: English Heritage.

CLARKE, C. P. 1998, *Excavations South of Chignall Roman Villa, Essex, 1977–81.* East Anglian Archaeology 83.

CLARKE, R. 2004, 'Rivenhall revisited: further excavations in the churchyard at St Mary and All Saints, 1999', *Essex Archaeol. Hist.* 35: 26–77.

COHEN, N. 2003, 'Boundaries and settlement: the role of the river Thames', *Anglo-Saxon Studies in Archaeology and History*, 12: 9–20.

COLES, R. 1939, 'Centuriation in Essex: an account of Roman agriculture in the county', *Essex Naturalist*, 26: 204–20.

COLLINS, R., and GERRARD, J. (eds.) 2004, *Debating Late Antiquity*. BAR British Series 365, Oxford: British Archaeological Reports.

COLMAN, S. 1999, 'Crown-post roofs', in Dymond and Martin (1999, 178–9).

——and BARNARD, M. 1999, 'Raised-aisled halls and queen-post roofs', in Dymond and Martin (1999, 180–1).

COOPER, J. 2001, *The Victoria History of the Counties of England: A History of the County of Essex*, x: *Lexden Hundred (Part)*. London: Institute of Historical Research.

COOPER, N. J. 2000, *The Archaeology of Rutland Water: Excavations at Empingham in Gwash Valley, Rutland, 1967–73 and 1990*. Leicester: University of Leicester Archaeological Services.

——and PRIEST, V. 2003, 'Sampling a medieval village in a day: the "big dig" investigation at Great Easton, Leicestershire', *Medieval Settlement Research Group Annual Report*, 18: 53–56.

CORBISHLEY, M. J. 1984, 'Excavations at St Mary's church Little Oakley, Essex, 1977', in Milton *et al.* (1984, 15–27).

CORCOS, N. 2002, *The Affinities and Antecedents of Medieval Settlement: Topographical Perspectives from Three Somerset Hundreds*. Oxford: BAR British Series 337.

COSTEN, M. 1992a, *The Origins of Somerset*. Manchester: Manchester University Press.

——1992b, 'Huish and Worth: Old English survivals in a later landscape', *Anglo-Saxon Studies in Archaeol. Hist.* 5: 65–83.

——1992c, 'Dunstan, Glastonbury and the economy of Somerset in the tenth century', in N. Ramsay, M. Sparks, and T. Tatton-Brown (eds.), *St Dunstan: His Life, Times and Cults*. Woodbridge: Boydell Press, 25–44.

——2007, 'Anonymous thegns in the landscape of Wessex 900–1066', in M. Costen (ed.), *People and Places: Essays in Honour of Mick Aston*. Oxford: Oxbow, 61–75.

COURTNEY, P. forthcoming, 'The Marcher lordships: origins, descent and organisation', in R. Howell and A. Hopkins (eds.), *Gwent County History*, ii: *Gwent in the Middle Ages 1070–1536*. Cardiff: University of Wales Press.

COWARD, H. 1978, 'The manor of Hutton in 1309', *SEARCH* [Journal of the Banwell Archaeological Society], 14: 33–50.

CREIGHTON, O. H. 2002, *Castles and Landscapes: Power, Community and Fortification in Medieval England*. London: Equinox.

CROCKELL, A. 1996, 'Archaeological sites along the Ilchester to Odcombe pipeline', *Proc. Somerset Archaeol. Natur. Hist. Soc.* 139: 59–88.

CROFT, R., and ASTON, M. 1993, *Somerset from the Air*. Taunton: Somerset County Council.

——and MYNARD, D. C. 1993, *The Changing Landscape of Milton Keynes*. Aylesbury: Buckinghamshire Archaeol. Soc. Monogr. 5.

CROMARTY, D. 1966, *The Fields of Saffron Walden*. Chelmsford: Essex Records Office.

CROSSLEY, D. W. 1963, 'List of hillforts and other earthworks in Pembrokeshire', *Bulletin Board of Celtic Studies*, 20: 171–235.

——1965a, 'Excavations at Merryborough Camp, Wiston', *Bulletin Board of Celtic Studies*, 21: 105–18.

——1965b, 'Excavations at Knock Rath, Clarbeston, 1962', *Bulletin Board of Celtic Studies*, 21: 264–75.

CROUCH, D. 1990, *William Marshall: Court, Career and Chivalry in the Angevin Empire 1147–1219*. London: Longman.

——and THOMAS, G. 1985, 'Three Goldcliff charters', *National Library of Wales Journal*, 24 (2): 153–63.

CROWSON, A., LANE, T., and REEVES, J. 2000, *Fenland Management Project Excavations 1991–1995*. Sleaford: Heritage Lincolnshire, Lincolnshire Archaeology and Heritage reports series No. 3.

————PENN, K., and TRIMBLE, D. 2004, *Anglo-Saxon Settlement on the Siltland of Eastern England*. Sleaford: Heritage Lincolnshire, Lincolnshire Archaeology and Heritage reports series No. 7.

CUNLIFFE, B. 1972, 'Saxon and medieval settlement patterns in the region of Chalton, Hampshire', *Medieval Archaeology*, 16: 1–12.

——1982, 'Iron Age settlement and pottery 650 BC–60 AD', in Aston and Burrow (1982, 53–62).

——1988, *Mount Batten, Plymouth: A Prehistoric and Roman Port*. Oxford: Oxford University Committee for Archaeology.

——1991, *Iron Age Communities in Britain*. 3rd edn. London: Routledge.

——2005, *Iron Age Communities in Britain*. 4th edn. London: Routledge.

CUSHION, B., DAVISON, A., FENNER, G., GOLDSMITH, R., KNIGHT, J., VIRGOE, N., WADE, K., and WADE-MARTINS, P. 1982, 'Some deserted village sites in Norfolk', *East Anglian Archaeology*, 14: 40–101.

DALE, R., MAYNARD, D., and COMPTON, J. 2005, 'Archaeology on the mid-Essex clay: investigations on the A130 by-pass: A12 Chelmsford by-pass to the A127 Southend arterial road, 1991–4 and 1999–2002', *Essex Archaeol. Hist.* 36: 10–54.

DALLAS, C. 1993, *Excavations in Thetford by B. K. Davison between 1964 and 1970*. East Anglian Archaeology 62.

DALLIMORE, J. 2001, *Newton St Loe, NE Somerset: A Study of the Vernacular Building Survey*. Bath: Bath and North East Somerset Council.

DARBY, H. C. 1952, *The Domesday Geography of Eastern England*. Cambridge: Cambridge University Press.

——1967, 'The south-western counties', in H. C. Darby and R. Welldon Finn (eds.), *The Domesday Geography of South-West England*. Cambridge: Cambridge University Press, 348–94.

——1973, *A New Historical Geography of England*. Cambridge: Cambridge University Press.

——1977, *Domesday England*. Cambridge: Cambridge University Press.

DARK, K. 2000, *Britain and the End of the Roman Empire*. Stroud: Tempus.

DAVEY, J. E. 2005, *The Roman to Medieval Transition in the Region of South Cadbury Castle, Somerset*. BAR British Series 399, Oxford: British Archaeological Reports.

DAVIES, J. 1999, 'Patterns, power and political progress in Iron Age Norfolk', in Davies and Williamson (1999, 14–43).

—— and WILLIAMSON, T. (eds.) 1999, *Land of the Iceni: The Iron Age in Northern East Anglia*. Norwich: Centre for East Anglian Studies.

DAVIES, M. 1973, 'Field systems of South Wales', in Baker and Butlin (1973a, 480–529).

DAVIES, M. F. 1939, *Pembrokeshire*, in L. D. Stamp (ed.), *The Land of Britain: The Report of the Land Utilisation Survey of Britain, Part 32*. London: Geographical Publications.

DAVIES, R. R. 1978, *Lordship and Society in the March of Wales, 1282–1400*. Oxford, Clarendon Press.

—— 1987, *Conquest, Co-existence and Change in Wales 1063–1415*. Cardiff: Cardiff University Press.

DAVIES, W. 1979, *The Llandaff Charters*. Aberystwyth: National Library of Wales.

DAVISON, A. 1982, 'Petygards and the medieval hamlet of Cotes', *East Anglian Archaeology*, 14: 102–7.

—— 1988, *Six Deserted Villages in Norfolk*. East Anglian Archaeology 44.

—— 1990, *The Evolution of Settlement in Three Norfolk Parishes*. East Anglian Archaeology 49.

—— 1995, 'Hargham', *Medieval Settlement Research Group Annual Report*, 10: 33.

—— 1996, 'Westacre', *Medieval Settlement Research Group Annual Report*, 11: 39.

—— 2001, 'Langford in Breckland', *Medieval Settlement Research Group Annual Report*, 16: 32–5, 51.

—— 2003a, 'The archaeology of the parish of West Acre part 1: field survey evidence'. *Norfolk Archaeol.* 44 (2): 202–21.

—— 2003b, 'Tittleshall: Godwick', *Medieval Settlement Research Group Annual Report*, 19: 65.

—— GREEN, B., and MILLINGTON, B. 1993, *Illington: A Study of a Breckland Parish*. East Anglian Archaeology 63.

DICKENS, A., MORTIMER, R., and TIPPER, J. 2006, 'The early Anglo-Saxon settlement and cemetery at Bloodmoor Hill, Carlton Colville, Suffolk: a preliminary report', *Anglo-Saxon Studies in Archaeol. Hist.* 13: 63–79.

DICKINSON, F. H. 1889, *Kirbys Quest for Somerset*. Somerset Records Society 3.

DICKS, T. R. B. 1967–8, 'Farming in Elizabethan Pembrokeshire 1588–1603', *National Library of Wales Journal*, 15: 215–25.

DILKE, O. 1971, *The Roman Land Surveyors*. Newton Abbot: David and Charles.

DODGSHON, R. A. 1980, *The Origins of British Field Systems: An Interpretation*. London: Academic Press.

—— 1981, 'The interpretation of sub-divided fields: a study in private or communal interests?', in Rowley (1981, 130–44).

DRAPER, S. 2004, 'Roman estates to English parishes', in Collins and Gerrard (2004, 55–64).

—— 2006, *Landscape, Settlement and Society in Roman and Early Medieval Wiltshire*. Oxford: BAR British Series 419.

DRURY, P. 1976, 'Braintree: excavations and research, 1971–6', *Essex Archaeol. Hist.* 8: 1–143.

DRURY, P. 1978, *Excavations at Little Waltham 1970–71*. CBA Research Report 26, London: Council for British Archaeology.

——and RODWELL, W. J. 1973, 'Excavations at Gun Hill, West Tilbury', *Essex Archaeol. Hist.* 5: 48–101.

————1978, 'Investigations at Asheldham, Essex: an interim report on the church and the historic landscape', *Antiquaries Journal*, 58 (1): 133–51.

————1980, 'Settlement in the later Iron Age and Roman periods', in Buckley (1980, 59–75).

——and WICKENDEN, N. P. 1982, 'An Early Saxon settlement within the Romano-British small town at Heybridge, Essex', *Medieval Archaeol.* 26: 1–40.

DUNNING, R. W. 1974, *Victoria County History of Somerset*, iv: *Kingsbury (East), Pitney, Somerton and Tintinhull Hundreds*. London: Institute of Historical Research.

——1981, *Victoria County History of Somerset*, iv: *Crewkerne, Martock and South Petherton Hundreds*. London: Institute of Historical Research.

——1985, *Victoria County History of Somerset*, v: *Whitley (Part) and Williton and Freemanors Hundreds*. London: Institute of Historical Research.

——1992, *Victoria County History of Somerset*, vi: *Andresfield, Cannington and North Petherton Hundreds*. London: Institute of Historical Research.

——1999, *Victoria County History of Somerset*, vii: *Bruton, Horethorne and North Ferris Hundreds*. London: Institute of Historical Research.

DYER, C. 1985, 'Power and conflict in the medieval village', in Hooke (1985, 27–32).

——2001, 'Review of *An Atlas of Rural Settlement in England*, by B. K. Roberts and S. Wrathmell', *Landscape Hist.* 23: 117–18.

——2003, *Making a Living in the Middle Ages: The People of Britain 850–1520*. London: Penguin.

——2004, 'Review of *Shaping Medieval Landscapes: Settlement, Society, Environment* by Tom Williamson', *Landscape Hist.* 26: 131–2.

——2007, 'A Suffolk farmer in the fifteenth century', *Agricultural History Review*, 55 (1): 1–22.

DYMOND, D., and MARTIN, E. 1999, *An Historical Atlas of Suffolk*. Rev. and enlarged edn. Ipswich: Suffolk County Council.

EAGLES, B. 1994, 'The archaeological evidence for settlement in the fifth to seventh centuries AD', in M. Aston and C. Lewis (eds.), *The Medieval Landscape of Wessex*. Oxford: Oxbow, 13–32.

EDWARDS, K. 1999, 'Palynology and people: observations on the British record', *Quaternary Proc.* 7: 531–44.

EDWARDS, N. 1997, *Landscape and Settlement in Medieval Wales*. Oxford: Oxbow.

——and LANE, A. 1988, *Early Medieval Settlement in Wales A.D. 400–1100*. Cardiff: University of Wales.

EKWALL, E. 1960, *The Concise Oxford Dictionary of English Place-Names*. Oxford: Oxford University Press.

ELLISON, A. 1983, *Medieval Villages in South-East Somerset*. Bristol: Western Archaeological Trust Survey 6.

——and PEARSON, T. 1981, *The Wincanton Bypass: A Study in the Archaeological Recording of Road Works*. Bristol: Committee for Rescue Archaeology in Avon, Gloucestershire and Somerset, Occasional Papers No. 8.

ENNIS, T. 2005, 'The Prittlewell prince and the Rayleigh paupers', *Current Archaeol.* 198: 298–301.

ERITH, E. J. 1948, 'The strip system of cultivation on Buckhurst Hill in the thirteenth century', *Essex Review*, 57: 97–9.

EVANS, D., and HANCOCK, A. 2006, 'Romano-British, late Saxon and medieval remains at the Old Showground, Cheddar: excavations in 2001', *Proc. Somerset Archaeol. Natur. Hist. Soc.* 149: 107–22.

EVERITT, A. 1977, 'River and wold: reflections on the historical origin of regions and pays', *Journal of Hist. Geogr.* 3: 1–19.

—— 1979, 'Country, county and town: patterns of regional evolution in England', *Trans. Royal Historical Society*, 5th Series, 29: 79–108.

—— 1986, *Continuity and Colonization: The Evolution of Kentish Settlement.* Leicester: Leicester University Press.

EVERSON, P. 1993, 'Pre-Viking settlement in Lindsey', in A. Vince (ed.), *Pre-Viking Lindsey.* Lincoln Archaeological Studies 1, 91–100.

—— and WILLIAMSON, T. (eds.) 1998, *The Archaeology of Landscape.* Manchester: Manchester University Press.

EVISON, V. I. 1981, 'Distribution maps and England in the first two phases', in V. I. Evison (ed.), *Angles, Saxons and Jutes.* Oxford: Clarendon Press, 126–67.

—— 1994, *An Anglo-Saxon Cemetery at Great Chesterford, Essex.* CBA Research Report 91, London: Council for British Archaeology.

FAIRBROTHER, J. 1990, *Faccombe Netherton: Excavations of a Saxon and Medieval Manorial Complex.* London: British Museum Occasional Paper 74.

FAITH, R. 1997, *The English Peasantry and the Growth of Lordship.* London: Leicester University Press.

FARMER, D. H. 1990, *Bede: Ecclesiastical History of the English People.* London: Penguin Books.

FAULKNER, N. 2000, 'Sedgeford: exploring an early English village', *Current Archaeology*, 171: 122–9.

—— 2004, 'The case for the Dark Ages', in Collins and Gerrard (2004, 5–12).

FAULL, M. 1976, 'The location and relationship of the Sancton Anglo-Saxon cemetery', *Antiq. J.* 56: 227–33.

FENWICK, V. 1984, 'Insula de Burgh: excavations at Burrow Hill, Butley, Suffolk 1978–81'. *Anglo-Saxon Studies in Archaeol. Hist.* 3: 35–54.

FIELD, J. 1993, *A History of English Field-Names.* London: Longman.

FILMER-SANKEY, W., and PESTEL, T. 2001, *Snape Anglo-Saxon Cemetery: Excavations and Surveys 1824–1992.* East Anglian Archaeology 95.

FINBERG, H. P. R. 1951, *Tavistock Abbey. A Study in the Social and Economic History of Devon.* Newton Abbot: David and Charles.

—— 1952, 'The open field in Devon', in W. G. Hoskins and H. P. R. Finberg (eds.), *Devonshire Studies.* London: Jonathan Cape, 265–88.

—— 1954, *The Early Charters of Devon and Cornwall.* Leicester: University of Leicester Department of English Local History Occasional Papers 2.

—— 1961, *The Early Charters of the West Midlands.* Leicester: Leicester University Press.

—— 1964, *The Early Charters of Wessex.* Leicester: Leicester University Press.

282   *References*

FINBERG, H. P. R. 1969, *West Country Historical Studies*. Newton Abbot: David and Charles.

—— 1974, *The Formation of England 550–1042*. London: Hart-Davis, MacGibbon.

FITZPATRICK, A., BUTTERWORTH, C. A., and GROVE, J. 1999, *Prehistoric & Roman Sites in East Devon: The A30 Honiton to Exeter Improvement DBFO Scheme, 1996–9*. Salisbury: Wessex Archaeology.

FLEMING, A. 1983, 'The prehistoric landscape of Dartmoor part 2: north and east Dartmoor', *Proc. Prehist. Soc.* 49: 195–241.

—— 1988, *The Dartmoor Reaves*. London: Batsford.

—— 1994, 'The Reaves revisited', *Proc. Devon Archaeol. Soc.* 52: 63–74.

—— 1998, 'Prehistoric landscapes and the quest for territorial pattern', in Everson and Williamson (1998, 42–66).

—— 2006, 'Post-processual landscape archaeology: a critique', *Cambridge Archaeological Journal*, 16 (2): 267–80.

—— 2007, 'Don't bin your boots', *Landscapes*, 8 (1): 85–99.

—— and RALPH, N. 1982, 'Medieval settlement and landuse on Holne Moor, Dartmoor: the landscape evidence', *Med. Archaeol.* 26: 101–37.

FOARD, G. 1978, 'Systematic fieldwalking and the investigation of Saxon settlement in Northamptonshire', *World Archaeol.* 9: 357–74.

—— 2001, 'Medieval woodland, agriculture and industry in the Rockingham Forest, Northamptonshire', *Med. Archaeol.* 45: 41–97.

—— HALL, D., and PARTIDA, T. 2005, 'Rockingham Forest, Northamptonshire: the evolution of a landscape', *Landscapes*, 6 (2): 1–29.

FOREMAN, S., and MAYNARD, D. 2002, 'A late Iron Age and Romano-British farmstead at Ship Lane, Aveley: excavations on the line of the A13 Wennington to Mar Dyke road improvement, 1994–5', *Essex Archaeol. Hist.* 33: 123–56.

FOSTER, I. D. L., MIGHALL, T. M., WOTTON, C., OWENS, P. N., and WALLING, D. E. 2000, 'Evidence for medieval soil erosion in the South Hams region of Devon, UK', *The Holocene*, 10 (2): 261–71.

FOWLER, P. J. 2000, *Landscape Plotted and Pieced: Landscape History and Local Archaeology*. London: Society of Antiquaries.

—— and THOMAS, C. 1962, 'Arable fields in the pre-Norman period at Gwithian', *Cornish Archaeology*, 1: 61–84.

FOX, A. 1952, 'Hill-slope forts and related earthworks in south-west England and South Wales', *Archaeol. J.* 109: 1–22.

—— 1954, 'Excavations at Kestor: an early Iron Age settlement near Chagford, Devon', *Rep. Trans. Devonshire Ass.* 86: 21–62.

—— 1958, 'A monastic homestead on Dean Moor, South Devon', *Med. Archaeol.* 2: 141–57.

—— 1995, 'Tin ingots from Bigbury Bay, South Devon', *Proc. Devon. Archaeol. Soc.* 53, 11–23.

FOX, C. 1932, *The Personality of Britain*. Cardiff: National Museum of Wales.

FOX, H. S. A. 1972, 'Field systems of east and south Devon, part 1: east Devon', *Trans. Devonshire Ass.* 104: 81–135.

—— 1973, 'Outfield cultivation in Devon and Cornwall: a reinterpretation', in M. Havinden (ed.), *Husbandry and Marketing in the South-West 1500–1800*. Exeter: Exeter University Press, 190–38.

—— 1981, 'Approaches to the adoption of the Midland system', in Rowley (1981, 64–111).

—— 1983, 'Contraction: desertion and dwindling of dispersed settlement in a Devon parish', *Medieval Village Research Group Annual Report*, 31: 40–2.

—— 1989a, 'Peasant farmers, patterns of settlement and pays: transformations in the landscapes of Devon and Cornwall', in R. A. Higham (ed.), *Landscape and Townscape in the South West*. Exeter: University of Exeter Press, 41–75.

—— 1989b, 'The people of the wolds in English settlement history', in M. Aston, D. Austin, and C. Dyer (eds.), *The Rural Settlements of Medieval England*. Oxford: Blackwell, 77–101.

—— 1991, 'Farming practice and techniques, Devon and Cornwall', in E. Miller (ed.), *The Agrarian History of England and Wales*, iii: *1348–1500*. Cambridge: Cambridge University Press, 303–23.

—— 1996, 'Introduction: transhumance and seasonal settlement', in H. S. A. Fox (ed.), *Seasonal Settlement*. Vaughan Papers in Adult Education No. 39, Leicester: University of Leicester, Department of Adult Education.

—— and PADEL, O. 2000, *The Cornish Lands of the Arundells of Lanherne, Fourteenth to Sixteenth Centuries*. Devon and Cornwall Records Society 41.

Fox, H. 2006, Foreword, in Turner (2006a, pp. xi–xvi).

FRANCIS, P. D., and SLATER, D. S. 1990, 'A record of vegetational and land use change from upland peat deposits on Exmoor part 2: Hoar Moor', *Proc. Somerset Archaeol. Nat. Hist. Soc.* 134: 1–26.

—— —— 1992, 'A record of vegetational and land use change from upland peat deposits on Exmoor part 3: Codsend Moors', *Proc. Somerset Archaeol. Nat. Hist. Soc.* 136: 9–28.

FULFORD, M. G. 1990, 'The landscape of Roman Britain: a review', *Landscape History*, 12: 25–32.

—— 1996, *The Second Augustan Legion in the West of Britain*. Cardiff: National Museum of Wales.

—— and WHITTLE, E. 1992, *Developing Landscapes of Lowland Britain*. London: Society of Antiquaries.

FYFE, R. M. 2000, 'Palaeochannels of the Exe catchment: their age and an assessment of their archaeological and palaeoenvironmental potential'. Ph.D. thesis, University of Exeter.

—— and RIPPON, S. J. 2004, 'A landscape in transition? Palaeoenvironmental evidence for the end of the "Romano-British" period in south west England', in Collins and Gerrard (2004, 33–42).

—— BROWN, A. G., and COLES, B. J. 2003a, 'Mesolithic to Bronze Age vegetation change and human activity in the Exe Valley, Devon, UK', *Proc. Prehist. Soc.* 69: 161–81.

—— —— and RIPPON, S. J. 2003b, 'Mid to late-Holocene vegetation history of Greater Exmoor, UK: estimating the spatial extent of human-induced vegetation change', *Vegetation Hist. and Archaeobotany*, 12: 215–32.

—— —— —— 2004, 'Characterising the late prehistoric, "Romano-British" and medieval landscape, and dating the emergence of a regionally distinct agricultural system in south west Britain', *Journal of Archaeological Science*, 31: 1699–714.

FYFE, R. M., BROWN, A. G., and COOK, N. forthcoming, 'Late-Holocene palaeoclimatological data from an upland soligenous mire: Moles Chamber, Exmoor, UK', *The Holocene*.

GAFFNEY, V., and TINGLE, M. 1989, *The Maddle Farm Project: An Integrated Survey of Prehistoric and Roman Landscapes on the Berkshire Downs*. BAR British Series 200, Oxford: British Archaeological Reports.

GAIMSTER, M., and BRADLEY, J. 2001, 'Medieval Britain and Ireland', *Med. Archaeol.* 45: 252–379.

——— 2002, 'Medieval Britain and Ireland', *Med. Archaeol.* 46: 146–264.

GALLANT, L., and SILVESTER, R. J. 1985, 'An excavation on the Iron Age hillfort at Berry Down, Newton Abbot', *Proc. Devon Archaeol. Soc.* 43: 39–48.

——LUXTON, N., and COLLMAN, M. 1985, 'Ancient fields on the south Devon limestone plateau', *Proc. Devon Archaeol. Soc.* 43: 23–37.

GARDINER, M., and RIPPON, S. 2007, *Medieval Landscapes*. Landscape History after Hoskins 2, Macclesfield: Windgather Press.

GARROW, D., LUCY, S., and GIBSON, D. 2006, *Excavations at Kilverstone, Norfolk: An Episodic Landscape History*. East Anglian Archaeology 113.

GARWOOD, A. 1998, 'A Late Iron Age and Roman site at Shillingstone Field, Great Sampford', *Essex Archaeol. Hist.* 29: 33–47.

GEAKE, H. 1997, *The Use of Grave Goods in Conversion Period England, c.600–c.850*. BAR British Series 261, Oxford: British Archaeological Reports.

GEAREY, B., and CHARMAN, D. 1996, 'Rough Tor, Bodmin Moor: testing some archaeological hypotheses with landscape palaeoecology', in D. J. Charman, R. M. Newnham, and D. G. Croot (eds.), *Devon and East Cornwall Field Guide*. London: Quaternary Research Association, 101–19.

——WEST, S., and CHARMAN, D. J. 1997, 'The landscape context of medieval settlement on the south-western moors of England: recent palaeoenvironmental evidence from Bodmin Moor and Dartmoor', *Med. Archaeol.* 41: 195–209.

——CHARMAN, D. J., and KENT, M. 2000a, 'Palaeoecological evidence for the prehistoric settlement of Bodmin Moor, Cornwall, southwest England, part I: the status of woodland and early human impacts'. *J. Archaeol. Soc.* 27 (5): 423–38.

——————— 2000b, 'Palaeoecological evidence for the prehistoric settlement of Bodmin Moor, Cornwall, southwest England, part II: landuse changes from the Neolithic to the present', *J. Archaeol. Soc.* 27 (6): 423–38.

GELLING, M. 1992, 'A chronology for Suffolk place-names', in Carver (1992, 53–64).

——1997, *Signposts to the Past: Place-Names and the History of England*. 3rd edn. Chichester: Phillimore.

GENT, H., and QUINNELL, H. 1999a, 'Excavations of a causewayed enclosure and hillfort on Raddon Hill, Stockleigh Pomeroy', *Proc. Devon Archaeol. Soc.* 57: 1–76.

——————— 1999b, 'Salvage recording on the Neolithic site at Haldon Belvedere', *Proc. Devon Archaeol. Soc.* 57: 77–104.

GENT, T. H 1997, *Archaeological Evaluation of WWB Rivers Diversion and Tipping Area, Teigngrace, Devon*. Exeter Archaeology Report 97.01 (copy in Devon HER, site no. 37247).

GERMANY, M. 2001, 'Fieldwalking at Crondon Park, Stock', *Essex Archaeol. Hist.* 32: 178–88.

—— 2003a, *Excavations at Great Holts Farm, Boreham, Essex, 1992–94*. East Anglian Archaeology 105.

—— 2003b, 'A causewayed enclosure at St. Osyth, near Clacton', *Essex Journal*, 38 (2): 39–43.

—— 2007, *Neolithic and Bronze Age Monuments and Middle Iron Age Settlement at Lodge Farm, St Osyth, Essex*. East Anglian Archaeology 117.

—— 2008, 'Monument 24858 Gilden Way, Harlow, Essex: archaeological evaluation'. Unpublished report, Essex County Council Field Archaeology Unit.

GERRARD, C., with ASTON, M. 2007, *The Shapwick Project*. Society for Medieval Archaeology Monograph.

GERRARD, S. 1997, *Dartmoor*. London: English Heritage.

—— 2000, *The Early British Tin Industry*. Stroud: Tempus.

GIBSON, C., and MURRAY, J. 2003, 'An Anglo-Saxon settlement at Godmanchester, Cambridgeshire', *Anglo-Saxon Studies in Archaeology and History*, 12: 136–217.

GIFFORD and Partners 1999, 'Report on an archaeological evaluation at The Old Ranges, Shoeburyness, Essex'. Unpublished report, Gifford and Partners (copy in Southend-on-Sea Museum).

GILLARD, M. 2002, 'The medieval landscape of the Exmoor region: enclosure and settlement in an upland fringe'. Unpublished thesis, University of Exeter.

GILMAN, P. J., and BENNETT, A. 1995, 'Archaeology in Essex 1994', *Essex Archaeology and History*, 26: 238–58.

GODWIN, H. 1968, 'Studies in the post-glacial history of British vegetation 15: organic deposits at Old Buckenham Mere, Norfolk', *New Phytologist*, 67: 95–107.

—— and TALLANTIRE, P. 1951, 'Studies in the post-glacial history of British vegetation 12: Hockham Mere, Norfolk', *Journal of Ecology*, 39: 285–307.

GOING, C. 1996, 'The Roman countryside', in Bedwin (1996, 95–107).

GONNER, E. C. K. 1912, *Common Land and Enclosure*. London: Macmillan.

GOODARD, S., and TODD, M. 2005, 'Medieval Rudge, Morchard Bishop', *Proc. Devon Archaeol. Soc.* 63: 209–10.

GOSSIP, J. 2005a, 'Richard Lander School development, Threemilestone, Cornwall: archaeological recording areas A–K: archive report'. Unpublished report, Historic Environment Service (Projects), Cornwall County Council.

—— 2005b, 'Richard Lander School development, Threemilestone, Cornwall: archaeological recording—pipeline and access road: archive report'. Unpublished report, Historic Environment Service (Projects), Cornwall County Council.

—— 2006, 'Truro College playing fields, Truro College, Cornwall: archaeological recording: archive report'. Unpublished report, Historic Environment Service (Projects), Cornwall County Council.

GOVER, J. E. B., MAWER, A., and STENTON, F. M. 1931, *The Place-Names of Devon Part 1*. English Place-Names Society VIII. Cambridge: Cambridge University Press.

GRAHAM, A. 2005, 'Evidence for the medieval hamlets of Pykesash and Ash Boulogne: archaeological excavations at Ash', *Proc. Somerset Archaeol. and Natur. Hist. Soc.* 148: 11–40.

—— and DAVIES, S. M. 1993, *Excavations in Trowbridge, Wiltshire, 1977 and 1986–1988*. Salisbury: Wessex Archaeology Report 2.

GRANT, N. 1995, 'The occupation of hillforts in Devon during the late Roman and post-Roman periods', *Proc. Devon Archaeol. Soc.* 53: 97–108.

Gray, H. L. 1915, *English Field Systems*. Cambridge, Mass.: Harvard University Press.

Green, S. 1999, *The Essex Landscape: In Search of its History*. Chelmsford: Essex County Council.

Greene, J. P., and Greene, K. T. 1970, 'A trial excavation on a Romano-British site at Clanacombe, Thurlestone, 1969', *Proc. Devon Archaeol. Soc.* 28: 130–6.

Gregory, T., and Gurney, D. 1986, *Excavations at Thornham, Warham, Wighton and Caistor St Edmund, Norfolk*. East Anglian Archaeology 30.

Gregson, N. 1985, 'The multiple estate model: some critical questions', *Journal of Historical Geography*, 11 (4): 339–51.

Griffith, F. M. 1984, 'Roman military sites in Devon: some recent discoveries', *Proc. Devon Archaeol. Soc.* 42: 11–32.

——1988a, 'A Romano-British villa near Crediton', *Proc. Devon Archaeol. Soc.* 46: 137–42.

——1988b, *Devon's Past*. Exeter: Devon Books.

——1994, 'Changing perceptions of the context of prehistoric Dartmoor', *Proc. Devon Archaeol. Soc.* 52: 85–99.

——and Quinnell, H. 1999, 'Iron Age to Roman buildings, structures and coin and other findspots', in Kain and Ravenhill (1999, 74–6).

——and Weddell, P. 1996, 'Ironworking in the Blackdown Hills: results of recent survey', in P. Newman (ed.), *The Archaeology of Mining and Metallurgy in South West Britain*. Matlock: Peak District Mines Historical Society/Historical Metallurgy Society, 27–34.

Gurney, D. 1994, 'The Roman period', in Wade-Martins (1994, 34–5).

——and Penn, K. 1998, 'Excavations and surveys in Norfolk in 1997', *Norfolk Archaeol.* 43 (1): 193–211.

————1999, 'Excavations and surveys in Norfolk in 1998', *Norfolk Archaeol.* 43 (2): 369–86.

————2000, 'Excavations and surveys in Norfolk in 1999', *Norfolk Archaeol.* 43 (3): 521–42.

————2001, 'Excavations and surveys in Norfolk in 2000', *Norfolk Archaeol.* 43 (4): 707–28.

————2002, 'Excavations and surveys in Norfolk in 2001', *Norfolk Archaeol.* 44 (1): 162–77.

————2005, 'Excavations and surveys in Norfolk in 2004', *Norfolk Archaeol.* 44 (4): 751–64.

Guthrie, A. 1969, 'Excavations of a settlement at Goldherring, Sancreed, 1958–1961', *Cornish Archaeol.* 8: 5–39.

Gutiérrez, A. 2007, 'The pottery: Brent Knoll vicarage'. Unpublished report.

Guttman, E. B. A. 2000, 'Excavations on the Hatfield Heath to Matching Tye rising main, north-west Essex', *Essex Archaeol. Hist.* 31: 18–32.

Hadley, D. 2000, 'Burial practices in the northern Danelaw, *c.*650–1100', *Northern History*, 36 (2): 199–216.

——2002, 'Burial practices in northern England in the later Anglo-Saxon period', in S. Lucy and A. Reynolds (eds.), *Burial in Early Medieval England and Wales*. Society for Medieval Archaeology Monograph 17, 209–28.

Hall, D. 1981, 'The origins of open field agriculture: the archaeological fieldwork evidence', in Rowley (1981, 22–38).

—— 1982, *Medieval Fields*. Aylesbury: Shire.

—— 1983, 'Fieldwork and fieldbooks: studies in early layout', in Roberts and Glasscock (1983, 115–32).

—— 1985, 'Late Saxon topography and early medieval estates', in Hooke (1985, 61–9).

—— 1988, 'The Late Saxon countryside: villages and their fields', in D. Hooke (ed.), *Anglo-Saxon Settlements*. Oxford: Blackwells, 99–122.

—— 1995, *The Open Field of Northamptonshire*. Northamptonshire Records Society.

—— 1996, *The Fenland Project, Number 10: Cambridgeshire Survey, Isle of Ely and Wisbech*. East Anglian Archaeology 79.

—— and MARTIN, P. W. 1979, 'Brixworth, Northamptonshire: an intensive field survey', *J. Brit. Archaeol. Ass.* 132: 1–6.

HAMEROW, H. 1991, 'Settlement mobility and the "Middle Saxon Shift": rural settlements and settlement patterns in Anglo-Saxon England', *Anglo-Saxon England*, 20: 1–17.

—— 1993, *Excavations at Mucking*, i: *The Anglo-Saxon Settlement*. London: English Heritage.

—— 2002, *Early Medieval Settlements: The Archaeology of Rural Communities in North-West Europe 400–900*. Oxford: Oxford University Press.

HANSON, L., and WICKHAM, C. (eds.) 2000, *The Long Eighth Century: Production, Distribution and Demand*, Leiden: Brill.

HARRISON, J. 1997, 'The composite manor of Brent: a study of a large wetland-edge estate up to 1350'. Unpublished thesis, University of Leicester.

HARRISON, S. 2002, 'Open fields and earlier landscapes: six parishes in south-east Cambridgeshire', *Landscapes*, 3 (1): 35–54.

HARVEY, M. 1982, 'Irregular villages in Holderness, Yorkshire: some thoughts on their origins', *Yorkshire Archaeological Journal*, 54: 63–72.

HARVEY, P. D. A. 1989, 'Initiative and authority in settlement change', in M. Aston, D. Austin, and C. Dyer (eds.), *The Rural Settlements of Medieval England*. Oxford: Blackwells, 31–43.

HASSAL, C. 1815, *A General View of the Agriculture of the County of Monmouth*. London: The Board of Agriculture.

HATCHER, J. 1970, *Rural Economy and Society in the Duchy of Cornwall 1300–1500*. Cambridge: Cambridge University Press.

HATTON, J. M., and CASELDINE, C. J. 1991, 'Vegetation change and land use history during the first millennium AD at Aller Farm, East Devon as indicated by pollen analysis', *Proc. Devon Archaeol. Soc.* 49: 107–14.

HAVERFIELD, F. 1920, 'Centuriation in Roman Essex', *Trans. Essex Archaeol. Soc.* NS 15: 115–25.

HAVIS, R. 2001, 'A Roman site at Radwinter', *Essex Archaeol. Hist.* 32: 241–3.

—— and BROOKS, H. 2004a, *Excavations at Stanstead Airport, 1986–91*, i: *Prehistoric and Romano-British*. East Anglian Archaeology 107.

—— —— 2004b, *Excavations at Stanstead Airport, 1986–91*, ii: *Saxon, Medieval and Post-Medieval: Discussion*. East Anglian Archaeology 107.

HAWARD, B., and AITKINS, P. 1999, 'Medieval church roofs', in Dymond and Martin (1999, 170–3).

HAWKINS, S. 2005a, 'Vegetation history and land-use change in the Blackdown Hills, Devon, U.K.' Unpublished report, Community Landscapes Project, University of Exeter.

——2005b, 'Vegetation history and land-use change in the Clyst Valley, Devon, U.K.' Unpublished report, Community Landscapes Project, University of Exeter.

——2005c, 'Vegetation history and land-use change in the Hartland peninsula, Devon, U.K.' Unpublished report, Community Landscapes Project, University of Exeter.

HAYES, P. P. 1988, 'Roman to Saxon in the south Lincolnshire fens', *Antiquity*, 62: 321–6.

——and LANE, T. 1992, *The Fenland Survey, Number 6: Lincolnshire Survey, the South West Fens*. East Anglian Archaeology 55.

HEDGES, J. D., and BUCKLEY, D. G. 1985, 'Anglo-Saxon and later features excavated at Orsett, Essex, 1975', *Med. Archaeol.* 29: 1–25.

HENDERSON, C. G. 1988, 'Exeter (*Isca Dumnoniorum*)', in G. Webster (ed.), *Fortress into City: The Consolidation of Roman Britain, 1st Century AD*. London: Batsford, 91–119.

——and WEDDELL, P. J. 1994, 'Medieval settlement on Dartmoor and in west Devon: the evidence from excavations', *Proc. Devon Archaeol. Soc.* 52: 119–40.

HENIG, M. 2004, 'Remaining Roman in Britain AD 300–700: the evidence of portable art', in Collins and Gerrard (2004, 13–23).

HERRING, P. 1993, 'Examining a Romano-British boundary at Foage, Zennor', *Cornish Archaeol.* 32: 17–28.

——1994, 'The cliff castles and hillforts of West Penwith in the light of recent work at Maen Castle and Treryn Dinas', *Cornish Archaeol.* 33: 40–56.

——1996, 'Transhumance in medieval Cornwall', in H. Fox (ed.), *Seasonal Settlement*. Leicester: University of Leicester, 35–43.

——1997, 'The prehistoric landscape of Cornwall and west Devon: economic and social contexts for metallurgy', in P. Budd and D. Gale (eds.), *Prehistoric Extractive Metallurgy in Cornwall*. Truro: Cornwall Archaeology Unit, 19–21.

——1998, *Cornwall's Historic Landscape: Presenting a Method of Historic Landscape Characterisation*. Truro: Cornwall Archaeology Unit.

——2000, *St Michael's Mount, Cornwall: Reports on Archaeological Works, 1995–1998*. Truro: Cornwall Archaeological Unit.

——2006a, 'Cornish strip fields', in Turner (2006a, 44–77).

——2006b, 'Cornish medieval fields, a case-study: Brown Willy', in Turner (2006a, 78–103).

——2007 in press, 'Historic landscape characterisation in an ever-changing Cornish landscape', *Landscapes*, 8 (2).

——forthcoming, 'Commons, fields and communities in prehistoric Cornwall', in A. Chadwick (ed.), *Recent Approaches to the Archaeology of Land Allotment*. BAR International Series, Oxford: British Archaeological Reports.

——and HOOKE, D. 1993, 'Interrogating Anglo-Saxons in St Dennis', *Cornish Archaeology*, 32: 67–76.

——and LEWIS, B. 1992, 'Ploughing up gatherer-hunters: Mesolithic and later flints from Butterstor and elsewhere on Bodmin Moor', *Cornish Archaeol.* 31: 5–14.

HESSE, M. 1997, 'The early parish and estate of Ickworth, West Suffolk', *Proc. Suffolk Instit. of Archaeol. Hist.* 39 (1): 6–27.

HEY, G. 2004, *Yarnton: Saxon and Medieval Settlement and Landscape: Results of Excavations 1990–96*. Oxford: Oxford Archaeology Thames Valley Landscapes Monogr. No. 20.

HEYWOOD, S. 1988, 'The round towers of East Anglia', in J. Blair (ed.), *Minsters and Parish Churches: The Local Church in Transition 950–1200*. Oxford: Oxford University Committee for Archaeology monogr. 17, 169–78.

HINES, J. 1984, *The Scandinavian Character of Anglian Britain in the Pre-Viking Period*. BAR British Series 124, Oxford: British Archaeological Reports.

HINTON, D. A. 1997, 'The "Scole-Dickleburgh system" examined', *Landscape Hist.* 19: 5–12.

—— 2005, 'Debate: south Hampshire, "east Wessex" and the *Atlas of Rural Settlement in England*', *Landscape Hist.* 27: 71–5.

HOBBS, B., and ROBERTSON, D. 2004, 'Medieval activity on the site of the former village hall, Little Cressingham', *Norfolk Archaeol.* 44 (3): 546–8.

HODDER, I. 1982, *Wendens Ambo: The Excavation of an Iron Age and Romano-British Settlement*. London: Passmore Edwards Museum.

HOLBROOK, N. 1987, 'Trial excavations at Honeyditches and the nature of the Roman occupation at Seaton', *Proc. Devon Archaeol. Soc.* 45: 59–74.

—— 2001, 'Coastal trade around the south-west peninsula of Britain in the later Roman period: a summary of the evidence', *Proc. Devon Archaeol. Soc.* 59: 149–58.

—— and BIDWELL, P. 1991, *Roman Finds from Exeter*. Exeter: Exeter Archaeol. Rep. 4.

HOLLINRAKE, C., and HOLLINRAKE, N. 1989, 'Compton Dundon, Court Orchard', in J. Bradbury and R. A. Croft, 'Somerset archaeology 1989', *Proc. Somerset Archaeol. Natur. Hist. Soc.* 133: 157–85.

—— —— 1997, 'An archaeological evaluation in the Old Showground, Cheddar'. Unpublished report no. 116 (copy on Somerset HER, PRN 57178).

—— —— 2001, 'A Late Saxon comb handle from Bawdrip', *Proc. Somerset Archaeol. Natur. Hist. Soc.* 144: 213–14.

—— —— 2004, 'An archaeological evaluation at 7 Coronation Road, Highbridge', Unpublished report no. 300.

HOMANS, G. C. 1941, *English Villagers of the Thirteenth Century*. Cambridge, Mass.: Harvard University Press.

—— 1969, 'The explanation of English regional differences', *Past and Present*, 42: 18–34.

HOOKE, D. 1981, 'Open field agriculture: the evidence from the pre-Conquest charters of the West Midlands', in Rowley (1981, 39–63).

—— (ed.) 1985, *Medieval Villages*. Oxford: Oxford University Committee for Archaeology monogr. 5.

—— 1994, *The Pre-Conquest Charter-Bounds of Devon and Cornwall*. Woodbridge: Boydell Press.

—— 1998, *The Landscape of Anglo-Saxon England*. London: Leicester University Press.

—— 1999, 'Saxon conquest and settlement', in Kain and Ravenhill (1999, 95–104).

HOPE, J. H. 1984, 'Excavations at All Saints Church, Cressing, Essex, 1979', in Milton *et al.* (1984, 28–42).

HORNER, W. S. 1993, 'A Romano-British enclosure at Butland Farm, Modbury', *Proc. Devon Archaeol. Soc.* 51: 210–15.

HORNER, W. S. 2001, 'Secrets of the sands', *Devon Archaeol. Soc. Newsletter May 2001*, 1: 8–9.

——2006, 'What's under your school?', *Devon Archaeol. Soc. Newsletter*, 94: 1–2.

HOSKINS, W. G. 1952, 'The making of the agrarian landscape', in W. G. Hoskins and H. P. R. Finberg, *Devonshire Studies*. London: Jonathan Cape, 289–334.

——1954, *Devon*. London: Collins.

HOUSLEY, R. A., STRAKER, V., CHAMBERS, F. M., and LAGEARD, J. G. A. 2007, 'An ecological context for the post-Roman archaeology of the Somerset moors (south west England, UK)', *Journal of Wetland Archaeology*, 7.

HOWELL, R. 2001, 'Roman survival, Welsh revival: the evidence of re-use of Roman remains', *Monmouthshire Antiquary*, 17: 55–60.

HOWELLS, B. 1967–8, 'The distribution of customary acres in South Wales', *National Library of Wales Journal*, 15: 226–33.

——1987, 'Land and people, 1536–1642', in B. Howells (ed.), *Early Modern Pembrokeshire, 1536–1815*. Haverfordwest: Pembrokeshire Historical Society, 1–31.

HUDSON, H. 2002, *The New Wedmore Chronicles*. Wedmore: private publication.

HUGGINS, P. J. 1978, 'Excavation of Belgic and Romano-British farm with Middle Saxon cemetery and churches at Nazeingbury, Essex 1975–6', *Essex Archaeol. Hist.* 10: 29–117.

——1988, 'Excavations on the north side of Sun Street, Waltham Abbey, Essex 1974–5: Saxon burials, precinct wall and south-east transept', *Essex Archaeol. Hist.* 19: 117–53.

HUGHES, M. 1984, 'Rural settlement and landscape in Late Saxon Hampshire', in M. Faull (ed.), *Studies in Late Anglo-Saxon Settlement*. Oxford: Oxford University Department for External Studies, 65–80.

HULL, G. 2002, 'Barkingwic? Saxon and medieval features adjacent to Barking Abbey', *Essex Archaeol. Hist.* 33: 157–90.

HUMPHREY, R. 2002, 'A Roman agricultural landscape at the golf course site, Mill Hill, Braintree', *Essex Archaeol. Hist.* 33: 103–22.

HUNTER, J. 1993a, 'The historic landscape of Cressing Temple and its environs', in D. Andrews (ed.), *Cressing Temple: A Templar and Hospitaller manor in Essex*. Chelmsford: Essex County Council, 25–35.

——1993b, 'The age of hedgerows on a Bocking estate', *Essex Archaeol. Hist.* 24: 114–18.

——1995, 'Settlement and farming patterns on the mid-Essex boulder clays', *Essex Archaeol. Hist.* 26: 133–44.

——1999, *The Essex Landscape: A Study of its Form and History*. Chelmsford: Essex Records Office.

——2003, *Field Systems in Essex*. Colchester: Essex Society for Archaeology and History, Occasional Papers, NS 1.

ISSERLIN, R. M. J. 1995, 'Roman Coggeshall II; excavations at "The Lawns", 1989–93', *Essex Archaeol. Hist.* 82–104.

IVENS, R. 1995, *Tattenhoe and Westbury*. Aylesbury: Buckinghamshire Archaeol. Soc. Monogr. 8.

JACOBSEN, G. L., and BRADSHAW, R. H. 1981, 'The selection of sites for palaeoecological studies', *Quaternary Research*, 16: 80–96.

JAMES, H. 1987, 'Excavations at Caer, Bayvil, 1979', *Archaeologia Cambrensis*, 136: 51–76.

——and WILLIAMS, G. 1982, 'Rural settlement in Roman Dyfed', in Miles (1982, 289–313).

JARVIS, K. 1976, 'The M5 motorway and the Peamore/Pocombe link', *Proc. Devon Archaeol. Soc.* 34: 41–72.

——and MAXFIELD, V. 1975, 'The excavation of a first century Roman farmstead and a late Neolithic settlement, Topsham, Devon', *Proc. Devon Archaeol. Soc.* 33: 209–65.

JENKINS, D. 1986, *The Law of Hywel Dda*. Llandysul: Gomer Press.

JOHNSON, D. A., MOORE, C., and FASHAM, P. 1998–9, 'Excavation at Penhale Round, Fraddon, Cornwall', *Cornish Archaeol.* 37–8: 72–120.

JOHNSON, M. 1999, *Archaeological Theory*. Oxford: Blackwell Publishing.

——2007, *Ideas of Landscape*. Oxford: Blackwell Publishing.

JOHNSON, N., and ROSE, P. 1982, 'Defended settlement in Cornwall: an illustrated discussion', in Miles (1982, 151–207).

————1994, *Bodmin Moor: An Archaeological Survey*, vol. i. London: English Heritage.

JONES, A. M. 1998–9a, 'The excavation of a Later Bronze Age structure at Callestick', *Cornish Archaeol.* 37–8: 5–55.

——1998–9b, 'The excavation of a Bronze Age enclosure at Liskeard Junior and Infant School', *Cornish Archaeol.* 37–8: 56–71.

JONES, B., and MATTINGLY, D. 1990, *An Atlas of Roman Britain*. Oxford: Blackwell.

JONES, G. R. J. 1979, 'Multiple estates and early settlement', in P. H. Sawyer (ed.), *English Medieval Settlement*. London: Edward Arnold, 9–34.

——1981, 'Early customary tenures in Wales and open-field agriculture', in Rowley (1981, 202–25).

——1985, 'Multiple estates perceived', *Journal of Hist. Geogr.* 11 (4): 339–51.

JONES, R., and PAGE, M. 2004, 'Characterising rural settlement and landscape: Whittlewood Forest in the Middle Ages', *Med. Archaeol.* 47: 55–83.

————2006, *Medieval Villages in an English Landscape*. Macclesfield: Windgather Press.

JONES, T. 1952, *Brut y Tywysogyon, or The Chronicle of the Princes: Peniarth MS 20 Version*. Cardiff: Cardiff University Press.

JONES, W. T. 1980, 'Early Saxon cemeteries in Essex', in Buckley (1980, 87–95).

JOPE, E. M., and THRELFALL, R. I. 1958, 'Excavation of a medieval settlement at Beere, North Tawton, Devon', *Med. Archaeol.* 2: 112–40.

KAIN, R. J. P., and OLIVER, R. 2001, *Historic Parishes of England and Wales*. Colchester: History Data Service.

————2004, *The Enclosure Maps of England and Wales, 1595–1918*. Cambridge: Cambridge University Press.

——and RAVENHILL, W. (eds.) 1999, *Historical Atlas of South-West England*. Exeter: Exeter University Press.

KEEVILL, G. D. (1992) 'Life on the edge: archaeology and alluvium at Redlands Farm, Stanwick, Raunds', in S. Needham and M. G. Macklin (eds.), *Alluvial Geoarchaeology in Britain*. Oxford: Oxbow Monograph 27, 177–85.

KEIL, I. J. E. 1964, 'The estates of the abbey of Glastonbury in the later Middle Ages'. Unpublished Ph.D. thesis, University of Bristol.

KENYON, D., and COLLARD, M. 2004, 'Anglo-Saxon and medieval remains at Kents Place, Sherbourne Street, Lechlade: excavations in 2000', *Trans. Bristol and Gloucestershire Archaeol. Soc.* 122: 117–26.

——and WATTS, M. 2006, 'An Anglo-Saxon enclosure at Copsehill Road, Lower Slaughter: excavations in 1999', *Trans. Bristol and Gloucestershire Archaeol. Soc.* 124: 73–110.

KISSOCK, J. 1990, 'The origin of the village in South Wales: a study in landscape archaeology'. Ph.D. thesis, University of Leicester.

——1992, 'Planned villages in Wales', *Medieval World*, 6: 39–43.

——1993a, 'Some examples of co-axial field systems in Pembrokeshire', *Bulletin Board of Celtic Studies*, 40: 190–7.

——1993b, 'Historic settlement project: South Pembrokeshire'. Unpublished report, Project Record No. 38882, Dyfed Archaeological Trust.

——1997, ' "God made nature and man made towns": post Conquest and pre-Conquest villages in Pembrokeshire', in Edwards (1997, 123–38).

KNOX, R. 2004, 'The Anglo-Saxons in Leicestershire and Rutland', in P. Bowman and P. Liddle (eds.), *Leicestershire Landscapes*. Leicester: Leicestershire Museums Archaeological Fieldwork Group Monograph 1, 95–104.

LAMBOURNE, A. 2004, 'According to the logic of the landscape: a critical examination of the significance of the Dartmoor Reaves for the wider Devon landscape of today'. Unpublished MA dissertation, University of Exeter.

LANE, T. W. 1995, *The Archaeology and Developing Landscape of Ropsley and Humby, Lincolnshire*. Sleaford: Heritage Lincolnshire.

——and HAYES, P. 1993, 'Moving boundaries in the fens of south Lincolnshire', in J. Gardiner (ed.), *Flatlands and Wetlands*. East Anglian Archaeology 50, 58–70.

LAVENDER, N. J. 1996, 'A Roman site at the New Source Works, Castle Hedingham: excavations 1992', *Essex Archaeol. Hist.* 27: 22–34.

——1997, 'Middle Iron Age and Romano-British settlement at Great Dunmow: excavations at Buildings Farm 1993', *Essex Archaeol. Hist.* 28: 47–92.

——1998a, 'Prehistoric and Romano-British activity at the William Edwards School, Stifford Clay Road, Grays; excavations 1997', *Essex Archaeol. Hist.* 29: 19–32.

——1998b, 'A Saxon building at Chadwell St. Mary: excavations at Chadwell St Mary County Primary School 1996', *Essex Archaeol. Hist.* 29: 45–58.

——2004, 'A131 Great Leighs by-pass: archaeological investigations 1993–2002', *Essex Archaeol. Hist.* 35: 196–204.

LAWSON, A. J. 1983, *The Archaeology of Witton, near North Walsham, Norfolk*. East Anglian Archaeology 18.

LEACH, P. 2001, *Roman Somerset*. Wimbourne: Dovecot Press.

——2006, 'Medieval remains at Downs Farm, Walton', *Proc. Somerset Archaeol. Natur. Hist. Soc.* 149: 145–7.

LEECH, R. 1982, 'The Roman interlude in the South West: the dynamics of economics and social change in the Romano-British south Somerset and north Dorset', in Miles (1982, 209–67).

LETCH, A. 2005, 'A Bronze Age, Roman and Saxon site at Bishops Park College, Jaywick Lane, Clacton-on-Sea: excavation 2003', *Essex Archaeol. Hist.* 36.

LEWIS, C. 2005, 'Test pit excavation within occupied settlements in East Anglia in 2005', *Medieval Settlement Research Group Annual Report*, 20: 9–16.

——forthcoming, 'New avenues for the investigation of medieval rural settlement: observations from the Education Field Academy', *Med. Archaeol.* 51.

——MITCHELL-FOX, P., and DYER, C. 1997, *Village, Hamlet and Field*. Manchester: Manchester University Press.

LIDDELL, D. M. 1930, 'Report on the excavations at Hembury Fort, Devon, 1930', *Proc. Devon Archaeol. Exploration Soc.* 1: 40–63.

——1931, 'Report on the excavations at Hembury Fort, Devon, second season, 1931', *Proc. Devon Archaeol. Exploration Soc.* 1: 90–120.

——1932, 'Report on the excavations at Hembury Fort, Devon, third season, 1932', *Proc. Devon Archaeol. Exploration Soc.* 1: 90–120.

——1935, 'Report on the excavations at Hembury Fort, Devon, 4th and 5th seasons, 1932', *Proc. Devon Archaeol. Exploration Soc.* 2: 135–75.

LIDDLE, P. 1996, 'The archaeology of Anglo-Saxon Leicestershire', in J. Bourne (ed.), *Anglo-Saxon Landscapes in the East Midlands*. Leicester: Leicestershire Museums Arts and Records service, 1–10.

LINDEN, H. VAN DER 1982, 'History of the reclamation of the western Fenlands and of the organizations to keep them drained', in H. de Bakker and M. W. van den Berg (eds.), *Proceedings of the Symposium on Peatlands below Sea Level*. Wageningen: IRRI Publications, 42–73.

LLOYD, T., ORBACH, J., and SCOURFIELD, R. 2004, *The Buildings of Wales: Pembrokeshire*. New Haven: Yale University Press.

LOCOCK, M. 2000, 'Buried soils of the Wentlooge formation', *Archaeol. in the Severn Estuary*, 10: 1–10.

——and WALKER, M. 1998, 'Hill Farm, Goldcliff: Middle Iron Age drainage on the Caldicot Level', *Archaeol. in the Severn Estuary*, 9: 37–44.

LOSCO-BRADLEY, S., and KINSLEY, G. 2002, *Catholme: An Anglo-Saxon Settlement on the Trent Gravels in Staffordshire*. Nottingham: Department of Archaeology, University of Nottingham.

LUFF, R. 1993, *Animal Bones from Excavations in Colchester 1971–85*. Colchester: Colchester Archaeological Report 12.

MACGOWAN, K. 1987, 'Saxon timber structures from the Barking Abbey excavations', *Essex Journal*, 22: 35–8.

MCINTOSH, M. K. 1986, *Autonomy and Community: The Royal Manor of Havering, 1200–1500*. Cambridge: Cambridge University Press.

MCKITTERICK, R. 1994, *Carolingian Culture: Emulation and Innovation*. Cambridge: Cambridge University Press.

MACKNEY, D., HODGSON, J. M., HOLLIS, J. M., and STAINES, S. J. 1983, *Legend for the 1:250,000 Soil Map of England and Wales*. Harpenden: Soil Survey of England and Wales.

MACKRETH, D. F. 1996, *Orton Hall Farm: A Roman and Early Anglo-Saxon Farmstead*. East Anglian Archaeology Report No. 76.

Maldon Archaeological Group n.d., 'Lofts Farm Project'. Unpublished reports.

MALIM, T. 1993, 'An investigation of multiperiod cropmarks at Manor Farm, Harston', *Proc. Cambridgeshire Antiq. Soc.* 82: 11–54.

MARTIN, E. 1999a, 'Suffolk in the Iron Age', in Davies and Williamson (1999, 44–99).

—— 1999b, 'Place-name patterns', in Dymond and Martin (1999, 50–1).

—— 2007, ' "Wheare most Inclosures be": the making of the East Anglian landscape', in Gardiner and Rippon (2007, 122–38).

—— and SATCHELL, M. forthcoming, *'Wheare most Inclosures be': East Anglian Fields: History, Morphology and Management*. East Anglian Archaeology.

——PLOUVIEZ, J., and ROSS, H. 1982, 'Archaeology in Suffolk 1981', *Proc. Suffolk Instit. Archaeol. Hist.* 35 (2): 155–65.

——————and FIELDMAN, H. 1986, 'Archaeology in Suffolk 1985', *Proc. Suffolk Instit. Archaeol. Hist.*, 36 (3): 225–46.

——————1987, 'Archaeology in Suffolk 1986', *Proc. Suffolk Instit. Archaeol. Hist.* 36 (3): 225–46.

——————1988, 'Archaeology in Suffolk 1987', *Proc. Suffolk Instit. Archaeol. Hist.* 36 (4): 309–20.

——PENDLETON, C., and PLOUVIEZ, J. 1992, 'Archaeology in Suffolk 1991', *Proc. Suffolk Instit. Archaeol. Hist.* 38(1): 378.

——————1993, 'Archaeology in Suffolk 1992', *Proc. Suffolk Instit. Archaeol. Hist.* 38 (1): 79–101.

——————1994, 'Archaeology in Suffolk 1993', *Proc. Suffolk Instit. Archaeol. Hist.* 38 (2): 206–19.

——————1995, 'Archaeology in Suffolk 1994', *Proc. Suffolk Instit. Archaeol. Hist.* 38 (3): 335–62.

——————1996, 'Archaeology in Suffolk 1995', *Proc. Suffolk Instit. Archaeol. Hist.* 38 (4): 457–85.

——————and THOMAS, G. 2000, 'Archaeology in Suffolk 1999', *Proc. Suffolk Instit. Archaeol. Hist.* 39 (4): 495–531.

——————and GEAKE, H. 2002, 'Archaeology in Suffolk 2001', *Proc. Suffolk Instit. Archaeol. Hist.* 40 (2): 201–33.

MATTINGLY, D. 2007, *An Imperial Possession*. London: Allen Lane.

MATTINSON, R. 2005, 'A phased summary and assessment of the excavation at North Camp, Shoeburyness, Essex'. Unpublished report, Pre-Construct Archaeology (copy in Southend-on-Sea Museum).

MAXFIELD, V. A. 1999, 'The Roman army', in Kain and Ravenhill (1999, 77–9).

MEDDENS, F. M., and BEASLEY, M. 2001, 'Roman seasonal wet pasture exploitation near Nash, on the Caldicot Levels, Wales', *Britannia*, 32: 141–84.

MEDLYCOTT, M. 1994, 'Iron Age and Roman material from Birchanger, near Bishops Stortford; excavations at Woodside Industrial Park, 1992', *Essex Archaeol. Hist.* 25: 28–45.

—— 1996, 'A medieval farm and its landscape: excavations at Stebbingford, Felsted 1993', *Essex Archaeol. Hist.* 27: 102–81.

—— 2000, 'Prehistoric, Roman and post-medieval material from Harlow: investigations at Church Langley 1989–1994', *Essex Archaeol. Hist.* 31: 33–93.

—— 2003, *Great Wakering: Historic Settlement Assessment Report*. Chelmsford: Essex County Council/Epping Forest District Council.

—— 2004, *Roydon: Historic Settlement Assessment Report*. Chelmsford: Essex County Council/Epping Forest District Council.

—— 2005, 'Archaeological fieldwalking in Essex, 1986–2005', *Essex Archaeology and History*, 36: 1–9.

—— and GERMANY, M. 1994, 'Archaeological fieldwalking in Essex, 1985–1993: interim results', *Essex Archaeol. Hist.* 25: 14–27.

MELLOR, V. 2004, 'Archaeological evaluation on land at Church Close, Whissonsett, Norfolk'. Unpublished report by Archaeological Project Services, Sleaford.

METCALF, D. M. 1993, *Thrymsas and Sceattas in the Ashmolean Museum Oxford*. London: Royal Numismatic Society.

—— 2001, '"As east as A, B, C": the mint-places of early sceatta types in the South East', *British Numismatic J.* 71: 34–48.

MILES, D. (ed.) 1982, *The Romano-British Countryside*. BAR British Series 103, Oxford: British Archaeological Reports.

—— 1994, *The Description of Pembrokeshire, by George Owen of Henllys*. Welsh Classics, Llandysul: Gomer Press.

MILES, H. 1975, 'Excavations at Woodbury Castle, east Devon', *Proc. Devon Archaeol. Soc.* 33: 183–208.

—— 1977, 'The Honeyditches Roman villa, Seaton, Devon', *Britannia*, 8: 107–48.

MILLETT, M. 1987, 'The question of continuity: Rivenhall reviewed', *Archaeol. J.* 144: 434–44.

—— 1990, *The Romanization of Britain*. Cambridge: Cambridge University Press.

—— and JAMES, S. 1983, 'Excavations at Cowdery's Down, Basingstoke, Hampshire', *Archaeological Journal*, 140: 151–279.

MILLS, A. D. 1990, *A Dictionary of English Place-Names*. Oxford: Oxford University Press.

MILTON, B. 1987, 'Excavations at Barrington's Farm, Orsett Cock, Thurrock, Essex, 1983', *Essex Archaeol. Hist.* 18: 16–34.

—— CORBISHLEY, M. J., HOPE, J. H., and TURNER, R. 1984, *Four Church Excavations in Essex*. Chelmsford: Essex County Council Archaeology Section Occasional Papers 4.

MOORE, I. E., PLOUVIEZ, J., and WEST, S. 1988, *The Archaeology of Roman Suffolk*. Ipswich: Suffolk County Council.

MOORE, J. S. 1982, *Domesday Book: Gloucestershire*. Chichester: Phillimore.

MOORE, P. D., MERRYFIELD, D. L., and PRICE, M. D. R. 1984, 'The vegetation and development of blanket mires', in P. D. Moore (ed.), *European Mires*. London: Academic Press, 203–35.

MORELAND, J. 2000, 'The significance of production in eighth-century England', in Hanson and Wickham (2000, 69–104).

MORRILL, J. 1987, 'Ecology and allegiance in the English Revolution', *Journal of British Studies*, 26: 451–79.

MORRIS, B. 2005, 'The Roman to medieval transition in the Essex landscape: a study in persistence, continuity and change', *Medieval Settlement Research Group Annual Report*, 20: 37–44.

—— 2006, 'The Roman–medieval transition in the Essex landscape: a study in persistence, continuity and change'. Ph.D. thesis, University of Exeter.

MORRIS, C. D. 1997, 'Tintagel Island 1994: an interim report', *Cornish Archaeol.* 36: 208–14.

MORRIS, J. 1983, *Domesday Book: Dorset*. Chichester: Phillimore.

MORRIS, R. 1989, *Churches in the Landscape*. London: J. M. Dent and Sons.

——and ROXAN, J. 1980, 'Churches on Roman buildings', in W. Rodwell (ed.), *Temples, Churches and Religion: Recent Research in Roman Britain with a Gazetteer of Romano-Celtic Temples in Continental Europe*. BAR British Series 77 (1), Oxford: British Archaeological Reports, 175–209.

MORTIMER, R. 2000, 'Village development and ceramic sequence: the Middle to Late Saxon village at Lordship Lane, Cottenham, Cambridgeshire', *Proc. Cambridge Antiq. Soc.* 39: 5–33.

——REGAN, R., and LUCY, S. 2005, *The Saxon and Medieval Settlement at West Fen Road, Ely: The Ashwell Site*. East Anglian Archaeology 110.

MUDD, A. 2002, *Excavations at Melford Meadows, Brettenhams, 1994: Romano-British and Early Saxon Occupations*. East Anglian Archaeology 99.

MURPHY, K. 1997a, 'The castle and borough of Wiston, Pembrokeshire', *Archaeologia Cambrensis*, 144: 71–102.

——1997b, 'Small boroughs in south-west Wales: their planning, early development and defences', in Edwards (1997, 139–56).

MURPHY, P. 1985, 'The cereals and plant remains', in West (1985, 100–10).

——1994, 'The Anglo-Saxon landscape and rural economy: some results from sites in East Anglia and Essex', in Rackham (1994, 23–39).

MURRAY, J. 2005, 'Excavations of a medieval cemetery at Crowland Road, Haverhill', *Proc. Suffolk Instit. Archaeol. Hist.* 41 (1): 5–42.

——and McDONALD, T. 2005, 'Excavations at Station Road, Gamlingay, Cambridgeshire', *Anglo-Saxon Studies in Archaeol. Hist.* 13: 173–330.

MUSGROVE, D. 1999, 'The medieval exploitation of the peat moors of the Somerset Levels'. Unpublished Ph.D. thesis, University of Exeter.

MYNARD, D. C. 1994, *Excavations on Medieval Sites in Milton Keynes*. Aylesbury: Buckinghamshire Archaeological Society.

——and ZEEPVAT, R. J. 1991, *Great Linford Deserted Medieval Village*. Aylesbury: Buckinghamshire Archaeological Society.

NEWMAN, J. 1992, 'The late Roman and Anglo-Saxon settlement pattern in the Sandlings of Suffolk', in Carver (1992, 25–51).

——2003, 'Exceptional finds, exceptional sites? Barham and Coddenham, Suffolk', in T. Pestel and K. Ulmschneider (eds.), *Markets in Early Medieval Europe*. Macclesfield: Windgather Press, 97–109.

——2005a, 'Survey in the Deben Valley', in M. Carver (ed.), *Sutton Hoo: A Seventh-Century Princely Burial Ground in its Context*. London: British Museum Press, 477–88.

——2005b, 'A landscape in hiding: the living and the dead 400–800 AD', *Saxon: Newsletter of the Sutton Hoo Society*, 42: 8–9.

NEWTON, K. C. 1960, *Thaxted in the Fourteenth Century*. Chelmsford: Essex County Council.

NOWAKOWSKI, J. A., and THOMAS, C. 1992, *Grave News from Tintagel: An Account of a Second Season of Archaeological Excavation at Tintagel Churchyard, Cornwall, 1992*. Truro: Cornwall Archaeological Unit.

O'BRIEN, E. 1999, *Post-Roman Britain to Anglo-Saxon England: Burial Practices Reviewed*. BAR British Series 289, Oxford: British Archaeological Reports.

OKASHA, E. 1993, *Corpus of Early Christian Inscribed Stones on South-West Britain*. London: Leicester University Press.

O'NEIL, B. H. ST J. 1933, 'The Roman villa at Magor farm, near Camborne, Cornwall', *J. Brit. Archaeol. Ass.* 39: 117–75.

OOSTHUIZEN, S. 1993, 'Saxon commons in south Cambridgeshire', *Proc. Cambridge-shire Antiq. Soc.* 82: 93–100.

—— 1997a, 'Prehistoric fields into medieval furlongs? Evidence from Caxton, Cambridgeshire', *Proc. Cambridgeshire Antiq. Soc.* 84: 145–52.

—— 1997b, 'Medieval settlement relocation in West Cambridgeshire: three case-studies', *Landscape Hist.* 19: 43–55.

—— 1998, 'The origins of Cambridgeshire', *Antiquaries J.* 78: 85–109.

—— 2002, 'Medieval greens and moats in the central province: evidence from the Bourne Valley, Cambridgeshire', *Landscape Hist.* 24: 73–88.

—— 2003, 'The roots of the open fields: linking prehistoric and medieval field systems in west Cambridgeshire', *Landscapes*, 4: 40–64.

—— 2005, 'New light on the origins of open-field farming', *Med. Archaeol.* 49: 165–95.

—— 2006, *Landscapes Decoded: The Origins and Development of Cambridgeshire's Medieval Fields*. Hatfield: University of Hertfordshire Press.

Ordnance Survey 2001, *Historical Map and Guide: Roman Britain*, 5th edn. Southampton: Ordnance Survey.

ORWIN, C. S., and ORWIN, C. S. 1938, *The Open Fields*. Oxford: Clarendon Press.

OWEN, H. 1911–18, *A Calendar of the Public Records Relating to Pembrokeshire*. London.

PADEL, O. 1985, *Cornish Place-Name Elements*. Nottingham: English Place-Name Society vols. 56–7.

—— 1999, 'Place-names', in Kain and Ravenhill (1999, 88–94).

PAGE, M. and JONES, R. forthcoming, 'Stability and instability in medieval village plans: case-studies in Whittlewood', in Gardiner and Rippon (2007, 139–52).

PARKER PEARSON, M., VAN DE NOORT, R., and WOOLF, A. 1993, 'Three men and a boat: Sutton Hoo and the East Saxon kingdom', *Anglo-Saxon England*, 22: 27–50.

PARKES, L. N., and WEBSTER, P. V. 1974, 'Merthyrgeryn: a grange of Tintern', *Archaeologia Cambrensis*, 123: 140–54.

PARRY, S. 2006, *Raunds Area Survey*. Oxford: Oxbow Books.

PASSMORE, A. J. 2005, 'A Roman enclosure and probable Roman trackway at Newland Mill, North Tawton', *Proc. Devon Archaeol. Soc.* 63: 33–41.

PATTISON, P. 1999, 'Challacombe revisited', in P. Pattison, D. Field, and S. Ainsworth (eds.), *Patterns in the Past*. Oxford: Oxbow, 61–70.

PEARCE, S. 1978, *The Kingdom of Dumnonia*. Padstow: Lodenek Press.

—— 1999, 'Bronze Age metalwork', in Kain and Ravenhill (1999, 69–73).

—— 2004, *South-Western Britain in the Early Middle Ages*. London: Leicester University Press.

PEARSON, T. 1978, 'Late Saxon and early medieval pottery from the deserted medieval village of Barrow(?) in Odcombe parish', *Proc. Somerset Archaeol. Natur. Hist. Soc.* 122: 79–82.

PEGLAR, S. M., FITZ, S. C., and BIRKS, H. J. B. 1989, 'Vegetation and land-use history at Diss, Norfolk, UK', *Journal of Ecology*, 77: 203–22.

PENHALLURICK, R. D. 1986, *Tin in Antiquity*. London: Institute of Metals.

PENN, K. 1994, 'The early Saxon settlement', in P. Wade-Martins (ed.), *An Historical Atlas of Norfolk*. Norwich: Norfolk Museum Service.

PENOYRE, J. 2005, *Traditional Houses of Somerset*. Taunton: Somerset Books.

——and PENOYRE, J. 1999, 'Somerset Dendrochronology Project, phase 3', *Proc. Somerset Archaeol. Natur. Hist. Soc.* 142: 311–15.

PERCIVAL, S. and WILLIAMSON, T. 2005, 'Early fields and medieval furlongs: excavations at Creake Road, Burnham Sutton, Norfolk', *Landscapes*, 6 (1): 1–17.

PESTEL, T. 2005, *Landscapes of Monastic Foundation: The Establishment of Religious Houses in East Anglia c.650–1200*. Woodbridge: Boydell Press.

PETTS, D. 2004, 'Burial in western Britain, AD 400–800: late antique or early medieval?', in Collins and Gerrard (2004, 77–87).

PEVSNER, N. 1958, *The Buildings of England: South and West Somerset*. London: Penguin Books.

PEWSEY, S., and BROOKS, A. 1993, *East Saxon Heritage: An Essex Gazetteer*. Stroud: Alan Sutton.

PHILLIPS, E. N. M. 1966, 'Excavation of a Romano-British site at Lower Well Farm, Soke Gabriel, Devon', *Proc. Devon Archaeol. Soc.* 23: 2–62.

PHILPOT, R. 1991, *Burial Practice in Roman Britain*. BAR British Series 219, Oxford: British Archaeological Reports.

PHYTHIAN ADAMS, C. 1987, *Rethinking English Local History*. Leicester: Leicester University Press.

——1993, 'Introduction: an agenda for English local history', in C. Phythian Adams (ed.), *Societies, Cultures and Kinship 1580–1850*. Leicester: Leicester University Press.

PITCHFORTH, H. 2001, *A Hidden Countryside: Discovering Ancient Tracks, Fields and Hedges Based on a Study of Witham in Essex*. Witham: private publication.

PLOUVIEZ, J. 1995, 'A hole in the distribution map: the characteristics of small towns in Suffolk', in A. E. Brown (ed.), *Roman Small Towns in Eastern England and Beyond*, Oxford: Oxbow, 69–80.

——1999, 'The Roman period', in Dymond and Martin (1999, 42–4).

POLLARD, J., and REYNOLDS, A. 2002, *Avebury: The Biography of a Landscape*. Stroud: Tempus.

POLLARD, S. M. H. 1966, 'Neolithic and Dark Age settlements on High Peak, Sidmouth, Devon', *Proc. Devon Archaeol. Soc.* 23: 35–59.

——1974, 'A Late Iron Age settlement and a Romano-British villa at Holcombe, near Uplyme, Devon', *Proc. Devon Archaeol. Soc.* 32: 59–161.

PONSFORD, M. 2003, 'Excavations at a Saxon-Norman settlement, Bickley, Cleeve, 1982–89', *Proc. Somerset Archaeol. Natur. Hist. Soc.* 147: 47–112.

POOS, L. R. 1983, 'Population and resources in two fourteenth century Essex communities: Great Waltham and High Easter 1327–1389'. Ph.D. thesis, University of Cambridge.

——1991, *A Rural Society after the Black Death: Essex 1350–1525*. Cambridge: Cambridge University Press.

POSTAN, M. M. 1972, *The Medieval Economy and Society*. London: Weidenfeld and Nicolson.

POSTGATE, M. R. 1973, 'Field systems of East Anglia', in Baker and Butlin (1973a, 281–324).

PRESTON-JONES, A., and ROSE, P. 1986, 'Medieval Cornwall', *Cornish Archaeol.* 25: 135–85.

PRIDDY, D., and BUCKLEY, D. G. 1987, 'An assessment of excavated enclosures in Essex together with a selection of cropmark sites', *East Anglian Archaeology*, 33.

QUINN, G. F. 1995, 'A new survey of the prehistoric field system on Kerswell Down and Whilborough Common', *Proc. Devon Archaeol. Soc.* 53: 131–4.

QUINNELL, H. 1986, 'Cornwall during the Iron Age and the Roman period', *Cornish Archaeol.* 25: 111–34.

—— 1988, 'The local character of the Devon Bronze Age and its interpretation in the 1980s', *Proc. Devon Archaeol. Soc.* 46: 1–14.

—— 1993, 'A sense of identity: distinctive Cornish Stone artefacts in the Roman and post-Roman periods', *Cornish Archaeol.* 32: 29–46.

—— 1994, 'Becoming marginal? Dartmoor in later prehistory', *Proc. Devon Archaeol. Soc.* 52: 75–83.

—— 1997, 'Excavations of an Exmoor barrow and ring cairn', *Proc. Devon Archaeol. Soc.* 55: 1–38.

—— 2004, *Excavations at Trethurgy Round, St. Austell*. Truro: Cornwall Archaeology Unit.

—— and HARRIS, D. 1985, 'Castle Dore: the chronology reconsidered', *Cornish Archaeol.* 24: 123–40.

RACKHAM, J. (ed.) 1994, *Environment and Economy in Anglo-Saxon England*. York: Council for British Archaeology Research Report 89.

RACKHAM, O. 1976, *Trees and Woodland in the British Landscape*. London: Dent.

—— 1980, 'The medieval landscape of Essex', in Buckley (1980, 103–7).

—— 1986a, *The History of the Countryside*. London: J. M. Dent and Sons.

—— 1986b, *The Ancient Woodland of England: The Woods of South East Essex*. Rochford: Rochford District Council.

—— 1988, 'Woods, hedges and forests', in Aston (1988a, 13–31).

RAHTZ, P. A. 1993, *Glastonbury*. London: Batsford/English Heritage.

—— HIRST, S., and WRIGHT, S. M. 2000, *Cannington Cemetery*. London: Britannia Monogr. 17.

RATCLIFFE, J. 1995, 'Duckpool, Morwenstow: a Romano-British and early medieval industrial site and harbour', *Cornish Archaeol.* 34: 80–175.

RAVENHILL, W. L. D. 1967, 'Cornwall', in H. C. Darby and R. Welldon Finn (eds.), *The Domesday Geography of South-West England*. Cambridge: Cambridge University Press, 296–347.

RCHME 1923, *An Inventory of the Historical Monuments in Essex*, iv: *South East*. London: HMSO.

REANEY, P. H. 1935, *The Place-Names of Essex*. English Place-Names Society XII, Cambridge: Cambridge University Press.

REDKNAP, M. 1991, 'The Saxon pottery from Barking Abbey: part 1, the local wares', *London Archaeologist*, 6 (13): 353–9.

Reece, R. 1986, 'Review of *Rivenhall: investigations of a villa, church and village 1950–1977*', *Essex Archaeol. Hist.* 17: 180.

Reed, S. J. 2005, 'Evaluation excavations of Post-Roman features at Wembury Bay near Plymouth', *Proc. Devon Archaeol. Soc.* 63: 55–64.

—— and Manning, P. T. 2000, 'Archaeological recording of a hillsope enclosure at North Hill Cleave, Bittadon, North Devon', *Proc. Devon Archaeol. Soc.* 58: 201–14.

—— and Turton, S. D. 2005, 'Romano-British structures at Parsonage Cross near Littlehempston', *Proc. Devon Archaeol. Soc.* 63: 43–53.

Rees, W. 1951, *An Historical Atlas of Wales from Early to Modern Times*. Cardiff: University College Cardiff.

—— 1953, *A Survey of the Duchy of Lancaster Lordships in Wales 1609–1613*. History and Law Series XII, Cardiff: Board of Celtic Studies.

Reidy, K., and Maynard, D. 2000, 'Possible Saxon burials at Hatfield Peverel: an evaluation at Smallands Farm, 1993', *Essex Archaeol. Hist.* 31: 279–80.

Reynolds, A. 1999, *Later Anglo-Saxon England: Life and Landscape*. Stroud: Tempus.

—— 2000, 'Yatesbury', *Current Archaeology*, 171: 113–18.

—— 2006, 'The early medieval period', in N. Holbrook and J. Jurica (eds.), *Twenty-Five Years of Archaeology in Gloucestershire*. Cirencester: Cotswold Archaeology/Bristol and Gloucestershire Archaeological Report No. 3.

—— forthcoming, *Anglo-Saxon Deviant Burial Customs*. Oxford: Oxford University Press.

Rhodes, J. 2002, *A Calendar of the Registers of the Priory of Llanthony by Gloucester 1457–1466, 1501–1525*. Gloucestershire Records Series 15.

Richards, M. 1969, *Welsh Administrative and Territorial Units*. Cardiff: University of Wales Press.

Richardson, I. 2006, 'Medieval settlement on the Holnicote Estate'. Unpublished report for the National Trust.

Rickett, R. 1995, *The Anglo-Saxon Cemetery at Spong Hill, North Elmham, Part VII: The Iron Age, Roman and Early Saxon Settlement*. East Anglian Archaeology 73.

Riddler, I. 2004, 'Anglo-Saxon Kent: early development *c*.450–*c*.800', in T. Lawson and D. Killingray (eds.), *An Historical Atlas of Kent*. Chichester: Phillimore, 25–8.

Riley, H. 2006, *The Historic Landscape of the Quantock Hills*. London: English Heritage.

—— and Wilson-North, R. 2001, *The Field Archaeology of Exmoor*. London: English Heritage.

Rippon, S. 1991, 'Early planned landscapes in south-east Essex', *Essex Archaeol. Hist.* 22: 46–60

—— 1993, 'Landscape evolution and wetland reclamation around the Severn estuary'. Unpublished Ph.D. thesis, University of Reading.

—— 1995, 'Roman settlement and salt production on the Somerset coast: the work of Sam Nash—a Somerset archaeologist and historian 1913–1985', *Proc. Somerset Archaeol. Natur. Hist. Soc.* 139: 99–117.

—— 1996a, *Gwent Levels: The Evolution of a Wetland Landscape*. York: Council for British Archaeology Research Report 105.

—— 1996b, 'Essex *c*.700–1066', in Bedwin (1996, 117–28).

—— 1997, *The Severn Estuary: Landscape Evolution and Wetland Reclamation*. London: Leicester University Press.

—— 1999, 'The Rayleigh Hills in south east Essex: patterns in the exploitation of rural resources in a "woodland" landscape', in Green (1999, 20–8).

—— 2000a, *The Transformation of Coastal Wetlands*. London: British Academy.

—— 2000b, 'The historic landscapes of the Severn estuary Levels', in S. Rippon (ed.), *Estuarine Archaeology: The Severn and Beyond*. Archaeology in the Severn Estuary 11, 145–62.

—— 2000c, 'The Romano-British exploitation of coastal wetlands: survey and excavation on the North Somerset Levels, 1993–7', *Britannia*, 31: 69–200.

—— 2001, 'The historic landscapes of the Severn estuary', in S. Rippon (ed.), *Estuarine Archaeology: The Severn and Beyond*. Exeter: Severn Estuary Levels Research Committee, 119–35.

—— 2004a, *Historic Landscape Analysis: deciphering the palimpsest*. York: Council for British Archaeology.

—— 2004b, 'Making the most of a bad situation? Glastonbury Abbey and the exploitation of wetland resources in the Somerset Levels', *Med. Archaeol.* 48: 91–130.

—— 2006a, *Landscape, Community and Colonisation: the North Somerset Levels during the 1st to 2nd millennia* AD. CBA Research Report 152, York: Council for British Archaeology.

—— 2006b, 'Landscapes of pre-medieval occupation', in R. Kain (ed.), *England's Landscape*, iii: *The South West*. London: Collins/English Heritage, 41–66.

—— 2007a, 'Focus or frontier? The significance of estuaries in the landscape of southern Britain', *Landscapes*, 8 (1): 23–38.

—— 2007b in press, 'Historic landscape characterization: its role in contemporary British archaeology and landscape history', *Landscapes*, 8 (2).

—— FYFE, R. M., and BROWN, A. G. 2006a, 'Beyond villages and open fields: the origins and development of a historic landscape characterised by dispersed settlement in south west England', *Med. Archaeol.* 50: 31–70.

—— SMART, C., and WAINWRIGHT, A. 2006b, *The Living Past: The Origins and Development of the Historic Landscape of the Blackdown Hills: Phase 1 Archive Report*. Exeter University, Department of Archaeology Report for the Blackdown Hills Rural Partnership.

ROBERTS, B. K. 1973, 'Field systems of the west Midlands', in Baker and Butlin (1973a, 188–231).

—— 1987, *The Making of the English Village*. London: Longman.

—— 1992, 'Dating villages: theory and practice', *Landscape Hist.* 14: 19–30.

—— and GLASSCOCK, R. E. 1983, *Villages, Fields and Frontiers: Studies in Rural Settlement in the Medieval and Early Modern Periods*. BAR International Series 185, Oxford: British Archaeological Reports.

—— and WRATHMELL, S. 2000, *An Atlas of Rural Settlement in England*. London: English Heritage.

—— —— 2002, *Region and Place*. London: English Heritage.

ROBERTSON, D. 2003, 'A Neolithic enclosure and Early Saxon settlement: excavations at Yarmouth Road, Broome, 2001', *Norfolk Archaeol.* 44 (2): 222–50.

—— 2004, 'Neolithic, Bronze Age, Iron Age, Early Saxon and medieval activity in the Norfolk Breckland: excavations at Grange Farm, Snetterton, 2002', *Norfolk Archaeol.* 44 (3): 482–521.

Robinson, D. 1988, *Biglis, Caldicot and Llandough: Three Late Iron Age and Romano-British Sites in South-East Wales. Excavations 1977–9.* BAR British Series 188, Oxford: British Archaeological Reports.

Robinson, M. 1992, 'Environment, archaeology and alluvium on the river gravels of the South Midlands', in S. Needham and M. G. Macklin (eds.), *Alluvial Archaeology in Britain.* Oxford: Oxbow, 197–208.

Roden, D. 1973, 'Field systems of the Chiltern Hills and their environs', in Baker and Butlin (1973a, 325–76).

Rodwell, K. A. 1983, 'The excavation of a Romano-British pottery kiln at Palmer's School, Grays, Essex', *Essex Archaeol. Hist.* 15: 11–35.

—— and Rodwell, W. 1981, 'Barton on Humber', *Current Archaeol.* 7 (7): 208–14.

Rodwell, W. 1966, 'Wickford: interim report', *Trans. Essex Archaeol. Soc.* 2 (1): 95–6.

—— 1976, 'Archaeological notes: some unrecorded archaeological discoveries in Essex, 1946–75: Bradwell-on-Sea', *Essex Archaeol. Hist.* 8: 234–8.

—— 1978, 'Investigations at Asheldham, Essex: an interim report on the church and the historic landscape', *Antiq. J.* 58: 133–57.

—— 1993, *The Origins and Early Development of Witham, Essex.* Oxford: Oxbow Monograph 26.

—— and Rodwell, K. 1977, *Historic Churches: A Wasting Asset.* London: Council for British Archaeology Research Report 19.

—— —— 1986, *Rivenhall: Investigation of a Villa, Church and Village, 1950–1977.* CBA Research Report 55, London: Council for British Archaeology.

—— —— 1993, *Rivenhall: Investigation of a Villa, Church and Village, 1950–1977, ii: Specialist Studies and Index to Volumes 1 and 2.* CBA Research Report 80, London: Council for British Archaeology.

Rogerson, A. 2005, 'New models of landscape change', *Saxon: Newsletter of the Sutton Hoo Society,* 42, 3–4.

—— Ashley, S., Williams, P., and Harris, A. 1987, *Three Norman Churches in Norfolk.* East Anglian Archaeology 32.

—— Davison, A., Pritchard, D., and Silvester, R. 1997, *Barton Bendish and Caldecote: Fieldwork in South-West Norfolk.* East Anglian Archaeology 80.

Rose, P., and Preston-Jones, A. 1995, 'Changes in the Cornish countryside AD 400–1100', in D. Hooke and S. Burnell (eds.), *Landscape and Settlement in Britain AD 400–1066.* Exeter: Exeter University Press, 51–68.

Round, H. 1903, 'The Domesday survey', in *The Victoria County History of Essex,* i. 333–598.

Rowlands, I. W. 1980, 'The making of the March: aspects of the Norman settlement of Dyfed', *Anglo-Norman Studies,* 3: 142–57.

Rowley, T. (ed.) 1981, *The Origins of Open Field Agriculture.* London: Croom Helm.

Ryan, P. 2000, 'The buildings of rural Ingatestone, Essex, 1556–1601: "great rebuilding" or "housing revolution"', *Vernacular Architecture,* 31: 11–25.

Ryder, L. 2006, 'Change and continuity: a study in the historic landscape of Devon'. Unpublished thesis, University of Exeter.

Salvatore, J. P., and Knight, M. 1991, 'Sections through the Roman road from Exeter to North Tawton', *Proc. Devon Archaeol. Soc.* 49: 99–106.

SAUNDERS, C. 1972, 'The excavations at Grambla, Wedron, 1972: interim report', *Cornish Archaeol.* 11: 50–2.

SAWYER, P. 1968, *Anglo-Saxon Charters: An Annotated List and Bibliography.* London: Royal Historical Society.

SCOTT, S. 2000, *Art and Society in Fourth-Century Britain.* Oxford: Oxford University School or Archaeology Monograph 53.

SCULL, C. 1992, 'Before Sutton Hoo: structures of power and society in early East Anglia', in Carver (1992, 3–23).

—— 2001, 'Burials in emporia in England', in D. Hill and R. Cowie (eds.), *Wics: The Early Mediaeval Trading Centres of Northern Europe.* Sheffield: Sheffield Academic Press, 67–74.

—— and BAYLISS, A. 1999, 'Dating burials of the seventh and eighth centuries; a case study from Ipswich, Suffolk', in J. Hines, K. Høilund Nielsen, and F. Siegmund (eds.), *The Pace of Change: Studies in Early-Medieval Chronology.* Oxford: Oxbow, 80–8.

SEEBOHM, F. 1890, *The English Village Community.* London.

SHAW, M. 1993/4, 'The discovery of Saxon sites below fieldwalking scatters: settlement evidence at Brixworth and Upton', *Northamptonshire Archaeol.* 25: 77–932.

SHORT, B. 2006, *England's Landscape: The South East.* London: Harper Collins/English Heritage.

SHORTER, A. H., RAVENHILL, W. L. D., and GREGORY, K. J. 1969, *South West England.* London: Thomas Nelson and Sons.

SILVESTER, R. J. 1978a, 'A hillslope enclosure at Collomoor, Bittadon', *Proc. Devon Archaeol. Soc.* 36: 245–9.

—— 1978b, 'Cropmark sites at North Tawton and Alverdiscott', *Proc. Devon Archaeol. Soc.* 36: 249–54.

—— 1980, 'An enclosure in Staverton Ford Plantation', *Proc. Devon Archaeol. Soc.* 38: 119–21.

—— 1981, 'Excavation at Honeyditches Roman villa, Seaton, 1978', *Proc. Devon Archaeol. Soc.* 39: 37–87.

—— 1988, *The Fenland Survey, Number 3: Norfolk Survey, Marshland and the Nar Valley.* East Anglian Archaeology 45.

—— 1993, ' "The addition of more-or-less undifferentiated dots to a distribution map": the Fenland Project in retrospect', in J. Gardiner (ed.), *Flatlands and Wetlands: Current Themes in East Anglian Archaeology.* East Anglian Archaeology 50, 24–39.

—— and BALKWILL, C. J. 1977, 'Three hillslope enclosures in the Lyd Valley, West Devon', *Proc. Devon Archaeol. Soc.* 35: 81–4.

SIMPSON, S. J., GRIFFITH, F. M., and HOLBROOK, N. 1989, 'The prehistoric, Roman and early post-Roman site at Hayes Farm, Clyst Honiton', *Proc. Devon Archaeol. Soc.* 47: 1–28.

SIMS, R. E. 1978, 'Man and vegetation in Norfolk', in S. Limbrey and J. Evans (eds.), *The Effect of Man on the Landscape: The Lowland Zone.* CBA Research Report 57, London: Council for British Archaeology, 57–62.

SLATER, G. 1907, 'The inclosure of common fields considered geographically', *Geogr. J.* 29 (1): 35–55.

SLEE, A. H. 1952, 'The open fields of Braunton', *Trans. Devonshire Ass.* 84: 142–9.

SMITH, G. 1996, 'Archaeology and environment of a Bronze Age cairn and prehistoric and Romano-British field system at Chysauster, Gulval, near Penzance, Cornwall', *Proc. Prehist. Soc.* 62: 167–219.

SMITH, K., COPPEN, J., WAINWRIGHT, G. J., and BECKETT, S. 1981, 'The Shaugh Moor Project: third report—settlement and environmental investigations', *Proc. Prehist. Soc.* 47: 205–74.

SMOOTHY, M. D. 1989, 'A Roman rural site at Rayne, Essex: excavations 1987', *Essex Archaeol. Hist.* 20: 1–29.

SMYTH, J. 1883, *The Lives of the Berkeleys: Lords of the Honour, Castle and Manor of Berkeley in the County of Gloucester from 1066–1618*. Gloucester: John Bellows.

SPURGEON, G. J. 1963, 'Two Pembrokeshire earthworks', *Archaeologia Cambrensis*, 112: 154–8.

SSAVBRG 1982, *Long Load and Knole, Long Sutton: Their Houses, Cottages and Farms, Settlement and People*. Somerset and South Avon Vernacular Building Research Group.

—— 1984, *The Vernacular Buildings of West and Middle Chinnock*. Somerset and South Avon Vernacular Building Research Group.

—— 1986, *The Vernacular Houses with Farms and Farmsteads of Alford and Lovington*. Somerset and South Avon Vernacular Building Research Group.

—— 1988, *The Vernacular Buildings of Batcombe*. Somerset and South Avon Vernacular Building Research Group.

—— 1993, *The Houses, Cottages and Farms of Chiselborough*. Somerset and South Avon Vernacular Building Research Group.

—— 1994, *Haselbury Plucknett: Evolution and Change of Land, Society and Buildings*. Somerset and South Avon Vernacular Building Research Group.

STACEY, N. R. 1972, 'The estates of Glastonbury Abbey, c.1050–1200'. Unpublished Ph.D. thesis, University of Leeds.

STEEDMAN, K. 1994, 'Rigby Crossroads', *Lincolnshire Archaeology and History*, 28: 1–20.

STENNING, D. F. 1996, 'Standing timber-framed buildings', in Bedwin (1996, 136–42).

—— 2003, 'Small aisled halls in Essex', *Vernacular Architecture*, 34: 1–19, 101–2.

STOPGATE, B. 1986, 'Llanfihangel near Rogiet: a shrunken village in south east Gwent', *Gwent Local History*, 61: 9–15.

STRACHAN, D. 1998, *Essex from the Air*. Chelmsford: Essex County Council.

STRAKER, V. 1997, 'Sourton Down, a study of local vegetation change and human impact on the landscape: pollen analysis of buried soils, sediments and peat', in P. J. Weddell and S. J. Reed, 'Excavations at Sourton Down Okehampton 1986–91', *Proc. Devon Archaeol. Soc.* 55: 95–128.

—— and CRABTREE, K. 1995, 'Palaeoenvironmental studies on Exmoor: past research and future potential', in H. Binding (ed.), *The Changing Face of Exmoor*. Dulverton: Exmoor Books, 43–51.

STRATTON, C. 1909, *Survey of the Lands of William, First Earl of Pembroke, 1567* (SRO Li/K2/A).

SVBRG 1996, *The Vernacular Buildings of Shapwick*. Somerset Vernacular Building Research Group.

—— 2001, *Vernacular Houses and Farms of Butleigh*. Somerset Vernacular Building Research Group.

—— 2004, *The Traditional Houses and Farms of Compton Dundon*. Somerset Vernacular Building Research Group.

SWANTON, M. 1996, *The Anglo-Saxon Chronicle*. London: Dent.

TAYLOR, A. 1994, 'Field-work in Cambridgeshire: October 1993–September 1994', *Proc. Cambridgeshire Antiq. Soc.* 83: 167–76.

—— MALIM, T., and EVANS, C. 1994, 'Field-work in Cambridgeshire: October 1993–September 1994', *Proc. Cambridgeshire Antiq Soc.* 83: 167–76.

TAYLOR, C. C. 1977, 'Polyfocal settlement and the English village', *Med. Archaeol.* 21: 189–93.

—— 1983, *Village and Farmstead*. London: George Philip and Son.

—— 1989, 'Whittlesford: the study of a river edge village', in Aston *et al.* (1989, 207–30).

—— 1992, 'Medieval rural settlement: changing perceptions', *Landscape Hist.* 14: 5–18.

—— 2002, 'Nucleated settlement: a view from the frontier', *Landscape Hist.* 24: 53–72.

—— 2004, 'Landscape history, observation and explanation: the missing houses in Cambridgeshire villages', *Proc. Cambridgeshire Antiq. Soc.* 93: 121–32.

—— and FOWLER, P. 1978, 'Roman fields into medieval furlongs?', in H. C. Bowen and P. J. Fowler (eds.), *Early Land Allotment*. BAR British Series 48, Oxford: British Archaeological Reports, 159–62.

TAYLOR, G. 2003, 'An Early to Middle Saxon settlement at Quarrington Lincolnshire', *Antiquaries Journal*, 83: 231–80.

TAYLOR, H. M. 1978, *Anglo-Saxon Architecture*, vol. iii. Cambridge: Cambridge University Press.

—— and TAYLOR, J. 1965, *Anglo-Saxon Architecture*, vols. i–ii. Cambridge: Cambridge University Press.

TAYLOR, R. J. (ed.) 1997, *Mawgan Porth: A Settlement of the Late Saxon Period on the North Cornish Coast: Excavations 1949–52, 1954 and 1974*. London: English Heritage.

THEW, N. 1994, 'Geology and geoarchaeology in the Yeo Valley at Ilchester', in P. Leach (ed.), *Ilchester*, ii: *Archaeology, Excavations and Fieldwork to 1984*. Sheffield: Department of Archaeology and Prehistory, University of Sheffield, 157–71.

THIRSK, J. 1964, 'The common fields', *Past and Present*, 29: 3–29.

—— 1966, 'The origins of the common fields', *Past and Present*, 33: 142–7.

—— 1967, 'The farming regions of England', in J. Thirsk (ed.), *The Agrarian History of England and Wales*, iv: *1500–1640*. Cambridge: Cambridge University Press, 1–112.

—— 1984, *The Agrarian History of England and Wales*, v: *1640–1750, 1: Regional Farming Systems*. Cambridge: Cambridge University Press.

—— 2000, *The English Rural Landscape*. Oxford; Oxford University Press.

THOMAS, C. 1958, *Gwithian: Ten Years' Work*. West Cornwall Field Club.

—— 1978, 'Types and distributions of pre-Norman fields in Cornwall and Scilly', in H. C. Bowen and P. J. Fowler (eds.), *Early Land Allotment*. BAR British Series 48, Oxford: British Archaeological Reports, 7–15.

—— 1981, *A Provisional List of Imported Pottery in Post-Roman Western Britain and Ireland*. Redruth: Institute for Cornish Studies.

THOMAS, C. 1990, ' "Gallici Nautae de Galliarum Provinciis": a sixth/seventh century trade with Gaul, reconsidered', *Med. Archaeol.* 34: 1–26.

——1993, *Tintagel: Arthur and Archaeology*. London: English Heritage.

——1994, *'And Shall These Mute Stones Speak?' Post-Roman Inscriptions in Western Britain*. Cardiff, University of Wales Press.

THORN, F., and THORN, C. 1980, *Domesday Book: Somerset*. Chichester: Phillimore.

————1983, *Domesday Book: Herefordshire*. Chichester: Phillimore.

————1985, *Domesday Book: Devon*. Chichester: Phillimore.

THORNDYCRAFT, V. R., PIRRIE, D., and BROWN, A. G., 2002, 'An environmental approach to the archaeology of tin mining on Dartmoor', in P. Murphy and P. Wiltshire (eds.), *The Environmental Archaeology of Industry*. Oxford: Oxbow, 19–28.

——————2004, 'Alluvial records of medieval and prehistoric tin mining on Dartmoor, SW England', *Geoarchaeology*, 19 (3): 219–36.

THORPE, L. (ed.) 1978, *Gerald of Wales: The Journey through Wales/The Description of Wales*. London: Penguin.

THREIPLAND, L. M. 1956, 'An excavation at St Mawgan-in-Pyder, Cornwall', *Archaeol. J.* 113: 33–81.

TIMBY, J., BROWN, R., BIDDUPH, E., HARDY, A., and POWELL, A. 2007, *A Slice of Rural Essex: Archaeological Discoveries from the A120 between Stanstead Airport and Braintree*. Oxford Wessex Archaeology Monogr. 1.

TINGLE, M. 1991, *The Vale of the White Horse: The Study of a Changing Landscape in the Clay Lowlands of Southern Britain from Prehistory to the Present*. Oxford: Tempus Reparatum.

——1998, *The Prehistory of Beer Head*. BAR British Series 270, Oxford: British Archaeological Reports.

TIPPER, J., LUCY, S., and DICKENS, A. forthcoming, *The Anglo-Saxon Settlement and Cemetery at Bloodmoor Hill, Carlton Colville, Suffolk*. East Anglian Archaeology.

TIPPING, R. 2002, 'Climatic variability and "marginal" settlement in upland British landscapes: a re-evaluation', *Landscapes*, 3 (2): 10–29.

TODD, M. 1987, *The South West to AD 1000*. London: Longman.

——1992, 'The hillfort of Dumpdon', *Proc. Devon Archaeol. Soc.* 50: 47–52.

——1998, 'A hillslope enclosure at Rudge, Morchard Bishop', *Proc. Devon Archaeol. Soc.* 56: 133–52.

——2005, 'Baths or baptisteries? Holcombe, Lufton and their analogies', *Oxford J. Archaeol.* 24 (3): 307–11.

TOLAN-SMITH, M. 1997, 'The Romano-British and later prehistoric landscape: the deconstruction of a medieval landscape', in C. Tolan-Smith (ed.), *Landscape Archaeology in Tynedale*. Newcastle: University of Newcastle, Tyne-Solway Ancient and Historic Landscapes Research Programme Monogr. 1, 69–78.

TOORIANS, L. 1990, 'Wizo Flandrensis and the Flemish settlement in Pembrokeshire', *Cambridge Medieval Celtic Studies*, 20: 99–118.

——1996, 'Flemish settlements in twelfth-century Scotland', *Revue belge de philologie et d'histoire*, 74: 659–93.

——2000, 'Flemish in Wales', in G. Price (ed.), *Languages in Britain and Ireland*. Oxford: Blackwell, 184–6.

TOULMIN SMITH, L. 1906, *The Itinerary in Wales of John Leland in or about the years 1536–1539*. London: George Dent.

TRIMBLE, G. 2001, 'An early Anglo-Saxon settlement at Bishee Barnabee Way, Bowthorpe: excavations 2001', *Norfolk Archaeology*, 44 (3): 525–35.

—— 2006, 'Church Close, Whissonsett, Norfolk: assessment report and updated post excavation project design'. Unpublished report, NAU Archaeology Report No. 1159.

TURNER, M. E. 1978, *A Domesday of English Enclosure Acts and Awards*. Reading: University of Reading.

TURNER, R. 1984, 'Excavations at St Mary's Church, West Bergholt, Essex, 1978', in Milton *et al.* (1984, 43–63).

—— 1999, *Excavations of an Iron Age Settlement and Roman Religious Complex at Ivy Chimneys, Witham, Essex 1978–83*. East Anglian Archaeology 88.

—— 2004, 'The Great Tower, Chepstow Castle, Wales', *Antiq. J.* 84: 223–318.

TURNER, S. 2003, 'Making a Christian landscape: early medieval Cornwall', in M. Carver, (ed.), *The Cross Goes North: Processes of Conversion in Northern Europe*, AD *300–1300*. Woodbridge: Boydell Press, 171–94.

—— 2004, 'Coast and countryside in "late antique" southwest England, *c.* AD 400–600', in Collins and Gerrard (2004, 25–32).

—— 2005, 'Converting the British landscape', *British Archaeol.* 84: 20–5.

—— (ed.) 2006a, *Medieval Devon and Cornwall: Shaping an Ancient Countryside*. Macclesfield: Windgather Press.

—— 2006b, 'The medieval landscape of Devon and Cornwall', in Turner (2006a, 1–9).

—— 2006c, 'The Christian landscape: churches, chapels and crosses', in Turner (2006a, 38–43).

—— (ed.) 2006d, *Making a Christian Landscape*. Exeter: Exeter University Press.

—— 2007, *Ancient Country: The Historic Character of Rural Devon*. Exeter: Devon Archaeological Society Occasional Paper 20.

TYERS, I., HILLAM, J., and GROVES, C. 1994, 'Trees and woodland in the Saxon period: the dendrochronological evidence', in Rackham (1994, 12–22).

TYLER, S. 1986, 'Goldhanger: note on loom weights from site 1, Chigborough Farm', *Essex Archaeol. Hist.* 17: 147–8.

—— 1996, 'Early Saxon Essex AD 400–700', in Bedwin (1996, 108–16).

—— and MAJOR, H. 2005, *The Early Saxon Cemetery and Later Saxon Settlement at Springfield Lyons, Essex*. East Anglian Archaeology 111.

—— and WICKENDEN, N. P. 1996, 'A late Roman and Saxon settlement at Great Waltham', *Essex Archaeol. Hist.* 27: 84–91.

UGLOW, J. 2000, 'Three Romano-British sites in the Lower Exe Valley', *Proc. Devon Archaeol. Soc.* 58: 227–47.

UNDERDOWN, D. E. 1985, *Revel, Riot and Rebellion: Popular Politics and Culture in England 1603–1660*. Oxford: Oxford University Press.

—— 1987, 'A reply to John Morrill', *Journal of British Studies*, 26: 468–79.

UPEX, G. S. 2002, 'Landscape continuity and the fossilization of Roman fields', *Archaeol. J.* 159: 77–108.

VINCE, A., and JENNER, A. 1991, 'The Saxon and early medieval pottery of London', in A. G. Vince (ed.), *Aspects of Saxon and Norman London 2: Finds and Environmental Evidence*. London: London and Middlesex Archaeological Society Special Paper 12, 19–119.

VINOGRADOFF, P. 1892, *Villeinage in England*. Oxford: Clarendon Press.

VINOGRADOFF, P. 1905, *The Growth of the Manor*. London: Macmillan.

VYNER, B. 1982, 'Excavations at Woodbarn Rath, Wiston, 1969', *Archaeologia Cambrensis*, 131: 49–57.

—— 1986, 'Woodbarn, Wiston: a Pembrokeshire rath', *Archaeologia Cambrensis*, 135: 121–33.

WADE, K. 1980, 'A settlement site at Bonhunt Farm, Wicken Bonhunt, Essex', in Buckley (1980, 96–102).

WADE-MARTINS, P. 1980, *Fieldwork and Excavation on Village Sites in Launditch Hundred, Norfolk*. East Anglian Archaeology 10.

—— 1989, 'The archaeology of medieval rural settlement in East Anglia', in Aston *et al.* (1989, 149–65).

—— 1994, *An Historical Atlas of Norfolk*. Norwich: Norfolk Museums Service.

WAINWRIGHT, G. J. 1971a, 'The excavation of a fortified settlement at Walesland Rath', *Britannia*, 2: 48–108.

—— 1971b, 'Excavations at Tower Point, St Brides, Pembrokeshire', *Archaeologia Cambrensis*, 120: 84–90.

WALKER, H. 2001, 'An Ipswich-type Ware vessel from Althorne Creek', *Essex Archaeol. Hist.* 32: 243–4

WALKER, R. F. 1991, 'The manor of Manorbier, Pembrokeshire, in the early 17th century', *National Library of Wales J.* 27 (2): 131–74.

WALLIS, S., and WAUGHMAN, M. 1998, *Archaeology and the Landscape in the Lower Blackwater Valley*. East Anglian Archaeology 82.

WARNER, P. 1987, *Greens, Commons and Clayland Colonisation: The Origins and Development of Greenside Settlement in East Suffolk*. Leicester; University of Leicester, Department of English Local History Occasional Papers, Fourth Series, No. 2.

—— 1996, *The Origins of Suffolk*. Manchester: Manchester University Press.

WATERHOUSE, R. 2000, 'East Portlemouth heritage appraisal: an archaeological history of the parish'. Unpublished report, The Coast and Countryside Service, Totnes.

WATON, P. V. 1982, 'Man's impact on the chalklands: some new pollen evidence', in M. Bell and S. Limbrey (eds.), *Archaeological Aspects of Woodland Ecology*. Oxford: BAR International Series 146, 75–91.

WEBSTER, C. J. 1999, 'Somerset archaeology in 1998', *Proc. Somerset Archaeol. Natur. Hist. Soc.* 142: 193–218.

—— 2001, 'Somerset archaeology in 2000', *Proc. Somerset Archaeol. Natur. Hist. Soc.* 144: 223–46.

—— 2003, 'Somerset archaeology in 2002', *Proc. Somerset Archaeol. Natur. Hist. Soc.* 146: 131–73.

—— 2004, 'Somerset archaeology in 2003', *Proc. Somerset Archaeol. Natur. Hist. Soc.* 147: 188–225.

—— and BRUNNING, R. 2004, 'A seventh-century AD cemetery at Stoneage Barton Farm, Bishop's Lydeard, Somerset and square-ditched burials in post-Roman Britain', *Archaeol. J.* 161: 54–81.

—— and CROFT, R. A. 1990, 'Somerset archaeology 1990', *Proc. Somerset Archaeol. Natur. Hist. Soc.* 134: 207–29.

—— —— 1994, 'Somerset archaeology 1994', *Proc. Somerset Archaeol. Natur. Hist. Soc.* 138: 165–86.

———— 1997, 'Somerset archaeology in 1996', *Proc. Somerset Archaeol. Natur. Hist. Soc.* 140: 133–59.

WEDDELL, P. 1987, 'Excavations within the Anglo-Saxon enclosure at Berry Meadow, Kingsteignton, in 1985', *Proc. Devon Archaeol. Soc.* 45: 75–96.

—— 1991, 'Archaeological assessment of the published route (preliminary) of the A30 Honiton to Exeter improvement'. Unpublished report, Exeter Museums Archaeological Field Unit, report 91.22.

—— 2000, 'The excavation of a post-Roman cemetery near Kenn, South Devon', *Proc. Devon Archaeol. Soc.* 58: 93–126.

—— and REED, S. J. 1997, 'Excavation at Sourton Down, Okehampton 1986–1991: Roman road, deserted medieval hamlet and other landscape features', *Proc. Devon Archaeol. Soc.* 55: 39–147.

———— and SIMPSON, S. J. 1993, 'Excavation of the Exeter–Dorchester Roman road at the river Yarty and the Roman fort ditch and settlement site at Woodbury, near Axminster', *Proc. Devon Archaeol. Soc.* 51: 33–134.

WEEKS, R. 2002, 'The "lost market" settlements of Pembrokeshire', *Medieval Settlement Research Group Annual Report*, 17: 21–30.

WELLDON FINN, R., and WHEATLEY, P. 1967, 'Somerset', in H. C. Darby and R. Welldon Finn (eds.), *The Domesday Geography of South-West England*. Cambridge: Cambridge University Press, 132–222.

WEST, S. 1985, *West Stow, the Anglo-Saxon Village*. East Anglian Archaeology 24.

—— 1998, *A Corpus of Anglo-Saxon Material from Suffolk*. East Anglian Archaeology 84.

—— 1999, 'The early Anglo-Saxon period', in D. Dymond and E. Martin (eds.), *An Historical Atlas of Suffolk*. Ipswich: Suffolk County Council.

—— and McLAUGHLIN, A. 1998, *Towards a Landscape History of Walsham le Willows*. East Anglian Archaeology 85.

—— and SCARFE, N. 1984, 'Iken, St Botolph and the coming of East Anglian Christianity', *Proc. Suffolk Instit. Archaeol. Hist.* 35 (4): 279–301.

—— CHARMAN, D., and GRATTAN, J. 1996, 'Palaeoenvironmental investigations at Tor Royal, central Dartmoor', in D. J. Charman, R. M. Newnham, and D. G. Croot (eds.), *Devon and East Cornwall Field Guide*. London: Quaternary Res. Ass., 62–80.

WHEELER, J., and LAING-TRENGROVE, D. 2006, 'A Roman tile kiln on Hatherleigh Moor and the sources of some Roman tile in Devon', *Proc. Devon Archaeol. Soc.* 64: 53–70.

WHEELER, R. E. M. 1935, *London and the Saxons*. London: London Museum.

WHITELOCK, D. 1955, *English Historical Documents*, i: *c.500–1042*. London: Eyre and Spottiswoode.

WHITFIELD, M. 1981 'The fields of south-east Somerset', *Proc. Somerset Archaeol. Natur. Hist. Soc.* 125: 17–29.

WICKHAM, C. 2005, *Framing the Early Middle Ages*. Oxford: Oxford University Press.

WILKES, E. 2004, 'Survey and excavation at Mount Folly, Bigbury-on-Sea', *Devon Archaeol. Soc. Newsletter*, 87: 5.

—— 2006, 'Mount Folly, Bigbury-on-Sea, 2003–6', *Devon Archaeol. Soc. Newsletter*, 93: 14–15.

WILKINSON, T. J. 1988, *Archaeology and Environment in South Essex: Rescue Archaeology Along the Grays By-Pass*. East Anglian Archaeology 42.

WILKINSON, T. J. and MURPHY, P. L. 1995, *The Archaeology of the Essex Coast*, i: *The Hullbridge Survey*. East Anglian Archaeology 71.

WILLIAMS, A. G. 1993, 'Norman lordship in south-east Wales during the reign of William I', *Welsh History Rev.* 16 (4): 445–66.

WILLIAMS, D. H. 1965, 'Tintern Abbey: its economic history', *Monmouthshire Antiquary*, 2 (1): 1–32.

—— 1970–1, 'Goldcliff Priory', *Monmouthshire Antiquary*, 3 (1): 37–54.

—— 1990, *Atlas of Cistercian Lands in Wales*. Cardiff: University of Wales Press.

WILLIAMS, G. 1988, 'Recent work on rural settlement in later prehistoric and early historic Dyfed', *Antiq. J.* 68 (1): 30–52.

—— and MYTUM, H. 1998, *Llawhaden, Dyfed: Excavations on a Group of Small Defended Enclosures, 1980–4*. BAR British Series 275, Oxford: British Archaeological Reports.

WILLIAMS, R. J. 1993, *Pennyland and Hartigans: Two Iron Age and Saxon Sites in Milton Keynes*. Aylesbury: Buckinghamshire Archaeological Society Monograph Series No. 4.

WILLIAMSON, T. 1984, 'The Roman countryside: settlement and agriculture in N.W. Essex', *Britannia*, 15: 225–30.

—— 1986, 'The development of settlement in N.W. Essex: the results of a recent field survey', *Essex Archaeol. Hist.* 17: 120–32.

—— 1987, 'Early co-axial field systems on the East Anglian boulder clays', *Proc. Prehist. Soc.* 53: 419–31

—— 1988, 'Settlement chronology and regional landscapes: the evidence from the claylands of East Anglia and Essex', in D. Hooke (ed.), *Anglo-Saxon Settlements*. Oxford: Blackwells, 153–75.

—— 1993, *The Origins of Norfolk*. Manchester: Manchester University Press.

—— 1998, 'The "Scole-Dickleborough field system" revisited', *Landscape Hist.* 20: 19–28.

—— 2000, *The Origins of Hertfordshire*. Manchester: Manchester University Press.

—— 2002, *The Transformation of Rural England*. Exeter: University of Exeter Press.

—— 2003, *Shaping Medieval Landscapes*. Macclesfield: Windgather Press.

—— 2005, 'The Angles and Saxons geographically considered', *Saxon: Newsletter of the Sutton Hoo Society*, 42: 10.

—— 2006a, *England's Landscape: East Anglia*. London: Harper Collins/English Heritage.

—— 2006b, 'Mapping field patterns: a case-study from eastern England', *Landscapes*, 7 (1): 55–67.

—— 2007, 'The distribution of champion landscapes', in Gardiner and Rippon (2007, 89–104).

WILTSHIRE, P. E. J. 1999, 'Palynological assessment of a mire peat sequence in the Eriswell Valley, Suffolk'. Unpublished report for the Ministry of Defence.

—— forthcoming, 'Palynological assessment and analysis', in *A Roman Settlement in the Waveney Valley: Excavations at Scole, 1993–4*. East Anglian Archaeology.

WINCHESTER, A. 1990, *Discovering Parish Boundaries*. Princes Risborough: Shire.

WOOD, J. 1997, 'New perspectives on West Cornwall courtyard houses', *Cornish Archaeol.* 36: 95–106.

WOOD, P. D. 1963, 'Open field strips, Forrabury Common, Boscastle', *Cornish Archaeol.* 2: 29–33.

WYMER, J. J., and BROWN, N. R. 1995, *Excavations at North Shoebury: Settlement and Economy in South-East Essex 1500 BC–AD 1500.* East Anglian Archaeology 75.

YORKE, B. 1990, *Kings and Kingdoms of Early Anglo-Saxon England.* London: Routledge.

YOUNG, A. 1804, *General View of the Agriculture of Norfolk.* London.

Index